THE ULTIM
DO-IT-YOURS
BOOK

THE ULTIMATE DO-IT-YOURSELF BOOK

a complete practical guide to home improvement

Consultant Editor: JOHN McGOWAN

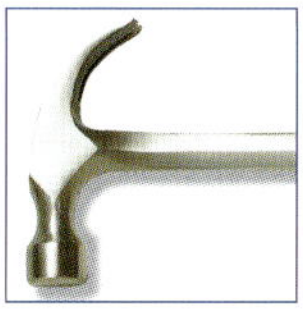

MIKE COLLINS, DAVID HOLLOWAY,
BRENDA LEGGE, DIANE CARR

Special Photography: COLIN BOWLING

HERMES HOUSE

This edition is published by Hermes House

Hermes House is an imprint of Anness Publishing Ltd
Hermes House, 88–89 Blackfriars Road,
London SE1 8HA
tel. 020 7401 2077; fax 020 7633 9499;
info@anness.com

A CIP catalogue record for this book is available from the British Library.

Publisher: Joanna Lorenz
Managing editor: Judith Simons
Art manager: Clare Reynolds
Senior editor: Doreen Palamartschuk
Editor: Ian Penberthy
Editorial reader: Diane Ashmore
Indexer: Janet Smy
Designer: Paul Calver
Illustrator: Peter Bull
Photographer: Colin Bowling
Photography consultant: Simon Gilham
Technical assistant: John Ireland
Production controller: Wendy Lawson

Previously published as *Do-It-Yourself*

10 9 8 7 6 5 4 3 2 1

Contents

PLANNING

The hardest part of any do-it-yourself project is deciding precisely what you want and planning how to achieve it. The decisions may involve simply choosing a colour scheme, or may be more complex, perhaps involving major changes to style, layout of a room, features and fittings. The secret of success is careful preparation, an understanding of basic colour scheming, and learning how to make the best use of the wide range of tools and materials available to the do-it-yourself enthusiast.

GETTING STARTED

Whether you are faced with a fairly simple job, such as decorating a small bedroom, installing cabinets and shelves, or repairing a fence, or something far more ambitious, such as adding a porch or cladding a whole room or ceiling, the same approach to the work is needed. The whole job has to be planned thoroughly so that you get a good result.

CHANGING YOUR ENVIRONMENT

Houses and flats, converted barns and studios are, on their own, merely structures of wood, glass, concrete and masonry. They spring into life and blossom only when the personality of the occupier is stamped upon them. Where you live should be how you live; it is more than just a place to sleep. It should be a microcosm of your whole lifestyle in terms of created space, room design, colour schemes, furniture, fittings, lighting, garden layout and all that goes with loving and caring for the home.

For this to be true we need to put in a lot of quality time thinking about, experimenting with, and enhancing our own environments, and much of this is possible with relatively few skills.

The most important thing to remember is that do-it-yourself is a practical and deeply satisfying pursuit, which fosters craftsmanship and pride in one's environment through practical achievement.

LEFT It is vital to carefully think through an idea before proceeding. Consider how you will tackle features such as installing this large wooden floor and adding the sweeping, open tread staircase.

LEFT Choosing and using the right materials and equipment for the job is vital.

THE WIDER WORLD

Just knowing how things are built and appreciating the time and skills that went into the concept, design and manufacture of them, hugely increases our appreciation of the material world, and leads to an enhanced understanding of cultural achievement, manifest in the buildings around us. Being able to exercise a skill is an enriching experience that adds to the fullness of life, especially so if one's working time is normally spent in an academic or sedentary job. There is also the pleasure of learning and using a new skill successfully.

HIDDEN ASSETS

The money saved in working on your own projects at home is an obvious advantage and, in a healthy property market, this creates an asset that grows over the years.

For many people, the physical nature of do-it-yourself also gives much-needed exercise in the evenings or weekends, which is all important for a healthy lifestyle. Hanging wallpaper, knocking-up cement, planing wood or climbing up and down ladders all contribute to keeping us in trim.

Individual expression

In an age that drives relentlessly on to standardization in all things, it is good to be able to produce individual work that reflects your personality, that suits your own needs entirely and that can be altered or added to at your own pleasure. Doctors tell us, "we are what we eat" and this could perhaps be stretched to, "we are how we live." This does not refer to the pressured sense of earning a living, but to the time we relax at home, where we have the freedom of choice, at least to some extent, over our immediate environment.

Having the imagination and the will to transform your home is a great start, but you also need practical skills and money, both of which can be built up over time. Fairly basic skills, such as painting, are learned largely through practical experience, by simply doing the job. A large amount of useful information is also available on the products themselves and at the point of sale in the form of instructional leaflets.

Undertaking complex jobs is often dictated by necessity. It may be that you need to make more of your living space because of an addition to the family, or perhaps you suddenly find you have more room available because the children are leaving home.

It is wise to live in a property for some time before starting major alterations, just to get the feel of the place; most necessary alterations will suggest themselves automatically.

Hands on

Specialized skills, such as bricklaying and carpentry, do need the experience of actually handling the tools regularly to gain manual dexterity, and the best way to obtain this experience is to do a few outside jobs that are not particularly important. Repairing a fence or wall, perhaps laying a few slabs or building a small tool shed or garden frame will help you develop skills remarkably quickly and boost your confidence. As confidence grows, it feeds the imagination, and in a short time, projects for inside the home begin to take shape in the mind.

Beginners should seek as much advice as possible from experienced professionals or at least read up on the particular project or task in mind so that the more common pitfalls can be avoided. Many colleges offer evening classes where, for a modest sum, the beginner can learn carpentry, brickwork and general do-it-yourself skills. These are worth investigating and can be very rewarding. The advantage of do-it-yourself is that your time is free, so never rush a job: haste encourages mistakes, leads to disappointment, and can be expensive in the cost of spoiled materials.

ABOVE FAR LEFT Paper hanging is a useful skill and fairly easily learned.

ABOVE LEFT Basic carpentry skills can be put to good use by fixing a garden gate.

ABOVE Bricklaying and pointing skills take practice and time to learn properly.

BELOW Virtually any floorcovering can be laid perfectly if the sub-floor is well prepared.

Forward Planning

Planning ahead is an essential ingredient of successful projects. It is important to remember that some schemes may involve a room or rooms being out of bounds for some days or even weeks, and provision must be made for this. Similarly, it is generally wiser to schedule the painting of the outside of your property for the summer months when there is at least a likelihood of good weather.

Infrastructure

There is little point in decorating any part of the house if you envisage having it rewired in the near future, or perhaps adding central heating. These major domestic services will need to be installed first. If you are planning an extension in a year or so, much the same will apply, so it is best to work out an overall scheme that considers major items.

Be prepared

It may be that at some point in a job you will need another pair of hands to hold or pass tools in an awkward spot, or to help with moving heavy objects. Just arranging for someone to be there at the right time can be a problem. When beginning a job such as decorating, be sure that everything is to hand; it is no use pasting wallpaper then finding that you are too short to reach the top of the wall to hang it and that you need to go looking for a trestle or a pair of steps. All these things must be well prepared and in position.

Costs

Plenty of projects have failed through lack of funds, so it is well worth costing your job carefully. If the job is to be done in stages as the money becomes available, make sure that you can put it "on hold" without any detrimental effects. Stripping the paint from exterior woodwork then leaving it for months to absorb moisture is asking for trouble. Removing old windows before the new ones are actually on site is tempting the gods!

Viability

This is the most important consideration of all. Viability not only covers whether a job can be done, but also whether it is beneficial to do it. Cladding good brickwork with stone, flush-panelling fine old panelled doors, and ripping out ornate skirting (base) boards will only detract from the value of your home, so if you live in a house with a particular architectural style, keep it that way.

ABOVE Keep the bulk of the exterior upkeep to do in the summer time.

BELOW LEFT Keep all your tools for the specific job near to hand.

BELOW All of these items will prove invaluable for drawing plans for your projects: graph paper; a sketch pad; a clipboard or drawing board; masking tape; a pair of compasses; dividers for the accurate transfer and duplication of measurements; drawing pens; pencils; eraser and pencil sharpener; a set square and protractor; templates for necessary shapes; rules; and a scale rule and a calculator for converting measurements and making calculations.

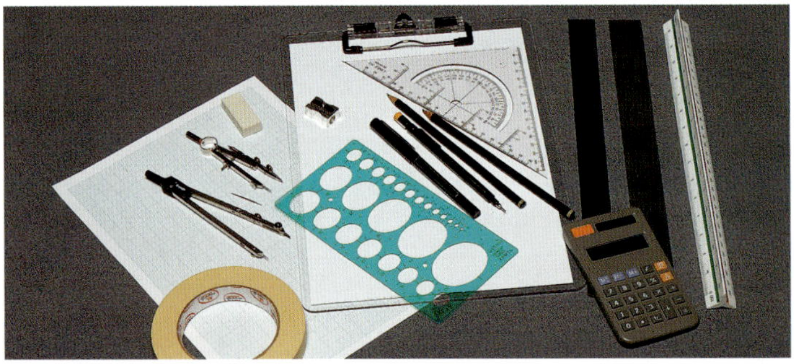

Checklist

Use this checklist to help in organizing your do-it-yourself project and to draw up a record of the tools, equipment and materials that are required.

Task	Materials	Tools/Equipment
1 Remove furniture from affected room(s)		
2 Remove fixtures and fittings: go to 7 if not executing major work. Order new fixtures and fittings		
3 Relocate room contents		
4 Carry out structural alterations		
5 Alter/extend/improve services, e.g. improve wiring/plumbing		
6 Replace features that are to be altered such as doors, mouldings (trims)		
7 Remove old wall and floorcoverings if being replaced		
8 Make good any damaged surfaces		
9 Wash painted/ceiling surfaces, apply primer sealer as necessary		
10 Wash painted woodwork, clean room before starting to decorate		
11 Level and repair floors as necessary		
12 Replace fixtures and fittings, such as light switches		
13 Fix wall tiles, cladding or panelling		
14 Paint or paper ceilings		
15 Paint or paper walls		
16 Paint woodwork (if papering walls, do this first)		
17 Add decorative moulding (trim), borders etc		
18 Replace shelf brackets, curtain (drapery) track, built-in furniture		
19 Lay new floorcoverings and clean room		
20 Reposition furniture		
21 Add soft furnishings		

Using Professionals

A do-it-yourself project can be as simple as hanging a picture or putting up a shelf, or as complex as creating a new room in the roof. In extreme cases, it can even mean building a full-scale house. Most of us do not go that far, but there are many jobs, especially in plumbing and electrics, where professional help is welcome and indeed necessary.

Regulations

Some projects require professional input by law, such as when local planning (zoning) permission is required or, more commonly, when the work must comply with building regulations. In this case, when applications must be made to a local authority, it is well worth securing the services of an architect, or at least a professional draughtsman, to draw up plans. He or she will be familiar with the building regulations of the local area and almost certainly will save you time and money in presenting the plans effectively to the right people.

Perhaps, more importantly, such a professional can advise you in advance if your project is likely to fail for a reason you may not even have considered.

Hands on

As a do-it-yourself enthusiast, you have to be familiar with several trades, but it is often well worth employing a professional for structural work to save time and possibly money. For example, a small extension to your home could be brick-built with the roof put on and tiled in a few weeks, which would leave you plenty of time to have the wiring installed, then plaster the walls, make all secondary fixings such as floors, doors, skirting (base) boards and to decorate the extension in relative comfort.

You also have to remember that many aspects of building work require stamina and strength on the part of the operative. Digging a foundation trench is not ideal for someone not used to a physical challenge, indeed, it could lead to back problems or other injuries. Jobs such as carrying bricks or blocks up a ladder or moving concrete around are tough going. Even working in unfavourable weather conditions and without the necessary clothing may lead to health problems.

Many building jobs require specialist equipment that a builder will supply – for example, an excavator, concrete mixer, roof ladder, scaffolding, and so on. If you take on jobs that require this type of apparatus, then you will have to pay for them, either by hiring or buying.

BELOW LEFT A competent builder will construct a block or brick wall quickly and efficiently.

BELOW Hacking off defective plaster is a time-consuming and strenuous job for the beginner.

Levels of competence

Being able to run pipes and electrical cables is a very different matter from knowing what is necessary in the way of safety or operational and building regulations. Understanding the capacity requirements of pumps and fuses together with a wide range of other knowledge is absolutely necessary to ensure that installations work and are safe.

Incorrectly installed plumbing and electrical systems can produce potentially disastrous, even fatal, results. Therefore, employing an advisor to oversee these requirements is essential if you have the slightest doubt about your own ability. Indeed, in many countries, it is a legal requirement that all such work is carried out by licensed tradespeople. Many contractors will offer advice for a small fee.

It can be very costly in terms of both time and money if plumbing or electrics are incorrectly installed and have to be taken out and done again.

Choosing help

Recommendations by word of mouth in the building trade are paramount and are especially valuable if the contractor you choose not only works, but also lives in your local area. Ask for the addresses of jobs the contractor has done recently in the area and make arrangements to go and see them – it is the best recommendation of all.

When you have made a shortlist of likely builders or contractors (at least three is usual) ask each of them for an estimate cost for the work to be done. Make sure that each has the same, detailed list of the jobs involved. When you have decided on the one to use (never automatically opt for the cheapest – consider all the relevant factors), ask for a firm quotation for the work.

When you have chosen your builder, plumber or electrician, then go through the whole job with him or her and get all the decisions in writing, which can save disputes later on.

Practical tips

- When you are employing a builder, carpenter, plumber or electrician, get a clear, written agreement on the method of payment. Some builders will complete a job before seeking payment, others will ask for stage payments.

- Always agree, before any work starts, that you will withhold a proportion of the costs (5–10 per cent is usual) for an agreed period of time after the job is finished. This will cover any snagging or work that has to be done again through faulty workmanship or materials.

- If you decide to make concrete yourself, consider buying a second-hand concrete mixer, and selling it again when the job is complete – it should save you money on buying or hiring costs.

ABOVE Employ a qualified electrician to carry out electrical work, as incorrectly installed electrics can be lethal. At least, get a qualified person to check out your work.

ABOVE Approach every job methodically. When decorating a room, clear it completely if possible. Check that all necessary equipment and materials are to hand.

ABOVE Whereas a builder is often able to work by him or herself, the do-it-yourself enthusiast will on occasions have to get a helper. It requires special handling skills to work alone.

Safety Equipment

A complete book could be devoted to the subject of safety in the home, and there is a wide range of equipment designed to minimize our capacity for hurting ourselves. Nevertheless, there is one requirement that we cannot buy, without which all that equipment is virtually useless, namely concentration. This is particularly important when working alone.

Awareness

Concentration is essential when using any form of power tool, especially a saw, where one slip can mean the loss of a finger, or worse. The dangers of accidents involving electricity are well documented, as are those involving falls from ladders, spillages of toxic materials, and burns and injuries caused by contact with fire or abrasive surfaces. In almost every case, there is a loss of concentration, coupled with poor work practices and inadequate protective clothing or equipment. So, although the items shown here are all useful, concentrating on what you are doing is the best advice to prevent accidents from occurring around the home and workshop.

ABOVE Rubber knee pads for floor work avoid damage to both the floor and person.

LEFT The "bump" cap is more stylish than the hard hat and will cope with most accidents.

Basic equipment

Overalls are a good investment because they not only protect clothing, but also most are designed to be close-fitting to prevent accidental contact with moving machinery. Industrial gloves, although not worn by those engaged in fine work, can provide very useful protection against cuts and bruises when doing rougher jobs, such as fencing and garden work. Similarly, safety boots should be worn when heavy lifting or the use of machinery is involved. They are essential when using a chainsaw.

Knee pads are necessary for comfort when laying a floor, stripping one for varnishing or carrying out any other job that requires a lot of kneeling. They will also protect the wearer from injury if a nail or similar projection is knelt on accidentally. Finally, a bump cap is worth considering. This will protect the head from minor

FAR LEFT Wear overalls for protection when painting and decorating.

ABOVE LEFT Gloves are essential when handling rough materials.

LEFT Safety boots with steel toe caps will protect your feet.

injuries and bumps, but is not so cumbersome as the hard hat required on building sites.

It is inevitable that minor cuts and abrasions will occur at some point so a basic first aid kit is another essential for the home or workshop.

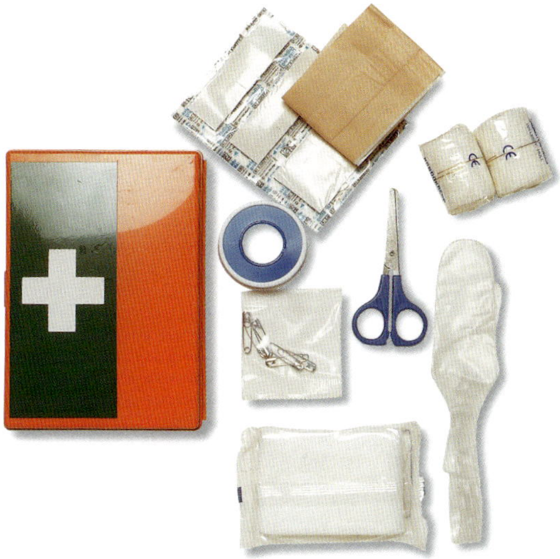

LEFT Keeping a basic first aid kit is a common and wise precaution even before any do-it-yourself work is envisaged. It should always be prominently displayed for people unfamiliar with the workshop.

Airborne dangers

When you are working with wood, the most common airborne danger is dust, mainly from sawing and sanding. This can do long-term damage to the lungs. Many do-it-yourself enthusiasts do not do enough work to warrant a workshop dust extractor, but it would be worth considering if funds allowed. Such a device can be wall-mounted or portable. In the latter case, it can be moved around the house or workshop to suit any tool in use.

A simple face mask, however, will offer adequate protection for occasional jobs. These can also be purchased for protection against fumes, such as from solvents, which can be very harmful. Dust, of course, also affects the eyes, so it is worth investing in a pair of impact-resistant goggles, which will protect the wearer from both fine dust and flying debris. Full facial protection is available in the form of a powered respirator for those working in dusty conditions over long periods.

Excessive noise is another airborne pollutant that can be dangerous over a long period. Woodworking machinery, such as planers and circular saws, is often the culprit. Earplugs are the simplest solution and can be left in the ears over a long period. If you need to be able to hear between short bouts of working, ear protectors are the answer. These can be worn in conjunction with other facial protection quite easily.

Practical tip

- Perhaps the most basic advice is to never work alone with machinery and if it is possible always have a friend or colleague nearby to help. If there is no telephone, having a mobile (cell) phone is handy in the workshop.

ABOVE Ear defenders are good for really loud noise but should be used sparingly.

ABOVE Dust extraction is the first line of defence in the workshop.

ABOVE A simple face mask can filter out the worst dust pollution.

Electrical and Ladder Safety

Most safety considerations concerning the use of power tools will be set out by the manufacturers in the operating instructions, so it is essential always to read the manuals on purchase and follow these to the letter. Using ladders, however, needs some direct input from the user by way of common sense, since no two situations are ever the same.

Electrical safety

Some tools have removable switches that allow the user to immobilize the tool and prevent any unauthorized use. Provisions for the use of padlocks are also common on machinery, and it is wise to buy tools with such facilities.

To safeguard against electrocution, which can occur if the flex (power cord) is faulty or is cut accidentally, the ideal precaution is a residual current device (RCD). This is simply plugged into the main supply socket (electrical outlet) before the flex and will give complete protection to the user. Extension leads (power cords) can be purchased with automatic safety cut-outs and insulated sockets and are ideal for both outside and inside work.

The danger of electrocution or damage caused by accidentally drilling into an existing cable or pipe can be largely prevented by using an electronic pipe and cable detector, which will locate and differentiate between metal pipes, wooden studs and live wires through plaster or concrete to a depth of approximately 50mm (2in). These are not too expensive and will be very useful around the home.

The danger of fire is ever present in both the home and workshop, so a fire extinguisher (possibly two or three) is necessary for every do-it-yourself enthusiast. It should be wall-mounted in plain view and tested and serviced regularly.

ABOVE AND LEFT Pipe and cable detectors give information which can largely eliminate any danger from electrocution.

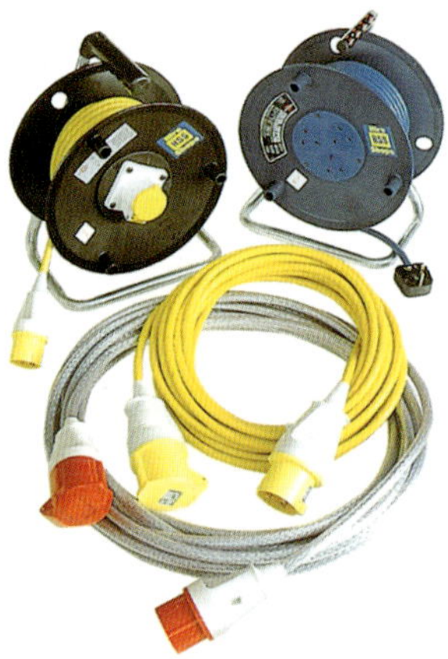

ABOVE Proper cable reels and insulated sockets protect the user from electrocution.

ABOVE A fire extinguisher is absolutely essential in the workshop or at home. Make sure the one you have is adequate for the size and type of workshop, and the type of fire source.

LEFT A simple circuit breaker can save a life.

ABOVE A ladder platform will ensure a firm footing, especially if heavy footwear is worn.

Slipping and falling

Steps and ladders can be hazardous, so make sure they are in good condition. Accessories to make a ladder safer to use include the roof hook, which slips over the ridge for safety; the ladder stay, which spreads the weight of the ladder across a vertical surface, such as a wall to prevent slippage; and the standing platform, which is used to provide a more comfortable and safer surface to stand on. The last often has a ribbed rubber surface and can be attached to the rungs of almost all ladders. Even more stable is the moveable workstation or a board or staging slung between two pairs of steps or trestles. These can often be used with a safety rail, which prevents the operator from falling even if a slip occurs.

ABOVE RIGHT A moveable workstation simplifies the whole process.

RIGHT Platforms supported by trestles are the safest way to paint from a height.

RIGHT Keeping tools on a stable surface when working at heights adds to your personal safety.

BELOW RIGHT A ladder attachment over the ridge of a roof improves safety and avoids damage to the roof covering.

BELOW Make sure that your ladder is secure at ground level. This is one of the most important steps to safe working practice.

Practical tips

- Never over-reach when working on steps or a ladder; climb down and reposition it.
- Never allow children or pets into areas where power tools or strong solvents are being used.
- Do not work when you are overtired. This causes lapses in concentration, which can lead to silly and/or dangerous mistakes.
- Keep the work environment tidy. Flexes (power cords) should not be walked on or coiled up tightly, because it damages them internally. Moreover, trailing flexes can be a trip hazard and long extension leads (cords) can be prone to overheating.

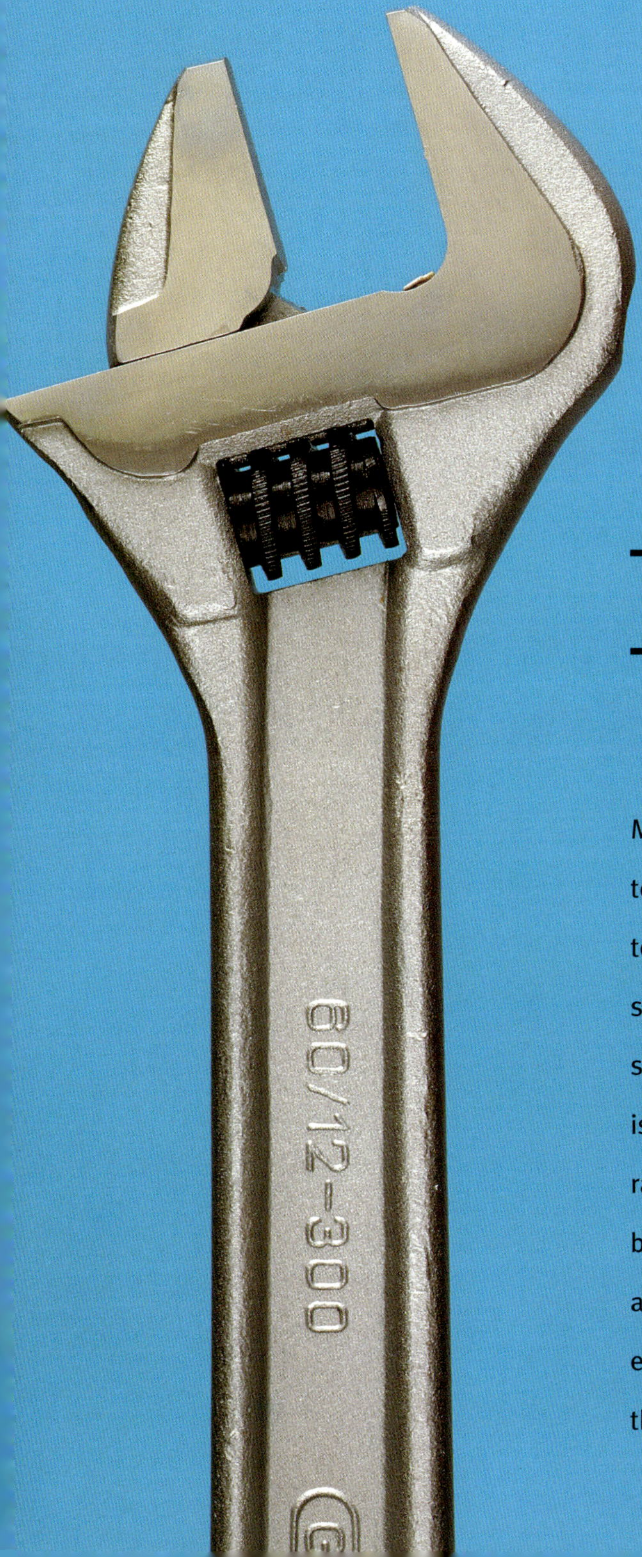

Tools and Techniques

Most tool kits grow organically as specific tools are added when the need arises. The tools featured on the following pages show a useful selection to have when starting your own projects. If your budget is tight, it is best to buy several hand tools rather than one power tool. This has the benefit of improving your manual skills at an early stage, which will give encouraging results as well as increasing the range of jobs you can undertake.

Measuring and Marking

Accurate measuring and marking out are very basic but essential skills for the do-it-yourself enthusiast to master. Time spent on perfecting them is never wasted. The golden rule is to measure twice and cut once. Buy some good quality tools – poor measuring and marking devices can lose their accuracy very quickly and spoil your work.

How to measure

There are dozens of types of flat, rigid rules for marking out, most of which are calibrated in both metric and imperial units. They may be wood or steel, although some cheaper varieties are plastic. Where curves are involved, greater accuracy will be achieved with a flexible steel rule or even a retractable steel tape, which can be bent around the work.

The T-square is useful for marking out large sheets of manufactured board such as plywood, MDF (medium-density fiberboard) or blockboard. Remember, however, that it must be used on a perfectly straight edge to give a 90-degree line across the sheet. Any small discrepancy will be greatly magnified across the sheet width and even more so along the length.

T-square

Short and long spirit levels

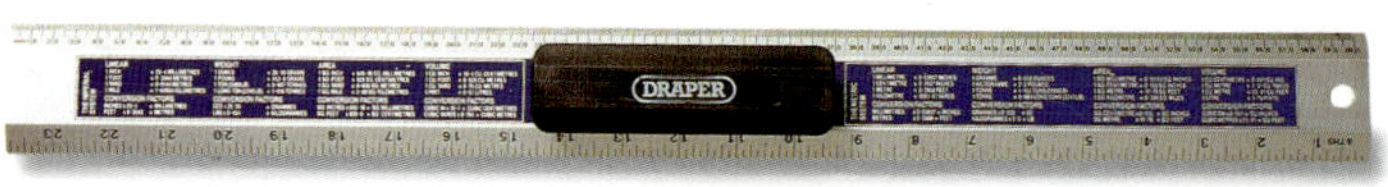

Straightedge

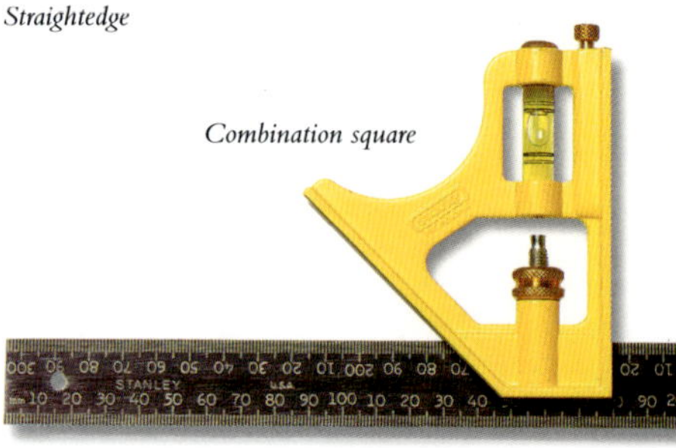

Combination square

Measuring tape

Fitting pre-made structures

When fitting previously-assembled cabinets or shelving to a wall, the most accurate method is to mark out the wall using a spirit level. Do not rely on existing lines, such as architraves (trims) around doors, picture rails or skirting (base) boards, as these may not be truly horizontal.

Where you need to mark off a series of equal spacings, simply set a pair of dividers or callipers to the correct distance, using a flat wooden or steel rule, and step off the divisions.

Transferring measurements from one point to another can also be done with a straightedge, and although this is very similar to a heavy steel rule, the bevelled edge gives it the added advantage of being very easy to cut or to mark against.

When marking out for fine work, a marking knife, with a bevel on one side of the blade only, is the tool to use. Such knives can be obtained with bevels on either side and are well worth having.

Converting measurements

On small work in particular, never be tempted to convert from metric to imperial or vice-versa. Some quite large errors can occur with standard conversions. Always work in the unit specified.

Sliding bevel

Marking knife

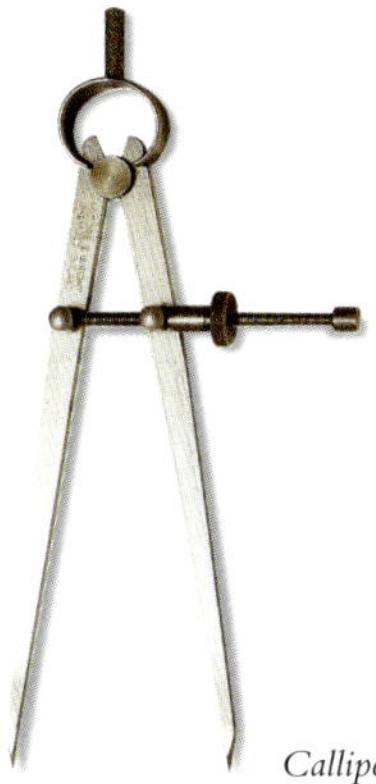

Callipers

Try square

Mortise gauge

Marking out

Never use a magic marker or a ballpoint pen when marking out, since the marks are virtually impossible to remove and will spoil your work.

ABOVE Use a carpenter's pencil, pencil, or chinagraph for marking measurements.

Marking joints

This does need a fair degree of accuracy, so the first thing to ascertain is that your prepared wood is flat and square, which is done with a combination square or a try square. Either of these tools should be slid down the length of the timber to be cut to ensure its uniformity and squareness.

For marking out a mortise, use a mortise gauge and set the points to the width of the chisel you intend to use to cut the mortise, not from a rule. This is far more accurate, as well as being much more convenient.

For marking angles on a piece of square timber, especially if they are to be repeated, such as when setting out treads for a staircase, use a sliding bevel.

A good alternative for marking frequently repeated angles, which are encountered in projects such as staircases, is to make up a jig or template that can be laid on to the stringer (the long diagonal part of the staircase) and mark the treads accordingly. Most workshops keep a range of templates made in hardboard or perspex.

FAR LEFT Use a try square for marking right angles. Keep it clean and make sure the blade is not loose. It can be used with a pencil or a marking knife as required.

LEFT Use a mortise gauge to scribe directly on to the wood. The two steel pins of the mortise gauge are independently adjustable on accurate brass slides, while the sliding stock runs against the face of the work. There is a single pin on the opposite side for marking a single scribed line, used to gauge thickness.

Drills and Bits

These come in a bewildering array of sizes and types but just a few are all that are needed for the home workshop, such as dowel bits for flat-bottomed holes; flat bits, which work with a scraping action and cut large holes very rapidly; and the ordinary twist bit that is used for making small holes and for starting screws. Beware of buying cheap sets of drill bits.

Drills

Accurate drilling is an important do-it-yourself technique, and it is much easier with a hand-held power drill and even more so with a bench-mounted pillar drill.

Drilling by hand with a carpenter's brace still has a place and a hand drill is useful for smaller jobs, especially in sites far removed from electric power. However, even in these circumstances, the cordless power drill has largely overcome the difficulty of needing a source of electric power.

Cordless drill/driver

This is worth its weight in gold in situations without power, and it is particularly safe near water. This hand-held power tool is rechargeable and usually comes with a spare battery. The variable torque and speed settings make it ideal for doubling as a screwdriver. Although generally not as powerful as a mains-powered drill, it is more than adequate for most jobs. Use it for drilling clearance holes for screws, fitting and removing screws, and drilling holes for dowels.

Practical tip

- **Never interfere with the centre-point of a drill, if it has one, as this will almost certainly affect its concentricity and effectiveness.**

Heavier work, especially that which involves using flat bits or Forstner bits for removing very large areas of wood, is best undertaken with a mains-powered electric drill to save time and avoid constant recharging of the battery.

Cordless drill

Hand drill

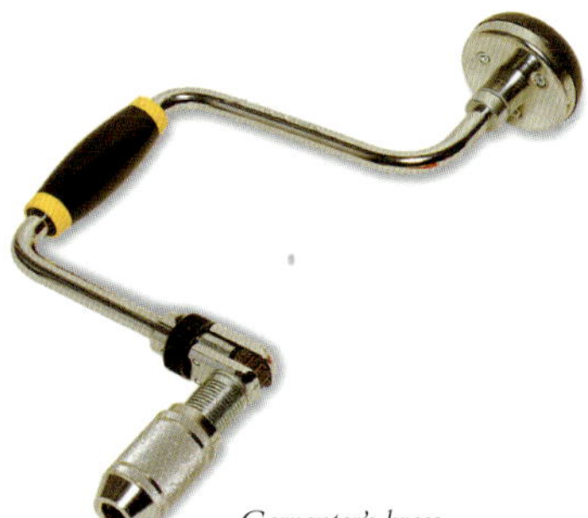

Carpenter's brace

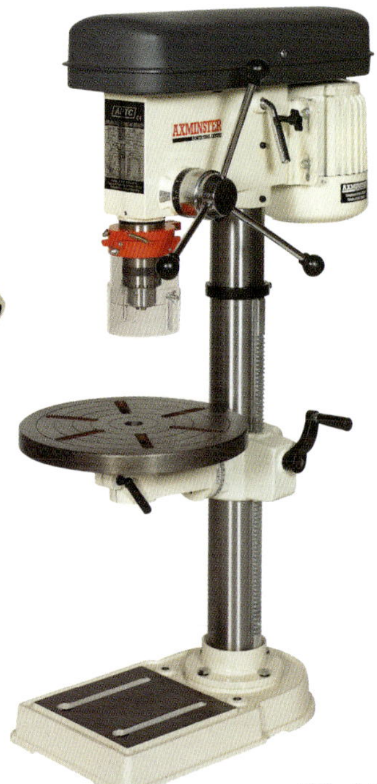

Pillar drill

Pillar drills

When using a pillar drill to bore holes that pass through the wood, place a piece of scrap wood beneath the workpiece so that the bit will emerge cleanly and not splinter the surface. Always run a pillar drill at the correct speed, as shown on the tool. This will always be slower for large-diameter drills and faster for smaller ones.

Varieties of bit

Great advances have also been made in the pattern of drill bits. For example, there are bits designed for setting dowels. Dowel jointing is often used in projects built with manufactured boards, such as chipboard and plywood, and the bits produce flat-bottomed holes.

There are also flat bits that work with a scraping action, cutting large holes very rapidly, although these are not as accurate as conventional twist bits. The latter are used for making small holes in wood, metal and other rigid materials. For the home worker on a limited budget, an adjustable bit is a good investment, but these can only be used in a hand brace. Engineering bits can all be used in woodwork.

Drilling accessories

Plug cutters are useful additions to any workshop, especially when quality work is undertaken. The cutter is fitted in a pillar drill and used to remove plugs from a piece of scrap wood. The plugs are then glued into holes in the workpiece to conceal fixing screws. Most cutters come with a special matching bit that bores a screw clearance hole and plug countersink in one operation.

ABOVE Many drill bits can be sharpened with a specialized grinding attachment designed to be run off a hand-held power drill.

Another common drilling accessory is the countersink bit. This allows the head of a screw to be set flush with the surface of the wood. Again, this is best used in a pillar drill with a depth stop to ensure accuracy.

Forstner bits are designed to drill large, flat-bottomed holes that do not pass through the wood, such as holes that might be needed to fit kitchen cabinet hinges. The bits will drill deep holes accurately, even in the end grain of timber, which is usually very difficult.

Screws and Screwdrivers

The holding power of screws is much greater than that of nails, and screwed work can easily be taken apart again without damage to any of the components, unless of course it is also glued. Driving screws does take longer than nailing and is also more expensive, but it will give the appearance of quality and craftsmanship to most work.

Types of screw

The most frequently used wood screws are made of mild steel or brass, often with countersunk heads that may be flat or raised. There are many different plated finishes available, ranging from chrome, used for internal fixings such as mirrors, to zinc, which will resist rust.

Brass screws will not rust at all and are commonly used in timbers such as oak, where steel would cause blue staining due to the tannic acid in the sap.

Screw sizes and head patterns

There are various types of screw head used for both hand and power driving. The most common in woodworking is the slot-head screw, followed by the Phillips head and the Pozidriv, both of which have a cross pattern in the head to take the screwdriver blade. A small selection of slot-head, Phillips and Pozidriv screwdrivers will cover most needs. Slot-head screwdriver blades can be shaped on a grindstone to restore their condition if necessary. Never use a screwdriver that is too small, as you will ruin the blade and the screw. Screw sizes are complex, combining the diameter (gauge) and the length: for example, "inch-and-a-half eight" describes a screw that is 1½in (40mm) long and gauge 8.

There is no need to delve too deeply into screw sizes, other than to say that wood screws come in gauges 1–14, and the most commonly used are gauges 6–10 from ½–2in (12–50mm). Generally, metric sizes in screws are not found, although one or two are just beginning to be used.

A selection of small screws for cabinet work

ABOVE From left to right: A Pozidriv screw head, a Phillips screw head and a slotted screw head.

Practical tips

- When screwing into hardwood, drill a pilot hole slightly smaller than the screw's diameter to ease the screw through.

- When fitting brass screws, first assemble the project with steel screws of the same gauge and length. Brass is very soft and the screws may shear off if used to cut their own threads.

Slot screwdriver

Stubby screwdriver

Pozidriv screwdriver

Small Pozidriv screwdriver

Phillips screwdriver

Small Phillips screwdriver

Screwdriver types

For woodworking, the traditional hand screwdriver has an oval wooden handle and is used to drive slot-head screws only. This is widely available in a variety of sizes. A range of plastic-handled tools of various sizes are also available, designed to drive Phillips and Pozidriv screws, as well as slot-heads.

Power screwdrivers and drill/drivers vastly increase the rate of work. They can offer various torque settings that allow the screw heads to be set just flush with the work surface. Power drivers are also very useful for dismantling screwed joints and furniture because they will run in reverse.

Keeping the head of a slotted-screwdriver correctly ground to prevent it from slipping is very important. Remember also that the blade width must equal the length of the screw slot for the greatest efficiency and to prevent both slipping and damage to the screw head. Always use the correct size of screwdriver with Phillips and Pozidriv screws, otherwise both the screw head and the screwdriver will be damaged.

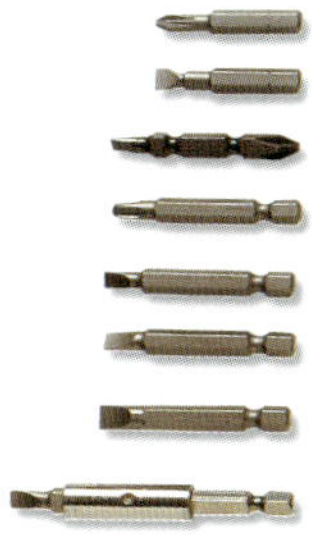

A selection of drill bits

Cordless electric drill and screwdriver

Using screws

Drilling a screw is a more skilled operation than nailing. It is usually advisable to drill pilot holes first to ease the screws' passage through the wood and to ensure that they go in straight. In hardwoods, pre-drilling is vital, otherwise the screws will just shear off when pressure is exerted by the screwdriver. Brass screws are particularly soft and need steel screws inserted before them (and then removed) to pre-cut the thread.

FAR LEFT Always drill pilot holes for brass hinge screws.

LEFT When fitting slot-head screws in a line, a neat finish can be achieved by setting all the heads so that they face the same way.

BELOW FAR LEFT Where possible, use the screwdriver with both hands to prevent slippage.

BELOW LEFT Screw holes should be marked very carefully when fitting hinges.

BELOW The correct way to bore and countersink when joining two planks of timber.

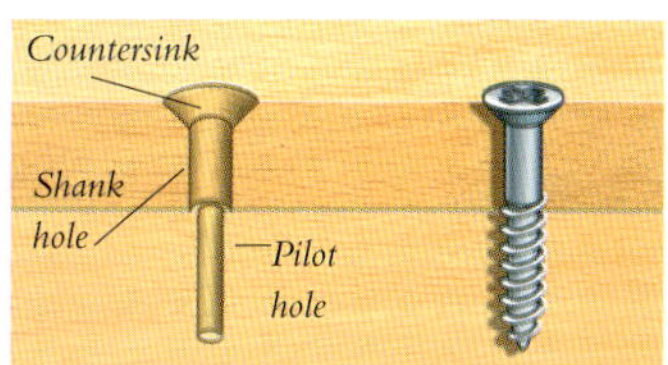

Saws

Sawing by hand and with power saws is a skill that must be learned well. Power saws do not take the skill out of sawing, or at least not all of it; they simply reduce the amount of hard work involved. You need to understand what types of saw are used for what purposes, and why, for the best results. There are dozens of special saws, but those covered here are all commonly used.

Cross-cut hand saw

Hardpoint hand saw

Tenon saw

Hand saws

The most common saw in the home workshop is the hand saw. This is used for cross-cutting (across the grain) and ripping (along the grain), and the teeth of the saw are set accordingly, so you will need to ask your tool supplier for the correct one. There are also general-purpose hand saws that are reasonably suited to both tasks, and these are quite often hardpoint saws, which cannot be sharpened, but their specially hardened teeth give them a long life.

The tenon saw, sometimes called a backsaw, because of the solid strengthening bar along its top edge, is made specifically for cutting the tenons for making mortise-and-tenon joints and other fine work. Really fine work is done with a dovetail saw, which is similar to a tenon saw, but has more teeth to the inch to give a finer cut.

The tenon saw is often used with a bench hook for accurate cutting, and one can be made quite easily as a do-it-yourself project. They usually measure about 300 x 150mm (12 x 6in). The mitre box is another handy aid for use with a tenon saw, allowing 90- and 45-degree angles to be cut accurately, but the beginner is best advised to buy one rather than attempt to make one since accuracy is vital.

Mitre box

Bench hook

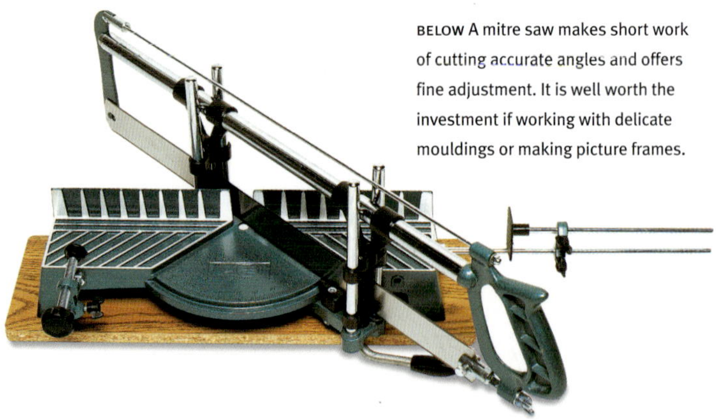

BELOW A mitre saw makes short work of cutting accurate angles and offers fine adjustment. It is well worth the investment if working with delicate mouldings or making picture frames.

Sawing techniques

When beginning a cut with a hand saw, draw the saw back toward your body to sever the wood fibres and produce a small kerf – the groove in which the saw blade will run. Always cut on the waste side of the marked line for perfect results.

When using a mitre box to make an angled cut, begin with the back of the saw raised slightly. This will make the cut easier to start. The bench hook also makes cross-cutting very easy at 90 degrees.

Power tools

A hand-held circular saw can be used for both cross-cutting and ripping, and many are supplied with a dual-purpose, tungsten-carbide-tipped blade for a long life. It is almost a necessity for the home woodworker and is an excellent investment; there are many quite inexpensive and reliable brands.

Another very handy tool is the jigsaw (saber saw). This comes into its own for cutting curves, but it can also save a lot of hard work when used to cut curved shapes from manufactured boards.

If a lot of curved or shaped work is envisaged, a small bandsaw is a useful addition to the workshop. These can be inexpensive.

Fret/scroll saws are very similar to jigsaws, having a reciprocating movement. They are used for fine pierced and detail work, and are capable of producing very delicate results. Most jigsaws come into their own when cutting manufactured boards, such as medium-density fibreboard, plywood or chipboard.

ABOVE LEFT Draw the saw back to start the cut.

ABOVE CENTRE Use a tenon saw for cutting small components or sawing tenons and the like. Point the nose of the saw downwards initially to start the cut.

ABOVE Use a bench hook for cross-cutting.

Practical tips

- Most cheap saws are not worth owning. Buy good ones, and hang them up or keep the blades guarded when they are not in use. Keep them dry, sharp, well set and lightly oiled.

- Always find a comfortable position to saw in. It will produce better results and reduce the risks of back strain or other injury.

FAR LEFT A circular saw will make light work of cutting timber, but be sure not to overload it, and always have the guards in place. Use a good-quality hand saw for smaller jobs.

LEFT A jigsaw (saber saw) is very good for cutting out curves and circles. Be sure your work is well clamped to keep it steady and firmly in place.

Nails, Hammers and Punches

There is no such thing as an "ordinary" nail. All nails have been derived for specific uses, although some can be put to several uses. Similarly, various types of hammer are available – always use the correct tool for the job. Wooden-handled hammers have a natural spring in the handles, which makes them easier to control than steel-handled ones.

Nails

The wire nail can be used for many simple tasks, such as box making, fencing and general carpentry, as can lost head and oval nails where there is no need for a flat head or when it is desirable for the nails to be concealed, such as when fixing cladding or boards. These wire nails can be considered as general-purpose fixings.

Oval wire nails can be driven below the surface of the work with less likelihood of them splitting the wood. They should be driven with their heads in line with the grain.

The cut nail is stamped from metal sheet and has a tapering, rectangular section, which gives it excellent holding properties. They are largely used for fixing flooring.

Panel pins (brads), as their name suggests, are used for fixing thin panels and cladding. They are nearly always punched out of sight below the surface, as are veneer pins.

When there is a need to secure thin or fragile sheet material, such as roofing felt or plasterboard (gypsum board), large-headed nails are used. These are commonly called clout nails, but may also be found under specific names, such as roofing nails and plasterboard nails. Their large heads spread the pressure and prevent the materials from tearing or crumbling. They are usually galvanized to protect against rust when used outdoors. Zinc nails are used for roofing because they are rustproof and easy to cut when renewing slates.

Dovetail nailing

When several nails are being driven into one piece of timber, avoid putting them in straight; slanting them will help prevent splitting.

Cross, or dovetail, nailing is a simple and useful method of holding a butt joint strongly in end grain.

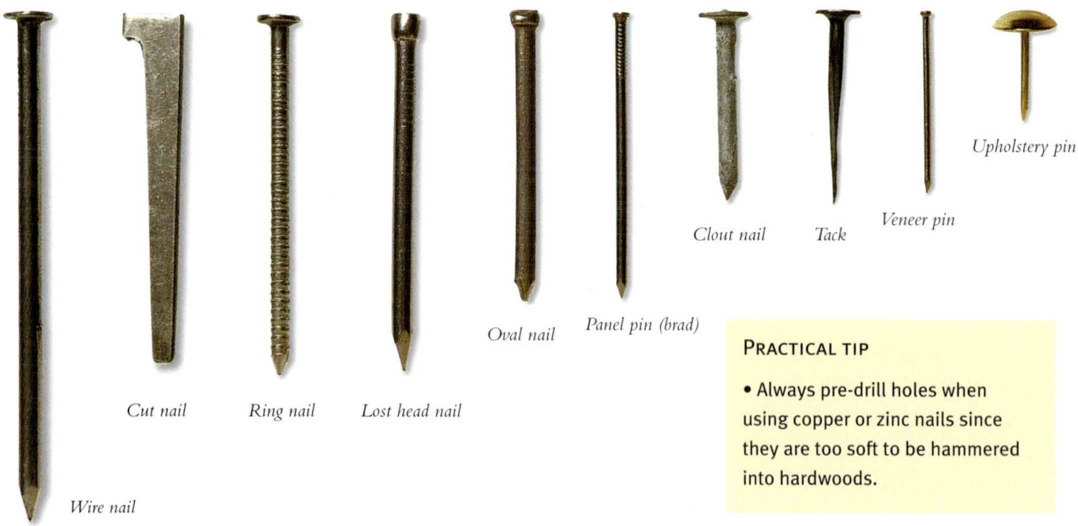

Practical tip

- Always pre-drill holes when using copper or zinc nails since they are too soft to be hammered into hardwoods.

Claw hammer

Cross-pein hammer

Pin hammer

Carpenter's mallet

HAMMERS

The most essential hammer for the woodworker is the claw hammer. About 365–450g (13–16oz) is a good weight to aim for, since the hammer should be heavy enough to drive fairly large nails. It is a mistake to use a hammer that is too light, as this tends to bend the nails rather than drive them.

For lighter nails, a cross-pein or Warrington hammer is useful, since the flat head can be used to start the nail or pin without risk of hitting your fingers. For even smaller panel pins (brads), the pin hammer is used.

THE MALLET

It should be remembered that the carpenter's mallet, often made from solid beech, is a form of hammer, but it should never be used for striking anything other than wood or similar soft materials or serious damage will result.

REMOVING AND HIDING NAILS

Nails or pins can be removed from a workpiece by using a specialized tool such as a nail puller. You might need to use this if you have bent the nail or perhaps if you are working with previously-used timber. Alternatively, the claw of a claw hammer can be easily employed.

Very often, we need to punch nail heads below the surface of the work and fill the resulting small holes with a wood filler. Nail sets are used for this, and they come in various sizes. Each has a very slightly concave tip to cover the nail head and prevent slipping. Nail sets should not be confused with centre punches, which are used to mark metal for drilling.

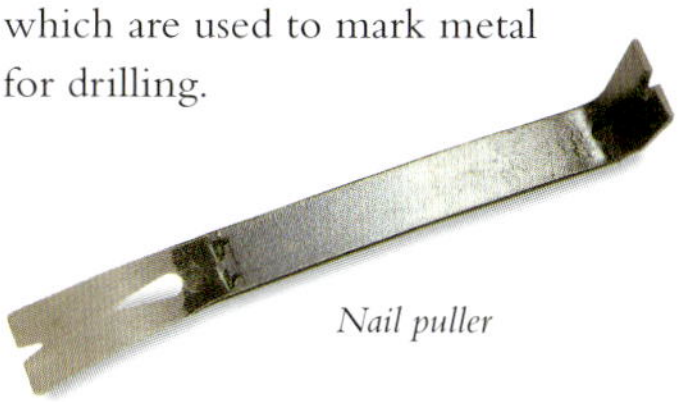

Nail puller

Centre punch

Nail sets or punches

ABOVE The claw hammer's ability to extract, as well as drive, nails makes it a useful tool for the carpentry shop.

Sanders

Although the term "sanding" is generally used for do-it-yourself projects, it is something of a misnomer. A truer description would be "abrading", because what we call "sandpaper" is, in fact, "glasspaper". In addition, we also use garnet paper, and silicon-carbide and aluminium-oxide abrasive papers, all of which shape wood very efficiently.

Grit size

One thing abrasive papers all have in common is classification by grit size, and the golden rule is to work progressively down through the grit sizes, from coarse to fine, when smoothing a piece of work. For example, 400 grit is finer than 200 grit and should be employed later in the finishing process. Abrasives can be used by hand or with a variety of machines, both hand-held and stationary. Sanders are also suitable for shaping work, using coarse abrasives for rapid material removal.

Types of sander

A tool commonly used for heavy-duty shaping and sanding is the belt sander. These normally have a 75mm (3in) wide belt, running continuously over two rollers and a dust collection facility in the form of a cloth bag.

Most home craftsmen are likely to own an orbital sander, which is useful for general light sanding work such as finishing boards. These sanders are designed to accept either half or a third of a standard-size abrasive sheet and quite often have dedicated sheets made for them. Random orbital sanders are similar, but often employ self-adhesive abrasive sheets that are easy to fit. They can be small enough to be used with one hand in tight spots, but still give a good finish to most types of work. A newcomer to the sanding armoury is the power abrader. This tool can remove material rapidly and should be regarded as a shaping or sculptural tool rather than a pure sander.

Practical tips

- **Most clogged-up sanding discs and belts can be cleaned by pressing a piece of plastic pipe, such as garden hose, on to the belt with the motor running.**

- **Always finish off your sanding by hand, working along the grain of the wood.**

Belt sander

Orbital sander

Random orbital sander

Palm orbital sander

Detail sander

LEFT AND ABOVE Power sanders are most useful for the quick removal of waste stock before finishing by hand. A belt sander is worth considering if you have a lot of heavy-duty work, but does not produce an acceptable finish on its own. For general use, an orbital sander is by far the most versatile power tool to buy.

Hand sanding

This is used to finish fine cabinet work. Always work along the grain of the wood. Use a cork or rubber block on flat surfaces to obtain the right amount of flexibility that you will need. Clear the dust away as you work to avoid clogging the paper, particularly on resinous and oily wood. To finish off a rounded edge, wrap a square of paper around a section of moulded timber with the correct profile for the job.

Static sanders

Very inexpensive and well worth owning is the combination sander. This consists of a belt and disc sander combined and is invaluable in the home workshop. Static sanders are almost exclusively shaping and trimming tools, rather than smoothers, since the workpiece is taken to them. Many have mitre fences for multi-angled cutting, and worktables that can be adjusted to exactly 90 degrees for the work in hand. They can be very aggressive unless handled with care.

Making a sanding block

1 Fold your sheet of abrasive paper to size and tear it along a sharp edge.

2 Wrap the abrasive around a cork block or similar soft material before starting to sand.

ABOVE Dedicated belt and disc sanders are now reasonably priced and they are very useful tools in the home workshop.

ABOVE The belt sander can be inverted and secured in a woodworking vice. Use the rounded ends of the belt to shape concave curves.

ABOVE The fast action of the belt sander means that it must be held with both hands to prevent it from running away.

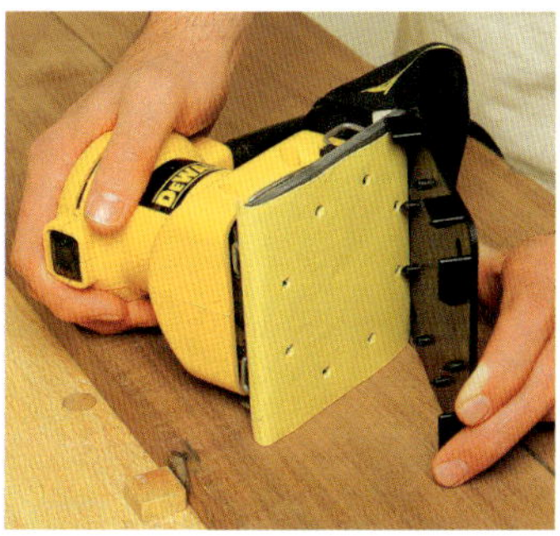

ABOVE The orbital sander is a much less ferocious cutter than the belt sander and is easy to control. They are sold as half-sheet, third-sheet and quarter-sheet models. Standard-sized paper fits the base.

ABOVE The power abrader has many uses, one of which is as a sculptural tool for shaping different kinds of wood.

Planes

Unplaned wood is known as "sawn" and comes in sizes such as 50 x 25mm (2 x 1in) or 100 x 50mm (4 x 2in). In spite of the ready availability of prepared (planed/dressed) timber, the do-it-yourself enthusiast must still learn to use at least one hand plane in the pursuit of this craft – for trimming joints and joining faces, and for the general cleaning up of timber surfaces.

Using planes

By using a hand plane to remove wood, a beginner will gain a better understanding of the characteristics of the wood being worked. The most commonly used variety is the small jack, or smoothing plane.

Good-quality examples are sufficiently weighty to avoid "chatter", which occurs when the plane skips over the surface of the wood without cutting properly.

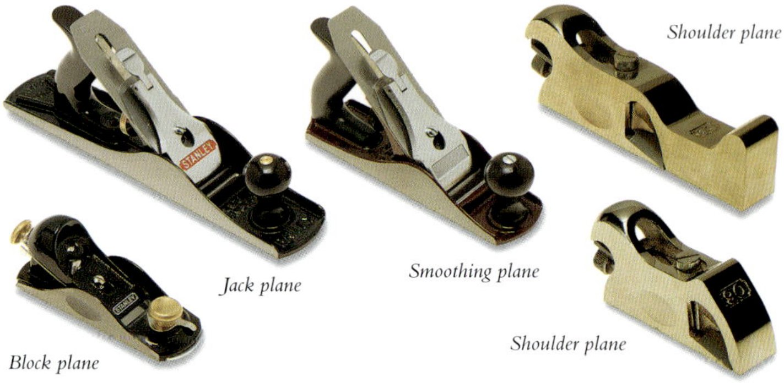

Hand planing techniques

Body weight plays a large part in planing technique. Position your body with your hips and shoulders in line with the plane, and your feet spaced comfortably apart.

At the beginning of the stroke, apply pressure to the front handle of the plane, switching to a general downward pressure during the middle of the stroke, and finish off by applying most of the pressure to the back of the plane at the end of the board.

Starting to plane

1 The correct body position helps to achieve the desired result.

2 Keep the pressure on the back of the plane at the end of your stroke.

3 To keep the plane centralized, tuck your fingers under the sole plate as a guide.

4 If you have identical edges to plane, clamp them together and work on both at once.

Practical tips

- Cheap planes often serve to blunt enthusiasm by poor performance. Always buy the best you can afford and keep them sharp.

- Check for sharpness and adjustment each time a plane is used – and make sure the wood to be planed is held firmly.

Planing end grain and boards

A block plane is often used for planing end grain because its blade is set at a low angle that severs the wood fibres cleanly. To avoid splitting the ends of the wood, work in from each side toward the middle.

A useful technique for planing wide boards is to work diagonally, or even at right angles, across the grain of the boards. This method will remove material efficiently. To finish, it will be necessary to make cuts with the grain for a smooth surface.

Chamfer cutting

This is often a quick operation, but it is easy to get carried away. So, for accuracy, always mark the extent of the desired chamfer with a pencil or marking knife before planing.

The electric planer

Electric planers can be aggressive when removing stock, so hold the tool with both hands and keep it moving so that it does not cut for too long in one spot. An electric planer can also be used across the grain of wide boards for quick results, provided final finishing is with the grain. Although the electric planer is very fast, the hand-held version rarely gives the quality of finish that can be achieved with a well-set and sharpened bench plane.

Making chamfers

1 Mark out a chamfer to ensure an even removal of the material.

2 Plane a chamfer by hand with a firm grip and tool control.

Planing

Above Use two hands to plane end grain with an electric planer to ensure complete control.

Above Plane across wide boards with an electric planer to give quick results.

Sharpening plane irons

Apply a coat of thin oil to the oilstone and rest the bevel of the iron on the stone. Hold the blade at 35 degrees to the oilstone and maintain a constant angle while working it backward and forward on the stone. Honing jigs, which set the angle exactly, are readily available, but most craftsmen soon learn to do this accurately by hand. Lay the back of the iron flat on the oilstone and slowly rub off the burr formed by the sharpening process. Clean any debris from inside the body of the plane before reassembly, and apply a drop of oil to the moving parts of the adjustment mechanism.

1 Keep the block at a steady angle along the sharpening stone.

2 Remove the burr or "back off" from a newly sharpened blade.

Knives

When we think of knives in relation to woodworking, the most common application is the marking or striking knife. However, the do-it-yourself enthusiast will need a variety of other knives, some of which have very specific functions. Some do not actually conform to the conventional idea of a knife at all, but all have metal blades and are essentially cutting tools.

Marking knives

The purpose of a marking knife is to mark a sawing line by lightly cutting the surface wood fibres and assist in the beginning of a sawcut. Not only does this provide a permanent guide line, but it also prevents the fibres from splintering as the saw cuts through. These tools are usually about 200mm (8in) and make a much finer line than a pencil.

They are normally used in conjunction with a steel rule, straightedge or square and are bevelled on one side only so that they can be used tight against the steel edge for accuracy. They are available in both left- and right-handed versions.

Marking knives without pointed ends are also frequently used, and these are bevelled on either the left- or right-hand side, depending on the needs of the user.

Twin-bladed knives are available and are adjusted by a set screw and locking knob. Typically, the blades can be set to a spacing of 3–19mm (⅛–¾in). This type of knife is used for marking parallel lines, gauging mortises and cutting thin strips from veneers for inlay work.

ABOVE Mark a line across the grain with the knife held firmly against the steel edge of a try square. This gives a very fine line of severed wood fibres, which is ideal to work to with either a saw or a chisel.

Marking out

A typical example of a marking knife being used in conjunction with a steel rule. Note how the fingers of the hand are spread to keep a firm and even downward pressure on the rule, allowing the knife to be used hard against the rule's edge.

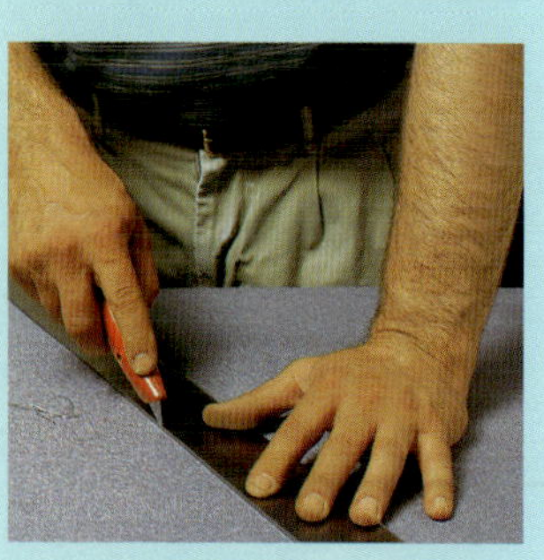

Striking knife with blade and point

Marking knife with bevel on one side

Twin-bladed adjustable marking knife

Heavy-duty retractable blade knife

General-purpose knives

By far the most common and useful general-purpose knife is the craft, or "Stanley" knife, that stores replacement blades in the handle. This is an indispensable tool in any workshop, and it can be used for many purposes, including marking out.

Another very handy tool in the workshop is the scalpel. More delicate and invasive than the craft knife, a scalpel is ideal for cutting out templates and particularly useful for cleaning up deeply indented cuts in carvings and routed work. Scalpels are made with a variety of handles and have replaceable blades.

Miscellaneous knives

Putty knives often find their way into the do-it-yourself enthusiast's tool kit. They have specially shaped ends to their blades to make "cutting off" easier. This means withdrawing the knife from the work without damaging the soft putty that is being applied to a window pane or moulding for example.

The filling knife is a familiar decorator's tool with a flexible spring-tempered blade that is ideal for forcing soft material, such as wood filler, into knot holes, cracks and blemishes in timber, and plaster filler into cracks in walls. These come in a variety of shapes and sizes and are often confused with stripping knives, which have thicker and less flexible blades.

> **Practical tips**
>
> - Never use a scalpel or craft knife with excessive pressure. The blade may snap off and pieces fly up into your unprotected eyes.
> - Always place the hand not holding the knife behind the blade of a trimming knife. This prevents injury if the blade slips.

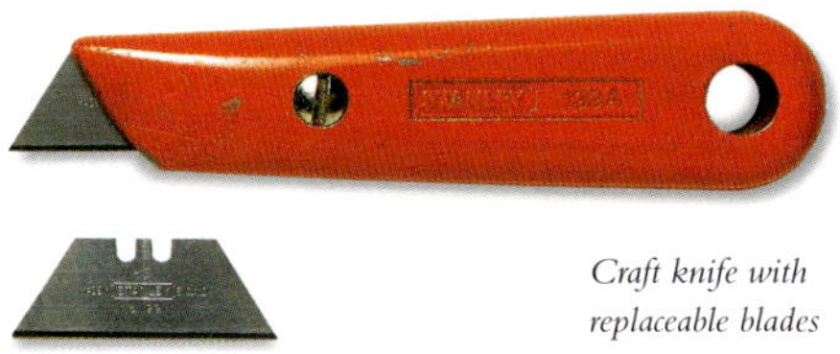

Craft knife with replaceable blades

Putty knives (above and below)

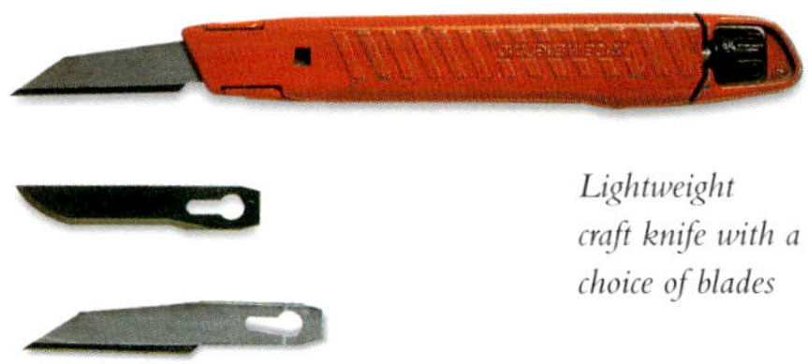

Lightweight craft knife with a choice of blades

A decorator's knife

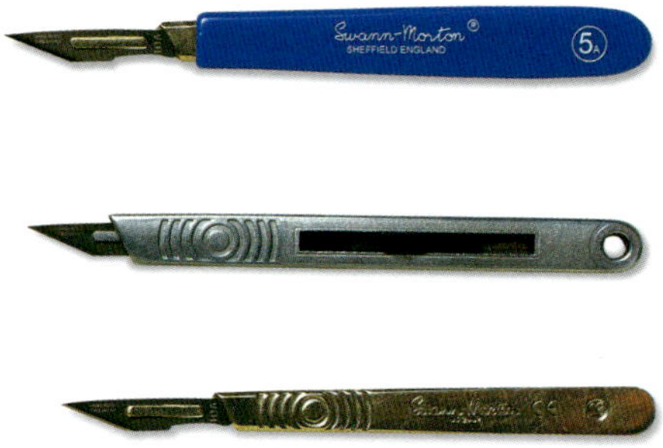

A selection of scalpels

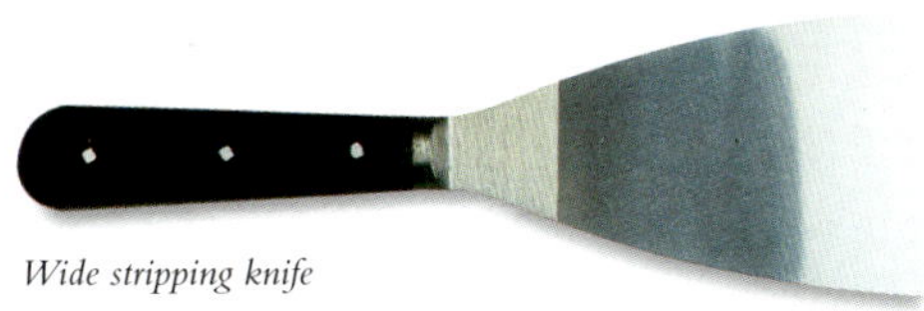

Wide stripping knife

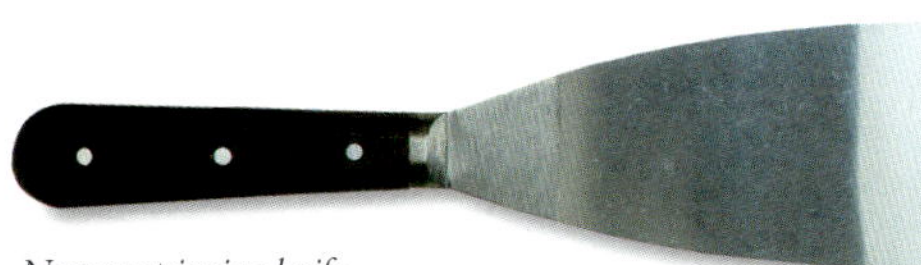

Narrow stripping knife

Tackers

Staple guns, or tackers, have a wide variety of uses around the home and are particularly useful when working alone. They can quickly secure light materials in position for fixing with nails or screws later. Moreover, they can be used one-handed, allowing the other hand to stretch and position the material for fixing, which can often produce more accurate results.

Fixing sheet materials and cables

Tackers come into their own for fixing virtually any sheet material, either to solid timber or manufactured boards such as chipboard, plywood and blockboard. The more powerful models are capable of fixing into plaster and soft masonry. A tacker is an essential item for upholstery work, ideal for fitting hardboard to floors and securing carpet underlay, as well as fixing roofing felt and ceiling tiles, and it can even be used to secure low-voltage electrical cables such as those used for door bells. Few are recommended for attaching cables carrying mains electricity, but special wiring tackers can be bought that will fire U-shaped staples for fixing cables up to 6mm (¼in) diameter.

Tacker types

Many tackers are similar to the hand-operated staplers found in every office. Electrically powered tools, for either light or heavy duty, pack a real punch. Those operated by compressed air are generally for heavy-duty use and are ideal for jobs such as fixing wire mesh, netting and heavy sheeting.

Many tackers will operate with either staples or nails and some are dedicated nailers only. The latter may fire up to 30 nails per minute.

Picture framers use smaller dedicated tools that fire special flexible points into the frame to hold both the glass and the backing. Some have an adjustable power control to match the hardness of the timber, as

Wiring tacker

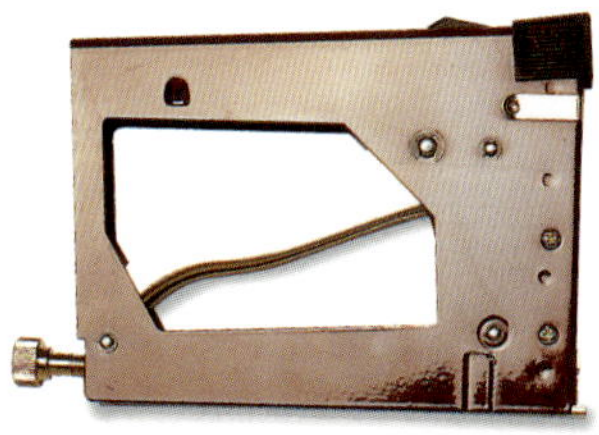

Picture framer's tacker

Glazier's tacker

Compressed air-powered nailer

Compressed air-powered nailer and tacker

do many of the more expensive general-purpose tackers.

Glaziers use a frame tool that fires brads up to 19mm (¾in) long to secure the glass in a window frame. It leaves the heads projecting about 4mm (3/16in) before glazing with putty. A more general application of this tool is for temporary fixings where the projecting head makes the brad or panel pin easy to remove.

General-purpose tackers

A hand-operated, heavy-duty staple gun is worked by gripping the body and squeezing down with the handle. Many have a small window that allows the contents of the magazine to be checked. A heavy-duty electronic tacker machine fires single staples, nails or pins and will accept staple widths of 4 and 10mm (3/16 and ⅜in) with lengths up to 23mm (⅞in). It also takes nails and pins up to 23mm (⅞in) long. It is ideal for fixing tongued-and-grooved cladding and heavy sheeting such as hardboard.

A typical nailer/tacker multiple-impact tool with electronic adjustment is ideal for upholstery work and general fixing around the home. Single-shot, continuous tacking or tacking two staples at a time can be achieved with this general-purpose tool.

Used in much the same way as a hammer, a hammer tacker feeds and drives staples as fast as the operator can use it. More suited to speed than accuracy, it earns its keep when something needs fixing in place quickly or if the finished result is not visually important.

Practical tips

- Never point a nail gun or powered tacker at anybody. New tools have safety devices to prevent operation when not in contact with the workpiece, but it is not worth taking chances, especially with an older tool.

- Always buy a brand of tacker that uses a standard size of nail or staple, making sure these are available locally.

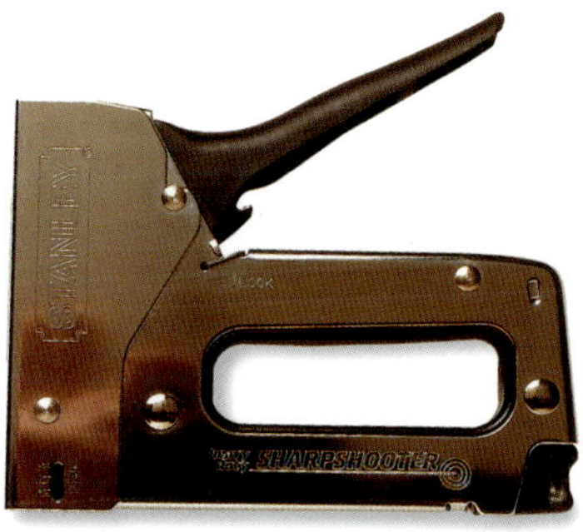

Hand-operated, heavy-duty staple gun

Stapler/nail gun

Hammer tacker

Electronic staple gun

Clamps

Many do-it-yourself tasks require two or more sections of a workpiece to be held together temporarily while a more permanent fixing is made, often with glue. A variety of clamps is available for this purpose, many of them with specific uses. Keen woodworkers may make their own clamps (or cramps as they are often called) from scrap wood or other materials.

Commonly used clamps

The most common clamp in the workshop is the G- (C-) clamp. This is a general-purpose tool that is available with a variety of throat sizes. It may be used on its own or in conjunction with others when, for example, working on the surface of a wide board or holding boards together for gluing.

The sash clamp was specifically designed for assembling window frames, or sashes, but it is also often used when edge-jointing boards to form large panels for table tops and similar items.

Sometimes, it is useful to be able to apply a clamp with one hand while holding the workpiece in the other, which is when the single-handed clamp comes into its own. It works on a simple ratchet system, rather like a mastic (caulking) gun.

For picture framing and heavier items with 45-degree mitres at the corners, there is the mitre clamp. This can be quite a complex affair with screw handles or a very simple clothes-peg (pin) type arrangement, that is applied very quickly.

Sash clamp

A selection of different-sized F-clamps or screw clamps

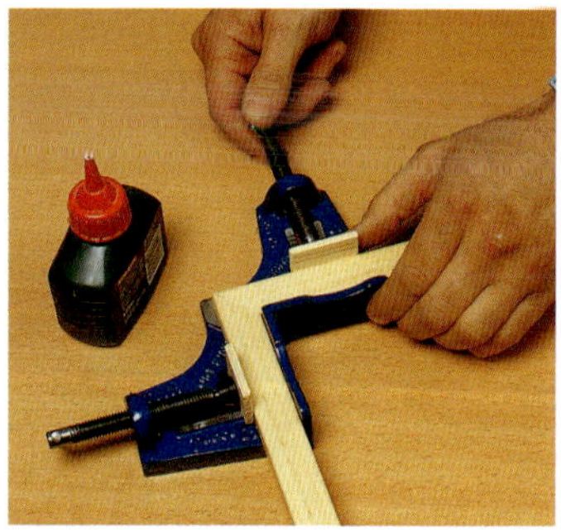

ABOVE Small wooden picture frames and mirrors can be easily joined with inexpensive mitre clamps.

Quick (spring) clamp

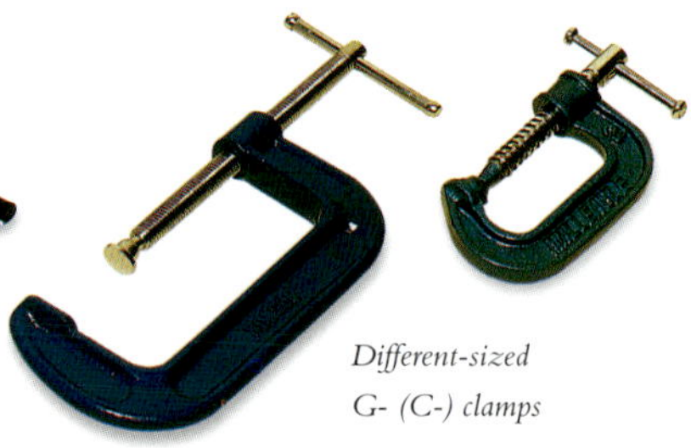

Different-sized G- (C-) clamps

ABOVE This clever little clamp works on spring pressure and can be applied quickly.

Web clamp

Mitre clamp

Special-purpose clamps

There are many of these, but one that the do-it-yourself enthusiast may find useful is the cam clamp, which is wooden with cork faces. This is a quickly operated clamp often used by musical instrument makers. Its advantages are its speed in use, its lightness and its simplicity. The cam clamp is ideal for small holding jobs around the home, although it cannot exert a great deal of pressure.

Another useful standby is the web, frame or strap clamp. This is perfect for holding unusually-shaped items,

Cam clamp

which can be pulled together from a single point.

They are most commonly used to join coopered work, such as barrels and casks, or multi-faceted shapes such as hexagons or octagons used in decorative frames and mirrors. The components to be joined usually lie flat on a horizontal surface, as shown.

ABOVE The web or strap clamp is ideal for multi-sided shapes that are difficult to hold. The strong nylon webbing extends around the work and is tightened with a spanner, applying tension equally around the work.

ABOVE Use sash clamps to edge-joint boards to form a panel such as a table top. Reverse the central clamp to even out the pressure.

ABOVE Home-made clamps used for the same purpose, but this time the pressure is exerted by means of wedges.

Clamps in use

Apply pressure to a joint or the assembly you are working on as soon as possible after gluing – make a habit of preparing everything you need in advance. Keep a box of small scraps of wood handy and use them to protect the surface of the work. It is often said that you can never have too many clamps, and you will soon start collecting a selection of different types and sizes to suit all kinds of assembly technique. Many of these you can make yourself.

ABOVE A home-made frame clamp being used on a picture frame. There are grooved blocks at the corners to hold the string.

ABOVE The G- (C-) clamp in a typical application. Note the packing pieces beneath the jaws to prevent bruising of the wood.

Practical tips

- Do not be tempted to release clamps too quickly. Be patient, allowing plenty of drying time for the glue.

- Think through the sequence for the clamping process and make sure you have enough clamps to hand before you apply any glue. You may decide you need another person to help.

Workbenches and Vices

A solid and stable surface is essential for producing good work, and serious thought should be given to this by the enthusiast. A good bench need not be too expensive, nor too pretty; the prime requirements are sturdy construction, a flat top surface and at least one good vice somewhere on the front of the bench.

Workbenches

A basic bench with a front vice can be improved by the addition of a tail vice and bench dogs. The bench can be improved still further by incorporating a cabinet and drawers. The bench dogs are set at a convenient length into a series of holes in the top of the bench and they work in conjunction with the tail vice for holding long pieces of timber along the top of the bench. They can easily be removed and reset at will.

ABOVE Bench dogs can be home-made in wood, plastic or metal.

ABOVE A wooden workbench with a front and tail vice.

LEFT A wooden workbench with drawers for useful storage of tools.

Portable supports

By far the most popular form of portable support is the foldaway workbench. This is really convenient to use, both in the workshop and the home, both internally and externally. It has the ingenious feature of a bench top that is in two halves and is capable of acting as a vice. It is handy for holding awkward shapes, such as pipes and large dowels.

Another form of a simple, portable bench is the saw horse, or trestle. A pair of these will support large workpieces such as doors. It is an ideal first-time project for a do-it-yourself enthusiast to make, providing experience in cutting angles and simple jointwork.

ABOVE A portable foldaway workbench with adjustable bench top.

ABOVE Wooden sawhorses come in pairs and are often home-made.

ABOVE Plastic, light-weight sawhorses can be useful if you are undertaking small jobs.

Vices

Your main workshop vice should be heavy and sturdy. It is normally screwed to the underside of the work bench or worktop, close to one of the legs. Make sure you buy one that is designed for woodworking, preferably with a quick-release action on the front of the vice that allows you to open and close the jaws quickly, turning the handle for final adjustments. You should certainly be able to fit false wooden jaws to prevent bruising of the work.

Additional ways of protecting the work in the vice take the form of magnetic vice jaws faced with cork, rubber or aluminium, which fit inside the main jaws of the steel bench vice.

Another useful, portable, addition to the bench that is cheaper than a woodworking vice is the swivelling bench-top vice. This can easily be fitted and removed very quickly, usually by means of a screw clamp. It is particularly handy for holding down small pieces of work in awkward positions, when carving for example. However, it is too lightweight to hold work that is to be struck hard.

The mitre clamp can also be considered as a bench vice of sorts and is useful to picture framers. Most woodworkers will keep one near the bench to hold any assemblies that require clamping at 45 degrees. Good quality ones are made from metal, since plastic will tend to flex when pressure is applied.

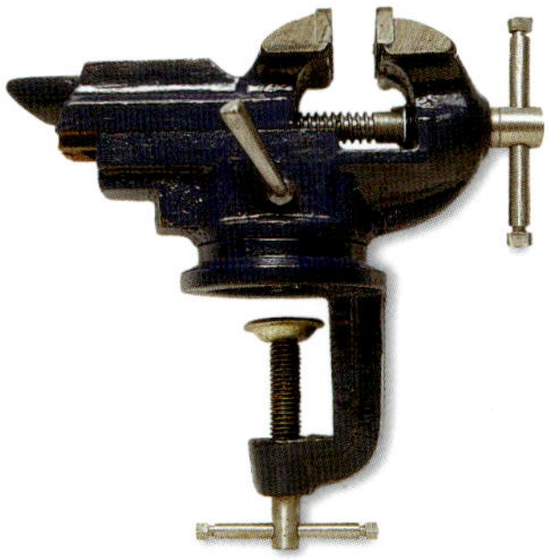

ABOVE A swivelling bench-top vice is handy for work that needs to be turned or that is an awkward shape to work.

ABOVE False faces for vices come in rubber, cork and aluminium and prevent damage to the wood being worked.

ABOVE A picture framer's vice is best made from metal rather than plastic.

RIGHT A solid carpenter's vice is an absolute essential tool in the workshop, second only to the workbench itself.

Practical tips

- Always buy the best-quality vice you can afford; second-hand ones can be particularly good value.
- Spend time adjusting your workbench to the exact height that suits you. An incorrect height can prove to be very tiring and is not good for your back. Never shorten the legs of a bench if it is too high; work off a duckboard if necessary.

Folding bench vice

The worktop acts as two vice jaws, one of which can be slewed to grip tapered items of work or straightened up to fit parallel-sided wood using the vice controls at the side of the bench. On some makes, the adjustable jaw can also be set vertically to provide downward clamping pressure. You can also clamp a piece of wood to the top of the bench between the plastic clamping pegs to hold awkwardly shaped pieces.

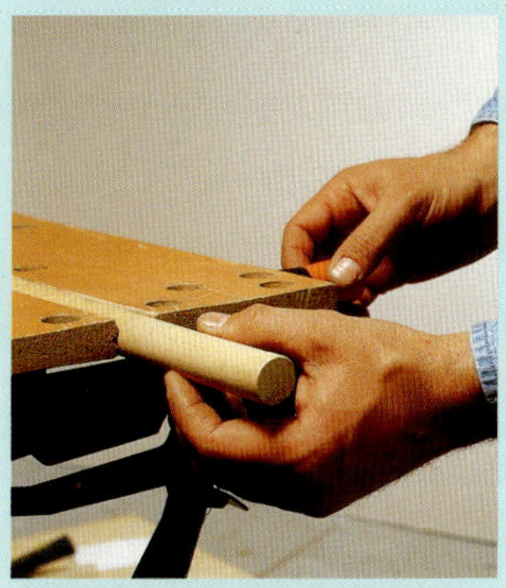

Put the piece of wood or other item you wish to saw between the vice jaws.

Pincers and Pliers

Every do-it-yourself enthusiast's tool kit should include a range of hand tools for gripping small items. Chief among these are pincers, used for removing nails and similar fixings, and general-purpose combination pliers, which offer a variety of gripping and cutting features. Many other special-purpose tools of similar design are also available.

Removing nails and tacks

A good pair of pincers will remove nails and tacks with little trouble. The rolling action required to remove a nail with pincers is very similar to that used with a claw hammer. Pincers are essential to the woodworker, an ideal length is about 175mm (7in) to ensure good leverage. The jaws should touch along their entire width and be properly aligned to provide maximum grip.

It is important that pincers have good leverage and do not damage the work, and for this reason, broad jaws – about 25mm (1in) wide – that will spread the load are best.

Some pincers come with a handy tack lifter on one of the handles. Purpose-made tack lifters are very useful for upholstery work, and if you intend doing any furniture making or restoration, it is well worth investing in one.

Another special tack and nail remover is the nail puller, or "cat's-paw", as it is sometimes known. This tool has a standard tack remover at one end and a large, right-angled claw at the other for getting under the heads of stubborn nails. The claw can be tapped under the head of an embedded nail with a small hammer.

LEFT The flat behind the claw of this Japanese nail puller can be tapped with a hammer to drive the claw under the nail head.

Reusing nails and wood

When removing an old nail from better-quality wood that is to be reused, protect the surface of the wood by slipping a piece of hardboard or thin plywood below the pincer head.

Pincers

Pincers with a tack remover

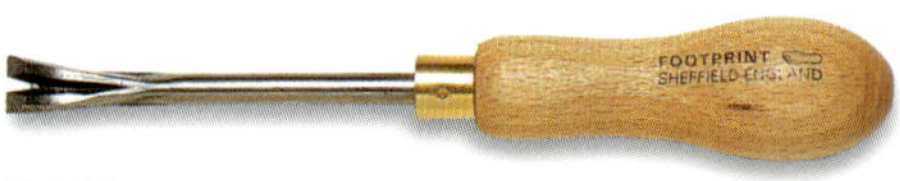

Tack lifter

Nail puller

Pliers

These come in a bewildering range of types and sizes, many of which have very specific uses.

Combination pliers are "Jacks of all trades" and are used for gripping, twisting and cutting. They come in various sizes, but a good pair would be about 200mm (8in) long and probably have plastic or rubber handle grips for comfort and insulation against shock.

Long-nosed (needlenose) pliers

These are rather more specialized and are used for gripping small objects in confined spaces. Some have cranked jaws at various angles for access to awkward places. They come in many sizes and some are designed for very fine work.

Specialized gripping and cutting tools

Glass pliers are used for gripping and shaping glass and ceramic tiles. They are usually made with bare steel handles to prevent any sharp particles from sticking to them.

Long-nosed, vice-grip pliers will hold very small objects in awkward spots and are useful for extracting small items embedded in wood.

Standard vice-grips are familiar to generations of craftspeople. They provide a powerful grip to hold all manner of objects in a variety of materials. Because they have locking handles, they can be very useful as miniature vices when gluing up small objects. Power cutters are less well known, but have razor-sharp replaceable blades for cutting sheet materials such as plastics and thin metals. They are handy in the workshop for making patterns and cutting templates.

Holding pliers

When using pliers, hold them firmly, keeping your palm away from the pivot, which can pinch your skin as the jaws close.

Long-nosed (needlenose) pliers

Glass pliers

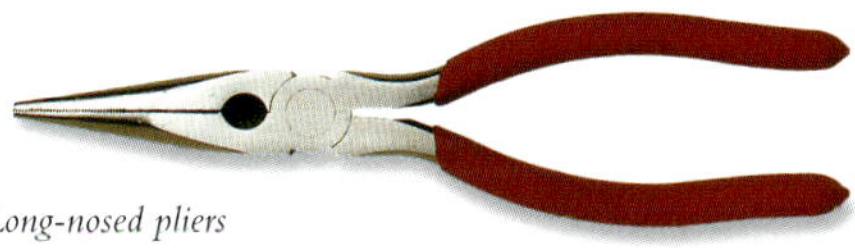

Long-nosed pliers

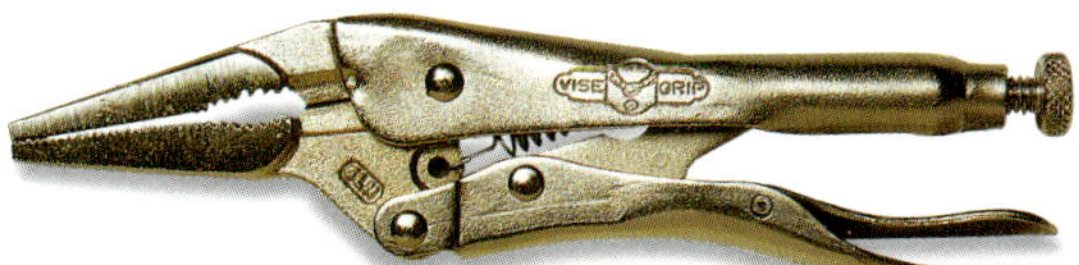

Long-nosed, vice-grip pliers

Combination pliers

Heavy-duty pliers

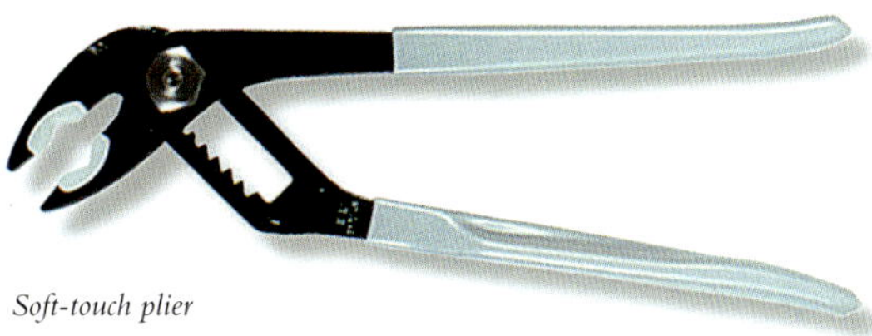

Soft-touch plier

Spanners and Wrenches

Although spanners and wrenches may be thought of as tools for the garage, there are many do-it-yourself tasks that require these gripping and twisting tools, particularly in the kitchen and bathroom, where you are likely to come into contact with pipes and their fittings. All home workshops need at least one comprehensive set of sockets or spanners.

Spanners

These are necessary in the home workshop where power tools and machinery are involved. They are needed for changing the blades on circular saws, for adjusting and setting bandsaw guides, and for assembling all manner of machinery stands, tool racks and benches. You should have a selection of wrenches and spanners in the home workshop. The combination spanner, open-ended spanner and the ring spanner are usually purchased in sets; the other tools are bought singly.

There is a large range to choose from, and it is essential to use a spanner that fits a nut or bolt perfectly, otherwise the fixing will be damaged and the user runs the risk of skinned knuckles. Spanners are graduated in specific sizes – metric, Whitworth and A/F are the most common. Open-ended spanners are the most usual. Some have jaws that are offset by about 15 degrees to allow them to get on to different flats of nuts when working in tight spots.

Ring spanners have enclosed heads that give a more secure grip. They may have six or 12 points and can be used on square or hexagonal nuts and bolts. The 12-point version needs only a very small movement for it to contact new flats on the nut or bolt head, so is very useful where there is limited room for movement.

ABOVE Socket sets are extremely useful in any home workshop and offer the owner a choice of types of drives (such as bars or ratchets) as well as sockets in a variety of sizes.

Open-ended spanner

Combination spanner

Ring spanner

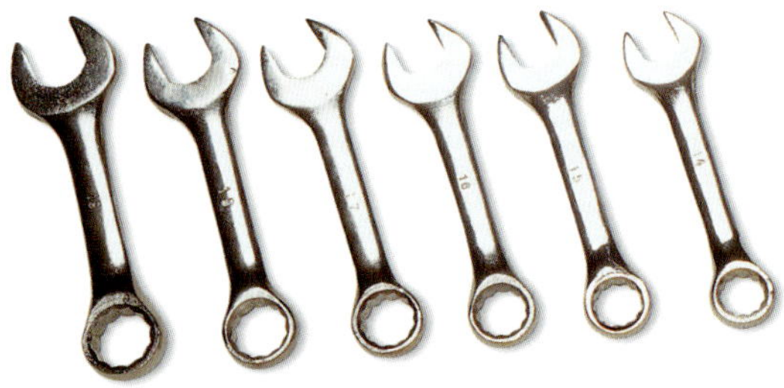

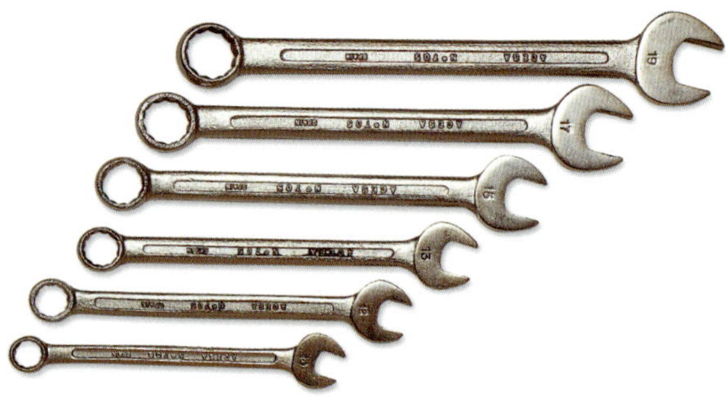

RIGHT Most spanners come in sets of six in both metric and imperial sizes.

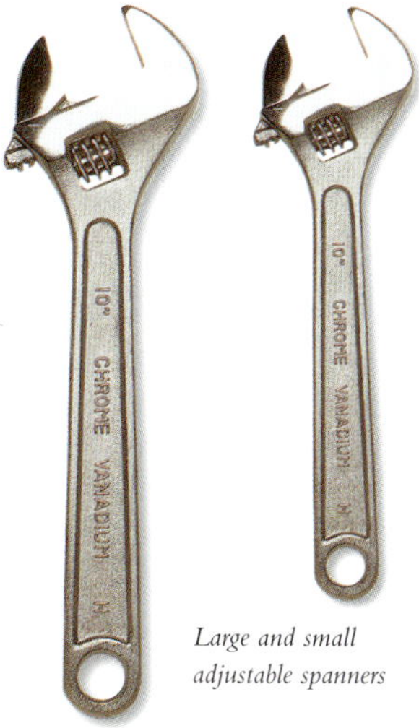

Large and small adjustable spanners

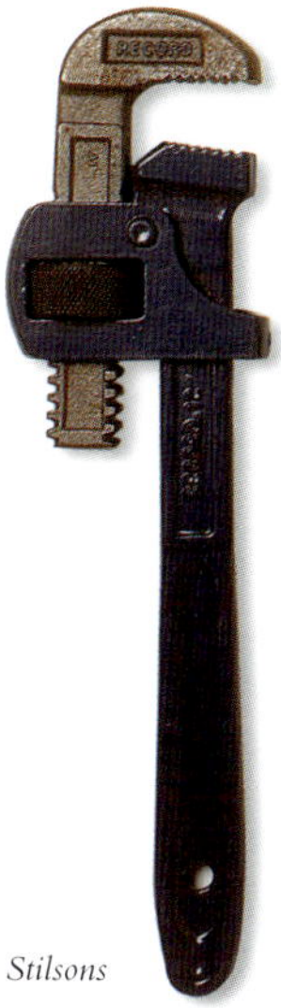

Stilsons

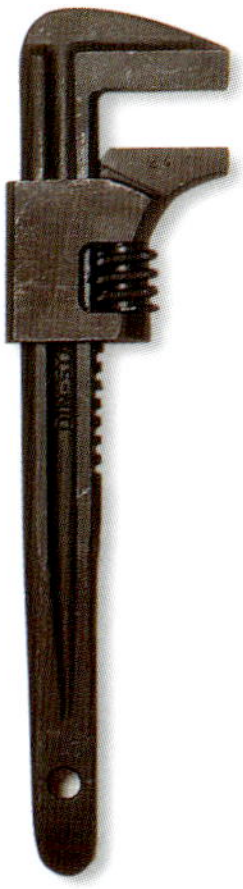

Pipe wrench

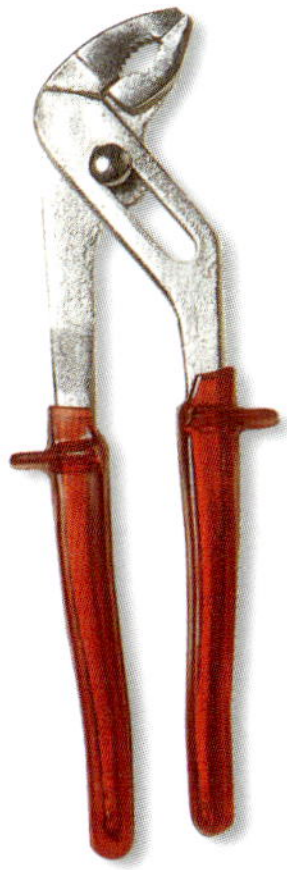

Swan necks

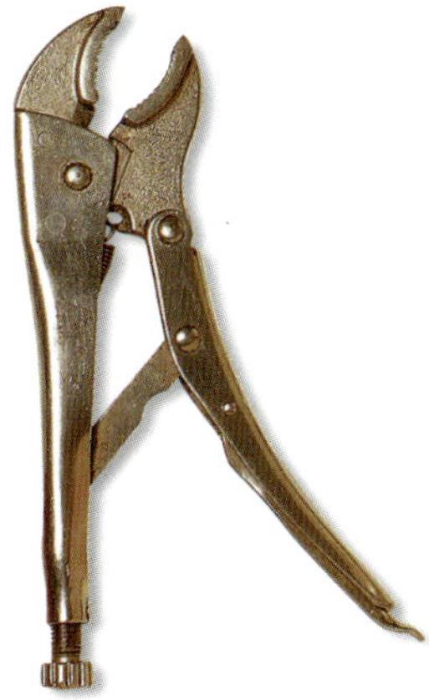

ABOVE The mole wrench is a specialized type of plier, which can be "locked" into position.

Sockets grip in the same manner as a ring spanner, but are designed to fit a variety of drive handles, of which the ratchet handle is the most useful. This enables the user to continue to turn a nut or bolt without having to remove the socket after each turn. Some large sets offer metric, Whitworth, BSF and A/F sizes. Small sets of additional sockets are available to complement your existing set, allowing you to build up a kit that meets your needs exactly.

The auto-adjustable wrench is quick and easy to use. Normally, the adjustable spanner is made from forged alloy steel. Self-grip wrenches, or vice grips, can be adjusted to fit pipework or on a nut or bolt head, and can then be locked to grip tightly. They are very versatile and useful tools. Water-pump pliers offer five or six settings by virtue of having an adjustable bottom jaw. They exert a heavy pressure because of their long handles.

ABOVE Allen keys are specially made for using with screws that have corresponding hexagonal holes in their heads.

Wrenches

Adjustable spanners and wrenches enable the user the grip various sizes and types of fittings. Some are designed for specific purposes, while others are suitable for more general household use.

Basic plumbing tools include adjustable pipe wrenches (known as Stilsons), an adjustable basin wrench, a double-ended basin wrench and water-pump pliers with soft jaws.

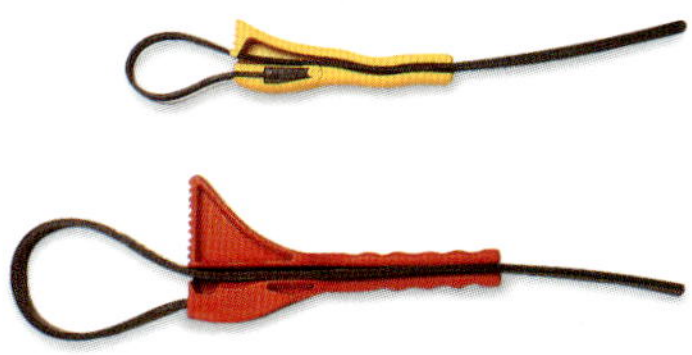

ABOVE These soft pliable grips, called "boa wrenches", can be used successfully on awkwardly shaped work, such as for opening containers or use them on polished surfaces.

Practical tip

- Never use a wrench on a nut or bolt if a spanner of the correct size is available. Wrenches are essentially for pipe work and will damage the corners of nuts and bolt heads very quickly. Use the correct tool wherever possible.

CHISELS

These come in a variety of shapes and sizes, all with specific uses. For jobs around the home, only three basic types are required. Most commonly used is the firmer chisel, which is a compromise between a mortise chisel and a bevel-edged chisel. It can be regarded as a general-purpose tool and has a strong blade of rectangular section designed for medium-heavy work.

SPECIAL-PURPOSE CHISELS

Bevel-edged and paring chisels have thinner blades than firmer chisels. The tops of the blades are bevelled along their length to allow better access into small recesses and corners, and to permit fine slicing cuts to be made in the wood.

The mortise chisel is a sturdy tool with a lot of steel just below the handle. It is used for chopping deep mortises across the grain so has to be able to withstand blows from a heavy mallet without damage. For this reason, a wooden-handled mortise chisel may have a metal band around the top of the handle to prevent it from splitting. The thickness of the steel blade also allows it to be used as a lever for cleaning the waste from the mortise. Many new chisels have shatter-resistant polypropylene handles that can be struck with a mallet, or even a hammer, without damage since the handles are virtually unbreakable. However, use a thin-bladed paring chisel with hand pressure only.

LEFT A selection of the many chisels available. A small selection will cover most needs. Keep them sharp and guarded when not in use. Always keep your hands behind the cutting edge. Only hit them with a wooden mallet if they are wooden handled. A hammer can be used on heavy plastic-handled varieties of chisel. Bevel-edged chisels are the most versatile type you can buy for most tasks. A firmer chisel has a stronger blade designed to accept heavier blows.

PRACTICAL TIPS

- Always make sure your chisel is really sharp. A blunt tool needs more pressure to force it through the work and is more likely to slip, possibly causing an accident.

- Do not leave chisels lying on the bench where the blades can come into contact with metal objects. Hang them up, fit them with plastic blade guards, or keep them in a cloth or leather chisel roll like the professionals.

BLADE WIDTHS

These usually range from 3 to 25mm (⅛in to 1in) in graduations of 3mm. After 25mm, it is usual for the graduations to increase by 6mm (¼in). Most home woodworkers will find 6mm (¼in), 12mm (½in), 19mm (¾in) and 25mm (1in) sufficient for their needs.

Firmer chisel

Mortise chisel

Bevel-edged chisel

Plastic-handled chisels such as this may be struck with a mallet or a hammer

Chiselling techniques

Always aim to remove as much excess wood as possible from the cut before using the chisel. For example, remove the wood with a saw before cleaning up with a chisel or, when cutting a mortise, drill out as much of the waste as possible and use the chisel to clean and square-up the sides to take the tenon.

When using a router to cut slots and rebates, square off the ends with a chisel by hand.

Remember to cut away from the marked line when chiselling so that any splitting will occur in the waste wood, and always cut away from yourself to avoid injury. Work patiently and never be tempted to make cuts that are too large. The chisel should be pushed or struck with one hand while being guided with the other. Paring with a chisel is a skilled and satisfying task, but a really sharp tool is essential. A blunt chisel can slip and cause a lot of damage as soon as it loses its edge.

ABOVE Remove the bulk of the waste from a dovetail with a saw before chiselling.

ABOVE To form a mortise, remove most of the waste with a drill, then finish with a chisel.

ABOVE Vertical paring by hand, and with a mallet, needs both hands for total control.

ABOVE Hold the chisel vertically and strike firmly with the wooden mallet.

Paring

1 Horizontal paring, working from both sides to the middle, prevents "break out" and results in clean work using less pressure.

2 To chamfer an edge, first use the chisel with the bevel down, then make the finishing cuts bevel up by making fine cuts.

3 When you are making the finishing cuts bevel up, note how the thumb controls the cutting edge of the chisel, close to the work.

Toolboxes and Tool Storage

Tidy and effective storage in the workshop pays off in many ways. Properly stored tools are protected from the atmosphere and will not rust or discolour. The sharp, cutting edges of saws and chisels are prevented from damage, as are the potential user's fingers, and tools can always be easily found near at hand when they are needed.

Storage

Efficient storage saves bench and floor space for other uses, and tools are more easily located, saving time and frustration. It is well worth taking the trouble to devise, and even make your own storage facilities. There are plenty of benches, cabinets, racks, clips and tool rolls on the market so that you can equip your workshop with exactly what you need. Remember, too, that storage for tools often needs to be portable, so tool pouches and carrying bags also need to be part of the overall picture.

Portable storage

The traditional carpenter's tool bag can still be obtained. Made from heavy canvas, it has two carrying handles and brass eyelets for closing.

Compact, compartmentalized plastic or metal toolboxes with drawers, carrying handles and safety locks are another option for carrying tools from one job to another.

A leather tool pouch can be worn around the waist and has loops and pockets for tools as well as screws and nails. Various sizes and styles are available. They are ideal for use on projects that require you to keep moving about.

Drill bits and chisels should always be carried in a tool roll with their tips covered for protection. Many saws are sold with a plastic snap-on blade guard to protect the teeth when not in use.

TOP RIGHT A carpenter's canvas toolbag.

RIGHT A tool pouch worn around the waist is very helpful when working in different parts of the home.

Engineer's toolbox

Bit roll

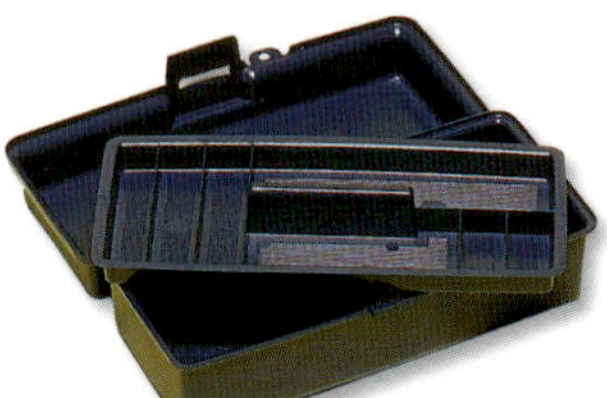

Removeable trays are very handy

Plastic toolbox with separate compartments

Static storage

The most important static storage space is that below the workbench top, and often this takes the form of cabinets or drawers. A useful device is the large tilting drawer, which can easily be made and is ideal for storing tools that are in frequent use, such as planes and chisels.

Wall-mounted cabinets with sliding doors are really practical in the workshop. The sliding doors allow them to be sited in confined areas and make it impossible to hit your head on them when they are open, which is especially important above the workbench. Fitted with a few pegs, shelves and compartments, they can be very useful.

Shelving units come in a variety of materials, shapes and sizes, and most proprietary brands can be added to as the need arises.

The tool board has the great advantage of not only displaying the tools, but also making it immediately obvious when a tool has not been replaced. To make a simple version, arrange the tools you wish to store on a flat board and draw around them with a felt-tipped pen or black marker pen. Then fit suitable hooks, pegs or clips needed to hold them in place.

Practical tips

- You can make a quick saw guard by simply cutting a slit along a length of garden hose and sliding it over the teeth of the saw blade.

- When not in a carrying roll, twist drills can be stored in a block close to the workbench or drill stand.

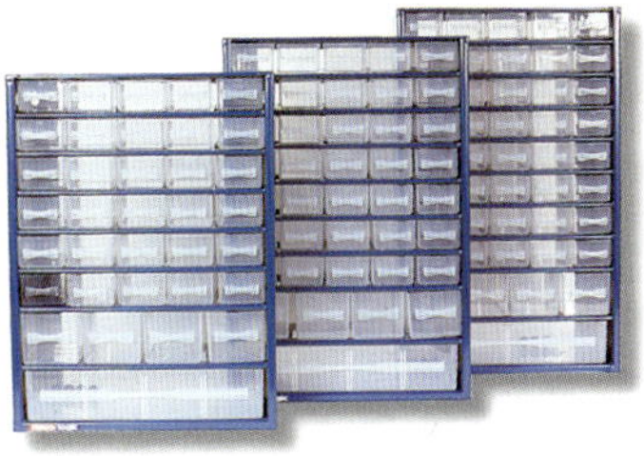

TOP AND ABOVE Specifically made in transparent plastics for easy identification of the contents, storage drawers for screws, nails, clips and a host of other small items are a must. They are best fitted to a wall at eye level, within reach of the bench.

ABOVE Make a home-made storage unit to keep your workshop drill bits tidy and easily accessible.

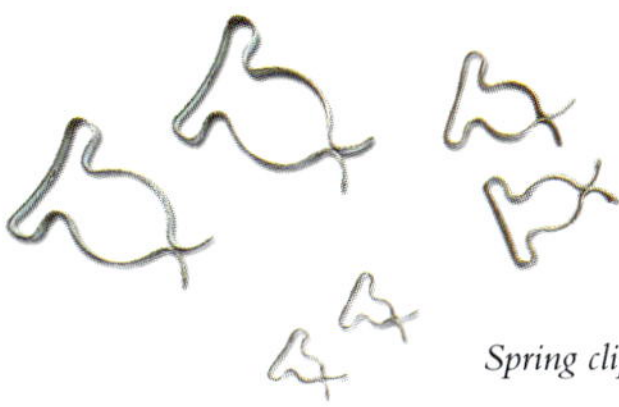

Spring clips

Tool boards

When making a tool board remember to leave space around each tool so that it can be lifted clear when the board is on the wall. The main drawback with tool boards is that they are usually in the open, which makes the tools prone to rust or theft.

ABOVE To make your own tool board, draw around the tools with a felt-tipped pen to indicate where they go. Hammer in nails or hooks that will hold them in place. Wall hooks will hold larger items, such as saws.

ABOVE Alternatively, you can buy a tool board made from plywood with holes from local builder's merchants. Insert spring clips that are widely available on the front of the tool board. These can also be fitted to the fronts of shelves.

EQUIPMENT AND MATERIALS

In the same way that many modern tools are designed specifically with the do-it-yourself enthusiast in mind, much of the equipment and many of the materials used around the home have been developed for amateur use. Sometimes, of course, you will have no choice but to use the traditional equipment and materials, but today even these are more user-friendly.

Plaster

In traditionally-built houses made of bricks and blocks, the purpose of plaster is to provide smooth wall surfaces. It is applied to the inner surfaces of the masonry walls that form the outer shell of the building and to both sides of any internal masonry walls. Plastering is a skill acquired only with a lot of practice. Do-it-yourself plasters make the job easier.

Using plaster

Most plaster used inside houses is based on lightweight gypsum; cement-based plasters (often referred to as renders) are used for finishing the outside of walls, but may be used for renovation work inside where there is a damp problem.

The main types of plaster

Conventional lightweight gypsum plaster is applied in two coats: undercoat around 10mm (⅜in) thick in two layers, and finish coat about 3mm (⅛in) thick in a single layer. If the surface you are working on is particularly absorbent, choose an HSB (high-suction background) version of the undercoat plaster; similarly, special undercoat plasters are made for dense, less absorbent surfaces. You may also find finish plaster specifically designed for creating a skim coat on plasterboard.

Do-it-yourself plasters

The one thing that all "professional" plasters have in common is that they are difficult to apply. They come in large unwieldy bags and have to be mixed with water; they normally set more quickly than the do-it-yourself enthusiast can cope with; it is easy to drag them off the wall when you are applying them; you need a lot of practice to obtain a smooth, even finish; and generally they can be put on only in thin layers.

Do-it-yourself plasters have been specifically designed to overcome all these problems. Two grades are available, repair and finish, and are usually available ready-mixed in small tubs, although sometimes as a powder for mixing with water.

Repair or one-coat plaster is much easier to apply than conventional undercoat plaster and can be used in thicknesses up to 50mm (2in). It can be employed either for filling deep holes – the kind you might be left with when a waste pipe has been removed from a wall – or to provide a base for the

ABOVE Some do-it-yourself finish plasters can be applied with a paintbrush.

Applying plaster

1 Mix do-it-yourself repair plaster in a bucket. Always add powder to water.

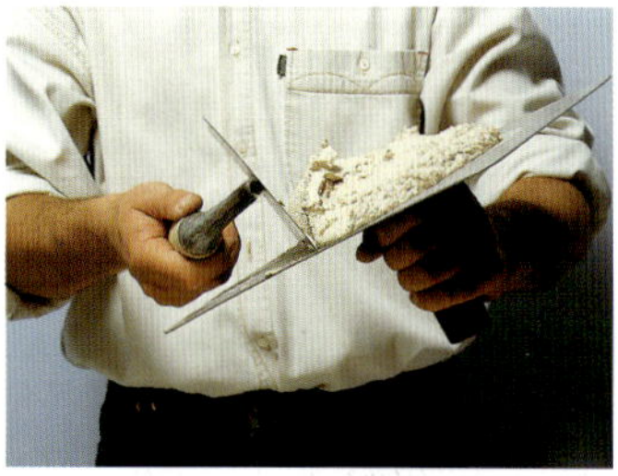

2 Scoop do-it-yourself repair plaster from the hawk with a plasterer's trowel.

3 Apply do-it-yourself repair plaster to a wall using a plasterer's trowel.

4 Level out the plaster with a straight length of wood, worked from side to side.

finish plaster, although do-it-yourself repair plasters are often smooth enough on their own as a basis for wall tiles and many wallpapers.

Do-it-yourself finish plaster, also known as plaster skim, can be applied up to 3mm (⅛ in) thick. As well as providing a finish over repair plaster, it can also be used for smoothing a rough surface and for covering over plasterboard.

How to apply plaster

All types of plaster can be applied with a plasterer's trowel. Carry the plaster to the wall on a hawk, a square flat board mounted on a short handle, and lift a small quantity of plaster off the hawk on to the wall using the plasterer's trowel. Spread it out with a sweeping motion. Always keep the trowel blade at an angle to the wall and allow the plaster to squeeze out through the gap between the bottom blade edge and the wall. When the plaster is starting to dry, it can be smoothed over, holding the trowel at an angle.

To ensure that a plaster repair is flush with the surrounding plaster, use a straight-edged length of wood and smooth over with a side-to-side motion, resting the ends on the nearby dry plaster surface.

Finish plaster is applied in the same way, but is polished with a flat trowel when almost dry. Some finishing plasters are applied with a brush, although a plastic spreader will be needed to give it a final smoothing.

External corners

If you need to apply plaster to an external corner, secure metal beading to the corner first, using dabs of plaster.

ABOVE On external corners, plaster should be applied over a corner bead.

Plasterboard

In a timber-framed house, the inner surfaces of exterior walls will be plasterboard (gypsum board), which is solid plaster contained by paper, as will the surfaces of all internal dividing walls. These may be given a skim coat of plaster to cover up the joints between adjacent sheets of plasterboard, or they can have the joints and nail holes filled before painting or papering. Some interior dividing walls in masonry walled houses may comprise plasterboard mounted on timber frames.

Replastering a bricked-up doorway

1 Remove any loose or crumbling plaster from the sides and top of the doorway.

2 Apply the first layer of undercoat plaster over wire mesh no more than 10mm (⅜in) thick.

3 Make scratches in the first layer to provide a "key" for the second layer of undercoat.

4 Apply the second layer of undercoat plaster and level it off with a timber straightedge.

5 When dry, apply the final layer of finishing plaster. Polish it smooth with a flat trowel.

Concrete and Mortar

Concrete is used to provide a solid and rigid surface as a floor, as paving or as a base for a garage or outbuilding. Mortar is the "glue" that holds the bricks together in a wall. The basis for both concrete and mortar is cement and sand (fine aggregate); concrete also contains stones (coarse aggregate). When mixed with water, the cement sets to bind the aggregates together.

Cement

Most cement used in the home is OPC (Ordinary Portland Cement). This is air-setting (that is, moisture in the air will cause it to harden unless bags are kept sealed). Ordinary Portland Cement is grey in colour and is sold in standard 50kg (112lb or 1cwt) bags in the UK, although smaller sizes are often available. Occasionally, two other types of cement are used in and around the home, White Portland Cement and Masonry Cement. The former is used where appearance is important, while the latter contains additives to increase the workability of mortars and renders.

Aggregates

Coarse aggregates are defined as those that will pass through a 20mm (¾in) sieve and are widely used for making concrete. Fine aggregates are often known simply as sand and are used in both concrete and mortar.

Two different types of sand are sold for building work. Sharp sand, sometimes known as concreting sand, is used for making concrete and mortar for laying paving slabs; soft sand, also known as bricklaying or building sand, is used in mortar for laying bricks and concrete blocks. You can also obtain all-in aggregate, often known as ballast, which contains both coarse and fine aggregates.

Buying concrete and mortar

There are three ways of buying concrete and mortar: as individual ingredients, as wet ready-mixed and as dry pre-mixed. Buying cement, sand and coarse aggregate separately for concrete is the cheapest option, but you do have to ensure dry storage for the cement. For big jobs, having wet ready-mixed concrete delivered is convenient, provided sufficient manpower is available to transport it from the truck to the site and to level it before it sets. For small jobs, bags of dry pre-mix are a good choice: the ingredients are in the correct proportions, and all you do is add water.

Mixing concrete

1 Start by measuring out the dry ingredients in the right proportions.

2 Mix the dry ingredients thoroughly until you have a consistent colour.

3 Make a small well in the centre of the pile and add a small amount of water.

4 Work from the edges of the pile, mixing the ingredients and adding more water.

5 Work the material with the edge of your spade to get the right consistency.

6 When the concrete is mixed, transfer it to a bucket or wheelbarrow.

Additives

Pigments can be added to the mix to change the colour of concrete, but need using with care. The most common additives affect the workability of concrete and mortar and often increase the time before it hardens. Many mortars need the addition of lime or a plasticizer to improve their workability.

Concrete and mortar mixes

The proportions of cement, sand and aggregate you need depend on the job you are doing: strong mixes are those with more cement; weak mixes are those with less. All proportions are by volume.

General-purpose concrete Good for most uses, except foundations and exposed paving. Mix one part cement, two parts sand and three parts 20mm (¾in) aggregate, or one part cement to four parts combined aggregate. This mix is known as 1:2:3 or 1:4.

Foundation concrete Use for wall foundations and bases and for precast paving. Mix 1:2½:3½ or 1:5.

Paving concrete Use for all exposed paving, especially drives, and garage floors. Mix 1:1½:2½ or 1:3½.

Normal mortar Use for bricklaying in normal conditions. Mix 1:5 to 6 (cement: soft sand) with a small amount of plasticizer or one part lime added for workability, or 1:4 to 5 (masonry cement: soft sand).

Strong mortar Use for brick walls in exposed conditions. Mix 1:4 to 4½ (cement: sand) with plasticizer or a quarter part lime added, or 1:2½ to 3½ (masonry cement: sand).

Mixing concrete and mortar

Even with bags of dry pre-mix, you will need a spot board, usually a sheet of hardboard or plywood, to mix the material with water.

Start by mixing the ingredients thoroughly. Measure out separate cement, sand and aggregate using a bucket in their dry state. Make a well in the centre of the pile and add some water using a different bucket.

Work material from the edges of the pile into the wet centre. Then make another well and add a little more water. Continue mixing and adding small quantities of water until it is all mixed and a uniform colour. The consistency is correct when you can just draw the back of your spade across it, leaving a smooth finish without water oozing out.

For large jobs, consider hiring a mixer. For concrete, start with half of the aggregate and water, then add the cement and sand in small batches plus the remainder of the aggregate and water. Clean the mixer with a small amount of coarse aggregate and clean water. A powered mortar mixer can also be hired to speed up the mixing process.

Concrete and mortar mixes

Concrete	Mix	Cement	Sand	Aggregate	Yield*	Area**
General-purpose	1:2:3	50kg (110lb)	100kg (220lb)	200kg (440lb)	0.15 (5.3)	1.5 (16)
Foundation	1:2½:3½	50kg (110lb)	130kg (290lb)	200kg (440lb)	0.18 (6.4)	1.8 (19.4)
Paving	1:1½:2½	50kg (110lb)	75kg (165lb)	150kg (330lb)	0.12 (4.2)	1.2 (13)
Mortar				**Lime*****		**Bricks laid**
Normal	1:5	50kg (110lb)	200kg (440lb)	50kg (110lb)	0.25 (8.8)	850
Strong	1:4	50kg (110lb)	150kg (330lb)	15kg (33lb)	0.19 (6.7)	650

* cubic metres (cubic feet) per 50kg (110lb) of cement

** area in square metres (square feet) of concrete 100mm (4in) thick

*** or plasticizer

ABOVE A powered concrete mixer can also be hired to speed up the mixing process. Empty the concrete into a wheelbarrow.

Roofing Materials

Two shapes of roof are used on houses: pitched and flat. Each employs different covering materials, although the basic framework is timber in both cases. If you are thinking about changing the roof covering on your house, bear in mind the style of other houses in the area and the weight of the roofing material the roof was designed for.

Pitched roofs

A pitched roof has a series of rafters supported at the bottom by the house walls and joined to a horizontal board at the ridge. Thin timber battens (furring strips) are nailed across the rafters to support the roof covering. Normally, felt is laid beneath the battens for additional weatherproofing, and some roofs have boards, known as sarking, below the felt. The main cladding materials are natural slate, manufactured slate and concrete and clay tiles.

Some roofs may have more than one pitch – on L-shaped houses and houses with front gables for example. Each section of the roof is covered separately; a lead-lined valley runs between the sections to collect rainwater.

Flat roofs

These actually have a gentle slope to remove rainwater. They are constructed from timber boards laid on top of joists, the boards being covered with asphalt or roofing felt. Felt is also used on the pitched roofs of outbuildings and sheds.

Natural slates

Although widely used on older houses, natural slates have become very expensive and are now rarely used as a new roofing material. However, second-hand slates can often be obtained for small jobs, repairs and replacement.

LEFT A professional roofer at work constructing this well-insulated roof. The horizontal battens have yet to be fitted; the vertical battens will provide ventilation to keep the sarking underneath dry.

Slates are held to the roofing battens by nails – either through two holes near the top of the slate (head nailing) or two holes in the middle of the slate (centre-nailing). In both cases, each slate covers about two-thirds of the two slates below it, so that all of the roof is covered by a thickness of at least two slates.

Natural slates are heavy and require handling with great care – they are fragile and have sharp edges. The nail holes can be made with an electric drill fitted with a masonry drill bit, though a professional slater uses the spike on his axe.

Natural stone roofing, which is even more expensive, is laid in the same way as slates.

Plain tiles

Clay plain tiles are another traditional material, but they are laid in a different manner – each tile has two

ABOVE Architectural salvage yards are the best place to find old slates and tiles.

ABOVE This "eyebrow" roof is made from plain concrete tiles.

FAR LEFT Modern concrete interlocking tiles on both house and garage. This style is known as "Double Roman".

LEFT Manufactured slates do not just have to be used on old roofs. Here, they are ideal for this modern building.

projecting lugs, known as nibs, on the back, which hook over the roofing battens. Some tiles are nailed in place as well, typically every fourth row and the tiles at the top, bottom and edges of the roof.

As with slates, each tile covers around two-thirds the length of the tiles underneath – thus the amount exposed is about one-third of the total tile length.

Plain clay tiles need a more steeply pitched roof than slates – a minimum of 40 degrees compared to around 20 degrees.

Plain concrete tiles are also available and are held on the battens in the same way as clay tiles.

RIGHT It would be difficult to find a more elegant roof covering than natural slate for this traditional-style building. To add contrasting colour, the ridge tiles are made from clay.

Interlocking tiles

Concrete tiles that are interlocking are widely used on modern homes and have yet another method of fixing. Like plain tiles, they hook over the roofing battens, but also interlock, each with its two neighbours, so that only one layer is needed and each tile only covers a small part of the tiles below.

There are many types of interlocking tile and the minimum pitch can vary from under 20 degrees to around 30 degrees. Interlocking clay tiles are also available, including decorative pantiles. To make replacement easy, the name and number may be embossed on the back.

Manufactured slates

Lighter, cheaper and easier to lay, manufactured slates have largely replaced natural slates. Made from resin, they often contain ground natural slate and may have "deckled" edges for a more realistic appearance. Many are held in place with clips, which makes them much easier to lay, although the roof itself needs to be truer in construction than is needed for natural slates.

Shingles

These are wooden tiles used for cladding walls and also for covering roofs. They are usually made from Western Red Cedar, which weathers naturally to a silver-grey colour. They are particularly suitable for use on steeply pitched roofs and are fixed in the same way as slates.

Flat roofing materials

Roofing felt varies in quality from simple bitumen sheet felt, employed for outbuildings, to expensive and long-lasting polyester felt used for garage roofs. New felt roofs for houses are often laid with hot bitumen – a job for professionals, as is laying a hot asphalt roof covering.

GUTTERING

These perform the very useful function of collecting the rainwater that falls on roofs and transferring it to underground drains. The size, shape and materials used can vary. The traditional material used for guttering was cast iron, but this has largely been replaced by plastic. Other materials that may be found include aluminium, galvanized steel and asbestos cement.

GUTTERING COMPONENTS

These can have one of three main shapes: half-round, square or moulded – ogee moulded is the traditional shape. Whatever its shape, most guttering comes in standard lengths, so it needs joints between the lengths. Each length will be supported by two or more brackets; some brackets are combined with joint units.

At a corner, a right-angle (90-degree) elbow joins two lengths together – 120- and 135-degree elbows are also available for bay windows – and at the edge of the roof, a stop-end is fitted. The gutter is connected via an outlet to the downpipe, which takes the rainwater to the drains; if this is at the end of the gutter, it is known as a stop-end outlet. The downpipe has its own brackets and elbows, plus some kind of outlet at the bottom to direct the water into the drainage gulley. Sometimes, and especially where there is more than one downpipe, a hopper head is fitted to a single downpipe and pipes from the gutters empty their water into the hopper head to be taken to the drains.

For the majority of houses, 115mm (4½in) guttering is used in combination with 70mm (2¾in) downpipes. On large houses, deep-flow guttering, with a greater capacity, is used. On garages, extensions and outbuildings, 75mm (3in) guttering plus 50mm (2in) downpipes will suffice.

LEFT Whatever type of guttering you choose for your home, keep to the same make and type for the whole house.

CAST-IRON GUTTERING

Although cast-iron is a rigid and a durable material, it is very heavy and brittle, and liable to rust if not kept painted. It is available in half-round and ogee profiles with a choice of round and square downpipes. Ornate cast-iron hopper heads are available, both new and second-hand.

The joints between lengths of gutter are made by the spigot of one length fitting into the socket of the next, with a layer of putty providing a waterproof seal between them once a bolt and nut have been used to lock the two lengths together.

ALUMINIUM GUTTERING

As a guttering material, aluminium has the advantage of being rigid and rustproof. Normally, it comes pre-finished in a range of colours and in a wide choice of profiles.

BELOW Here, the rainwater that falls from the top roof descends on to the lower roof where it is collected by the lower gutter. It then descends the lower downpipe to the drains.

Plastic guttering

Although less rigid than cast-iron and aluminium guttering, plastic guttering does not corrode, and is light and easy to handle.

Plastic guttering is available in a choice of colours. Half-round and square are the most common profiles, and are available in standard and deep-flow patterns, although both moulded and ogee forms are also available. Connectors are available for joining to existing plastic or cast-iron guttering; downpipes can be round, square or rectangular. Some half-round guttering is ribbed so that leaves can fall into the gutter, but water can still flow underneath them.

Plastic guttering may be sealed by rubber or neoprene gaskets fitted into the connectors; the gutters themselves are a simple snap-fit into the brackets, although sometimes notches need to be cut in the gutter to fit connectors.

Although they may have the same nominal size and the same profile, different makes of plastic guttering are often not compatible with one another. It is advisable to stick with one make and use it for all the guttering around your house.

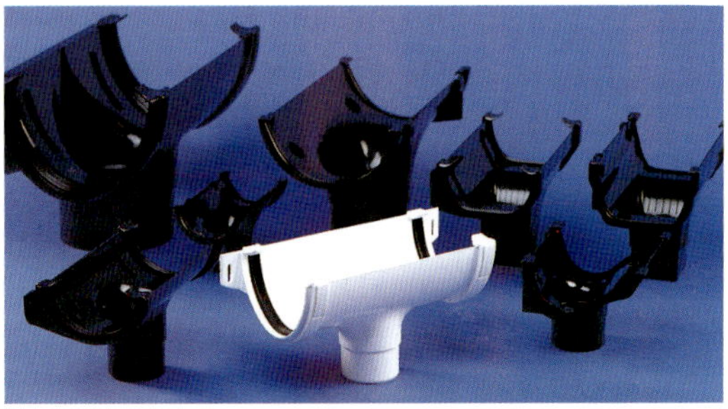

RIGHT Just some of the different shapes and sizes of plastic guttering available from a single manufacturer.

BELOW RIGHT If you are fitting guttering yourself, always have a good work platform beneath you and wear the correct safety equipment.

Fitting guttering

Many guttering manufacturers provide excellent literature, which will help you select replacement guttering for your home and give full instructions on how it should be fitted. One of the most important aspects is that the guttering has the capacity to cope with the amount of rainwater that falls on the house. It also needs to be laid with a slight fall from the highest point, usually the roof edge, to the lowest point, always the outlet to the downpipe. Check with your local authority or council for what arrangements are acceptable when getting rid of the rainwater.

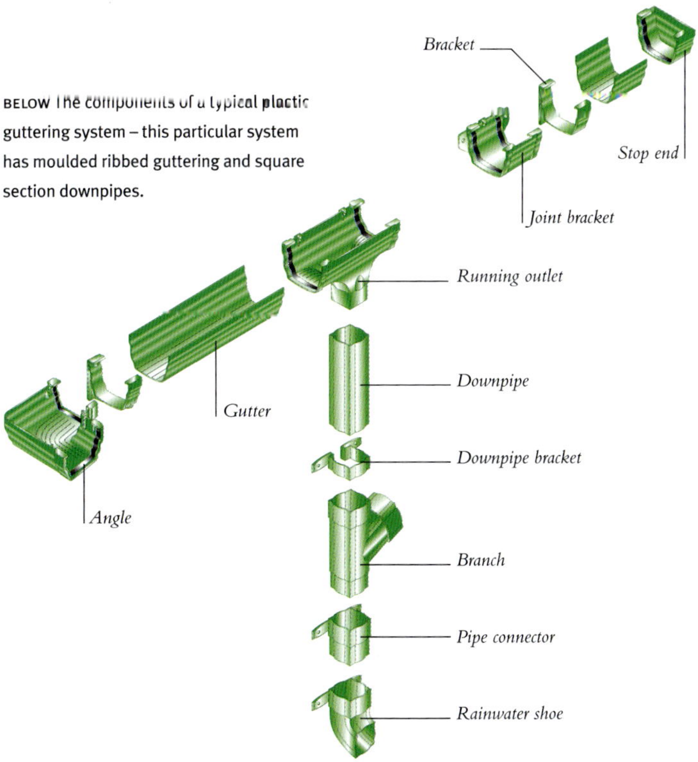

BELOW The components of a typical plastic guttering system – this particular system has moulded ribbed guttering and square section downpipes.

Adhesives and Sealants

A fantastic range of adhesives and sealants is available, some designed for specific uses, woodworking adhesive and bath sealant for example, and others formulated for more general use. You need a good selection of both adhesives and sealants in your do-it-yourself armoury, some of which you buy when you need them, others you keep in reserve for emergencies.

Woodworking adhesives

The majority of woodwork projects that require two or more pieces of wood to be glued together need a PVA (white) woodworking adhesive. This white liquid dries quickly, loses its colour, and has the advantage that excess adhesive can be removed with a damp cloth before it sets.

Where a joint has to withstand damp conditions, an exterior-grade of woodworking adhesive must be used; if the joint may need to be taken apart in the future, a traditional woodworking adhesive, such as animal glue or fish glue, can be used.

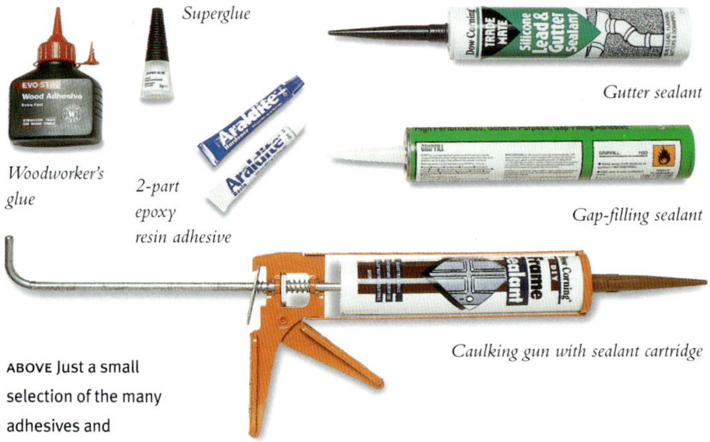

ABOVE Just a small selection of the many adhesives and sealants available for various types of job.

Two-part adhesives

These adhesives can be used on a wide range of materials and are very useful, as they are strong and can fill gaps between the two mating surfaces, which is often necessary when repairing broken china. Some two-part adhesives are even suitable for joining metal. For epoxy resin types, the two parts come in separate tubes and must be mixed together just before use; for two-part acrylic types, the adhesive is applied to one surface and the hardener to the other. Quick-setting versions are available, although drying time does depend on temperature, the warmer the better. You may need to experiment with different types when trying to glue plastics together.

ABOVE A range of household glues and tape for repair work.

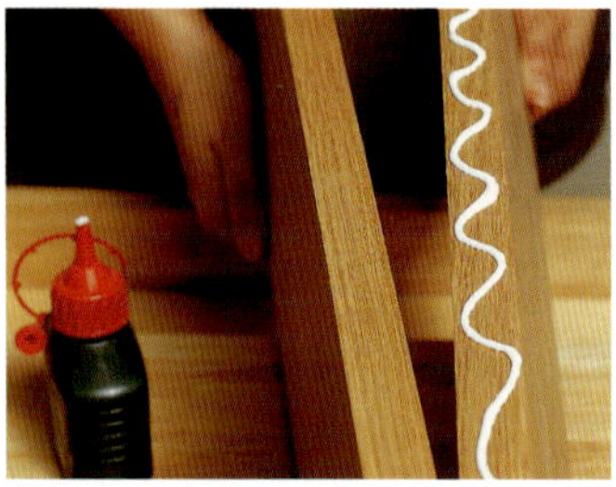

ABOVE A PVA woodworking adhesive used to join two boards together.

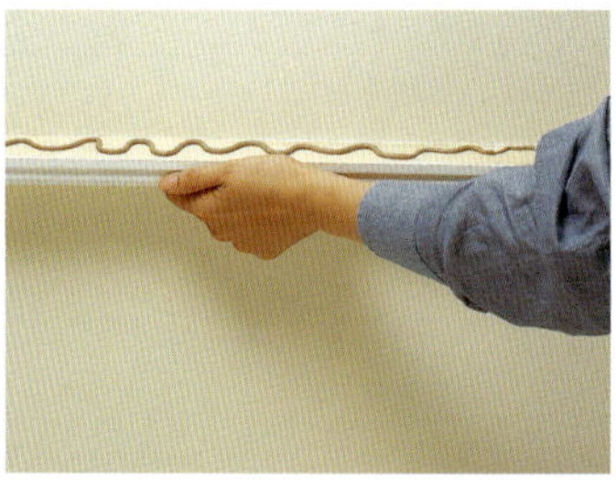

ABOVE Panel adhesive can be used to secure timber mouldings to walls.

ABOVE A two-part epoxy adhesive is ideal for repairing broken china.

Contact adhesives

This type of adhesive is used for joining sheet materials, for example, plastic laminate sheet to a timber worktop, and for repairing leather. Adhesive is applied to both surfaces and allowed to dry until it becomes tacky, then the surfaces are brought together. Some contact adhesives allow slight adjustment after the surfaces have been joined; with others, you have to get the positioning right the first time. Take care when using solvent-based contact adhesives, do not smoke and ensure there is adequate ventilation.

Superglue

This type of adhesive has the advantage that it sets almost immediately, so you can actually hold the two parts to be glued rather than fitting clamps, straps or weights. It has no gap-filling properties and no flexibility when set, but nevertheless is extremely useful. Make sure you have the correct release agent to hand in case you get any on your skin as it can glue fingers together.

Special adhesives

Some adhesives should only be bought when needed. These include:

- Glass adhesive that sets clear under the action of light with no obvious glue line.
- Panel adhesive, for securing manufactured boards.
- Specialized adhesives for wallpapering and tiling.
- Adhesives for repairing PVC.
- Specialized adhesives for laying soft floorcoverings.

Sealants

The majority of sealants come in cartridges designed to fit into a caulking gun. This is an essential, but inexpensive, tool and is easy to use after a little practice. If you retain the tip that you cut off the end of the cartridge nozzle before you can use it, it can be reversed and used to seal the cartridge after use.

The most useful sealants for use around the home are the building silicones and mastics (caulking), available in different colours and different grades depending on the final use. These have the advantage that they never set completely, so can be used for sealing between two materials that are likely to move slightly. Common examples are the gap between a bath, basin or shower tray and a wall, and the gap between a window or door frame and the surrounding brickwork; a rigid sealant or filler used here would crack quite quickly.

Various repair sealants, often incorporating bitumen, are available for mending cracks in gutters, downpipes and flat roofs; expanding foam fillers can be used for sealing really large gaps.

Practical tip

- When using most types of adhesive (superglues are the exception), you will need to clamp at least two surfaces together while the adhesive dries. Work out your clamping arrangement before applying the adhesive, so that you are certain that the two (or more) parts will be held together securely.

ABOVE Use mastic or silicon sealant indoors and outdoors to seal gaps between wood and masonry where a rigid filler might crack.

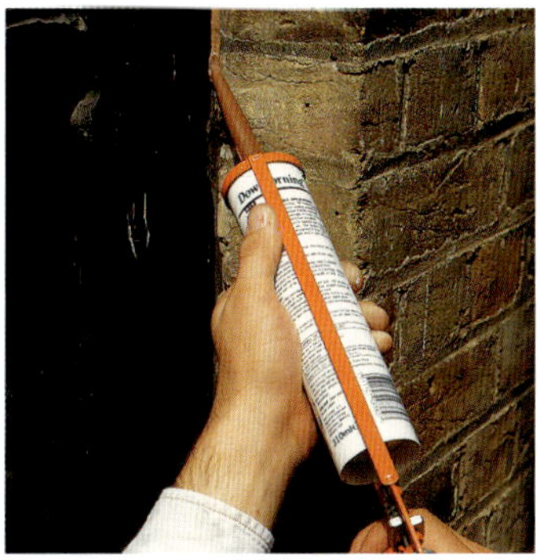

ABOVE Use a non-setting mastic or coloured building silicone sealant to fill gaps around a door frame.

ABOVE Use white waterproof sealant for the gap behind a wash basin. Apply it in one continuous movement.

Timber and Manufactured Boards

Do-it-yourself projects rarely involve expensive hardwoods such as mahogany, oak, ash and beech. These tend to be used by furniture makers and the joinery trade, owing to their high cost and relative difficulty in working. Softwoods, such as prepared pine, or manufactured boards are the basic materials used by the home craftsperson for most structural work.

Using wood

Hardwoods, as they are expensive, are often used as veneers over cheaper materials, as lippings around flat surfaces such as shelving and table tops, and for picture framing.

Softwoods, such as pine and, to a lesser extent, Douglas fir, are the most commonly used types of wood for do-it-yourself jobs such as wall frames, flooring, skirting (base) boards, picture and dado (chair) rails and a great variety of cladding, framing and fencing applications.

In addition to softwoods, there is a range of manufactured boards, which are cheap and come in convenient sizes that keep jointing to the minimum.

Practical uses

The two manufactured boards most often used are plywood and chipboard (particle board). The former, which has good mechanical strength and can be sawn easily, is suitable for structural work.

ABOVE A selection of manufactured boards.

Chipboard is more friable and less easy to work accurately, but is cheap. It is adequate for some flooring applications and a host of carcassing jobs, such as kitchen cabinets and bookcases. It is unwise to drive screws or nails into the edge of a chipboard panel, as the material will crumble.

Veneered finishes

Both plywood and chipboard are available with hardwood and coloured melamine veneer for improved appearance.

Practical tip

- **Like many manufactured boards, hardboard does not like damp conditions and has a tendency to buckle. Keep it away from steamy areas if possible, or make sure it is sealed with paint, polyurethane varnish or proprietary sealer.**

Blockboard, which consists of solid wooden blocks sandwiched between plywood skins, is a stable and strong structural material often used where some form of weight-carrying capacity is required. As with all manufactured boards, the extremely hard resins used to bond blockboard together rapidly blunts tools unless they are tungsten (carbide) tipped.

Pineboard is like the core of blockboard, but without the outer layers. Small strips of pine are glued together on edge and sanded smooth. It is ideal for instant shelving and carcassing.

MDF (medium-density fiberboard) is another useful material. Unlike

Common thickness of manufactured board

TYPE	3mm ⅛in	6mm ¼in	9mm ⅜in	12mm ½in	16mm ⅝in	19mm ¾in	22mm ⅞in	25mm 1in	32mm 1¼in
Plywood	x	x	x	x	x	x	x	x	
Plywood (D. Fir)				x		x			
Blockboard						x		x	
Chipboard				x	x	x	x	x	
Hardboard	x	x							
MDF		x	x	x		x		x	x

ABOVE Plywood is easy to cut and is very good for carcassing work.

ABOVE Sawing veneered chipboard is best done with the veneer face-up to avoid damage.

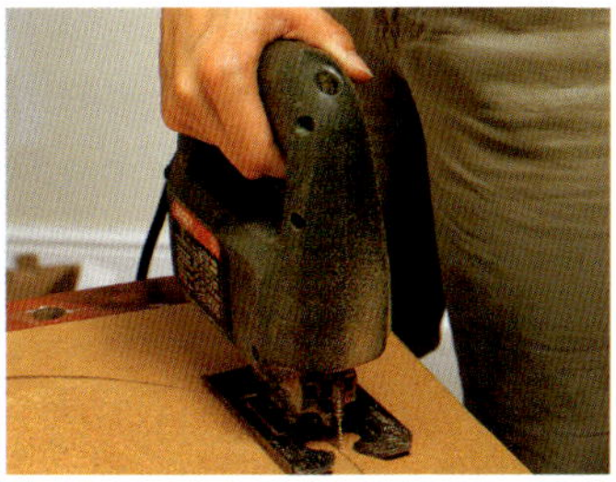

ABOVE Cutting a template from hardboard using an electric jigsaw.

most other boards, it can be worked to fine detail with saws and chisels, and it is often used for making quite delicate mouldings. Hardboard is ideal for covering floors prior to tiling or carpeting and, as it is light, for making back panels for cabinets or pictures. It can be used for making templates to establish correct shapes, especially when using expensive material for the finished object, helping to avoid mistakes.

Different uses for wood

Hardwoods, such as mahogany, oak, ash and beech, are readily available, but tend to be used in the furniture trades for making solid items such as chairs, which have few flat surfaces and need structural strength. Boards with hardwood veneers are often used for panelling and other flat surfaces such as table tops and interior doors.

Typical applications for softwoods include flooring, internal doors, skirtings and framing for projects that will be clad with a variety of materials. Tongued-and-grooved cladding has become popular over the years. It provides a relatively inexpensive decorative finish using solid timber. Tongued-and-grooved timber comes in a variety of species but the most commonly found is pine or a similar softwood such as hemlock. More exotic species will need to be specially ordered.

ABOVE LEFT The centre section of this display case was made from MDF and then painted.

LEFT The carcass of this bookcase is a box made of veneered MDF with solid wood trim.

BELOW A skirting (base) board, veneers, softwoods and hardwoods.

Paper-coated MDF skirting (base) board

Bird's-eye maple veneer

Cherry veneer

Pine softwood

Douglas fir softwood

Beech hardwood

Mahogany hardwood

FLOOR COVERINGS

Whether you have a solid concrete floor or a suspended timber floor, there is a wide range of floor coverings to choose from. Floor coverings can be divided into five main groups, including carpet; sheet materials, mainly vinyl and linoleum; soft floor tiles including vinyl, cork, rubber, linoleum and carpet tiles; hard floor tiles such as ceramic and quarry tiles; and timber floors.

CARPET

There are two main types of carpet: fabric-backed and foam-backed. The former requires special edge gripper strips and an underlay, and is difficult for an amateur to lay successfully, as it has to be stretched as it is laid. The latter requires no underlay, except paper to cover gaps in floorboards, and is easy to cut and to lay, using double-sided adhesive tape.

Carpet comes in a vast range of designs and qualities, and in different grades for a variety of situations: the heaviest wear grades are required in hallways and on stairs; the lowest grades in bedrooms. Water-resistant grades are needed in bathrooms. Carpet, except carpet tiles, is not recommended for kitchens.

LEFT A linoleum floor is ideal for kitchens as it is very durable and easy to keep clean. The cushioned types also offer extra warmth and softness underfoot. Borders can be used to frame individual tiles.

SHEET MATERIALS

Vinyl sheet flooring is easy to cut, easy to lay and easy to keep clean, making it ideal for use in bathrooms, kitchens and children's bedrooms.

Normal sheet vinyl is reasonably soft and warm underfoot, cushion vinyl even more so.

Durable linoleum (oil-impregnated sheet) is the traditional sheet flooring, but is more difficult to lay. However, modern linos come in a range of patterns and colourful designs that rival vinyl sheeting.

SOFT FLOOR TILES

All soft floor tiles are quiet, warm and comfortable underfoot. As they are also easy to clean, they are suitable for bathrooms, kitchens work rooms and bedrooms.

All soft floor tile materials must be laid on a surface that is absolutely dry and flat: a solid concrete floor

ABOVE A variety of natural floor coverings such as sea grass.

ABOVE Carpet tiles can be laid with any pattern.

ABOVE A selection of soft floor coverings, including cork.

ABOVE There is a vast array of hard flooring tiles available.

will probably require levelling, while a timber floor may need covering with sheets of hardboard.

Most soft floor tiles are laid in the same way. Individual tiles are stuck to the floor using the correct adhesive or by peeling off the backing from self-adhesive tiles. In general, carpet tiles are laid dry, with perhaps just a few secured with double-sided adhesive tape to keep the whole floor in place.

LEFT Quarry tiles are unglazed ceramic floor tiles with a brown, buff or reddish colour, and are a very popular choice for hallways, conservatories and country-style kitchens. Terracotta tiles are featured here.

Hard floor tiles

These materials are also easy to keep clean, so they can be used in the same rooms as soft floor tiles. They are much more durable, but are cold underfoot and noisy.

The main materials are ceramic (glazed clay), and quarry or terracotta. Ceramic floor tiles, which are thicker and stronger than ceramic wall tiles, are laid with a special adhesive, and grout is used to fill the gaps between them. Quarry and terracotta tiles are laid with a cement mortar, which is also used to fill the gaps. Hard floor tiles need a rigid, dry, flat surface. On a timber floor, this means laying thin plywood sheeting rather than hardboard.

Timber floor coverings

There are many timber floor coverings that can be laid on top of existing floors. Some are nailed down, some are stuck down and some are allowed to "float", not actually being secured to the floor underneath, but being free to expand and contract independently.

Timber flooring is available in thin strips, sometimes two or three boards wide, resembling floorboards. The strips are tongued and grooved and are glued together, but not to the floor underneath. Thicker timber strips can be laid in the same way, but can also be nailed to the floor below. Although some thick strips are made of hardwood, this timber is so expensive that in some cases, laminate flooring (a thin hardwood layer attached to a thick softwood layer) is used. Timber mosaic flooring, often known as imitation parquet flooring, consists of square tiles that are glued to the underlying floor; most types are self-adhesive. Each tile consists of four smaller tiles, and each smaller tile comprises a number of small timber "fingers", so the final effect is a basketweave design. True parquet flooring consists of thick blocks that are glued to the floor, typically using a black mastic (caulking), in a herringbone pattern. Achieving a flat level surface with this type of flooring is not easy. Timber floorboards themselves can be made to look good if varnished.

LEFT Woodstrip, laminated and mosaic flooring.

RIGHT A wooden floor can be warm and stylish.

FIXINGS

Often, home improvement projects involve joining together materials with very different properties, such as fixing wood to brickwork or plaster, or metal to brickwork or stone. The problems arising from this can be overcome in a variety of ways, not least by taking advantage of the many different fixings manufactured for use with new materials and hollow walls.

CHOOSING FIXINGS

Different types of fixing are required for hollow walls. Fixing wood to wood can be done in a variety of ways, including nailing, screwing and gluing, but there are many proprietary brackets, plates and knock-down joints that can make the job much quicker and often stronger. Knock-down joints also allow a project to be dismantled and reassembled at will. Often do-it-yourself projects can be made or marred by the choice of fixings, especially where they are visible. A good general rule is to make them as simple as possible, both visually and mechanically, particularly when choosing catches for cabinets and door furniture in general.

As a rule of thumb, never use a fixing that is too large or ostentatious so as to detract from the item of furniture.

RIGHT Fixing a batten (furring strip) to an exterior wall with a masonry nail is now a commonly applied method.

BELOW A cordless drill and a selection of wall plugs and screws.

MASONRY NAILS

These provide the most basic method of attaching timber to brickwork and plaster. They are hardened nails that can be driven into masonry and give a firm fixing. They are not used in the assembly of a wooden structure, but simply hold it to the wall.

FIXINGS FOR SOLID WALLS

Plastic wall plugs are the most common method of providing fixings in solid walls. They expand to grip the sides of the hole when a wood screw is driven home. They must be a snug fit in their holes, otherwise they will not hold. Wall plugs come in various sizes and are designed for moderate loads, such as shelves, curtain rails, mirrors etc.

Frame fixers are made specifically for fixing door and window frames directly to the masonry in one operation. They comprise a long wall plug, often supplied with a

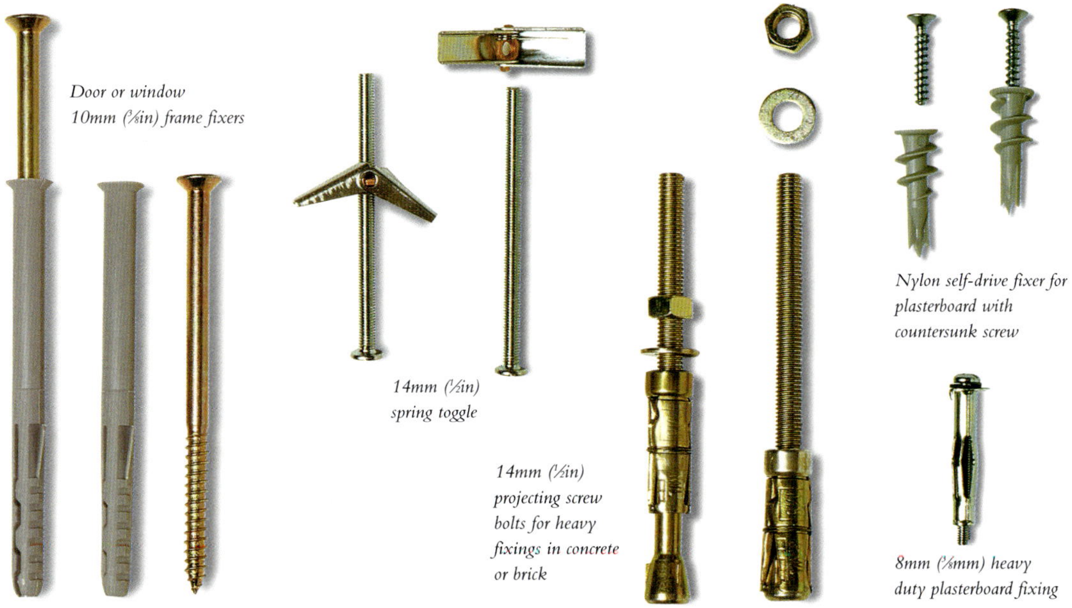

screw of the correct size. A hole is drilled through the frame with a wood drill and continued into the brickwork with a masonry drill. The fixer is tapped through the frame into the wall and the screw tightened in the normal way. Some types can be hammered home, but they will still need to be undone with a screwdriver.

Screw bolts are often used where a heavy load is expected, such as when fitting heavy timbers to brickwork. The bolt expands within the hole as the nut is tightened, providing a very strong grip. A washer should always be used under the nut to prevent damage to the wood as it is tightened since these exert a very strong grip.

Fixings for hollow walls and doors

Cavity fixings are designed to expand to grip the inner surface of chipboard (particle board) or hollow doors and are sufficient to hold moderate loads. They can also be used with lath-and-plaster walls often found in older buildings.

Spring toggles work in a similar way to other cavity fixings. They are pushed into the hole with the springs in compression and once the arms have passed through, they spring open to grip the back of the surface material. The device is then tightened with a screwdriver.

Often used for light fixings in plasterboard (gypsum board), the self-drive fixer taps its own thread in a hole drilled slightly smaller than the diameter of the plug. The plug will remain in place even when the fixing screw is removed.

Plasterboard can present its own particular problems with fixings owing to its fragile and crumbly nature. The golden rule is to get it right the first time.

ABOVE A range of fixings designed to overcome problems of getting a secure fixing in very different materials. Most of these have appeared in the last 40 years or so, and manufacturers continue to develop and improve quality constantly.

Practical tips

- **Always wear safety goggles when using masonry nails because, if struck incorrectly, they will not bend like a wire nail and may shatter and cause injury.**
- **Make sure that all fixings made in plaster are made when the material is dry, otherwise shrinkage may well cause problems later.**
- **Shelving designed to carry heavy weights will be heavy itself, and its weight should be considered when deciding on the fixings required.**

Joints and Hinges

There is a huge range of fittings available for making joints and connecting different materials. Any device that includes a pivot action can be called a hinge, and there are many different variations. Some are designed to be concealed within the framework of a cabinet, or the carcass, while others are intended as decorative features in their own right.

Joint plates and brackets

Flat mild-steel plates, drilled and countersunk to take wood screws, are a common means of making and strengthening butt joints in timber framing. Fixings are also available to make right-angled joints, lap joints, and for hanging joists.

Another very handy fixing is the trestle dog. With a pair of these and some timber, you can make a trestle. They are also useful for assembling impromptu benches and small scaffolds in a few minutes. The greater the weight they bear, the harder they grip.

Shelving aids

Simple metal brackets are readily available. They are fixed to the wall with screws and wall plugs, and then a wooden shelf is secured from below with screws. Shaped wooden brackets give a traditional look and are plugged to the wall in a similar way. Glass shelving for the bathroom may be fixed with shelf-grips, which are backed with adhesive strips for securing to ceramic tiles. Shelves over radiators are often of coated steel with a wood-grain decorative finish. They simply clip into place over the radiators.

Heavy-duty wall brackets are required to hold the weight of a television. These are made of metal and allow the television to be rotated through 360 degrees and tilted downward. Shelving systems are available from many sources. Often, they offer great flexibility and lots of add-on accessories. Many can be used as room dividers and as portable furniture.

ABOVE Trestle dogs provide a quick way of joining wood for an immediate work platform.

OPPOSITE A selection of the many different types and sizes of hinges that can be found, available in a variety of finishes.

BELOW Various traditional ways of joining timbers with metal brackets.

L-shaped corner reinforcing bracket

T-shaped fixing plate

L-shaped bracket

A simple 90 degree angle bracket

An ideal method used in crossing joints

A butt joint held on either side with brackets

Knock-down joints

These joints are often used with manufactured boards, such as chipboard (particle board) and plywood. They ensure good square connections and allow the unit to be dismantled and reassembled as required. For the best results, at least two should be used for every panel.

ABOVE The knock-down joint in its separate parts ready for putting together.

ABOVE When the parts are joined, they form a strong and accurate joint.

Hinges

There is a wide range of hinges in a choice of types, finishes, sizes and materials for a variety of tasks; some are functional, while others make decorative features in their own right. Many specialist outlets sell all manner of hinges, stays and catches, and most can be ordered by mail.

The selection of the correct hinges for a job is important, since they must be able to support the weight of the door, which could be quite considerable if it is an external door. Butt hinges are the most common type.

Special chipboard concealed hinges are a familiar sight on furniture such as kitchen cabinets. In the case of a bar counter, they must be able to fold back flat. For internal doors, rising-butt hinges will allow the door to rise as it is opened so that it clears a thick carpet, yet lets in no draught when closed.

Catches

These are usually made very simply and are more often seen on cabinets and garden gates than on fancy furniture. Modern ones are often sprung ball bearings.

75mm (3in) loose pin butt hinge

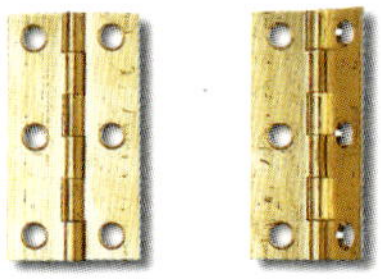

75mm (3in) brass butt hinge

75mm (3in) fasfit hinge

25mm (1in) steel backflap hinge

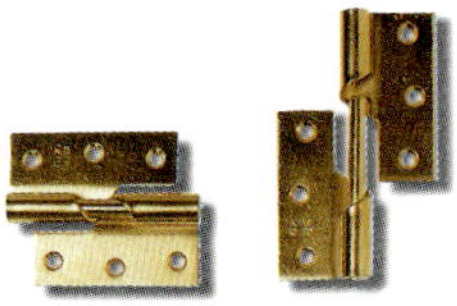

75mm (3in) rising butt hinge

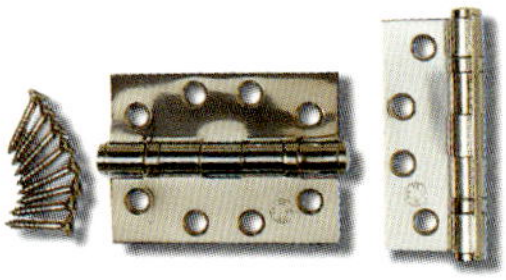

100mm (4in) stainless steel butt hinge

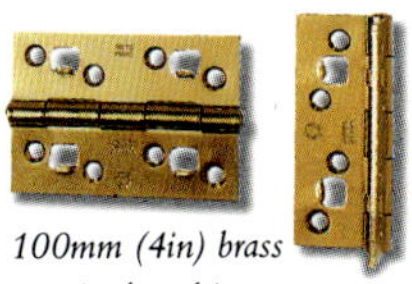

100mm (4in) brass security butt hinge

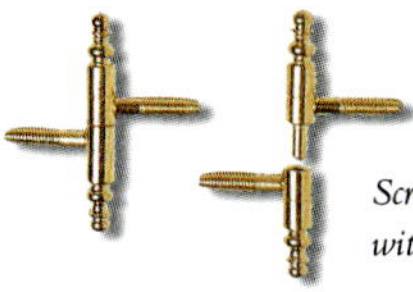

Screw-in barrel hinge with finials

75mm (3in) tee hinge

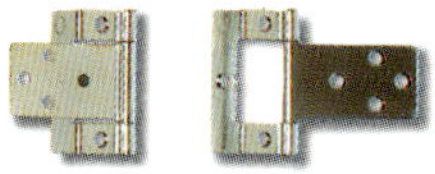

Easy hang, zinc-plated hinge

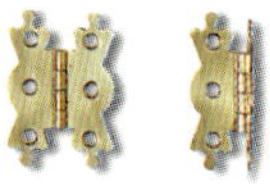

58mm (2¼in) brass butterfly hinge

75 x 14mm (3 x 9/16in) steel strap hinge

50mm (2in) antiqued brass H-hinge

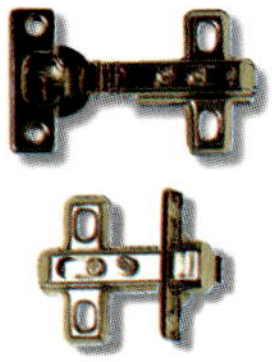

26mm (1in) concealed, steel unsprung hinge

Brass turn button

Cupboard catch

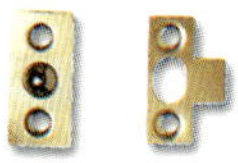

12mm (½in) bales (ball) catch

Painting Equipment

This is one aspect of do-it-yourself work where you cannot afford to skimp on materials. You will not achieve professional results by using cheap brushes that shed their bristles as you work, or cut-price rollers that disintegrate before the job is finished. Invest in the best quality equipment your budget allows if you are serious about your work.

Choosing brushes

Paintbrushes come in pure bristle, synthetic fibre and even foam versions. The last guarantees that you will not be left with brush strokes, and they are inexpensive enough to discard when you have finished. All natural brushes shed a few bristles in use, but cheap brushes are the worst offenders. Usually, these have fewer bristles to start with and they are often poorly secured. Regard pure bristle brushes as an investment; you can reuse them repeatedly, and many professional painters claim that their performance improves with age.

Synthetic brushes, usually with nylon bristles, have the big advantage of being moult-free, and they perform well with water-based paints. A more expensive version, made of polyester and nylon, is particularly easy to handle and said to give a superior finish.

Tool box essentials

Serious painters will need a range of brushes: slimline, 12 and 25mm (½ and 1in), for fiddly areas, such as window frames; medium sized versions, 50 and 75mm (2 and 3in), for doors, floors and skirting (base) boards; and large types, 100mm (4in), for quick coverage of walls and ceilings. You might like to add a few extras to this basic kit:

- A cutting-in (sash) brush, specially angled to cope with hard-to-reach areas, is particularly useful if you are painting around window frames. It comes in 12mm, 18mm and 25mm (½, ¾ and 1in) versions.
- A radiator brush, available with a plastic or metal handle and designed to reach the wall behind a radiator.
- Special-effects brushes, from stubby stencil brushes to mottlers, which allow you to create the distinctive look of woodgrain, and a range of artist's brushes for adding detail.

Practical tips

- Work new brushes across your palm to dislodge any loose bristles.
- Use an extension pole with your roller when painting ceilings.
- Imagine you are holding a pen when using lightweight brushes; this gives maximum control.

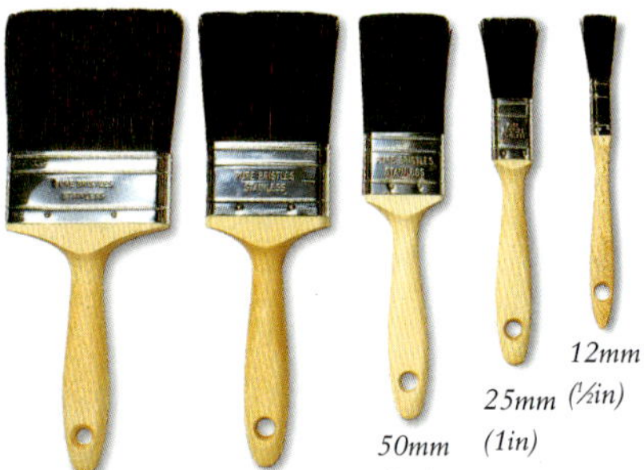

100mm (4in) brush

75mm (3in)

50mm (2in)

25mm (1in)

12mm (½in)

Dragging and colourwash brushes

Foam brushes

Stippling brush

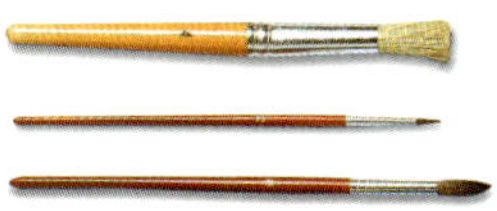

Stencil brush and artist's brushes

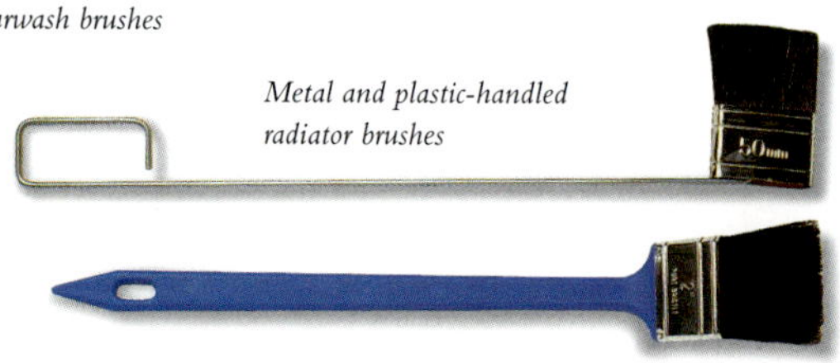

Metal and plastic-handled radiator brushes

Paint pads

If you are new to decorating, you may find that a paint pad is easier to handle than a brush. It gives a speedy and even finish, is light to handle and works particularly well with acrylic paints. Experiment with a single pad first before investing in a kit, to make sure you are happy with the tool.

Each pad consists of a layer of fibre on top of a layer of foam, which in turn is attached to a plastic handle. Use paint pads in conjunction with a paint tray. If you purchase a kit, a tray will usually be provided.

The right roller

If speed is of the essence, a paint roller will be an indispensable part of your decorating kit. Once you have purchased a roller, you can simply buy replacement sleeves that fit the existing handle.

Use sleeves with a short pile for smooth surfaces and for applying gloss paint. Medium-pile sleeves work well on smooth and lightly-textured surfaces, and with standard and solid emulsion (latex) paint. Use long-pile sleeves on uneven and textured surfaces.

ABOVE FAR LEFT Use a cutting-in brush on a window frame.

ABOVE LEFT Load paint on to the paint pad using the tray supplied with the pad.

ABOVE Use a power roller to paint large areas.

Power rollers are mains or battery-operated and in theory they can simplify the whole process, with the paint contained in a portable reservoir. However, they can result in drips and streaks, and many professional decorators prefer more conventional methods.

Paint pads

Cutting-in brush

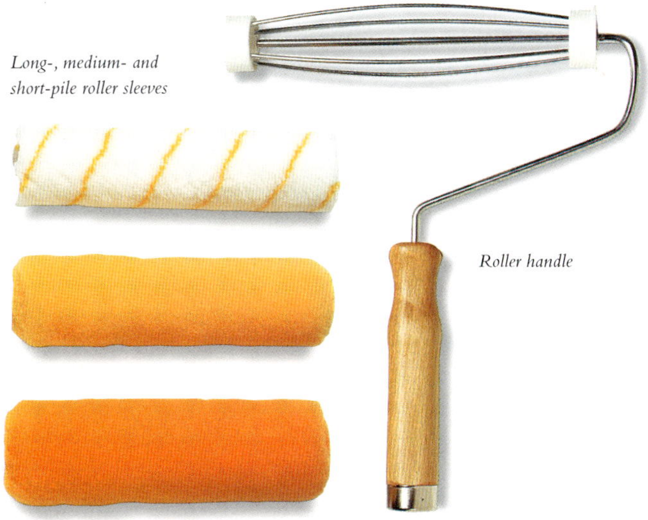

Long-, medium- and short-pile roller sleeves

Roller handle

Types of Paint

Today, there are so many different shades, textures, and thicknesses of paint to choose from that making the right choice can seem bewildering. In reality, having more choice can make the job easier. Whether you are painting your house interior: kitchen, bathroom, lounge, ceiling, floor; or exterior: shed, conservatory, fences, decking, drainpipes, there is a paint to meet your needs.

Different types of paint

All paints fall into one of two broad categories: water- or oil-based. Emulsions (latex) paints fit into the first category and are typically used on walls and ceilings. Oil-based paints, such as glosses and enamels, contain a solvent and they are ideal for wood surfaces such as doors, skirting (base) boards and window frames, and any metalwork. Both water- and oil-based paints come in matt (flat), mid-sheen (semi-gloss) and full gloss finishes.

If you are using emulsion paint, you will not need a separate undercoat, but you will need to apply at least two coats for good coverage. In general, gloss and enamel paints do require a separate undercoat, unless of the one-coat variety. One-coat emulsions are particularly useful when painting ceilings, reducing the amount of work involved.

Remember that if you are working with bare wood, metal, concrete or stone surfaces, you will need to apply a primer before the undercoat.

Paint consistency

The thickness of paint is influenced by various additives. When thinning paint make sure you use the correct diluent. At one end of the spectrum are fully-liquid paints, which require a certain amount of expertise to ensure a drip-free finish; at the other are non-drip, thixotropic or solid paints, which give a good finish whatever your skill level. Use them at cornice-level, on ceilings and above picture rails to avoid splashes.

ABOVE 1 powder pigments, 2 emulsion (latex) paints, 3 acrylic primer, 4 artist's acrylic colours, 5 acrylic scumble, 6 crackle glaze, 7 neutral wax, 8 methylated spirit (denatured alcohol), 9 brown shellac, 10 clear shellac.

BELOW FAR LEFT A selection of different-coloured paints, including watercolours, stencil paints and acrylics.

BELOW LEFT Before using, stir liquid paints with a wooden stick.

BELOW One-coat paints rapidly speed up paint decorating tasks.

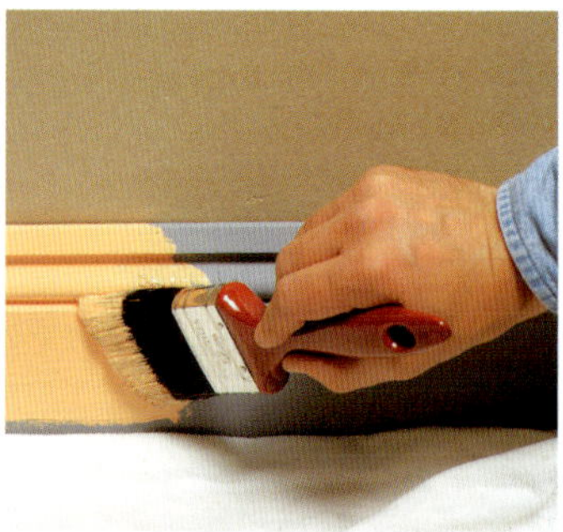

ABOVE FAR LEFT Textured paints are excellent for covering minor flaws in plasterwork.

ABOVE LEFT Turn off the heating, and allow the radiator to cool before applying paint.

ABOVE Start at the innermost corner and work outward when painting floors.

Special paints

Textured paints produce a relief pattern on internal walls and ceilings. They are best applied with a roller, which can be plain or have a textured patterned sleeve.

Enamel radiator paints are designed to withstand high temperatures and will not discolour like ordinary paints. You can choose from a range of bright colours to suit your decor, in satin or gloss.

Floor paints can enliven the dullest expanse of concrete, stone or wood. There is even a variety to transform tired vinyl and linoleum floors. Vary the effect with stripes, geometrical shapes or stencils for a unique look.

Kitchen and bathroom paints are specially formulated to cope with damp conditions. They contain a fungicide to stop mould growth and are considerably tougher than standard emulsions.

Microporous paints are also known as "breathing" paints. These water-based finishes, which are typically used on exterior wood, will expand and contract with the timber. These paints also let moisture escape so you will not end up with flaky or blistered paint surfaces.

The range of special paints is growing by the day. There are paints for use on MDF (medium-density fiberboard) and melamine surfaces, plus tried and tested outdoor paints, including masonry paints for rendered surfaces, colourful garden paints for walls, containers, fences and sheds, bituminous paints for pipes and guttering, and security paints, which remain tacky to prevent would-be felons from entering the house by climbing the drainpipes.

There are also traditional paints that use authentic materials; they come in various finishes, including matt, distemper, eggshell and gloss.

Practical tips

- On freshly plastered walls, make sure you use a new-plaster emulsion; standard types will not allow the plaster to dry out fully.
- If the paint can you are using is still quite full, seal it, upend it to allow the paint to form a protective seal around the lid. Store the can upside down until you need it.

RIGHT Traditional, or historic, paints are the perfect choice for period houses.

FAR RIGHT Fence paints come in a wide colour range and give a weatherproof finish.

Wallpapering Equipment

Using the correct tools will make the job of hanging wallpaper much easier, allowing you to achieve a more professional finish. Some are needed specifically for wallpapering; others are likely to be part of your standard do-it-yourself tool kit. When buying decorating tools, opt for quality rather than quantity – to make sure they last longer and produce better results.

Measuring and marking

A retractable steel tape is essential for taking accurate measurements, while a long metal straightedge, a spirit level and a pencil will be needed for marking levels, vertical guidelines on walls and the positions of fixtures.

Cutting and trimming

For cutting wallpaper to length and trimming edges, you will need a pair of paperhanger's scissors, which have long blades and curved tips used for creasing paper into angles. Choose scissors that are at least 250mm (10in) long and made from stainless steel, or have been specially coated so that they will not rust.

A sharp craft knife can also be used for trimming and will be easier to use with vinyl wallcoverings. Various trimming tools are also available, including the roller cutter, which enables you to crease and cut into edges with a single movement, and is accurate and simple to use.

Pasting

For mixing and applying paste, you will need a plastic bucket and a paste brush. Proper paste brushes have synthetic bristles and will be easier to clean than ordinary paintbrushes. A pasting table is not essential, but is extremely useful. They are also inexpensive and fold for easy storage. For ready-pasted wallcoverings, a polystyrene soaking trough is required.

ABOVE A paste table is not essential, but will make the job of pasting and hanging wallcoverings much easier. Also shown are the essentials for mixing and applying paste. Keep a decorator's sponge handy to wipe away traces of adhesive on the wallcovering or paste table.

ABOVE A polystyrene trough is needed for soaking ready-pasted wallcoverings. This will allow you to carry each drop to where it will be hung, and help to keep water off the floor.

Avoiding paste drips

A length of string tied tightly across the top of a wallpaper paste bucket makes a handy brush rest. Use the string rather than the side of the bucket for removing excess adhesive from the pasting brush.

ABOVE Take accurate measurements with a retractable steel tape.

ABOVE A sharp craft knife is useful for making awkward cuts, and trimming vinyl wallcoverings.

ABOVE Use spirit levels to ensure that wallcoverings are hung straight, and pattern repeats are level.

BELOW A plumbline provides a vertical guideline for hanging the first length of wallpaper on each wall.

LEFT Paperhanger's scissors have very long blades, making it much easier to cut wallpaper neatly.

BELOW A decorator's sponge holds water well and is good for washing down walls.

BELOW A soft-bristle paperhanger's brush is the best tool for smoothing ordinary wallpaper into place.

BELOW A seam roller gives a professional finish to wallpaper seams and the edges of borders, particularly vinyl wallcoverings.

Hanging

To ensure that wallpaper is hung straight and true, a plumbline or spirit level are essential. Hanging wallpaper may also involve working at heights, so access equipment will be required. A set of sturdy steps will be suitable for papering walls, but a safe work platform will be needed for ceilings and stairwells.

Finishing

A paperhanger's brush is the best tool for smoothing down wallpaper, although a sponge can be used for vinyl wallcoverings. For the best results, choose a brush with soft, flexible bristles and buy the largest size that you can manage comfortably. Do not use wallpaper brushes with a metal ferrule or collar on them for this job, as you might inadvertently tear or mark delicate wallcoverings.

Use a cellulose decorator's sponge rather than an ordinary household sponge. This type of sponge is made of a higher-density material, which is firmer and will hold water better. It can also be used for washing down walls before papering or painting.

A seam roller will give a neat finish to joints and the edges of borders, but should not be used on wallpaper with an embossed pattern. Various types made from wood and plastic are available. A soft plastic seam roller is the best option as it is less likely to leave marks on thin or overpasted wallpapers.

Practical tips

- A paste bucket will be easier to clean after use if it is lined with a plastic refuse sack first.
- An old flush door is a good alternative to a pasting table. Rest it between two chairs or across trestles.
- If you do not have a plumbline, improvise by using string and a large, heavy weight.
- A radiator paint roller makes an ideal tool for smoothing wallpaper in awkward corners and behind a wall fitting such as a radiator.

Types of Wallcovering

When choosing wallcoverings, it is important to take into consideration how practical it will be in the room you wish to decorate. Each room in your home has very different requirements and by choosing the right type of wallcovering, you will be sure of a decorative surface that will wear well and look good for years to come.

Lining paper

This provides a smooth base for wallpaper or paint on walls and ceilings. It is made in several grades from light 480 grade, suitable for new or near perfect walls, to extra-thick 1200 grade for use on rough and pitted plaster. A good-quality lining paper will be easier to handle than a cheap, thin paper and less likely to tear when pasted.

Wallpapers for painting

Woodchip paper is made by sandwiching particles of wood between two layers of paper. The thicker grades are easy to hang and cover uneven surfaces well, but woodchip is not easy to cut and can be difficult to remove, while the thinner grades tear easily. Woodchip is a budget-buy, but not particularly attractive or durable.

Relief wallpaper is imprinted with a raised, decorative surface pattern and is available in a wide choice of designs, as well as pre-cut dado (chair rail) panels and borders. It is quite easy to hang, although the thinner grades can tear when wet. It hides blemishes well and is durable once painted.

Textured vinyl has a deeply embossed surface pattern that masks

ABOVE Some wallcoverings are more hardwearing than others. Bear this in mind when choosing a pattern and material.

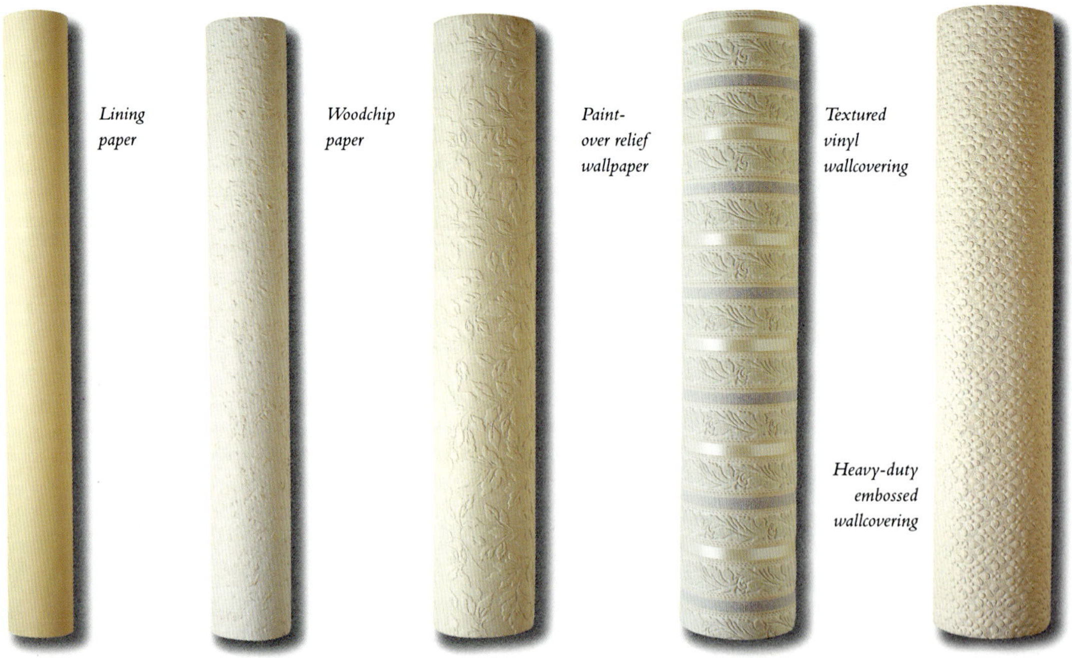

Lining paper

Woodchip paper

Paint-over relief wallpaper

Textured vinyl wallcovering

Heavy-duty embossed wallcovering

flaws and is uncrushable, so it is suitable for hardwearing areas such as the hall (lobby) and children's rooms. It is more expensive than relief wallpaper, but very easy to hang and usually dry strippable.

Embossed wallcovering comes in rolls and pre-cut panels made from a solid film of linseed oil and fillers fused on to a backing paper. It requires a special adhesive and will crack if folded, but it is not difficult to hang. It is very expensive, but is extremely hardwearing and durable, and the deeply-profiled, traditional designs are well suited to older and period properties.

Patterned wallcoverings

Printed wallpaper is available in an extensive choice of patterns and colours. The cheapest are machine-printed, but top-price designs are hand-printed and often untrimmed, so hanging is best left to the professionals. Printed wallpaper can be sponged, but is not particularly durable and is best used in rooms where it will not be subjected to much wear. The thinner grades tear easily when pasted.

Washable wallpaper also comes in a good choice of designs, but is more durable and has a thin plastic coating that allows the surface to be washed clean. It is priced competitively, fairly easy to hang and in some cases is dry strippable.

Vinyl wallcovering has a very durable surface layer of PVC that creates a hardwearing, often scrubbable, finish that resists steam, moisture and mould. There is a good choice of colours and patterns, as well as pearlized and embossed textured designs. Vinyl wallcovering is usually ready-pasted and dry strippable; paste-the-wall ranges are also available.

Sculptured vinyl is a thick, very hardwearing vinyl imprinted with a decorative design or tile effect. The waterproof finish resists steam, condensation, grease and cooking splashes, so it is a good choice for kitchens and bathrooms. It requires a heavy-duty adhesive, but is easy to hang and is dry strippable.

Special wallcoverings

Metallic foils and wallcoverings made from natural materials such as cork, silk and grasscloth can often be ordered from dedicated decorating outlets. They are expensive and difficult to hang, so employing a professional is advisable. In general, they are hard to clean, so they are best for low-wear areas of the home.

Printed wallpaper

Vinyl wallcovering

Paste-the-wall wallcovering

Sculptured vinyl wallcovering

Special metallic wallcoverings

Tiling Equipment

Tiles used for wall decoration are generally fairly thin, measuring 4–6mm (3/16–1/4in) thick, although some imported tiles (especially the larger sizes) may be rather thicker than this. The commonest kinds are square, measuring 108mm (4 1/4in) or 150mm (6in) across, but rectangular tiles measuring 200 x 100mm (8 x 4in) and 200 x 150mm (8 x 6in) are becoming more popular.

Tiling tools

For almost any ceramic tiling job, large or small, a good selection of tools will simplify the whole process.

A tile file makes light work of smoothing cut edges. A tile saw is useful for making shaped cuts to fit around obstacles such as pipework. Choose the coarse variety of abrasive paper for rubbing down paintwork. An all-in-one tile cutter, or tile jig, will make life easier for a beginner. Most incorporate a measuring device, trimmer and snapping mechanism in one neat unit. A standard tile cutter works well, but requires practice for best results.

Tile spacers are required when using standard field tiles. Other types have bevelled edges that create a grouting gap automatically when butted together.

A chinagraph (wax) pencil is suitable for marking glazed surfaces such as tiles. The marks are easy to erase when the job is finished.

A notched adhesive spreader will create a series of ridges in the adhesive, allowing it to spread when the tile is pressed home and ensuring that an even thickness of adhesive is applied. A squeegee will be needed at the grouting stage to force grout into the gaps between tiles.

Additions to this basic list are a spirit level for setting out horizontal and vertical guidelines; a straight-edge and tape measure; a sponge for cleaning off excess adhesive or applying grout; tile nippers for cutting off small pieces of tile; a glass cutter for cutting mirror tiles; a tile saw for cutting out complex shapes; and a pointing trowel for spreading adhesive on the wall. You will also need a tiling gauge for working out the positioning of tiles, made of lengths of softwood battening.

Practical tip

- The colour of an existing tiled surface can be given a quick makeover by applying tile primer and top coat, giving you "new" tiles at a fraction of the cost.

Snap-off tile file

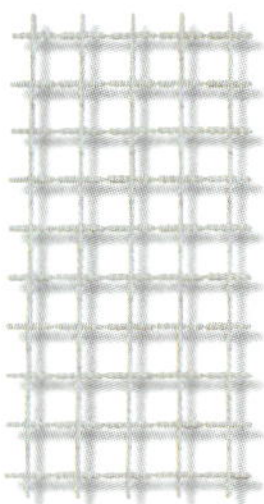

2mm (1/16in) tile spacers

Grout absorbent sponge

Notched spreader

Squeegee

Tile edge sander with abrasive strips

Pointed tiling trowel

Chinagraph pencil

Adhesive and grout

Both adhesive and grout for wall tiling are now usually sold ready-mixed in plastic tubs complete with a notched plastic spreader for your convenience. For areas that will get the occasional splash or may suffer from condensation, a water-resistant adhesive and grout is perfectly adequate, but for surfaces such as shower cubicles and around baths, which will have to withstand prolonged wetting, it is essential to use both waterproof adhesive and waterproof grout.

Always use waterproof grout on tiled worktops; ordinary grout will harbour germs. Some silicone sealant or mastic (caulking) may also be needed for waterproofing joints where tiling abuts, such as on baths, basins and shower trays.

It is important that you allow adhesive to dry for at least 24 hours before applying grout.

Grouting

This is generally white, but coloured grout is on sale and will make a feature of the grout lines (an effect that looks best with plain or fairly neutral patterned tiles).

Adhesive and grout are both sold in a range of quantities, sometimes labelled by weight, sometimes by volume. Always check the coverage specified by the manufacturer on the packaging when buying, so as not to buy too much or run out halfway through the job.

Tools for adhesive and grouting

Notched spreaders are used for creating a series of ridges in the adhesive, allowing it to spread when the tile is pressed home, and ensuring that an even thickness of adhesive is applied. They are available in various sizes. Grouting tools include a grout spreader, grout finisher and grout remover.

Tile saw

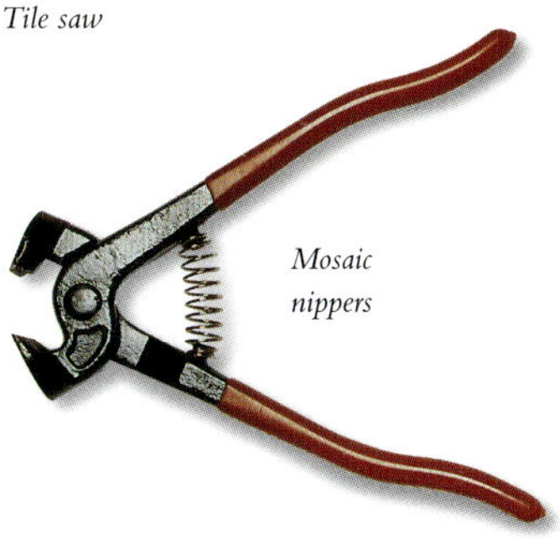

Mosaic nippers

Tile cutter with jaws

Grout refinishing kit

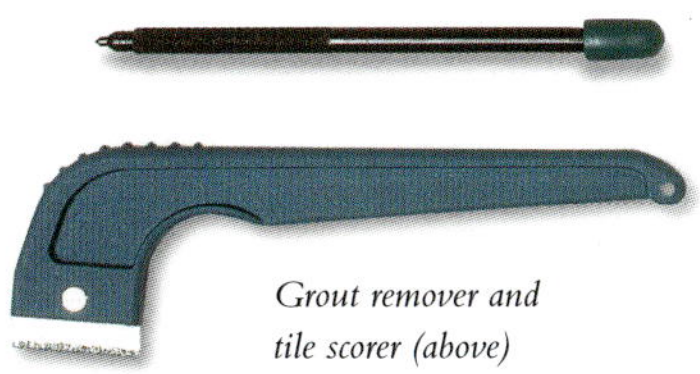

Grout remover and tile scorer (above)

Straightedge

Heavy-duty tile cutter with jaws

Tile jig with adjustable width and angle facility

MAINTENANCE AND REPAIRS

Where your home is concerned, prevention is often better, and certainly less expensive, than cure. A regular programme of inspection and maintenance will prevent small problems from becoming large and expensive ones. From time to time, however, repairs will be necessary, and their successful completion depends on having all the necessary tools and equipment to hand, and understanding how to use them.

Repairing and Replacing Floorboards

The majority of floors in older homes will have individual floorboards nailed to floor joists. In modern homes, sheets of flooring-grade chipboard (particle board) will be nailed or screwed to the joists. If a new floor covering is to be laid, it is essential that floors are in good condition. If floorboards are to be exposed, they need to be in even better condition, as any defects will be visible.

Lifting floorboards

To inspect the underfloor space or fit new floorboards, you will need to lift existing floorboards. You may find some that have been cut and lifted in the past to provide access to pipes or cables. These should be easy to lever up with the flat blade of a bolster (stonecutter's) chisel – do not use a screwdriver as you will damage the floorboard.

To lift boards that have not been cut, check first that they are not tongued-and-grooved – a tongue along one edge of each board fitting into a groove along the adjacent edge of its neighbour. If they are, use a floorboard saw or a circular saw with its cutting depth set to 20mm (¾in) to cut through the tongue.

Lever up the floorboard with your bolster chisel, and use a floorboard saw to make a right-angled cut across it. Make the cut exactly over a joist so that the two parts of the board will be supported when they are replaced.

Repairing joists

ABOVE Cut the new joist section to length and clamp it in place while you drill holes through it and through the old joist.

ABOVE Pass bolts through the holes and add a washer before securing the nuts with a spanner.

Chipboard sheets are easy to unscrew, but you may need to cut through tongues in the same way as for traditional floorboards.

Joist problems

Most of the problems associated with floor joists are due to dampness, which may occur if airbricks (vents) have become blocked or if there are not enough airbricks to ensure adequate ventilation of the underfloor space.

Lift a few floorboards and inspect the joists with a torch and a mirror, prodding any suspect areas with a bradawl (awl). If sections of joist are damaged, you should be able to cut and lift floorboards or chipboard sheets over the damage and bolt on a new section of joist of the same size, making sure that it is fixed to solid wood. Do not bother to remove the old joist unless it is actually rotten. If you do find signs of dry rot (typically white strands), all damaged

Removing a section of floorboard

1 If it is a tongued-and-grooved board, cut through the tongue with a circular saw.

2 Lift the end of the floorboard by levering with a bolster (stonecutter's) chisel.

3 Wedge the board up and cut, over a joist, with a floorboard saw.

Fitting floorboards

ABOVE Plane down floorboards if they are too wide to fill the gap.

ABOVE Use card or plywood packing pieces over the joists if the board is too shallow.

ABOVE Use a chisel to cut a slot to fit over a joist if the board is too thick.

wood must be removed by a firm of professionals. If you find signs of woodworm attack, treat the affected areas with a recommended woodworm eradicator or call in a professional firm.

Loose floorboards

If floorboards are loose, the best answer is to replace the nails holding them down with screws. Do not put a screw in the middle of a board – there could be a pipe underneath. If nail heads are protruding, use a hammer and nail punch to set them below the surface of the floorboards. This is essential before attempting to use a sanding machine or laying carpet or sheet vinyl.

Damaged floorboards

If floorboards are split or broken, the damaged section, at least, will need to be replaced. The most likely problem is that old floorboards will have become "cupped", or turned up at the edges. You can overcome this by hiring a floor sanding machine.

You do not need to replace a whole floorboard if only part of it is damaged; simply lift the board and cut out the damaged section, making the cuts over the centres of joists.

If replacement floorboard is too wide, plane it down to fit the gap – do not fit a narrower replacement floorboard, as you will get draughts. If the board is slightly thicker, chisel slots out of it where it fits over the joists; if it is thinner, use packing pieces of cardboard or plywood between the joists and the board.

Secure each floorboard with two floorboard nails at each joist, positioning them about 25mm (1in) from the edge of the board and exactly in the middle of the joist. It is a good idea to drill nail pilot holes in the board first.

Practical tip

- When laying new floorboards or new floor coverings, make sure that you can still gain access to pipes and cables underneath. If necessary, cut a removable inspection hatch in both the floor and the floor covering.

Fixing floorboards

ABOVE Drill pilot holes for floorboard nails to avoid splitting the wood.

ABOVE Hammer down protruding nails to prevent them damaging the floor covering.

ABOVE Secure loose floorboards by replacing the nails with screws.

Repairing Cracks and Holes in Floors

Before laying a new floorcovering, it is essential that the existing floor surface is sound and smooth. As well as repairing or replacing floorboards, you may have to fill cracks and holes in wooden floors, and deal with unevenness, and possibly damp, in solid floors. Any faults not rectified will eventually show through the floor covering and may damage it.

Filling holes in timber floors

Nail and screw holes can easily be plugged using a flexible wood filler applied with a filling or putty knife. If the floorboards are to be left exposed and treated with a clear sealer, try to match the wood filler, or stopping, to the colour of the surrounding floorboards – so do the filling after any sanding.

Larger recesses can also be filled with flexible filler, but if a knot has fallen out, leaving a large round hole, plug this by gluing in a short length of dowel and planing it smooth afterwards. Select a dowel that matches the colour of the floor or stain it once planed down.

Filling cracks in timber floors

You will find two main kinds of crack in timber floors: splits in the ends of the floorboards and gaps between the boards.

A split can often be cured by skew (toe) nailing – that is driving two nails through the end of the board at an angle toward the centre and down into the joist. As the nails are driven in, they should close up the split.

Gaps between floorboards are more difficult to deal with. If they are narrow, flexible wood filler will work, but for wider gaps, you must cut slivers of wood and glue them into place in the gaps. Once the glue has dried, plane or sand the slivers flush with the surrounding floor and stain to match if necessary.

If there are lots of wide gaps between floorboards, a better solution is to lift all the floorboards one by one, starting at one side of the room and working toward the other, and re-lay them tightly against one another. Floorboard clamps will help you do this, as they force a board against its neighbour while you nail or screw it down.

Levelling a wooden floor

Individual rough patches on a timber floor can be sanded down by hand, which you should do after using filler, but where floorboards have become cupped or are heavily encrusted with old paint, grease and polish, the best move is to hire an industrial-type sanding machine and re-sand the floor. Begin with coarse abrasive and progress through to the fine grades, working across the floorboards at an angle. Finish off by working along the floorboards with fine abrasive. Hire an edging sander as well, unless you own a belt sander, because the floor sander will not sand right up to the skirting boards.

Fixing gaps in floorboards

1 Drive glued slivers of wood between floorboards to fill large gaps.

2 Plane down the wood slivers flush with the floor when the glue has dried.

ABOVE Use flexible wood filler to cover the holes made by nail heads and screws.

ABOVE With a split board, first glue the split, then drive in nails at the end of the board.

Preparing solid floors

1 Brush a crack in a solid floor with diluted PVA (white) glue to help new mortar bond to it.

2 Apply quick-set repair mortar to a crack in a solid floor. Level it flush and leave to harden.

3 If excessively porous, seal it by brushing on a coat of diluted PVA adhesive.

Filling cracks and holes in solid floors

Provided a solid floor is basically sound and dry, you should be able to fill cracks and holes using a quick set repair mortar. All loose material should be removed and the cracks enlarged if necessary to give the mortar something to grip.

The surface of the crack or hole should be brushed with a solution of one part PVA (white) adhesive and five parts water to reduce absorbency and help the mortar adhere to the floor. Use the same PVA adhesive and water solution to make up the mortar, then trowel it into place, building up two or more layers in a deep hole. Level the surface with a plasterer's trowel.

Levelling solid floors

Little skill is required to produce a smooth, flat solid floor surface, as a self-levelling floor compound will do the job for you. Two types are available: both are powders and are mixed with either water or with a special latex emulsion.

Before you start, clear the room, removing all skirting (base) boards and doors; nail battens (furring strips) across thresholds to prevent the compound from spreading. Fill any cracks or holes more than 6mm (¼in) deep as described previously and brush the floor with the PVA/water solution. Mix the floor levelling compound in a bucket with water and tip it out on to the floor, spreading it out with a plasterer's trowel or a float. Leave it to settle. Once the compound has dried, at least 24 hours, you can refit the skirting boards and doors, but check that the latter will clear the higher floor when opened – you may need to trim a little off the bottoms.

Laying a self-levelling compound

1 Mix up self-levelling floor compound according to the manufacturer's instructions.

2 Starting from a corner farthest from the door, pour the compound on to the floor.

3 Using a plasterer's trowel, smooth the compound to a thickness of 3mm (⅛in).

Repairing Damaged Floorcoverings

Of all the types of floorcovering, tiled finishes can be the easiest to repair, since individual tiles can often be lifted and replaced. The way you do it depends on whether the tile is hard or soft and on how it has been secured to the floor. Even damaged carpet can be patched effectively, but care needs to be taken to avoid further damage to surrounding areas.

Ceramic and quarry tiles

These are among the most difficult tiles to replace, as first you will have to chip out the old tile. Drill a few holes in the tile with the biggest masonry drill you own, then use a club (spalling) hammer and cold chisel to chip out the tile, making sure you do not damage the surrounding tiles. Chip out all old adhesive or mortar from under the tile and grout from the edges.

Lay some new tile adhesive for ceramic tiles or mortar for quarry tiles and push the replacement tile gently into place. If it is not flush with its neighbours, lift it quickly and add or remove adhesive or mortar as necessary. Clean any excess mortar or adhesive off the face of the tile and leave to set before making good the gaps around the tile with grout for ceramic tiles or more mortar for quarry tiles. If re-laying several tiles, it helps if you make up some small spacers.

Replacing a quarry tile

1 Remove any cracked quarry (or ceramic) tiles with a club hammer and cold chisel.

2 Bed a new quarry tile on mortar, but use the recommended adhesive for ceramic tiles.

Mosaic timber tiles

There are two ways to replace these tiles. One is to lift the whole tile, which consists of four groups of timber strips, and replace with a new one. First drill or chisel out one strip and then lever the rest of the tile from the floor. The second method is to remove just the damaged strip or strips and glue in replacements taken from a spare tile, pressing them into place with a block of wood.

Carpet tiles

These are designed to be replaceable, so if you stain, burn or damage one in some other way, you have not ruined a whole carpet. Sometimes, the tile can simply be lifted and a new one put in its place, but some carpet tiles may be held down with double-sided adhesive tape, which will need replacing with the new tile – do not try to reuse any old tape.

Replacing a mosaic strip

1 First drill a sequence of holes through the damaged mosaic strip.

2 Carefully cut away the strip around the holes with a chisel.

3 Apply a little glue to the new mosaic strip. Using a block of wood, hammer it in place.

Soft floor tiles

Most soft floor tiles – vinyl, cork, lino and rubber – are replaced in the same way. First you have to soften the adhesive holding the tile in place, which is best done with a hot-air gun, starting at one corner and gradually peeling the tile back. This becomes easier once you can direct the hot-air gun beneath the tile. An old chisel can be used to remove any remaining adhesive. Check that the replacement tile is an exact fit.

Some soft tiles are self-adhesive, requiring only the removal of backing paper, while others require a separate adhesive. Always add the adhesive to the back of a replacement tile to avoid staining the other tiles. With the adhesive in place, or the backing paper removed, hold the tile against the edge of one of the surrounding tiles and lower it into place. You may only get one attempt at this, so take care to get it right.

Carpet

Provided you have a matching piece, you can patch most types of carpet, but it may be worth cleaning the carpet first, since the patch may be a brighter colour. First decide how large the patch should be – if the carpet is patterned, you may want to join along a pattern line – cut the patch about 25mm (1in) larger than this all round, with the same part of any pattern. Lay the patch over the carpet, lining up the pattern exactly, and secure it with adhesive tape.

Using a trimming knife fitted with a new blade and a metal straightedge, make a single cut down through both thicknesses of carpet along each edge of the patch. Remove the tape and lift both pieces of carpet – the patch should fit exactly into the hole in the carpet with the pattern matching. With foam-backed carpet, lay four strips of double-sided tape on the floor around the edges of the hole so that each strip overlaps the joint between the old carpet and the patch. Brush the edges of the patch and the hole with latex adhesive to prevent fraying, then press the carpet patch on to the tape. Remove excess adhesive with a damp cloth.

With fabric-backed carpet, use non-adhesive carpet repair tape and latex adhesive on the back and edges of the patch and the hole. Press the patch down into the hole with a wallpaper seam roller and wipe off any excess adhesive with a damp cloth.

Replacing a vinyl tile

1 Remove a vinyl or cork tile using a hot-air gun to soften the adhesive.

2 Apply adhesive to the back of the vinyl or cork tile and replace.

Patching foam-backed carpet

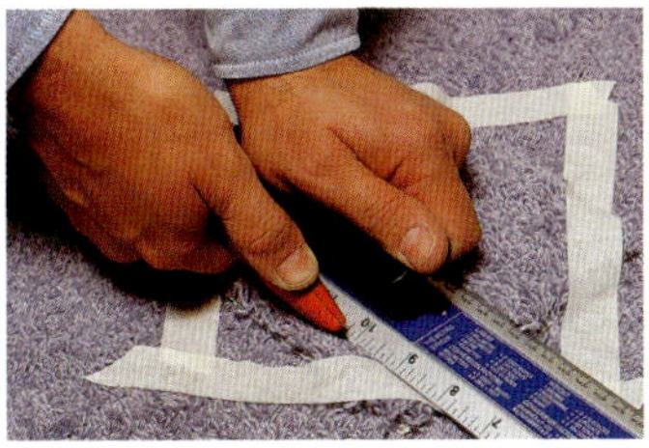

1 Use a trimming knife and straightedge to cut through both the carpet patch and the existing carpet.

2 Press the carpet patch on to double-sided adhesive tape. Brush the edges with latex adhesive to prevent fraying.

3 The finished patch of carpet should fit exactly into the hole and the joins should be invisible in longer pile carpet.

Repairing Ceilings and Walls

Before carrying out any redecorating, such as painting or papering, ceilings and walls must be in near-perfect condition if the best results are to be achieved, as any defects will show through. This means filling any cracks, holes or other imperfections to leave a smooth surface. Fortunately, there is an excellent range of products for making good those defects.

Filling cracks

A general-purpose filler can be used for the majority of cracks in ceilings and walls. This comes ready-mixed in tubs or as a powder for mixing with water. The filler is simply applied with a filling or putty knife, pressing it into the cracks and smoothing it flush with the surface. Some cracks need enlarging slightly to give the filler something to grip; fine cracks can be filled with special hairline crack filler.

Normal fillers are quite adequate if you are papering the ceiling or wall, but for paint, a fine surface filler is better. Most fillers take a short while to dry, after which they can be sanded flush with the surrounding surface. Instant fillers set very quickly and are good for last-minute minor repairs while you are actually painting or papering.

Most of these fillers are equally as suitable for wood as for plaster – provided the wood is to be painted – so all your crack and small hole filling can be done in one go, using the same material. For cracks between two different materials, for example the wall plaster and timber architrave (trim) moulding around a door, use a flexible filler. This will absorb the inevitable movement between the two materials without opening up.

Filling holes

Small holes, especially those left by screws, can be filled in the same way as cracks. Cut off any protruding wall plugs or, better still, remove them altogether so that you can obtain a smooth finish.

Larger holes are more of a problem. The kind of hole left by removing a waste pipe from a wall can be made good with do-it-yourself repair plaster, which can usually be applied in layers up to 50mm (2in) thick. Smaller recesses up to 20mm (¾in) deep can be treated with a special deep-gap filler, while really deep cavities can be filled with an expanding foam filler. Once set, this can be cut and sanded smooth, then painted or papered over. If an area of plaster has fallen off the wall, use a repair plaster, levelling it with the surrounding sound plaster with a straight length of wood.

For larger areas, nail timber battens (furring strips) to the wall to act as guides for your timber straightedge.

Practical tip

- If you are repairing damage to a plastered external corner, pin a batten (furring strip) to one side of the corner to support the filler while it sets. For whole corners, use metal corner beading held in place with plaster.

BELOW FAR LEFT Fill a fine crack with hairline crack filler, applied here with a putty knife.

BELOW LEFT Use a repair plaster for a deep hole, applied with a plasterer's trowel.

BELOW Use expanding foam filler to seal the gap around a window or door frame.

Repairing a hole in plasterboard

1 Use a padsaw to square up a hole in damaged plasterboard.

2 Attach a piece of string to the patch.

3 Butter the back of the patch with filler or coving adhesive.

Repairing plasterboard (gypsum board)

Surface damage and small holes in plasterboard can be repaired in the same way as cracks and holes in solid plaster, but if a large hole has been punched in the material – by a door handle, say – a different solution is required. In this case, a patch must be placed behind the hole to provide support for a layer of filler.

First use a padsaw to open out the hole, squaring the sides. Then cut a section of fresh plasterboard to a length slightly less than the diagonal dimension of the hole. This will allow you to pass it through the hole at an angle. Drill a tiny hole in the middle of the plasterboard patch and insert a piece of knotted string through it before adding filler or coving (crown molding) adhesive to the edges on the grey side of the plasterboard. This will secure it firmly to the back of the existing plasterboard panel.

Pass the patch through the hole and pull it back against the edges. Hold the string taut while adding filler to the hole, then leave this to set. Cut off the projecting string and make good with a final smooth coat of general-purpose filler or finish plaster, ensuring the surface is level.

4 Pass the plasterboard patch through the hole while holding the string.

5 Fill the hole with plaster while holding the patch tightly in place with the string.

Repairing lath-and-plaster

Holes in lath-and-plaster ceilings and walls can be repaired in the same way as holes in normal plastered surfaces, provided the laths are intact. First brush the laths with PVA (white) adhesive to reduce absorbency, then repair with general-purpose filler, deep-gap filler or repair plaster. If the laths have broken, cut back the plaster until you expose the vertical studs. Cut a piece of plasterboard (gypsum board) to size and nail it in place before filling the hole.

ABOVE To repair damaged lath and plaster, cut back the old plaster, removing any split wooden laths and square off the edges. Cut a new plasterboard patch to fit the hole and nail it in place. Add support strips if it is a large patch. Complete the repair by plastering over the patch after filling and taping the edges all around.

Concealing the Ceiling-to-wall Joint

Coving (crown molding), a quadrant-shaped moulding made from polystyrene, plaster or timber is fitted between the walls and ceiling of a room. It has two functions: to be decorative and to conceal the joint between the walls and ceiling. An ornate coving may be referred to as a cornice; old plaster cornices may be clogged with years of paint and need cleaning to reveal the detail.

Preparing for coving

Using a short length of coving as a guide, draw pencil lines all around the room, on the wall and ceiling, to indicate the position of the coving. Make sure the lines are straight and continuous. If you are fitting polystyrene or plaster coving, any wall and ceiling coverings must be stripped off between the pencil marks. Run a trimming knife along the lines, then lift the paper with a flat stripping knife, using water and wallpaper stripper if necessary.

If you are fitting plaster coving, score the surfaces of the walls and ceiling with the edge of a filling or putty knife, or trowel, to provide a key for the adhesive.

LEFT Plaster coving is held in place with adhesive (plus nails if heavy) and painted.

LEFT Timber coving is nailed in place and usually varnished or stained (nail holes filled).

LEFT Paper-covered polystyrene coving is held in place with adhesive and it is usually painted.

LEFT Plain polystyrene coving is held in place with adhesive and usually left untreated.

Dealing with corners

With polystyrene and plaster coving, you can often buy moulded internal and external corner pieces that fit over the coving at corners, saving you the trouble of having to make neat joints. With timber coving, you may find pre-scribed ends to fit both internal and external corners.

If you have no ready-made corners, you will have to cut 45-degree mitres on the ends of lengths of coving where they meet at a corner. Special jigs or paper templates are often sold with polystyrene and plaster coving to help with this. The alternative is a deep mitre box. For plaster and wood, use a fine-toothed panel or tenon saw to cut the coving; with polystyrene, use a sharp trimming knife. Be prepared to make slight adjustments to the mitres if the room is not absolutely square.

LEFT A template is used to guide a trimming knife to make mitres in polystyrene coving.

Practical tip

- When removing wire nails used to hold coving temporarily in place, employ pliers rather than pincers or a claw hammer, which could damage the mouldings.

Polystyrene coving

The corner pieces for polystyrene coving have square ends designed to be butted against the straight pieces. Start by fitting an internal corner, spreading the recommended adhesive and simply pushing the coving into place. Then fit the straight pieces, working toward the next corner, where you may have to cut a straight piece to fit.

If the walls are uneven, it is better to use ceramic tile adhesive rather than the coving adhesive, since it will provide a thicker adhesive bed.

Plaster coving

Special adhesive is available for fixing plaster coving, and it should be spread on the back edges of the mouldings. To hold the coving in place while the adhesive sets, drive wire nails into the wall and ceiling along the edges of the coving (not through the coving), after using a damp cloth to remove excess adhesive that is squeezed out along the joints. Once the adhesive has set, remove the pins and, if necessary, make good the corners and joints with plaster filler (spackle).

Putting up plaster coving

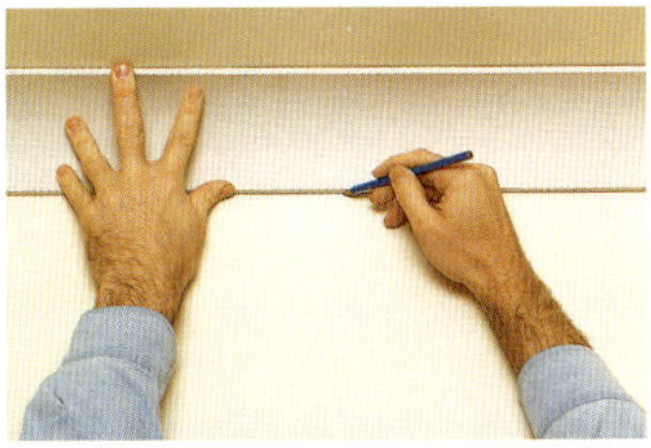

1 Use the coving and mark out two parallel guidelines on the wall and ceiling of the room.

2 Remove old coverings. Score the surface of painted or plaster walls to improve adhesion.

3 Cut the mitre for the corner, press the length into place and support with nails.

4 Cut a mitre using a mitre box and tenon or panel saw.

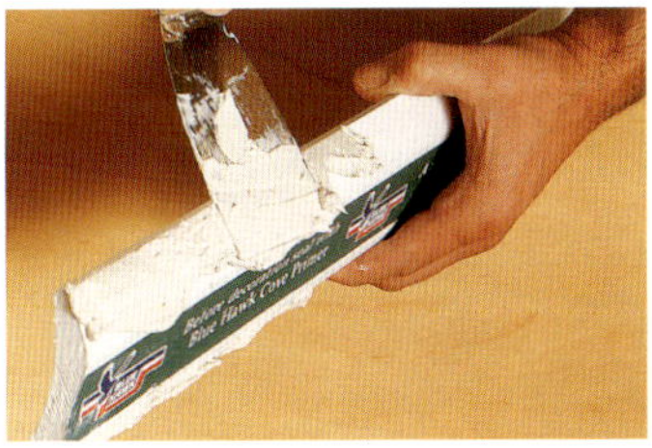

5 Butter the back edges of the plaster coving with good adhesive.

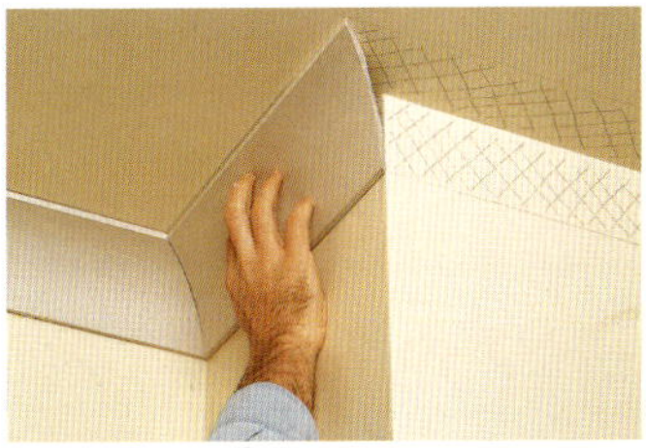

6 Fit the adjacent corner piece which has been carefully mitred for an external corner.

7 Complete the external corner with another length of coving, butting the ends together.

8 Fill any gaps at external and internal angles with cellulose filler and sand down once dry.

Timber coving

This could be put up with adhesive in the same way as plaster coving, but it is easier to use panel pins, making sure they will protrude about 20mm (¾in) from the back of the moulding. Drive them home with a nail punch, then use matching wood filler applied with a putty knife to conceal the holes.

As an alternative to mitring internal corners, they can be scribed – that is, the end of one piece of moulding is cut to the profile of the adjacent piece. The first piece is cut square to butt tightly into the corner, and the second piece fits over it.

External corners will have to be mitred, and all corners must be made good with wood filler once the coving is in place.

Fixing timber coving

1 Fix with a punch and panel pins (brads).

2 Fill the nail holes with matching wood filler.

Replacing Window Glass

Replacing broken window glass is a common do-it-yourself job, and something that is worth learning how to do properly. Working with normal window panes is quite straightforward (though care is needed), but replacing the glass in a leaded-light window is trickier. That said, it is well within the scope of anyone with patience and a practical frame of mind.

Types of glass

Most window glass used in our homes is 4mm (3/16in) float glass, although small panes may be 3mm (1/8in) and large panes may be 6mm (1/4in) or more in thickness.

Large panes of glass and glass in vulnerable areas, such as in doors, in panels next to doors or at low level, are likely to be one of two types of safety glass. Toughened glass is heat treated so that it is less likely to break, and when it does it shatters into tiny fragments; laminated glass comprises two thin panes of glass with a plastic layer between them, so that if the glass breaks, it remains stuck to the plastic interlayer.

In all cases, replace like with like. If in doubt, take a piece of the old glass to your supplier when buying a replacement.

Removing the old glass

The first step is to remove the old glass immediately, making sure you wear stout gloves that cover your wrists. Collect the glass in newspaper or a cardboard box and dispose of it safely and carefully; your glass supplier may be prepared to accept the broken pieces for recycling. An old chisel can be used to chop out all the old putty – do not use a good one, as its blade will be damaged by the sprigs (or clips in a metal frame) that hold the glass in place. Pull out the sprigs or clips and remove all the old putty from the recess.

Practical tip

• When removing broken glass from a window, apply a criss-cross pattern of adhesive tape to the pane to prevent the glass from flying around.

Replacing broken glass

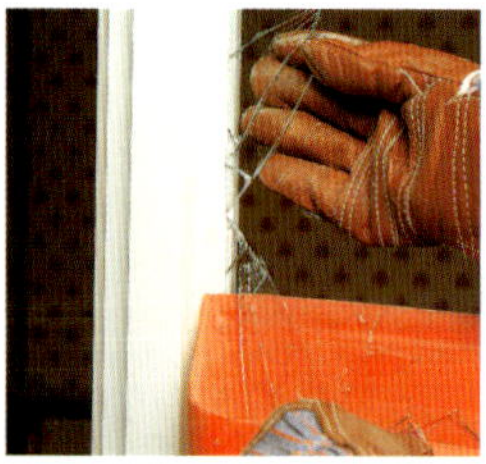

1 Remove the broken glass, wearing gloves to prevent cuts.

2 Use an old chisel to remove the old putty from the rebate.

3 Pull out the old glazing sprigs with pincers from the frames.

4 Squeeze a thin layer of putty into the corners of the frame.

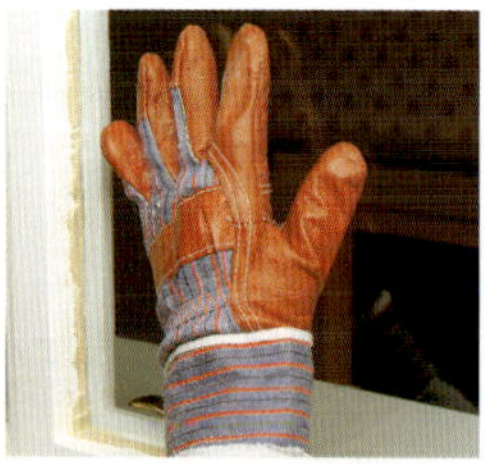

5 Position the new glass in place with equal clearance all round.

6 Tap in the glazing sprigs at 300mm (12in) intervals.

7 Add more putty and neaten it to a 45-degree bevel.

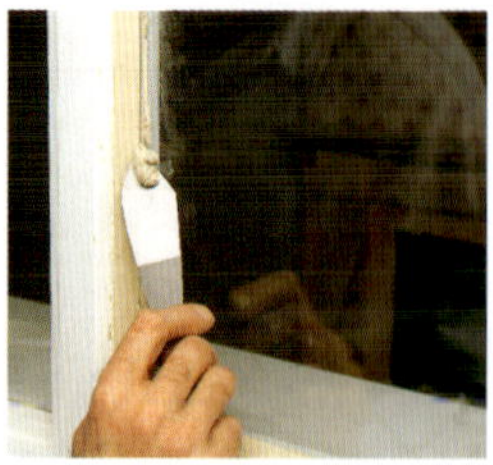

8 Trim the excess on the inside and outside. Leave to harden.

Measuring up

Take measurements of the width and height of the recess in several places. The size of glass you need is 3mm (⅛in) less than the size of the recess. If in doubt, cut a cardboard template to fit and take this with you to the glass supplier. Reckon on buying some new glazing sprigs or clips to hold the glass in place, and buy the correct type of putty – either for timber or for metal windows.

Fitting the new glass

Check that the glass fits the recess without binding anywhere, then put it in a safe place.

Take a small amount of putty and work it in your hands until it is pliable; if it sticks to your fingers, roll it out on newspaper to remove some of the oil. When it is workable, begin pressing a layer into the window recess, squeezing it out of the palm of your hand between thumb and forefinger rather like toothpaste.

Put the glass in place, resting it on a couple of matchsticks (wooden matches), and press it gently into the opening until putty is squeezed out at the back – press on the sides of the glass, not the centre. Then fit the glazing sprigs, sliding the head of the hammer along the surface of the glass, or re-fit the clips. Remove putty that has squeezed out on the inside of the window.

Finally, add more putty to the outside of the window, using the same thumb and forefinger technique, until you have a good bead all the way around the glass.

Take a putty knife and smooth off this bead at an angle of 45 degrees, pushing the putty into the edges of the frame as you draw the putty

Replacing glass in lead cames

1 Use a sharp trimming knife to cut through the cames at the corners at 45 degrees.

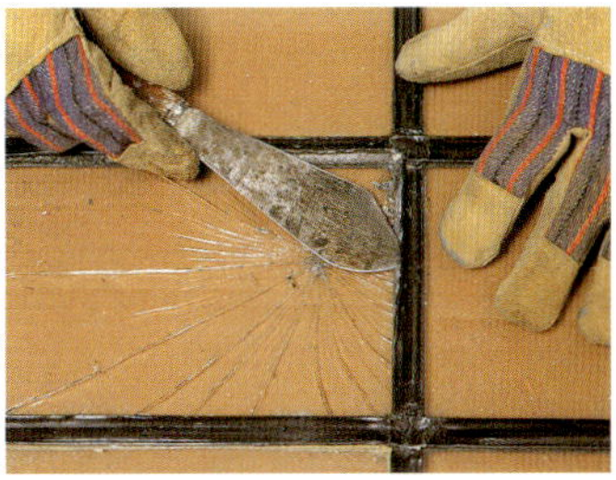

2 Lever up and fold back the cames all round the pane to remove the old glass.

3 With the new glass in place, press the cames back into place with a seam roller.

4 Fuse the lead together at the corners using a small electric soldering iron.

knife along it. Make neat mitres at the corners. If the knife sticks, wet it with water. Leave the putty for about 14 days before painting over it to disguise and seal the joints, allowing the paint to overlap on to the glass to prevent moisture from seeping down into the frame.

Replacing leaded lights

If the glass in a leaded-light window has broken, you will need a really sharp trimming knife to cut through the lead cames at the corners. Make each cut at an angle of 45 degrees so that you can lever up and fold back the edges of the cames securing the broken pane and lift the glass out. Measure the recess exactly and buy a piece of glass of the same thickness and slightly smaller all round. Put the replacement glass in its recess using a small amount of putty mixed with a little black powder paint.

Fold the lead cames back on to the glass neatly, pressing them down with something like the handle of a spoon or a rounded piece of wood and finishing off with a wallpaper seam roller. Finally, fuse the mitred corners together with a small electric soldering iron and some resin-cored solder.

Many leaded light windows will have one or more panes of coloured glass. The best place to look for authentic replacements for these will be in an architectural salvage yard. A glass merchant can cut a piece of old glass down to size for you.

Repairing Windows

The most obvious signs that there is something wrong with a window are when it starts to rattle in the wind or to stick, making it difficult to open and close. Rattling is most likely to be caused by worn hinges or wear of the window itself; sticking by swelling of the wood, build-up of paint or movement of the frame joints. All these faults can be repaired.

Repairing hinges

Loose or worn hinges are often a cause of window problems. To start with, try tightening the screws or replacing them with slightly longer screws of the same gauge. If that does not work, replace the hinges with new ones of the same size and type plus new screws. Remember that steel hinges will rust quickly, so apply suitable primer immediately and then repaint to match the window when this has dried.

Check the opening and closing of the window. If the window is sticking on the far edge, it may be necessary to deepen the recess for one or both hinges; if it binds on the closing edge, one or both recesses will be too deep and may need to be packed out with cardboard. A rattling window can often be cured by fitting draught-excluder strip. Measure the gap, then buy a suitable draught excluder.

ABOVE A loose window joint can be re-glued with fresh adhesive. Clamp it up while the adhesive dries.

Worn windows

Sash windows are particularly prone to wear. The best answer is to remove the windows and fit brush-pile draught excluder inside the sash channel. A new catch to hold the windows together may also be necessary. Fit a new inner staff bead around the window so that it fits more closely against the inner sash.

Warped windows

Timber, hinged windows can sometimes warp, so that they meet the frame only at the top or at the bottom. The best way to cure this is to fit some mortise window locks, which fit into holes cut in the actual window, with the bolts shooting into more holes in the frame. These allow the window to be held in the correct position (get someone to push from the outside while you lock it) so that the warp will self correct. You could position a tiny block of wood between the window and frame so that the warp is over-corrected – do not overdo this or you will break the glass.

Practical tip

- When replacing painted steel hinges with brass versions, always use brass screws to match.

Dealing with binding windows

ABOVE A binding window may be cured simply by tightening the hinge screws or replacing them with longer ones.

ABOVE If a window is binding on the far side, it may be that the hinge recesses need to be deepened with a chisel.

ABOVE A sticking window may be swollen or have too much paint on it. Plane down the leading edge of the window.

Reinforcing a window joint with dowels

1 To reinforce a glued window joint, drill holes across the joint.

2 Then, hammer in adhesive-covered dowels of the same size.

3 When the adhesive has dried, chisel or plane the dowels flush.

Sticking windows

Over time, a build-up of paint may cause windows to stick, especially when the weather is damp and the wood begins to swell. Use a plane to cut down the offending areas, which is much easier if you remove the window from its frame, then repaint before refitting the window.

Make sure that all bare wood is covered with paint, as this will prevent water from getting in, which causes the wood to swell. Also, check that the putty is in good condition and doing its job of keeping the water out and the glass in.

Loose window joints

If the paint on a timber window has been allowed to deteriorate, the joints may have dried out and shrunk, causing the window to sag and stick in the frame.

Remove the window and strip off the old paint. You will be able to see the gaps in a loose mortise-and-tenon joint, and it should be possible to work wood glue into these. Use sash clamps to keep the window square while the adhesive dries. There may be wedges in the mortise-and-tenon joint that you can replace with new glued-in wedges as with doors. If not, you can drill holes across the joint and glue in lengths of dowel to reinforce it. Use a proper dowel drill – 6, 8 or 10mm (¼, 5⁄16 or ⅜in) – and fit two dowels per joint. Chisel or plane the dowels flush once the adhesive has dried.

The alternative is to fit an L-shaped reinforcing bracket to each loose window corner. Make sure the window is perfectly square before you fit these and, for neatness, chisel out a recess in the face of the window so that the bracket is flush with the surface, or slightly below so that it can be covered with filler.

Reinforcing a window joint with a bracket

1 To fit an L-shaped corner reinforcing bracket, first chisel out a recess.

2 Screw the bracket in place so that it is below the surface.

3 Fill over the bracket and smooth down once the filler has dried.

Repairing Window Sills

A wooden sill is often the first part of a window to need repair, as the rain that falls on the window drips on to the sill and some of it may collect, resulting in flaking paint or crumbling, rotten wood. The treatment ranges from simple repainting to replacement. Since sills project from the wall, they are also prone to impact damage, which can affect concrete and stone sills.

Wet rot

This can be recognized by softening and darkening of the wood and often by severe splintering, the rotten wood falling out. Fortunately, it is fairly easy to repair; on the other hand, dry rot – recognizable by white strands on the surface and a musty smell – requires the services of a professional.

Provided the damage is not so severe that sill replacement is a better option, the first thing to do is remove all the rotten wood with a sharp chisel until you get back to sound, dry wood. Use a hot-air gun if necessary to dry out the wood.

Brush the wood with a wood hardener solution and leave this to dry. This prepares the wood for the application of exterior wood filler. Although this sets hard, it retains sufficient flexibility to be able to move with the wood as it expands and contracts with varying temperatures and humidity. The wood filler can be applied with a filling or putty knife and should be left to set. Substantial damage may need two or even three layers.

Once the filler has hardened, it can be sanded down and the whole area painted to match the surrounding wood – it is probably best to repaint the whole sill.

Some wet-rot repair systems include wood preservative sticks or tablets that you put in drilled holes in the wood surrounding the repair area to prevent future rot. The holes are concealed when the damaged area is filled.

A wet rot system cannot be used to make good dry rot, which can affect masonry as well as woodwork. In this situation, all damaged wood must be completely removed (along with any affected bricks and mortar) and the areas must be professionally sterilized before replacement materials are installed.

Repairing wet rot

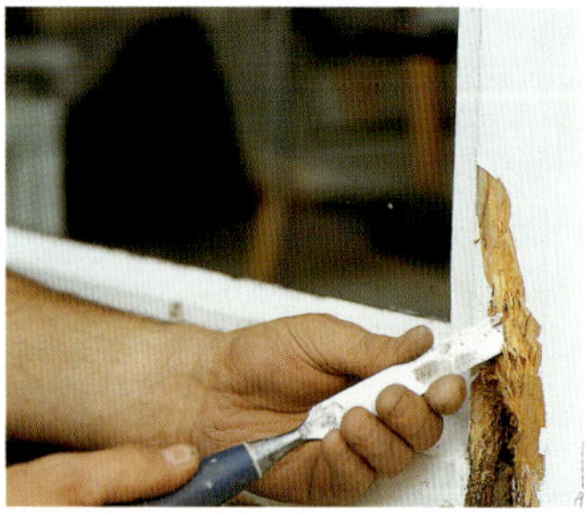

1 Chisel out all the rotten wood, making sure only sound wood is left.

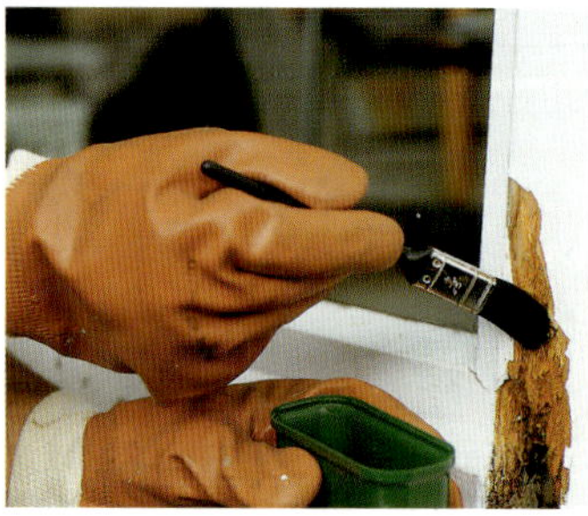

2 Brush the sound wood with hardener and leave to dry as recommended.

3 To fit wood preservative sticks, drill holes in the sound wood.

4 Push preservative sticks into the drilled holes and below the surface.

5 Fill the damaged area with exterior wood filler. Leave to dry before sanding.

Replacing a wooden sill

If only part of a sill needs replacing, you may be able to cut out the damaged section and fashion a replacement, screwing and gluing it in place. However, it is not always easy to achieve a perfect match.

Replacing the whole window sill may be easier than you think, and it can be done without removing the window frame.

First remove any opening windows and take out the glass from the fixed windows. Remove the window board, or inner sill, and saw down through the sill as close as possible to the jambs. Slide out the cut sill sections, then saw through the tenon joints between the jambs and the ends of the sill to remove them. Clean the brickwork below the sill and dry it if necessary.

Cut a new sill to the correct length and, if necessary, cut slots in the ends to fit under the jambs. Prime the sill and the ends of the jambs and leave to dry. Put the new sill in position on a mortar bed, driving in timber wedges to force it up against the bottom of the jambs before inserting countersunk screws at an angle through the jambs and into the sill. Fill the screw holes before painting.

Glue in wooden blocks to fill any gaps between the jambs and sill, and add more mortar under the window sill if necessary.

1 Cut out the old window sill close to the jambs after removing the inner window board.

2 Put in a new window sill, trimming it to fit underneath the jambs.

3 Secure the new window sill with screws angled down through the jambs.

Repairing a concrete or stone sill

A simple crack or small hole in a concrete or stone sill can be repaired in much the same way that you deal with a crack or hole in a wall or ceiling, using an appropriate exterior filler or ready-mixed mortar.

Damage to the edge is more difficult to repair, as it involves building timber shuttering to hold the new concrete while it sets.

Chisel away all loose concrete before fitting the shuttering, using temporary timber supports. Then fill the damaged area with fresh concrete – use dry readymix – using a trowel. Once the concrete has completely set, you can remove the shuttering. A similar arrangement is used to replace a whole concrete or stone sill, but in this case, it must take the form of a box with a length of rope pinned along the bottom to provide a former for the window sill's drip groove.

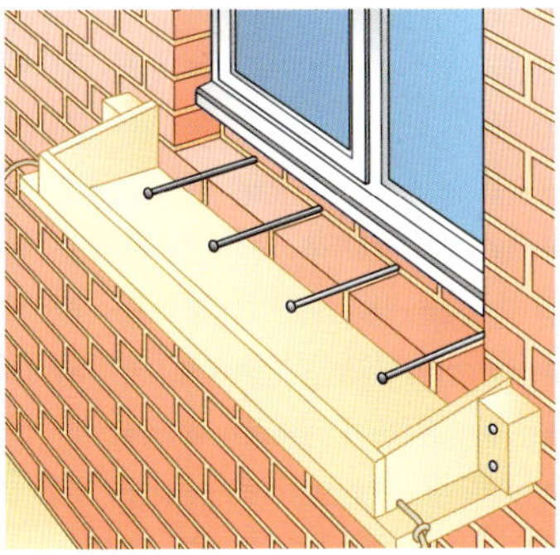

ABOVE Fit shuttering for a new concrete window sill with a drip groove rope.

ABOVE Fill the shuttering with concrete, making sure the surface is level.

Rehanging a Door

There may be occasions when the way in which a door opens is not the most convenient. Switching the hinges from one side to the other may provide a more attractive view of the room as the door is opened or allow better use of the wall space. Alternatively, making the door open outward may create more useful space. However, never have a door opening outwards on to a stairway.

Switching the hinged side

When switching the hinged edge of a door from one side to the other, you will need to cut a new mortise for the latch and drill new holes for the door handle spindles. The old latch mortise and spindle holes can be filled by gluing in small blocks of wood and lengths of dowel. Leave the blocks and dowels slightly proud of the surface, then plane and sand them flush when the glue has dried. If you reverse the door, you will be able to use the old latch and door handle spindle holes, but the latch itself will need to be turned around.

You will need to cut a new slot for the striker and striking plate (keeper) on the other side of the frame, and fill the old recess with a thin block of wood stuck in place. Again, make this oversize, planing and sanding it flush once the adhesive has dried.

You will also need to chisel out new recesses for the hinges in both the door and the frame; if the door is reversed, you may be able to use part of the old hinge recesses in the door and need only fill the unused portions. Fill the old hinge recesses with thin blocks of wood glued into place and sanded flush.

If the door has rising butts or other handed hinges, these will need to be replaced.

After re-hanging the door, the light switch may be in the wrong place if it is in the room the door opens into. There are two choices here: reposition it on the other side of the door (means running a new wire) or move it across the wall so that it is outside the room, but more or less in the same place (little or no new wire, but possible problems securing the switch mounting box).

Reversing doors

When re-hanging a door, it can reduce the amount of work required if you reverse the door – that is, turn it so that the side which faced inwards now faces outwards. This is very true when changing the hinges from left to right or the other way round. There are, however, two problems with doing this. The first is that the two sides of the door may be painted in different colours, which will mean a complete re-painting job.

The second is that the door may not fit properly the other way round. Doors and frames can both move slightly over time and while the door will operate perfectly well fitted one way it may bind or catch when fitted the other way.

Filling a recess

1 To fill an old hinge recess, cut a sliver of wood slightly over size.

2 Add adhesive and tap the wood sliver down into the recess.

3 When the adhesive has set, plane the surface flush and smooth.

In to out

When making a door open outward, you will be able to use the same latch and handle positions if the door is hung from the same side of the frame. You will have to reverse the latch, but will be able to make use of parts of the hinge recesses in the door. However, you will need to reposition the striking plate and make new hinge recesses in the frame, as described previously.

The one extra job will be to move the door stop, unless this is positioned centrally in the frame. Moving the door stop needs care to avoid splitting it – slide a chisel in behind the stop and lever it out. Remove the sides before the top, starting in the middle.

When repositioning the door stop, hang the door first, so that you can be sure that the stop fits snugly against the door all round. You can use the same nails to secure it, but reposition them and fill the old holes before repainting.

If you change the side of the frame from which the door is hung (as well as changing it from in to out), you can retain the existing door hinge, latch and door handle positions, although new recesses must still be cut in the frame for the hinges and striking plate, and the old ones filled.

Practical tip

- To prevent the paint from chipping when you remove a doorstop, run a trimming knife blade along the joint between doorstop and frame to cut through the paint.

Changing door handles

1 Remove the existing door handle and latch from the door, along with the door spindle.

2 Fill the latch recess (not shown) and plug the handle spindle hole with dowel. Fill holes.

3 On the other side of the door, cut a recess for the latch and drill a hole for the spindle.

4 Fit the latch and the door spindle. Now fit the new door handle (here with a keyhole).

Repositioning the door stop

1 Slide a chisel under the door stop in order to lever it out.

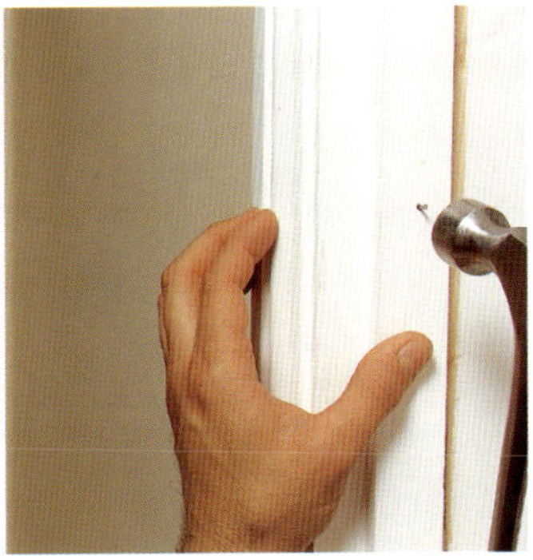

2 Nail it to the door frame in its new position and fill in any nail holes.

REPAIRING DOORS

Doors can develop all sorts of problems, from simple squeaks and rattles to suddenly refusing to open and shut properly. Fortunately, most of the problems are easy to solve, though for most door repairs you will need to remove the door from the frame. Some faults can be cured by fitting a draught excluder and others by fitting a weatherboard.

SQUEAKS

A door normally squeaks simply because the hinges need oiling. Often you can dribble sufficient oil on to the hinges with the door in place, but if they are caked in dirt and paint, it is best to remove the door and work the hinges back and forth with oil before replacing it.

A door may also squeak if the hinges are binding, usually because the recesses have been cut too deep into the door and/or frame. The solution is simple: unscrew each half of each hinge in turn, place a piece of cardboard behind the hinge and refit the screws. Experiment until the door hangs correctly – you may need more than one thickness of cardboard (or thin plywood).

A door can also bind because the screws are sticking out of the hinge. Normally these can simply be retightened; if they will not hold, fit longer ones of the same gauge, or a smaller size if the original screws had heads that were too large for the countersinks in the hinge.

RATTLES

The simplest way to stop any door rattling is to fit a draught excluder. With an internal door, you could also try moving the door stop; with all types of door, you could try moving the latch striking plate, although this is not easy – drilling out and filling the old screw holes with glued-in dowels helps.

BINDING

External doors often bind during cold, damp weather, becoming free again when the weather is dry and warm. This is a sign that the bottom of the door was not sealed when the door was painted, allowing moisture to get in and swell the door.

Binding doors can also be caused by a build-up of paint on the leading (non-hinge) edge. The cure is to remove the door and then to plane down the leading edge, repainting it once the door has been fitted. Add at least one coat of primer to the bottom of the door to prevent more moisture from getting in.

If a door binds at the bottom, it may be because the hinges have worked loose. Try tightening the screws, fitting larger or longer screws if necessary. If this does not work and the door joints have not worked loose, you will have to remove the door and plane down the part that is rubbing. Use a block plane, working toward the centre of the door. Then repaint the bottom of the door. With an internal door, you may be able to remove sufficient material by laying a sheet of sandpaper on the floor (abrasive side up) and working the door back and forth across it. A door can bind seriously when you have fitted a new carpet or other

PRACTICAL TIP

- Door hinge screws are often caked with paint and can be very difficult to turn. Clean the paint out with a sharp screwdriver, held at an angle to the slot and tapped gently with a hammer. To release a stiff screw, place the screwdriver blade in the slot and strike the end of the handle smartly with a hammer, trying, in effect, to push the screw further in. If this does not work, try tightening the screw before unscrewing it.

ADJUSTING HINGES

1 Pack a hinge with cardboard to prevent a door binding.

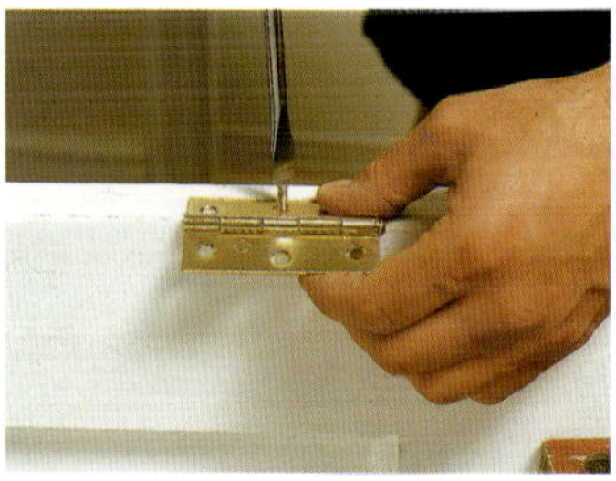

2 Fit longer screws to a hinge if the old ones have lost their grip.

ABOVE Take the door off its hinges and plane the leading edge of a door if it is sticking.

ABOVE Run the base of a door over sandpaper if it is binding.

ABOVE Use a door trimming saw to adjust the height after fitting a new carpet.

floorcovering. In this case, remove the door and cut a strip off the bottom with a circular saw fitted with a rip guide. If there are several doors to shorten, consider hiring a door trimming saw, which can be used with the doors in place.

LOOSE JOINTS

Most doors will have a mortise-and-tenon joint at each corner where the side members, or stiles, meet the top and bottom rails. These can work loose with age.

You do not need to take the door apart: simply remove it, prise out any wedges, cut new wedges and glue them in place. For added security or if there are no wedges, drill 10mm (⅜in) holes through each stile and the tenon, and glue in 10mm (⅜in) dowels, planing them flush once the adhesive has dried. When repairing a door in this way, use sash clamps first to square it up and then to hold it square while the glue dries.

WARPED DOOR

If a door has become warped, you can straighten it with pairs of clamps, stout lengths of wood and packing blocks. Mount the door between the timbers, say lengths of 50 x 100mm (2 x 4in), and position the packing blocks to force the door in the opposite direction to the warp. Force it beyond straight by tightening up the clamps and leave for as long as you can. When the clamps are removed, the door should be straight.

ABOVE Reinforce mortise-and-tenon joints with new tapering wedges.

ABOVE Straighten a warped door with timbers, clamps and packing blocks.

FITTING A WEATHERBOARD

A weatherboard is a shaped piece of wood screwed to the bottom of a door to throw rainwater clear. For the best result, drill clearance holes for the screws, then counterbore them with a drill of the same size as the screw heads. That way, the screw heads will be below the surface and can be concealed by gluing in timber plugs.

ABOVE Fit a weatherboard with screws tightened into pre-drilled holes.

Fitting Doors

There is quite a lot to do when fitting a new or replacement door – even if it is the right size. You will need to fit the hinges to the door, together with some form of latch and may need to cut new recesses in the frame for the hinges and striking plate. If the door latch has a lock, you will need to drill and chisel out keyholes.

Size

Doors come in standard sizes, but you may need to trim the sides of a door with a plane or the ends with a saw before fitting it. There needs to be around 3mm (⅛in) clearance at the sides and top, and 5mm (³⁄₁₆in) at the bottom. Always take equal amounts off each side or end, and if planing the top and bottom, work from the edges toward the centre to prevent the wood splitting.

Hinges

A solid hardwood external door will need three substantial hinges: typically 100mm (4in), but most internal doors can be hung on two 75mm (3in) hinges. If you are using brass hinges, always use brass screws.

Choose the hinge positions, using an existing door as a guide – some hollow flush doors incorporate hinge blocks of solid wood – and mark lines across the edge of the door with the aid of a try square. Then use either a hinge or a marking gauge set to the width of the hinge to mark out the recesses – each hinge should end up so that only the knuckle protrudes from the edge of the door. Also mark the thickness on the face of the door.

Cut out the recesses with a mallet and chisel, first cutting down along the lines with the chisel held vertically, then removing the wood with the chisel held at an angle, bevel down to prevent digging in. Take great care not to go beyond the marked recesses. When the hinges fit snugly, make pilot holes for the screws with a small drill or bradawl and screw the hinges in place.

Offer the door up to the frame, propping it on 5mm (³⁄₁₆in) blocks, and transfer the positions of the hinges on to the frame. Cut the recesses in the same way, check the fit, make pilot holes and, with the door propped on the blocks again, secure the hinges to the frame. Check that the door swings freely and closes properly without catching the frame. If necessary, remove the door and deepen the hinge recesses, or pack them out with cardboard.

Fitting hinges

1 Mark out the hinge using the hinge itself as a guide.

2 Cut a recess for the hinge with a chisel and wooden mallet.

3 Clean up the hinge recess, working from the side. Secure the hinge.

4 The hinge should sit snugly in its recess with the knuckle protruding.

Practical tip

- As a guide for drilling holes to a specific depth, wrap insulating or masking tape around the drill shank at the depth required.

Fitting a mortise lock

1 Mark out the mortise lock using a mortise gauge.

2 After drilling out the main recess, remove the rest of the wood with a chisel.

3 Cut out a keyhole and spindle hole. Fit the lock and spindle and then the handle.

Latches and locks

Most doors are fitted with a mortise latch, ranging from a simple spring-operated affair to a sturdy high-security lock. The method of fitting is the same, except that with a lock you will need to make keyholes.

Check the instructions and mark out the position of the latch or lock and the handle spindle holes on the door – some hollow flush doors will have a solid block to take the latch/lock. To make the mortise, first drill as many large holes as you can within the outline, then use a chisel to remove the remaining wood. Put the latch/lock in place and mark around the foreplate so that you can chisel out a housing for this – you may also need to deepen the main hole. Drill the handle spindle holes, checking the fit of the latch/lock and the positions of the handles.

Fit the latch/lock to the door and use it to transfer the position of the bolt to the door frame. Draw the outline of the striking plate, double checking its position in relation to the door stop – too close and the latch will not work, too far away and the door will rattle. Drill and chisel out recesses for the plate and screw it in place. Check the latch/lock operation; if necessary, reposition it.

Letter plate

This needs only a large rectangular hole and two smaller holes to fit it. Mark out the position of these on the door – in a solid central rail or bottom rail or, possibly, vertically on the closing stile. Drill the two small holes (for the letter plate securing bolts) and drill largish holes at each corner of the main outline to start the jigsaw (saber saw). Cut along the marked lines, working from the outside of the door, so that any splintering is covered by the letter plate. Do not force the saw or its blade will bend. Clean up the hole with a file and fit the letter plate.

Fitting a letter plate

1 Work from the outside of the door. Mark out the letter plate and drill holes for the bolts.

2 Drill holes at the corners of the marked out letter plate and finish cutting with a jigsaw.

3 Fit the letter plate from the outside, securing the nuts inside.

Repairing Stairs

The most common problem with stairs is that they creak. However, they may also suffer from physical damage and from missing parts, especially beneath the treads. The ease with which stairs may be repaired will depend partly on whether you have access to the underside. In some cases, plaster or boards may conceal it, which means working only from above.

How stairs are built

The flat parts of stairs that you walk on are called treads; the vertical sections connecting them are called risers. Treads and risers are joined to one another by various means: butt joints, housing joints or tongued-and-grooved joints. Both treads and risers are joined to the side timbers (strings) by butt joints if the strings are "open", that is shaped to follow the line of the treads and risers, or by housing joints if the strings are "closed", that is having parallel sides. The housing joints in closed strings are reinforced by long, thin glued-in wedges, while in both cases the joint between the front of each tread and the riser below is usually reinforced by small glued-in triangular blocks.

Blocks

Reinforcing blocks can work loose, and some may be missing altogether. If blocks are missing, you can make new ones by cutting diagonally down through a piece of 50mm (2in) square timber. When fitting new blocks, or refitting old ones, screw them to both tread and riser as well as applying wood adhesive. With an existing loose block, it may be possible to prise open the joint to squeeze in some adhesive.

Wedges

Tapered wedges are used to hold the risers and treads firmly in closed strings, but with age, the wedges may become loose. It is best to remove all loose wedges so that you can clean them and the grooves they fit in of all traces of old glue. If any wedges are missing, make replacements by cutting tapered strips from a piece of timber cut to length, using an old wedge as a guide.

Apply glue to the wedge and its groove, then hammer the vertical wedges home first, followed by the horizontal ones, which should make contact with the vertical wedges at the bottom.

Replacing blocks

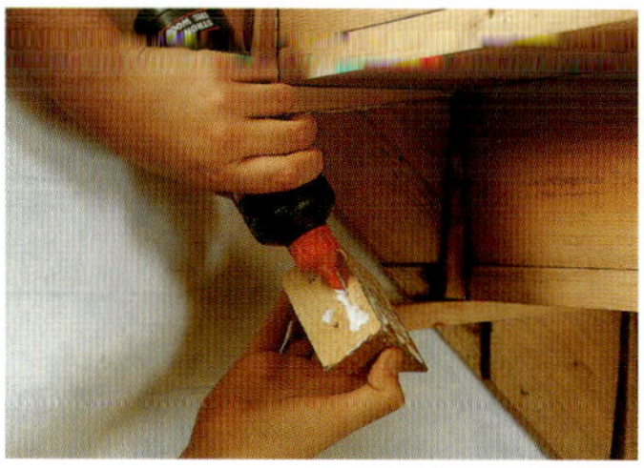

1 Clean the old adhesive off loose reinforcing blocks and add fresh adhesive on the two meeting sides.

2 When putting the blocks back into place, screw them to both the tread and the riser to hold them securely.

Replacing wedges

1 If any of the tapered wedges are missing, cut fresh ones from a block of wood.

2 Before applying each wedge, coat each side with adhesive. Remove excess afterwards.

3 Hammer the wedges into place; the horizontal ones under the vertical ones.

Securing treads

1 If you have access from underneath, drive screws up through the backs of treads into the bottom of the risers.

2 If access is denied, cut recesses towards the back of the tread and front of the riser and fit L-shaped brackets to secure the joint.

3 To secure the front of a loose tread, drill holes down exactly into the centre of the riser below and fit screws.

Securing treads

If the joint between the back of a tread and the riser above is loose, you can insert reinforcing screws from below, through the back of the tread into the bottom of the riser. Where access to the underside is impossible, reinforce this joint from above with a couple of L-shaped brackets recessed into the back of the tread and the front of the riser. Make the recesses slightly deeper than the thickness of the brackets and screw them in place.

If the joint between the front of a tread and the riser below is loose, and you cannot get below to reglue the blocks and/or wedges, you can reinforce the joint with screws. Drill pilot holes down through the tread into the riser, making sure they are centred in the riser, and enlarge the holes in the tread to clearance size before driving countersunk screws through the tread into the riser.

If possible, prise the joint apart with a bolster (stonecutter's) chisel, brush out any dirt and squeeze in some glue before screwing the joint together.

Repairing a damaged tread

It is very unlikely that an entire stair tread will need to be replaced. The more common fault is that part of the nosing, the front curved section, will have sustained damage. Fortunately, this can be replaced relatively easily.

Mark out as much of the nosing as you need to remove, drill holes and cut it out using a circular saw, cleaning up the cut with a chisel. Saw the ends to an angle of 45 degrees. Shape a new piece of timber to fit exactly into the space, drilling pilot holes through it and into the existing tread for the securing screws.

Enlarge the holes in the new section and countersink them before gluing and screwing it in place. Drive the screw heads below the surface and screw on a supporting batten (furring strip) while the adhesive dries. Fill the screw holes.

Practical tip

- When replacing stair treads in an older house, you may well find that the replacement timber you buy will be too small because the original tread was an imperial size (in) and the replacement is metric (mm). If this is the case, buy a larger size and plane it down.

Repairing a damaged tread

1 Use a circular saw or jigsaw to cut out the damaged section, finishing off the ends of the cut with a sharp chisel.

2 Cut and plane the replacement wood to size and shape before screwing or gluing it in place with a supporting batten.

Repairing Stair Balustrades

"Balustrade" is the name given to the combination of balusters (banisters), posts and handrails that run up the side of a staircase. Over time, these components may become loose or damaged, but repairs are quite straightforward and may range from simply regluing a cracked baluster or repairing a short length of handrail, to replacing the entire assembly.

Baluster repairs

The most likely problem with a balustrade is a cracked or broken baluster. Often, it will be possible to prise a split apart with a wood chisel, squeeze in some adhesive and tape up the split, or clamp it with a small G-clamp, while the adhesive dries. Sometimes, a short dowel glued into a hole drilled across the split will help.

If the baluster is broken, it will be necessary to remove it and either fit a new one or glue together the original piece, which may be your only option if you cannot find a replacement of the same style. You will need to work out how to remove the old baluster. Sometimes, this simply involves pulling out a couple of nails top and bottom. On other occasions, you may need to remove the nosing on the end of a tread, or prise out spacers fitted between the balusters under the handrail and in the base rail, or even cut through the baluster.

You can fashion replacement square balusters yourself and build up broken moulding on a damaged turned baluster with wood filler. If you need to replace a complete turned baluster, you may be able to buy a new one of the same style, if the staircase is not too old, or a second-hand one from an architectural salvage yard, if it is. Failing that, you could approach a local woodturner to make a new one. Otherwise, the broken piece will have to be repaired.

Repairing a handrail

You can buy handrail moulding to repair a broken section, but you need a special type of bolt to hold the sections together. This passes through holes drilled into the ends

Replacing a balustrade

1 If you have an old-fashioned balustrade like this, you may want to replace it completely.

2 Remove the old handrail and the wrought iron sections and prise up the base rail.

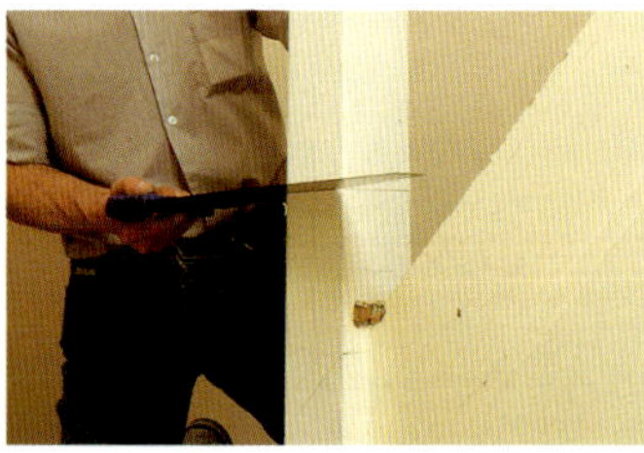

3 Cut through all newel posts with a panel saw, keeping the cut square to the post.

7 Hammer the newel post into place, using a piece of scrap wood to protect the top.

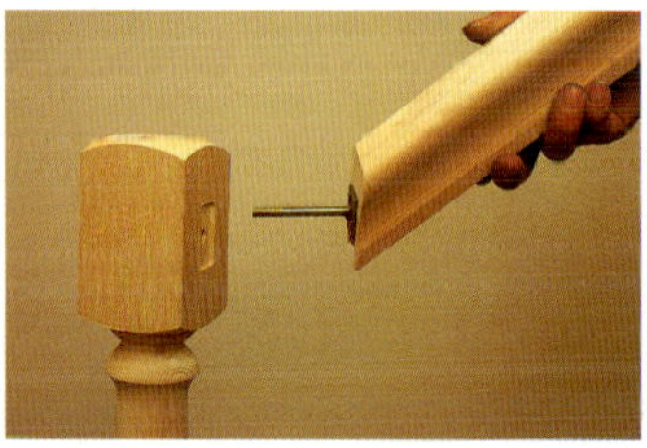

8 Cut the handrail to the correct length and angle before joining it to the newel post.

9 Fit a nut to the bracket bolt and tighten it with a socket spanner. Fit the cover plug.

of the new and old handrails, both cut square, and requires "pockets" to be cut out to accommodate the nuts of the bolt. Two additional holes need to be drilled for dowels that prevent the handrail from turning around the bolt. To position these correctly, drill the holes in one part, using a dowelling bit, and fit centre-points into the holes so that their positions can be transferred to the other part.

REPLACING A BALUSTRADE

You can buy kits for replacing a complete balustrade, using the bottom portions of the existing newel posts. The first step is to remove the existing balustrade – handrail, balusters and the bottom rail. Cut through the old newel posts with a panel saw close to the base, making sure the cuts are square. Then drill a large hole in each stump of newel post to take the end of the new newel post and shape the stump to a gentle curve. The new newel post is glued into place with a dowel to tighten it. The new handrail must be cut to length with the correct angle at each end and secured with the brackets supplied.

The base rail must also be cut to the correct length and angles. Then each baluster can be cut to length, again with the ends at the correct angle, and slotted into the base rail and the underside of the handrail. The balusters are held in place with wooden spacers nailed to the base rail and the underside of the handrail. Special accessories are available to accommodate staircases that have 90-degree turns or half-landings.

PRACTICAL TIPS

- To reinforce a straight break in a baluster, first drill a 10mm (3/8in) hole in the centre of one of the sound sections. Then make a right-angled cut through the baluster, using the thinnest saw blade you can find, such as a junior hacksaw, to remove a portion of the drilled baluster. Glue this to the other broken piece and leave for the adhesive to set. Continue the hole through the glued joint into sound timber. Finally, glue the whole baluster together with a 10mm (3/8in) dowel bridging the original break and the new saw cut.

- When buying a handrail, look for the type that has a grooved underside to hold the balusters firmly and in a straight line.

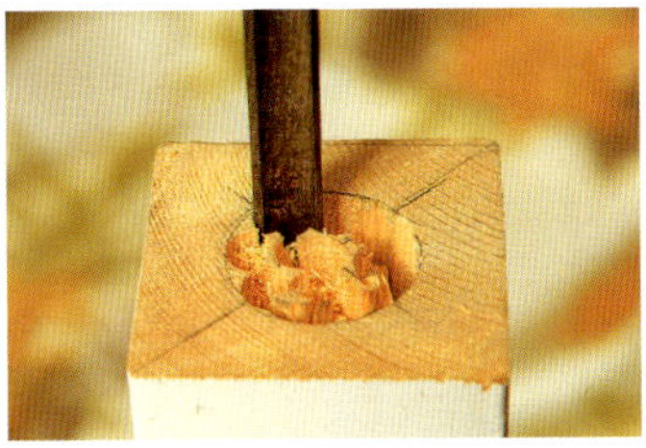

4 Mark out the hole for the new newel post, drill several holes and lever out the waste.

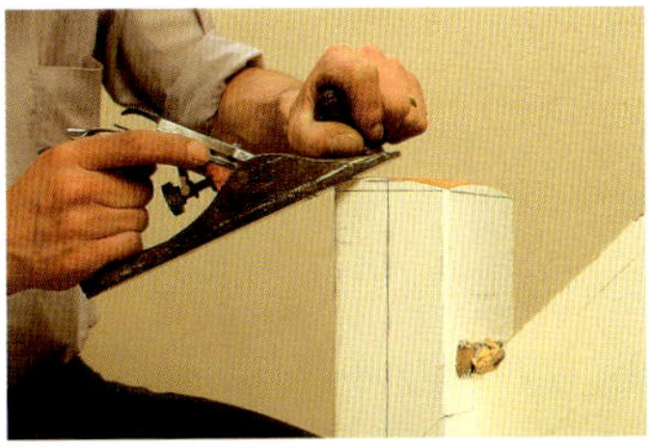

5 Use a plane (or a planer-file) to give the stump of the newel post a rounded top.

6 Using the dowel supplied, apply adhesive to the newel post and insert it into the hole.

10 Each baluster will have to be cut to the correct angle. Use a sliding bevel to mark it.

11 Spacers fitted to the handrail and to the bottom rail correctly space the balusters.

12 Enhance the final result by sanding and applying a stained varnish to the staircase.

Clearing Sinks and Drains

The waste pipes leading from sinks, basins, baths and showers can become blocked with all sorts of things – hair, food scraps, grease and so on – so that water will no longer drain freely. There are many tools with which to clean them. Larger soil pipes, to which waste pipes may be connected, and the soil pipes leading from toilets can also become blocked and need bigger versions of the same tools.

Plunging

A rubber basin plunger, a rubber cup on the end of a long handle, is used to clear blocked waste pipes by using water pressure.

With the basin, sink, or similar, full and the overflow blocked with a damp cloth, hold the plunger over the waste outlet and pump it up and down. This will force water down the waste pipe and should clear the blockage. A force pump and an aerosol clearer work on the same principle, but create more pressure and can be used with the sink empty.

ABOVE Blocked waste outlets can be cleared with a sink plunger or a force pump (as here).

ABOVE Use a sink auger, pushed down until it meets the blockage.

Sink Auger

A sink auger, or plumber's snake, is a flexible steel cable with a specially shaped head at one end and sometimes a turning handle at the other. It is passed down through the waste outlet and along the waste pipe until it reaches the blockage, where the head is turned to dislodge the blockage and allow water to flow freely. It cannot be used with a bottle-type trap.

Removing the Trap

If plunging or using a sink auger does not work, or if the trap is of the bottle type, you will have to remove the trap itself. Place a bucket beneath it and simply unscrew the connections by hand.

If the blockage is in the trap, you should be able to clear it out, dismantling the trap if necessary. If it is farther down the waste pipe, removing the trap will give you a clearer run with a sink auger. Refit the trap, making sure that it is tight.

Blocked Toilets

You can obtain larger versions of sink plungers and force pumps to use in toilets, and also a larger auger. The business end of the auger should be passed round the U-bend until you reach the blockage, when rotating the auger should clear it.

Practical Tip

- You can help to keep waste pipes, particularly sink wastes, clear by occasionally pouring some washing soda down the waste outlet. This will help to prevent grease from building up.

Chemical clearers can be used in the same way, but are not ideal for total blockages.

ABOVE Unscrew a bottle-type waste trap from a basin to check for blockages.

ABOVE Use rubber gloves and a large plunger to clear a blocked toilet.

ABOVE Use drain rods in an inspection chamber to remove a blockage.

ABOVE Use an auger in a waste gully to clear a blocked drain.

Blocked drains and soil pipes

A large auger can also be used to clear blocked underground drains. It should be passed down through an open gully and along the drain until you reach the blockage.

The main soil pipe will run vertically either inside or outside the house. If it is blocked, your best chance of clearing it will be to unscrew an inspection hatch and then either to use an auger or drain rods to dislodge the blockage.

Using drain rods

These are used for clearing drains when there is a blockage between one (full) inspection chamber and the next (empty) one. When you discover the empty chamber, go back to the last full one and rod from there. Drain rod sets come with a choice of heads – plungers to push the blockage along the pipe, scrapers to pull it back and wormscrews or cleaning wheels to dislodge it.

Start with a wormscrew connected to two rods, lowering it to the bottom of the chamber. Feel for the half-round channel at the bottom of the chamber and push the wormscrew along this until it enters the drain at the end. Push it along the drain, add more rods to the free end and only turn the rods clockwise, otherwise they may become unscrewed. Keep working at the obstruction until water flows into the empty chamber, then use the scraper and plunger to clear the underground drain section.

Inspecting a soil pipe

1 To clear a blocked soil pipe, start by unscrewing an inspection hatch.

2 Then remove the inner cover – make sure you are standing well out of the way!

3 Use an auger or drain rod to clear the soil pipe before replacing the cover.

Clearing and Repairing Gutters

The gutters and downpipes of your home are essential to remove rainwater. Nevertheless, they are exposed to the elements and are likely to become blocked, so regular maintenance is necessary to keep them clear and also to keep them in good condition. If you are replacing sections of plastic guttering, make sure you always use the same brand.

Clearing gutters and downpipes

Autumn is the ideal time to clear out gutters, removing leaves, birds' nests and general dirt and debris so that the winter rains can drain away freely. Use a garden trowel or gutter clearing tool to scoop out blockages from the gutters into a bucket, which should be secured to your ladder.

If there is a blockage near to the top of a downpipe, use something like a bent metal coat hanger to pull it out. Blockages farther down can be removed by using drain rods fitted with a wormscrew head.

Maintenance for cast-iron gutters and downpipes

Traditional cast-iron gutters may look very nice, but they can give no end of trouble.

To start with, they rust, so need regular painting to keep them looking good. A more serious problem, however, is that the putty used to seal the joints can dry out, causing leaks.

You may be able to overcome minor joint leaks by cleaning the gutter out and brushing the inside with bituminous paint, but a proper repair will mean unscrewing the joint and replacing the old putty with non-setting mastic (caulking).

Use a hacksaw to cut through the securing bolt if it has rusted in place. Then remove the screws holding the gutter to the fascia board and lift it clear. It will be very heavy – do not drop it, as it will shatter as well as possibly causing damage. Clean the joint faces, apply the mastic and replace the gutter, using a new nut and bolt to connect the sections.

Cleaning out gutters

ABOVE You can use a household garden trowel to clean out gutters.

ABOVE Alternatively, use gutter clearing tools specially designed for the job.

Repairing cast-iron gutters

ABOVE Prior to painting a cast-iron gutter, clear it out using a wire brush.

ABOVE Treat cast-iron guttering with black bituminous paint to seal leaks.

ABOVE Remove a cast-iron gutter bolt with a hacksaw if it is rusted in place.

Downpipes

A wire balloon fitted into the top of a downpipe will prevent birds from nesting and keep leaves and other debris out. If your downpipe does get blocked, clear with drain rods fitted with a wormscrew.

A crack or hole in a cast-iron gutter can be repaired with a glass fibre repair kit sold for use on car bodywork. Apply the glass fibre sheets over the damage and fill to the level of the surrounding metal with the resin filler provided with the kit. Glass fibre bandage can also be used in the same way for repairing cast-iron downpipes.

Maintenance for plastic gutters and downpipes

Plastic guttering has largely replaced cast iron and is easier to repair. It is also much easier to replace.

Leaks at the joints between lengths of plastic gutter are prevented by rubber seals, and if these fail it is usually quite easy to replace them. Take the old seal to the shop as a guide when buying a replacement. Otherwise, try cleaning them with some liquid soap to make them more efficient. If an end stop is leaking, replace the rubber seal in this in the same way.

The alternative is to use a gutter repair sealant, available in a cartridge for use with a caulking gun, forcing this into the joint to make a seal. Self-adhesive gutter repair tape is also available for sealing splits in plastic gutters and covering small holes in gutters and downpipes.

When separating and reconnecting lengths of plastic guttering, note that some types simply snap into their securing brackets, while others have notches cut near the gutter ends to take the clips.

Repairing gutter brackets

If a gutter is sagging, the most likely cause is failure of the screws that hold a bracket in place. First, remove the section of gutter above the offending bracket.

If the screws have worked loose, it may be possible to retighten them, perhaps replacing them with longer or larger screws; if the holes have become too large, move the bracket slightly to one side, making new holes in the fascia board for the bracket screws. A rise-and-fall bracket is adjustable in height and so allows correction of sagging gutters without the need to remove them.

ABOVE Wearing gloves, use glass fibre to repair a crack in a cast-iron gutter. Remove the gutter from the brackets to make it easier.

Repairing plastic gutters

ABOVE Rubber seals in the end stop of plastic guttering can be replaced if they fail.

ABOVE Gutter repair sealant can be used to fix a leaking joint between gutters.

ABOVE Repair a crack in a gutter with gutter repair tape applied to the inside.

Repairing Pitched Roofs

A pitched house roof may be covered with traditional slates, clay tiles or interlocking concrete tiles. All can fail and work loose; you can repair small areas of damage yourself, but large-scale repairs may mean wholesale replacement of the roof covering, which should be entrusted to a professional roof contractor. Never walk directly on a roof covering; use a proper ladder.

Slates

The most common cause of roof slates slipping is "nail sickness", that is one or both of the nails holding a slate rusting through. The slate itself may be undamaged and still be on the roof somewhere.

If only one nail has failed, use a slate ripper to cut through the other one. This tool is slid under the slate, hooked around the nail and given a sharp tug to break the nail.

With the slate removed, you will be able to see, between the two exposed slates, one of the timber battens (furring strips) to which the slates are attached. Cut a strip of zinc or lead, about 150 x 25mm (6 x 1in), and nail one end to the exposed batten so that the strip runs down the roof.

Slide the slate back into its original position and secure it by bending the end of the zinc or lead strip over the bottom edge. Note that slates at the edges of the roof have mortar fillets beneath them to prevent the wind from blowing debris into the roof space.

Slate ripper

Slater's axe (for cutting slates)

Replacing slates

1 Use a slate ripper to cut through a slate nail that is still holding the slate.

2 Slide out the damaged slate, taking care not to let it fall to the ground.

3 Fit a lead or zinc strip by nailing it to the batten (furring strip) under the slate.

4 Slide the old (or replacement) slate into place over the lead or zinc strip.

5 Bend the end of the lead strip over the bottom edge of the slate.

Replacing a dislodged tile

Most concrete and many clay tiles are held in place by hooks, or nibs, on the top edge, which fit over the roof battens. If these are still intact, a dislodged tile can simply be replaced by gently lifting the surrounding tiles, supporting them on wooden wedges and slipping the tile back into position. If the nibs have broken off, the tile can be replaced in the same way as a slate. Edge tiles also have a fillet of mortar beneath them.

Replacing ridge tiles

1 Remove loose ridge tiles, clean away debris and apply a fresh bed of mortar.

2 Put the old (or replacement) ridge tile in position, pushing it down into the mortar.

3 With the ridge tile firmly in place, smooth all joints and remove excess mortar.

Ridge tiles

The curved tiles that run along the top of a tile or slate roof are mortared into place. With age and weathering, one or two may have become loose.

To replace ridge tiles, you need a roof ladder with hooks that fit over the ridge and wheels that allow you to run it up the roof from the top of a conventional ladder. This will provide a safe means of access.

Once you have reached the ridge, remove the loose tiles, then use a small trowel to scrape away crumbling mortar until you reach sound mortar. Dampen the tiles and trowel on a bed of fresh mortar. Place each ridge tile gently into position, tapping it down with the handle of the trowel. Add mortar to the ends of each ridge tile to fill the joints with its neighbours and scrape off all excess mortar.

Valleys

If you have a dual-pitch roof – different parts of the roof pointing in different directions – there will be a lead-lined valley between them to allow rainwater to escape and provide a junction between the tiles. Cracks can occur in the lead, allowing water to leak through.

A severely damaged roof valley will need to be replaced completely – a job for professionals. But simple cracks can be repaired with self-adhesive flashing tape. Once the area around the crack has been cleaned, the tape is applied – sometimes, a primer is needed first – and rolled out flat using something like a wallpaper seam roller.

Practical tip

- **For securing loose ridge tiles and packing under edge tiles and slates, use a weak mortar mix – no more than three parts sand plus plasticizer to allow some movement and prevent cracking.**

Repairing valleys

1 Clear out any leaves and debris from a leaking roof valley using a stiff brush.

2 Roll out self-adhesive flashing tape to repair the roof valley.

ABOVE Lead flashing is used to seal between a pitched roof and a parapet wall.

Repairing Flat Roofs

Unless expensive materials have been used, the average life of a felted flat roof is about ten to 15 years. If a felted flat roof fails, it is not worth trying to repair it and you should re-cover it. However, there are things you can do to repair minor faults and to extend its life before it needs to be replaced. Failure to act can result in water leaking through to the timbers below and causing rot.

Repairing cracks and blisters

You will need bituminous mastic (caulking) to repair a crack or blister in a felted flat roof. Although quite messy, the job is straightforward.

First remove any loose chippings from around the damaged area with a brush. Using a hot-air gun, soften the felt first if necessary, and brush or scrape away dirt, moss and any other debris. With a crack or split in the roofing felt, pull back the edges; with a blister, make a cross-shaped pattern of cuts in the centre of the blister and peel back the four sections. If any seams are lifting, clean the area below them.

When the underlying surface has dried out – use a hot-air gun to speed this up if necessary – apply mastic to the exposed area and press down the edges of the crack, blister or lifted seam, using something like a wallpaper seam roller. If a crack cannot be closed up, use polyester reinforcing tape or flashing tape to strengthen the repair.

Some emergency roof repair compounds can be used to seal a leaking roof even if it is wet or under water. Instant repair aerosols can be used on damp roofs (and also on leaking flashing or guttering); check the manufacturer's instructions.

If a felted flat roof has several cracks and blisters, or is generally in bad condition, it is possible to waterproof it with either a bituminous emulsion or a longer-lasting elastomeric liquid rubber.

ABOVE A solar-reflective roof seal absorbs less heat, so stays more flexible and will not blister.

Patching a blister

1 Brush all solar-reflective chippings and dirt and debris away from the area to be repaired.

2 If necessary, use a hot air gun to soften the damaged roofing felt before scraping it away.

3 If the roofing felt has blistered, use a trimming knife to cut a cross shape.

4 Apply the repair mastic and work it into the cross and under the felt.

5 Flashing tape can be rolled out to cover up a crack that will not close up.

Re-covering a felted roof

1 Sweep the whole roof clear and treat the surface with fungicide.

2 Apply liquid rubber compound over the entire roof surface.

3 Clean up splashes and recover the roof with loose stone chippings.

The whole roof should be swept clean before treating the surface with fungicide to kill any mould. Carry out any local repairs, then cover the surface with the emulsion or liquid rubber, tipping it out from the container and spreading it with a soft brush or broom. Sponge away any splashes with solvent.

Some bituminous emulsions need a priming coat before the main coat; all liquid rubber compounds are one-coat treatments and they last longer because they remain flexible.

When the emulsion or liquid rubber coating has dried, reapply stone chippings. Use new chippings if the old ones are dirty or have lost their shine – the purpose of stone chippings on flat roofs is to keep them cool by reflecting sunlight.

Roof junctions

The junction between a flat roof and the house wall is particularly prone to damage, allowing water to seep through. The correct way to seal this joint is with lead flashing, inserted into one of the mortar courses of the wall.

If a mortar fillet has been used to seal the junction, or if lead flashing has split, the simplest way to effect a repair is by using a self-adhesive bituminous flashing tape. Choose the appropriate type of tape to the task in hand.

Clean the surfaces that are to be covered and apply any necessary primer before removing the backing paper and pressing down the flashing tape, first with your fingers, then a seam roller. Wear heavy gloves when doing this as it can be messy. The tape can be cut with scissors if required. Make good the mortar joints where any lead flashing meets the house wall, using fresh mortar.

Repairing junctions

1 Use flashing tape to seal porous felt or metal flashings. Brush on a coat of primer.

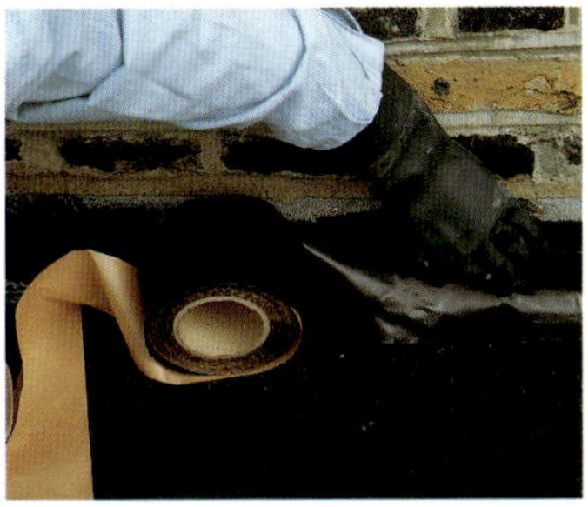

2 Unroll the flashing tape, peel off the release paper and press the strip into position.

3 Run a seam roller firmly along both edges of the strip to ensure the tape bonds well.

Refelting Flat and Pitched Roofs

If the damage to a felted roof is too serious to repair, refelting is the solution, provided the underlying structure is in good condition. Simple pitched roofs, such as those found on garden sheds, are the simplest; replacing a high-performance flat roof on a house extension or lean-to garage is likely to be much more difficult, though not impossible.

Pitched roofs

In general, a shed roof has only a single layer of felt, but with a fairly generous overlap between sheets to keep rain out. The first step is to rip off all the old felt and remove all the nails. Replace or repair the timber roof decking if necessary and check that the edging timbers are sound. Treat all timber with preservative.

New pieces of felt should be cut, making them 150–200mm (6–8in) longer than the shed roof. Lay the first strip along the bottom of one side of the roof, smoothing any creases with a length of wood. Make sure the ends overlap the ends of the roof evenly and that the bottom edge overlaps the edge of the roof sufficiently to be turned down and project just beyond the eaves. This allows rainwater to drip clear.

Using 13mm (½in) roofing nails, secure the top of the felt strip to the roof, the bottom to the eaves board and the ends to the fascias, folding the corners neatly, and repeat for the other side of the shed. Trim excess felt from the ends of the roof. If the shed is large, lay a second strip on each side nailed at the top but with the bottom overlapping the first sheet by at least 75mm (3in) and secured by felt adhesive. Fix it at the ends with nails. The final strip is laid over the ridge; cut it to width as well as length so that it overlaps the sheets on the sides of the roof by no more than 75mm (3in). Secure this with adhesive, but nail the ends.

Fit the fascia boards to cover the nailed edges at the ends of the roof.

Refelting a shed roof

1 Cut the felt longer than the roof and unroll the first strip along the bottom of one side.

2 Making sure it overlaps at each end and at the bottom, hammer nails along the top edge.

3 Apply a generous layer of felt adhesive along the top edge of the first strip of felt.

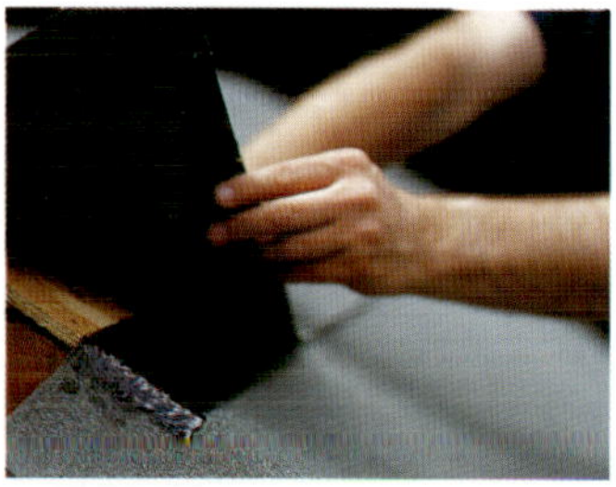

4 Apply the second strip of felt overlapping the first so that the nail heads are covered.

5 Make neat folds at the ends of the roof and nail the felt to the roof boards to secure it.

6 Make the corners waterproof with more felt adhesive. Nail the fascia boards at either end.

Re-covering a felted flat roof

Most flat roofs have two or three layers of felt, which will be a more durable type than that used on shed roofs. The top sheet will be capping felt, held down with adhesive.

The first step is to strip off all the existing felt down to bare timber and remove any guttering and flashing. When removing the old felt, notice how it is folded and cut at all corners and edges – make sketches that you can follow later. Check the condition of the roof timber, repairing or replacing it as necessary. Remove all nails and sweep the roof clean.

Most flat roofs have a raised angled lip along two sides to direct rainwater to the third open side, where it flows into a gutter. The fourth side meets the house wall.

Strips for the first layer of felt should be cut to slightly longer than the roof and nailed into place, working toward the gutter, using 18mm (¾in) clout nails. Allow an overlap of at least 50mm (2in) between strips. Make cuts so you can take the felt up and over the angled lips at the edges and up the angled fillet at the house wall, following the sketches you made earlier. Trim the felt flush at the eaves.

Cut a flashing strip about 150mm (6in) wide from the capping felt and lay this along the house wall so that it laps on to the roof. Tuck it into the lowest available mortar joint, having cut out some of the mortar first. If you are adding a second layer, stick it down to the first, using a continuous coat of felt adhesive. Cut the first strip to a different width so that the joints do not coincide with those of the first layer. Lay the first strip on the roof, roll it back halfway to apply adhesive underneath, then repeat the process for the other end. Carry on in this manner for the remaining strips, overlapping them by at least 50mm (2in) and applying felt adhesive along the overlap. Do not take the second layer over the the raised lips. The top layer should be stuck down in the same way as the second, but the detailing at the corners and edges will be different.

Finish off by laying a second flashing strip along the house wall, fixing it into a higher wall mortar joint with fresh mortar, and a folded "apron" along each lipped edge.

BELOW A cross section of a flat roof, showing how it is constructed.

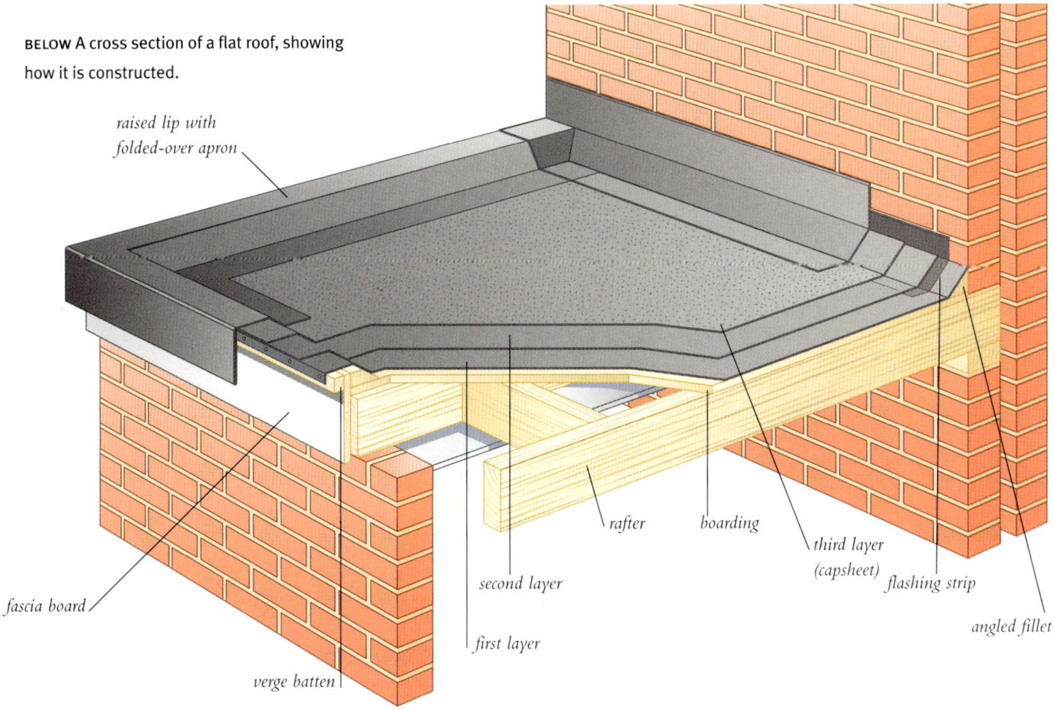

Repairing Fence Posts and Gates

Fences around your home serve the useful purpose of keeping children and pets in and intruders out, as well as providing privacy. However, since most fences are made of wood, they are likely to decay and need attention. There are many ways of overcoming rotting fences. Gates also suffer and must be maintained in good condition, otherwise the security your fence provides will be compromised.

Repairing fence posts

A fence relies on its posts to provide much of its strength and to keep it upright – but because the posts are set in the ground and can get wet, they are prone to rotting, leading to fence collapse.

The most vulnerable part of a fence post is the portion underground. Either this will be completely rotten, making the post unstable, or the post will have snapped off at ground level. In both cases, there are ways to effect a repair using the remaining sound piece of post.

If the fence post is still standing or is attached to a closeboard fence – overlapping vertical boards nailed to triangular-section horizontal (arris) rails – the best way to repair it is with a fence-post spur. This is a short concrete post that you set into the ground next to the broken post. Then you bolt the two together. Start by digging a hole roughly 30cm (1ft) square and 50cm (20in) deep in front of the broken post, that is on your side of the fence; you may need a long cold chisel and a club (spalling) hammer if you encounter concrete.

Place the spur in the hole so that it lines up with the post, then insert coach bolts in the holes in the spur, giving them a tap with a hammer to transfer their positions to the post. Drill holes in the post to take the bolts. Secure the spur to the fence post with the coach bolts and fill the hole around it, first with a layer of hardcore (rubble), then with concrete. If necessary, prop the main post upright while the concrete sets.

With a panel fence, release the adjacent panels from the post and saw through it at ground level. Then hammer a repair spike – a shorter version of the normal fence-post spike – over the rotten wood in the ground. Fit the sound portion of the post into the socket of the spike and replace the fence panels.

Fitting a fence spur

1 With the fence still standing, dig a large hole – around 30cm (1ft) square – next to the damaged post.

2 Place the fence-post spur in the hole in order to mark the coach bolt holes on the post ready for drilling.

3 Drill holes in the timber post, insert the coach bolts from the other side and secure the spur.

4 Fill the large hole first with hardcore (rubble) and then with concrete. Smooth down the surface and leave to set completely.

Repairing timber gates

If a timber gate is sagging and dragging on the ground, check first that the posts are upright, using a level and paying particular attention to the hinged side. If a post has rotted, replace it with a new one.

Fitting a repair spike

1 With the fence panels removed, saw through the damaged post at ground level.

2 Using the tool provided, hammer in the repair spike over the rotten post.

3 Fit a new post (or the old post) into the spike and secure it in place.

If it is leaning slightly, it may be possible to force it back, with the gate removed, and ram some hardcore or more concrete into the ground to hold it in place.

Timber gates may also sag if the joints have become loose. You can fit a variety of metal brackets to support the framework of a timber gate: flat L-shaped or T-shaped brackets at the corners where the vertical stiles meet the cross-rails or the diagonal brace, a right-angled bracket on the inside of the frame between stile and cross-rail, and straight flat brackets to repair simple splits. All will look better if they are recessed into the timber so they are flush with the surface. You could alternatively try replacing the main diagonal support brace or fitting longer hinges.

Repairing metal gates

First, check that the posts are vertical, then that you can move the adjusting nuts – often these will be rusted or clogged with paint. If this is the case, wire brush off the worst of the rust and paint and apply a silicone spray or penetrating oil until you can turn the nuts freely. Finally, adjust the hinges so that the gate no longer rubs on the ground and swings freely but closes properly.

ABOVE Four different types of post spike. From the left: a normal post spike for new posts; a repair spike for rotten posts; a spike for mounting in fresh concrete; a spike for bolting down to a hard surface.

Repairing a sagging gate

ABOVE Fit a replacement diagonal brace to support a timber gate.

ABOVE Using longer hinges is one way to secure a sagging timber gate.

Post levels

A post level can be strapped to a post to ensure it is vertical in both directions.

Repairing Fences and Walls

Timber fences are constantly exposed to the effects of rain, sun and wind. Sooner or later, parts of a fence will rot, split, break or simply fall off. Regular treatment with preservative or stain will prolong the life of a fence, but when repairs are necessary, do not delay, otherwise the fence will no longer do its job. Even masonry walls are not immune to the effects of weathering.

Closeboard fences

A closeboard fence consists of two or three horizontal triangular (arris) rails fitted between posts and supporting overlapping vertical lengths of tapered (feather-edge) boarding (pales). The result is an extremely durable and strong fence. Even so, arris rails can split and sag, while individual pales can become damaged. A horizontal gravel board will run along the bottom of the fence to protect the end grain of the vertical pales from ground moisture. Normally, this is easy to replace, as it is held with just a couple of nails or screws.

Usually, a single broken pale can be levered off with a claw hammer and the nails securing it prised out. If they will not budge, hammer them into the arris rail with a nail punch. Cut the replacement pale to the same length and slide its thin edge under the thick edge of the adjacent pale, having levered this clear of the arris rails slightly and removed the nails from it. Then nail through both pales – each nail holds two pales. If you are replacing several pales, use a short piece of wood as a gauge to ensure even overlapping of the pales.

Repairing closeboard fencing

1 Use an old chisel to lever out the damaged pale of a closeboard fence.

2 Slide the replacement pale into place and nail it to the horizontal arris rail.

3 Reinforce a broken arris rail by nailing on a galvanised repair bracket.

4 A flanged galvanized repair bracket will support the broken end of an arris rail.

Repairing arris rails

If an arris rail has split in the middle, you can buy a galvanized repair bracket that simply fits over the rail and is screwed or nailed in place. If necessary, have a helper lever the fence up, using a crowbar (wrecking bar) over a block of wood, while you fit the repair bracket.

A similar repair bracket, but with a flanged end, is available for reconnecting an arris rail that has broken where it is fixed to the fence post. This is screwed or nailed to both the rail and the post. You can use two of these brackets to replace a complete length of arris rail after sawing through the old rail at the ends and levering it from the fence.

Replacing fence panels

A panel fence has posts regularly spaced at 1.83m (6ft) intervals. The panels come in a variety of designs – interwoven, overlapping and imitation closeboard are the most popular – but are all fixed between the posts in the same way, with either clips or nails holding the panels to the posts.

If clips have been used, replacing a broken panel with a new one will be easy, since screws often secure the panel to the clips. If the panel has been nailed in place, you may destroy it as you lever it out.

The new fence panel should fit exactly between the posts and can be secured in the same way. If the new panel is a tight fit at any point, use a planer-file or rasp to trim it; if it is loose, trim a section of the timber from the old panel to fill the gap.

Repairing garden walls

A common problem with garden walls is that bricks suffer from spalling, that is the surface breaks up. This results from water getting into the brick and expanding as it freezes.

Depending on how well the wall has been built, it may be possible to remove the damaged brick and turn it around, using a masonry drill and a thin-bladed plugging chisel to remove the mortar from the joints. However, it is likely that mortar on the back of the brick will prevent its removal. Therefore, the only solution will be to break it up with a bolster and club hammer, then insert a new brick. Remove all old mortar from the hole, then lay a bed of fresh mortar on the bottom of the hole. Add mortar to the top and sides of the new brick and push it into place, forcing more mortar into gaps, before finishing off the joints to the same profile as the remainder of the wall.

A garden wall can crack along mortar lines, and this often shows a problem with the foundations. There is little alternative to demolishing at least the split section, investigating the problem and making good the foundations before rebuilding it.

Replacing a fence panel

1 To remove a fencing panel, start by levering out the nails holding it in place.

2 You may need to use something like a crowbar in order to lever out the panel.

3 If using clips, nail these in place before sliding the panel through them.

4 Nails are driven through the end section of the panel right into the supporting post.

Removing a damaged brick

1 Remove the mortar around the old brick.

2 Insert a new mortared brick.

3 Repoint the mortar around the replaced brick to the correct profile.

Repairing Steps and Repointing Brickwork

Solid concrete steps are very prone to damage, especially at the edges, while the mortar in brickwork all around the garden is likely to need replacing at some point, or at least freshening up. You need only a minimum of tools to carry out the necessary work, but make sure you have the right safety wear (gloves and safety shoes) and do not work in very cold weather.

Damaged steps

Minor damage in a concrete step, such as small cracks and holes, can be repaired in much the same way as repairing cracks and holes in plaster walls, except that you use an exterior-grade filler, quick-setting cement or mortar made from three parts fine sharp sand to one part cement. Brushing the damaged area with PVA adhesive (white glue) will help the repair compound to stick. Smooth off the surface of the repair compound with a trowel before it has finally set, as you will not be able to rub it down afterwards. Any repair involving a broken corner or edge, however, will require shuttering to contain the repair compound while it sets.

For small repairs to the edge of a step, you need only a block of wood propped in place; more extensive repairs need complete shuttering. Exterior-grade plywood is the best material for this. Use three pieces to make a three-sided mould of the correct height. Secure them at the back with timber anchor blocks screwed into wall plugs inserted in the wall alongside the step. For freestanding garden steps, use sash clamps to hold the shuttering.

Before fitting the shuttering, use a wire brush to remove any loose concrete and plant matter from the step. Hack off any split pieces of concrete and then brush the surface with PVA adhesive.

With the shuttering in place, trowel in the repair compound and smooth it off, using the top of the shuttering as a guide. As it begins to dry, when moisture has disappeared from the surface, roughen the surface with a stiff broom or hand brush, then use a small pointing trowel to round off the edges where they meet the shuttering. Remove the shuttering when the filler, cement or mortar has set.

Repairing a concrete step

1 Use a wire brush to remove loose and damaged concrete around the step.

2 Apply a coat of PVA adhesive to the surface to help the repair compound stick.

3 Fit a piece of wood shuttering to the step edge and prop this in place.

4 Using a trowel, fill in the step edge with repair concrete and smooth it out.

5 Remove the shuttering and if necessary, smooth out the surface of the concrete.

Brickwork

Failed mortar joints between bricks are not only unsightly, but they also allow water into the wall, damaging the bricks when it freezes. The solution is to repoint the joints with fresh mortar.

First, use a thin-bladed plugging chisel to remove all loose mortar until you reach sound material. Brush all dust from the joints and dampen them with a paintbrush dipped in water or a hand-held garden sprayer.

Use a pointing trowel – a smaller version of a bricklaying trowel – to push fresh mortar into the joints, working on the verticals first, then the horizontals. Carry the mortar to the wall on a hawk – a flat metal plate or wooden board on a handle – then hold this against the wall directly beneath the joint you want to fill. Use the pointing trowel to slice off a thin strip of mortar and press it into the joint.

When you have used one batch of mortar, go back over all the joints, shaping the surface of the mortar to the required profile:

- Weatherstruck – using the edge of the pointing trowel to create a sloping profile that sheds rainwater from the wall. Start with the vertical joints and slope them all in the same direction.
- Recessed – using a square-shaped stick, or special tool.
- Flush – using sacking to rub the surface and expose the sand aggregate in the mortar.
- Concave (or rubbed) – using a rounded stick or a piece of hosepipe and run along the joints to make the profile.

A weatherstruck profile is often used on house walls for its rain-shedding properties, while recessed joints are only appropriate to wall surfaces inside. A concave profile is a good choice for garden walls.

ABOVE The causes of cracked pointing should be investigated immediately and repaired.

Practical tips

- The secret of good repointing is to keep the mortar off the face of the brickwork. Take great care when forcing mortar into the joints, removing any excess immediately before it dries.
- Let the joints harden a little before you give them a profile.
- Clean all bricklaying tools immediately after use with clean water. They will be much more difficult to clean if the mortar is allowed to dry.

Repointing brickwork

1 Use a thin-blade plugging chisel with a club hammer to free loose mortar from the joints.

2 Brush out dust and debris from the joints and dampen the existing mortar with water.

3 Hold the hawk tightly against the wall and push mortar into the joint using a trowel.

4 Give the mortar the profile you want – here, a concave profile using a length of hosepipe.

Repairing Concrete and Asphalt Drives

There are many materials that can be used for surfacing paths, patios and drives, and in time most will need some form of repair or maintenance. The technique required depends on the material. Keeping paths, patios and drives in good condition is not simply a matter of appearance. If the surfaces are allowed to deteriorate, they can become dangerous to walk on, especially when wet.

Damaged concrete

Concrete is a popular choice for paving because it is relatively cheap and easy to lay. Nevertheless, it can crack, develop holes and crumble at exposed edges.

Before carrying out any repairs to concrete paving, it is a good idea to clean it thoroughly, and the best way of doing this is to use a pressure washer, which directs a high-velocity jet of water at the surface, removing all algae, slime, dirt and debris. Chip out any damaged areas until you have a solid surface to work on.

Minor holes and cracks can be repaired with exterior filler, quick-setting cement or mortar made with fine sharp sand rather than soft builder's sand. However, you should chip out holes to a depth of about 20mm (¾in) and enlarge cracks to allow the repair compound to grip properly. Any repairs involving edges will require the use of timber shuttering to contain the repair compound while it dries. Fitting shuttering is fairly simple, using stout timber boards. Solid timber pegs are driven into the ground so that the boards fit tightly against the edge of the existing concrete.

Spread the repair compound over the damaged area – some PVA adhesive (white glue) brushed over the surface will help it stick – and smooth it out with a trowel.

Before the repair compound sets completely, roughen the surface with a stiff brush, as smooth concrete surfaces are dangerous when wet. Finally, remove the shuttering and smooth off any rough areas with the trowel and a piece of sacking.

Apart from brushing, there are several ways you can make a concrete surface more attractive and less slippery. Embedding small stones in the surface is one method, or you could provide surface texture with a float or by rolling a heavy pipe over the concrete.

Repairing a concrete path

1 Clean the damaged path with a pressure washer to remove all dirt and algal growth.

2 Fit a piece of shuttering to the edge of the path and drive the pegs home to hold it.

3 Mix up the concrete repair compound in a bucket with a small amount of water.

4 Use a plasterer's trowel to apply the concrete right up to the existing edges.

5 Remove the shuttering once the repair compound has dried.

Repairing asphalt

Asphalt (tarmacadam) is an economical and hardwearing paving material. Provided it has been laid properly, an asphalt path or drive can last a long time. After all, it is basically the same material, small stones mixed with liquid bitumen, that is used for making roads.

However, many domestic asphalt paths and drives may have been laid badly and may start to crumble. If weeds begin to break through the surface, it is a sign that an insufficient thickness of asphalt has been laid, and the only sensible answer is to have a second layer professionally installed on top of the existing one. Laying a complete asphalt drive, which needs to be done with hot asphalt, is not a job for the amateur. However, small holes can be readily mended.

The first step is to sweep the existing drive thoroughly, paying particular attention to the area around the intended repair. If the surface adjacent to the damage has become distorted, you may be able to reshape it by heating the surface with a hot-air gun and tamping the asphalt down with a piece of wood.

Cold-lay asphalt repair compounds are normally laid after the application of a coat of bitumen emulsion.

Compact the repair compound into the hole or depression, using a stout piece of wood or a garden roller for a large area. Spray the roller with water to prevent the repair compound from sticking to it. If you want, scatter stone chippings over the asphalt and roll them in.

For really deep holes, it is best to fill them partially with concrete before adding the final layer of cold-fill compound.

Repairing an asphalt path

1 Brush the damaged area of the path or drive until you have a clean working area.

2 Apply asphalt repair compound and press it into the damaged area with a spade or trowel.

3 Tamp the filled area with a stout piece of wood or use a garden roller to flatten it.

4 If required, add stone chippings and then roll again.

Good drainage

If there are puddles forming on your paving or if rainwater does not clear away, it is a sign that the paving has not been laid to the correct slope (fall).

This does not need to be huge and around 1 in 100 is normally recommended, that is 1cm per metre (½in per 4ft).

The fall can be checked using a straight timber batten set on edge with a small block of wood under its lower end and a spirit level on top. The thickness of the wood block depends on the length of the batten; for a 3m (10ft) batten, you need a 30mm (1¼in) block.

Safety first

Many paving materials, especially paving slabs, are heavy and have rough edges. So it is important that you wear the correct safety gear – stout gloves and safety shoes as a minimum. Gloves will also protect your hands when using heavy hammers. If you are not strong enough, do not attempt to lift paving slabs by yourself as you could damage your back. Take care, too, when using tools such as angle grinders for cutting paving slabs to fit in corners and other awkward areas.

Repairing Slab and Block Paving

Concrete paving slabs are a common choice of paving for patios. The same slabs can also be used for paths, but for drives, stronger and thicker, hydraulically-pressed slabs must be laid on a much stronger base. Normally, paving slabs are set on dabs of mortar on a sand base, but they may also be laid on a solid bed of mortar, a method that is always used when laying heavy-duty slabs for a drive.

Repairing slab paving

A slab may have broken because something too heavy has been placed on it or as a result of something hitting it. Sometimes, individual slabs may become loose or may sink, in which case they will need to be lifted and re-laid.

If the joints around the slab have been filled with mortar, the first job will be to chip this out, using a narrow-bladed masonry chisel.

If possible, remove a broken slab from the centre, working outward, you can use a bolster chisel or a garden spade to lever up sections or whole slabs, but protect the edges of adjoining slabs with pieces of timber. Clean out the bottom of the hole, removing all old mortar, and level it using builder's sand tamped down with a stout piece of wood – allow about 10mm (⅜in) for the mortar. Mix up a batch of mortar using dry ready-mix and put down five dabs, one in the centre and one near each corner. Also lay a fillet of mortar along each edge.

Lower the new slab, or the old slab if it is undamaged, into position and tap it down with the handle of a club hammer. Check that the slab is level with its neighbours by placing a spirit level across them. Adjust as needed, then when perfectly level fill the joints with more mortar.

Replacing a concrete slab

1 Use a narrow-bladed masonry chisel to chip out the mortar around a damaged paving slab.

2 Lift or lever out the broken pieces, starting from the centre. Clean out the hole.

3 Add more sand and put down five blobs of mortar and apply mortar to the edges.

4 Lower the paving slab into position and make sure it lines up with surrounding slabs.

5 Use the handle of your club hammer to tap the slab into place until it is exactly level.

6 Add some more mortar to finish the joints, smoothing it down level with the paving.

ABOVE Crazy paving paths can be both functional and attractive.

Crazy paving

This form of paving employs pieces of real stone or broken slabs (whole slabs of real stone are prohibitively expensive) and is popular for paths, although larger areas may also be paved in this manner. It can be laid in one of two ways: on a bed of sand or a bed of concrete. Like full-size paving slabs, individual pieces may break, sink or work loose.

When repairing crazy paving, you may need to re-lay quite large areas. As when laying new crazy paving, work from the sides toward the centre, using the biggest pieces with the straightest edges along the sides, then filling in with smaller pieces.

Whichever way you lay crazy paving, the joints should always be well mortared, and the mortar finished flush or shaped with a pointing trowel to give V-shaped grooves around the slab.

Repairing block paving

Concrete blocks are also commonly used for paving: the individual blocks are bedded in a layer of sand and held tightly against one another by edging blocks or restraints set in mortar. Fine sand is brushed into the joints between blocks.

If an individual block becomes damaged, the main problem will be getting it out to replace it. Drill holes in it with the largest masonry drill you own, then break it up with a cold chisel and club (spalling) hammer. In this way, you will reduce the risk of damaging the surrounding blocks. Loosen the sand at the base of the hole and add a little more so that the new block sits proud of the surface by around 10mm (⅜in). Tap it down with the handle of the club hammer, then force it into its final position by hitting a stout piece of wood laid over the block with the head of the hammer. Brush fine joint sand into the cracks.

ABOVE A pressure washer is the most effective way of cleaning paving, but you need to be careful not to splash yourself (wear protective clothing in any case) and not to wash earth out of flowerbeds. Never point the spray directly at the house walls.

Replacing a damaged block

1 Use a large masonry drill to make a hole in a damaged paving block.

2 Use this hole to start chipping out the block with a cold chisel.

3 Clean up the hole, then add a little more sand to the bottom of the hole.

4 Push the new block into place. Tamp it down, using a block of wood to protect it.

Repairing Gravel Paths and Edges

One of the big advantages of gravel is that it makes a noise when you walk on it and provides a significant deterrent to potential intruders. It is also good for drives, as it can soak up oil drips from cars without showing permanent stains. However, gravel can become weedy and may blow about. It may also be trodden into the house and develop thin patches.

Maintaining a gravel surface

Regular raking and the application of weedkillers are required to keep a gravel drive or path looking good, and you can buy silicone resins that help bind the stones together without affecting their appearance. Thin areas can simply be filled by pouring on a bag of new gravel and spreading it with a garden rake.

To prevent gravel from spreading beyond its allotted area, add concrete edging strips. These should be set on a bed of mortar and held upright while the mortar sets. If you do not like the look of concrete edging consider using bricks or wood.

You can use the oil-catching properties of gravel to good effect by installing strips of it in a concrete drive where you park the car. The concrete will act to keep the gravel in place and the gravel will catch any oil drips.

To lay a new gravel path, dig out the area, add compacted hardcore, followed by sand and coarse gravel and finally fine gravel to level.

ABOVE Gravels naturally vary considerably in colour and size.

Laying a gravel path

1 Excavate the area to a depth of about 15cm (6in) and make the base firm.

2 Provide a firm edge to retain the gravel. For straight paths, secure battens with pegs.

3 Compact a layer of hardcore. Add a mixture of sand and coarse gravel, and tamp it firm.

4 Top up with fine gravel. Rake and roll repeatedly until the surface is firm and level.

Maintaining gravel paths

1 Apply weedkiller to a gravel path to keep it looking good.

2 Scatter new gravel on to a path to give it a fresh appearance, and rake it level.

ABOVE This narrow, concrete kerb edging has been used here to contain a gravel garden and to divide it from paving slabs.

ABOVE Handle Victorian-style rope edging carefully if it is made from clay, as it can easily chip or break.

ABOVE Wooden edgings are useful if you want to create a formal or old-fashioned effect. Secure in place with pegs.

Repairing edging

Edging is an important part of paving, as it can help to hold the main body of paving in place and prevent the edge slabs or blocks from being damaged. There are several kinds, of which the most common are concrete edgings, used with all types of paving, and self-edging where the paving material itself, concrete blocks for example, is used as the edging.

All masonry edging should be bedded in mortar, no matter how the remainder of the paving is laid.

Where edging has become loose, pull it out and chip and scrape away all the old mortar. Lay a bed of fresh mortar and push the edging pieces back into place, using a straightedge to align them with their neighbours. Drive in timber pegs to hold the edging vertical and tight against the paving; finish off by applying a 45-degree fillet of mortar along the base of the edging between the pegs.

When the mortar has set, remove the pegs and make good the peg holes with more mortar and conceal the fillet of mortar with soil or turf.

Practical tip

- Paths always make a smarter feature with a neat or interesting edging. If you have an older-style property, try a Victorian-style rope edging. If it is a country cottage, try something both subtle and unusual, such as green glass bottles sunk into the ground so that just the bottoms are visible. Or try bricks: they can be used on their sides, on end, or set at an angle of about 45 degrees.

Repairing a path edge

1 To replace loose edging, the first task is to remove the edging and to clean out all the old mortar, using a chisel if necessary.

2 Push fresh mortar firmly down into the hole, checking that you have enough to bring the edging level.

3 Push the edging piece back into place, lining it up and add an angled fillet of mortar along its bottom edge.

Insulating Roofs and Pipework

Good insulation reduces the rate at which expensive domestic heat escapes through the fabric of your home and helps to protect vulnerable plumbing systems from damage during cold weather. The different parts of your home can be insulated by various methods, and most jobs can be handled by a competent person. The cost will eventually be recouped through savings made on energy bills.

Roofs and plumbing

As with any do-it-yourself job, breaking the whole project down into manageable parts can help. Around 25 per cent of heat escapes through the roof, so it is a good place to start your insulation project. The roof is where pipework is at greatest risk of freezing, so this must be tackled as well.

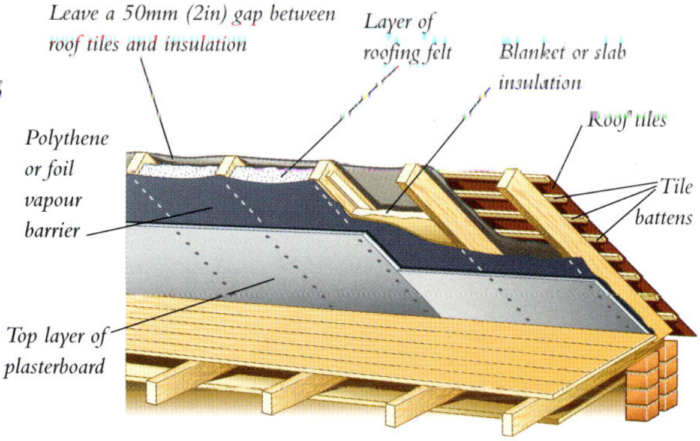

RIGHT A cutaway section of a roof showing the roofing felt or building paper, examples of sheet and blanket insulation between the rafters, the vapour barrier and the plasterboard (gypsum board) sheets.

Safety first

Invest in protective clothing. A basic kit should comprise:

- Well-fitting overalls and gloves to keep out dust particles.
- Protective goggles and face mask.
- A safety helmet, which is essential when working in confined spaces with limited headroom.

Most important of all, remember that unless you have laid suitable flooring in the roof area, you will only be able to walk on the joists. In between will be the exposed ceiling of the rooms below, which will be fragile and will not bear your weight. To avoid accidents, lay stout planks of wood across the joists and stand on them.

Insulation materials

A simple way to stop heat loss is to place insulation material between the joists. Your choice may be influenced by personal preference or ease of use – some varieties are much cleaner and less likely to cause skin irritation than others – or the decision may be made for you by the local authority if you are applying for a grant to complete the work.

Current recommendations suggest that the insulation should be laid to a depth of 200mm (8in). However, this may not be possible with some materials if the joists are of a shallower depth. Also, if the roof area has a floor, this may restrict the depth of the insulation. In the latter case, the floor will have to be lifted to put insulation between the joists.

Laying loose-fill insulation

1 Lay loose-fill insulation by pouring the material between the joists.

2 Level off with a spreader, which you can make from a strip of chipboard (particle board).

Loose-fill insulation

This is sold by the bag and is simply poured between the joists and levelled off with their top surfaces. Although easy to handle and spread, the dustier varieties, such as vermiculite, can be unpleasant to work with. Moreover, the material may be blown about if the roof area is prone to draughts.

Blanket insulation

This consists of rolls of glass fibre, mineral fibre or rock fibre, which are simply unrolled between the joists. Widths are available to match common joist spacings. A typical roll length would be 6–8m (20–26ft), but short lengths are also available, known as batts. Some types may cause skin irritation, so always wear gloves when laying the insulation.

Slab insulation

These products are light and easy to handle, but as with the blanket versions some types may cause skin irritation. Again, the slab widths match common joist spacings. Look out for high-density slabs if you want the bonus of an effective sound barrier.

Essential buys

Good insulation need not mean great expenditure. The most effective items are relatively cheap and could save you a great deal in the long term. Any water storage tanks in the roof must be insulated to protect them from freezing; indeed, some water suppliers may require this by law. Padded jackets are available for the purpose. Likewise, any exposed pipework in the roof should be fitted with thick insulating sleeves to prevent freezing.

Laying blanket insulation

1 Lay blanket insulation by unrolling the material and pressing gently into place.

2 Butt join two rolls of blanket insulation and press the two ends together leaving no gaps.

Practical tips

- Leave the space under a cold-water storage tank free from insulation. Warmth rises from rooms underneath to help prevent freezing.
- Insulate the roof access hatch with blanket insulation, backed with plastic, and glue or pin in place.

ABOVE FAR LEFT Fix reflective foil between rafters to act as a vapour barrier over insulation.

ABOVE LEFT Split foam pipe insulation.

ABOVE Seal pipe insulation with adhesive tape to make it secure.

FAR LEFT Secure an insulation blanket to a hot water cylinder.

LEFT Insulate a cold water cistern with a purpose-made jacket.

Insulating Walls and Floors

The walls of any house represent a huge part of the building and it is essential that they are well insulated. The type of insulation required depends on the fabric of your home – solid walls require one method, cavity walls another. It is also imperative to insulate your home at ground level, as around 15 per cent of heat can escape through the floors.

Heat loss in walls

The largest area of heat loss, some 35 per cent, is estimated to escape through house walls. However, the best solution, which is cavity-wall insulation, is a job that must be left to the professionals. Despite the extra outlay, the work is very cost-effective, and you can expect to see a return on your investment after a few years. This treatment, of course, is not possible if the house has solid walls. The usual procedure is to pump foam, pellets or mineral fibres into the cavity through holes drilled in the outer leaf of the wall. Make sure that the work is carried out by an approved contractor.

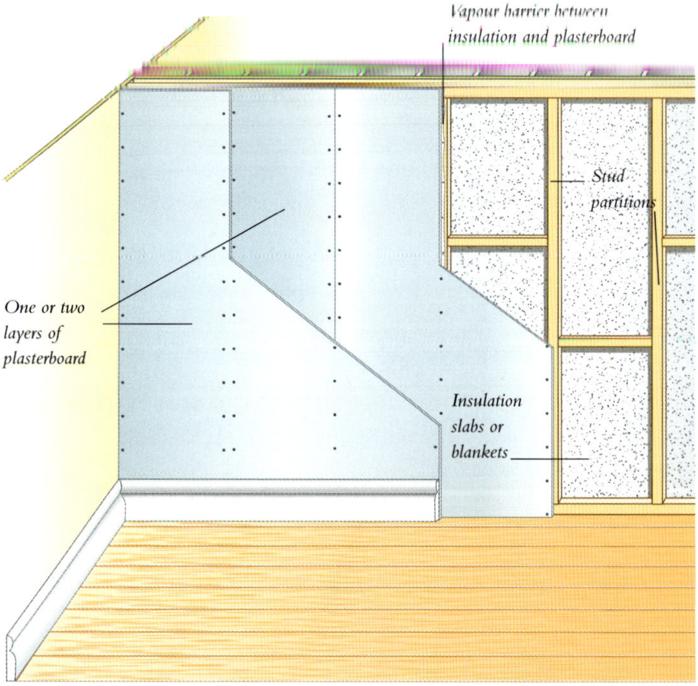

ABOVE A party wall can be insulated by erecting a stud partition wall in front of it, which is filled in with blanket or slab insulation behind it and two layers of plasterboard on the framework.

Do-it-yourself solutions

Applying insulation to the inner faces of walls is well within the scope of most people. One possibility is to use thermal plasterboard (gypsum board) to dry line external walls. Another is to add a timber framework to the wall, infill with slab or blanket insulation and face it with plasterboard. To prevent condensation, plastic sheeting should be stapled to the insulating material.

The disadvantage of both of these methods is that you will lose some of the floor area of the room. At least 50mm (2in) will be lost by using thermal plasterboard, and more if you create a new partition wall. However, in terms of comfort and cost-savings, this sacrifice may be worth making. Providing the plaster wall is sound, the boards can be fixed directly to it with adhesive. A vapour barrier is included as standard.

ABOVE Installing cavity wall insulation is a specialist job that can take up to three days.

Practical tips

- Fabric wallcoverings have good insulation properties. Similarly, rugs and wallhangings can keep heat in and reduce sound levels.
- Use acoustic slabs when dry-lining walls for a quieter life.

Draughty floors

If you draughtproof floorboards that have substantial gaps, bear in mind that it could involve disruptive work and should be avoided if possible. If you are prepared to lift and replace floorboards, the methods are very similar to laying roof insulation.

However, you will need to provide some means of supporting the insulation material between the joists. Nylon netting stapled to the sides of the joists is the usual method for holding glass fibre insulation blanket in place. Pull up the netting tightly before nailing down the boards so that the blanket does not sag and let cold air through. Lengths of wood fixed between the joists will support slab insulation.

An easier method of coping with a draughty floor is to choose a good underlay for your carpet and also repair any gaps or cracks between floorboards with sealant.

Larger gaps will need to be filled with strips of wood, carefully cut to fit tightly. Spread adhesive on the sides of each strip and tap it into the gap. Allow the glue to set, then plane down the strip so that it is flush with the surrounding floor.

Solid concrete, or direct-to-earth, floors are generally insulated by covering the area with sheets of rigid polystyrene, topped by a covering of polythene sheeting.

RIGHT Putting aluminium foil behind a radiator will help to save energy by reflecting heat back into the room.

FAR RIGHT Stop draughts at skirting (base) board level by sealing any gaps with mastic and quadrant (quarter-round) moulding. Secure the latter to the skirting with pins.

Filling gaps in floorboards

1 Tap slivers of wood in place to cure floorboard draughts. Leave the repair slightly proud of the surface.

2 Once the glue has set, sand down the raised area to a smooth finish with a power sander or planer.

A floating floor, comprising of tongued-and-grooved chipboard, is then installed over this.

A gap of 9mm (3/8in) should be left between the chipboard and the wall to allow for expansion. This gap will not be noticeable once a new skirting (base) board is installed. The layer of air trapped under the floating floor will help keep the area warm.

This work can be fairly disruptive, and as the new floor will be at a raised level, existing doors will need to be removed and planed down. Architraves around doors will also need to be shortened to accommodate the change.

Practical tips

- Position a shelf about 150mm (6in) above a radiator to project heat into the room.
- A papier-mâché mix made from pieces of newspaper and a thick solution of wallpaper paste can be used to repair small holes in floorboards. Add woodstain to match the surrounding boards, and then sand the repair smooth when dry.
- If floorboards are in very poor condition, cover the area with panels of hardboard or plywood.

Draughtproofing Doors and Windows

The smallest gaps and cracks in the fabric of your home can create the most uncomfortable living conditions. About 15 per cent of heat loss is attributed to poor or non-existent draughtproofing, yet fitting draughtproofing materials is quite easy and inexpensive. Effective draughtproofing not only stops heat from escaping, but also makes your home feel warmer by eliminating cold draughts.

A healthy balance

The main targets are windows, doors, chimney flues and the roof access hatch, but check also for gaps around skirting (base) boards and between floorboards. However, there is a healthy balance to be struck. If every draught is eradicated, you could create ideal conditions for condensation. The solution is to draughtproof all the obvious cold spots in your home, but also ensure that there is adequate ventilation, in the form of grilles, airbricks and extractor fans.

Doors and windows

These are the two main sources of draughts in the home, and many products have been designed to deal with the problem. Windows alone are responsible for about 10 per cent of heat loss. One solution is to replace single glazed units with double glazing, but this is the most costly remedy and it may take up to 20 years to recoup your investment in terms of energy savings.

Draught excluder strips are an inexpensive method of sealing gaps around windows and doors. The strips are self-adhesive and easy to apply, although foam strips offer variable levels of success. Avoid the

Closing holes

Draughts may not only pass around doors, but also through them. The problem is quite easy to solve. Keyhole covers are inexpensive, while a brush-type or rubber flap fixed to the inside of a letter plate will prevent anything other than the mail coming through.

ABOVE Fit a letter box with a rubber or brush seal to stop draughts.

ABOVE A simple cover plate, or escutcheon, will stop draughts.

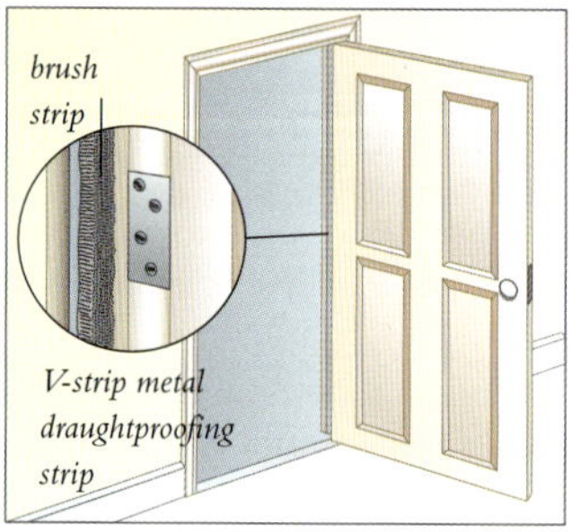

LEFT A metal draughtproofing strip can be fixed to a door frame, such as the example shown here, a V-strip type. The insert shows where the brush strip should be fixed.

BELOW Various types of threshold draught excluders. Most, with the exception of flexible strip excluders, are made for internal or external doors, so choose the correct size and type for your doors.

Flexible rubber strip held in place by screws.

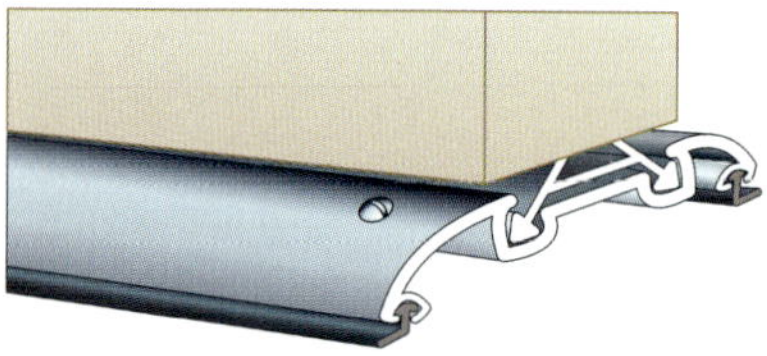

An aluminium flexible arch excluder.

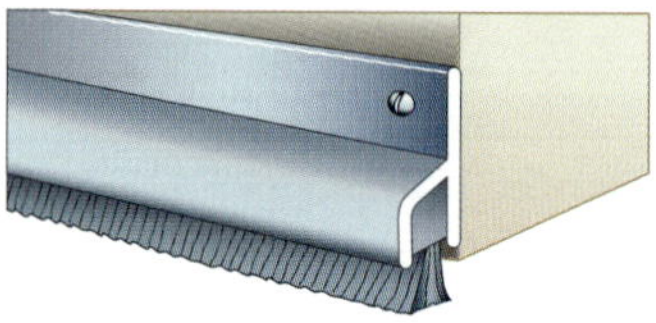

Brush-type strip fitted at the base of the door.

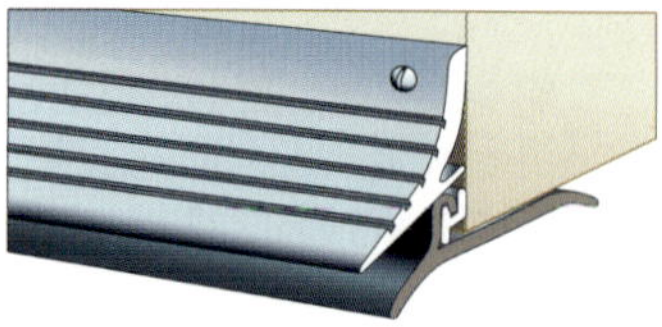

All-in-one door kit, with a trim to expel rainwater, plus a draught excluder.

cheapest varieties, as they may soon become compressed and will not do the job properly. Look for products that are guaranteed for between two and five years. These will be easy to remove and replace if you wish to upgrade the draughtproofing system.

Rubber strips, commonly with E- or P-shaped profiles, are dearer, but are better in terms of performance and longevity. Normally, casement windows are easier to draughtproof than the sash variety.

The most effective way of keeping draughts out at the sides of sashes is to fix nylon pile brush strips to the window frame. The top and bottom do not need special treatment, as any of the products recommended for casement windows can be used.

Silicone sealants (caulking) are good for filling large or irregularly shaped gaps around windows and doors. They come in white, brown and clear versions. Use a caulking gun for ease of application, although products that do not require a gun are also available. To make a repair with silicone sealant, clean the frame rebate (rabbet) and apply the sealant to the fixed frame. Brush soapy water on to the closing edge of the window or door. Close and immediately open the door. The soapy water acts as a release agent, preventing the door or window from sticking to the sealant.

SECONDARY GLAZING

This is a relatively inexpensive way to prevent draughts from windows. The cheapest method involves attaching a clear film to the inside of the window with tape. It can be discarded during the summer months and a fresh film applied in winter.

A sturdier option is acrylic sheet. If you opt for this method, make sure that at least one window is easy to open in case of an emergency.

Alternatively, you could buy a kit that allows the secondary glazing units to slide along a track.

ABOVE Apply sealant to a window.

ABOVE To apply secondary glazing film, stick double-sided adhesive to the frame, fix the film in place and heat it to iron out wrinkles.

PRACTICAL TIPS

- For good adhesion, always clean and dry window and door frames thoroughly before applying self-adhesive sealant.
- Consider adding trickle ventilators to windows to allow essential air into your home.
- When replacing windows, consider using panes of low-emissivity glass. This has a special coating that reflects heat back into the room and gives the same advantages as triple glazing, but for less money.

INSTALLING A RIGID GLAZING SYSTEM

1 Cut the channelling to fit the four edges of the glass or plastic sheet. Fix on to the sheet.

2 Hold the glazing over the window and mark the positions for the fixing holes.

3 Deepen the marked spots with a bradawl to provide pilot holes. Screw the glazing in place.

Providing Ventilation

Ventilation, a free flow of fresh air, is essential in a home, not only for humans to breathe, but also to prevent condensation occurring. There are three main areas of a home that need ventilation: the main living space, the spaces under suspended timber floors, and the roof space. You may also need to ventilate chimneys that have been sealed.

Ventilation for living

In older homes, there are likely to be so many gaps around doors and windows and through fireplaces that any additional ventilation will be unnecessary, although you may need to open a few windows from time to time. In modern homes, the combination of draughtproofed windows and doors and sealed or non-existent fireplaces means that some kind of additional ventilation is necessary. This may take the form of forced ventilation, through an extractor fan in a bathroom or kitchen, or background ventilation, for which the main item is the trickle ventilator.

A trickle ventilator allows a slow, but constant, stream of fresh air into a room and is simply fitted into a window frame. Holes are drilled through the frame and the ventilator fitted over them, thus allowing air to flow into and out of the room. A grille prevents insects from getting in, and there is usually some kind of control to vary the rate of flow.

Practical tip

- Where a room contains a gas boiler, current regulations may mean that you need an unobstructed ventilator fitted in an outside wall. Check with your gas supplier (or heating installer) whether you need to have one of these fitted.

Underfloor ventilation

A suspended timber floor consists of floorboards or sheets of flooring grade chipboard (particle board) supported on joists. To keep the joists and the flooring dry, and so avoid rot and woodworm attack, some kind of underfloor ventilation is essential. This takes the form of airbricks fitted in the outer walls.

The first thing to check is that all the existing airbricks are free of debris and have not been blocked up in the mistaken belief that this will save money on heating.

Next, check that there are enough airbricks – there should be one airbrick for every 2m (6ft) of wall length. Inserting a new airbrick is not difficult, as most match the size of standard bricks.

Decide where you want to put it, drill out the mortar around the existing brick and remove it. With a cavity wall, the most common, you will have to continue the hole through the inner wall and fit a terracotta liner to maintain the airflow. Use the corners of the hole in the outer wall to line up and drill four holes in the inner wall, then chip out the hole with a bolster (stonecutter's) chisel and club (spalling) hammer, working from the inside. You will need to lift floorboards to do this.

Fit the airbrick from the outside, applying mortar to the bottom of the hole and the top of the brick, pushing mortar in the sides. Point the mortar joints to the same profile as the surrounding joints. Mortar the liner in place from inside the house.

Ventilating roof spaces

If your house has a gable end wall, the roof space can be ventilated by fitting airbricks in the gable. If the house is semi-detached, ask your neighbour to do the same, and fit another airbrick in the party wall to allow the air to circulate freely.

Clearing an airbrick

ABOVE Airbricks can get blocked by soil, leaves or stones from nearby paths.

ABOVE Clear any debris around the airbrick and clean the holes with a vacuum.

The alternative is to fit ventilators in the timber soffits – the horizontal boards that overhang the eaves. All that is needed to fit these is to cut a hole in the timber using a padsaw or a jigsaw (saber saw), then push the ventilator in place, securing it with screws if necessary. There must be a clear space above each ventilator for air to flow into the roof, so make sure that any insulation material does not extend to the eaves. A badly ventilated roof space can lead to condensation and possible rot.

Blocked fireplaces

If a fireplace has been bricked or boarded up, the result could be condensation within the old chimney, leading to staining of the chimney breast (fireplace projection) especially if there is no airbrick.

Fit a metal ventilator to the bricks or panel where the fireplace used to be, after making a hole just smaller than the ventilator area. Some types are made to be screwed in place; others, for use with bricks, are held by plaster. If the chimney pot itself has also been removed and the chimney capped off, make sure that airbricks have been fitted into the chimney at the top.

Practical tip

- You may need to install more airbricks in a room where there is a solid concrete hearth (from an old cooking range, say). This can create "dead" areas which may need extra ventilation to prevent rot.

Fitting an airbrick

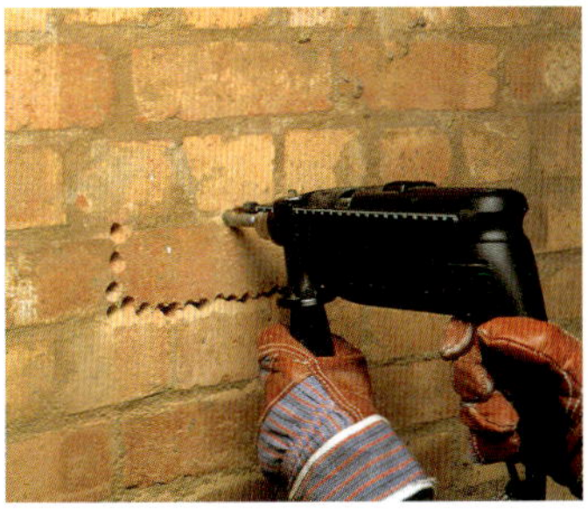

1 Airbricks are the same size as one, two or three bricks. To fit one, start by drilling a series of closely-spaced holes through the joint around a brick.

2 Then use the club (spalling) hammer and a wide bolster (stonecutter's) chisel to cut out the brickwork. With solid walls, drill holes right through and work from inside too.

3 Fit a cavity liner through to the inner wall if the wall is of cavity construction, then trowel a bed of fairly wet mortar on to the bottom of the opening.

4 Butter mortar on to the top of the airbrick and slide in place. Push more mortar into the gaps at the sides and pack it down. Use drier mortar to point neatly all around the airbrick.

5 As an alternative to the traditional terracotta airbrick, fit a two-part plastic version. The sleeves interlock to line the hole as the two parts are pushed together.

6 Slide the outer section into place, and point around it. Slide the inner section into place from the inside of the house. Fit its cover grille.

Fitting an Extractor Fan

If the basic ventilation measures have been undertaken, such as installing trickle ventilators and airbricks, and condensation is still a problem, the answer is to fit an extractor fan. These can be incorporated into walls, windows and ceilings and have the advantage that they get rid of moist and stale air from close to where it is produced.

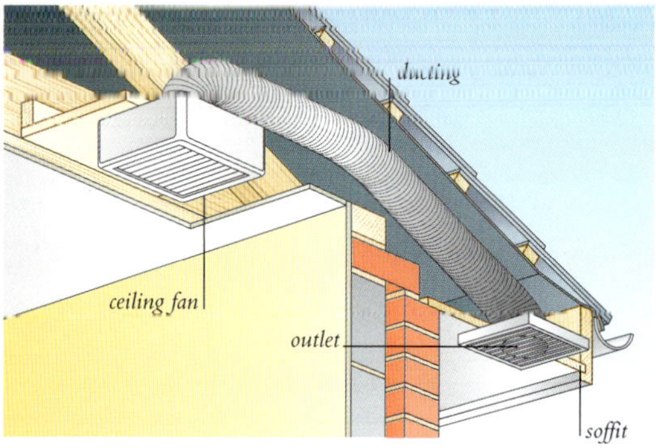

LEFT Fit an extractor fan in the ceiling so that it discharges via a duct to a hole with an outlet at the soffit.

Providing extra ventilation

An extractor fan provides positive ventilation where it is needed, in a kitchen, bathroom or toilet, removing stale or moist air before it can cause a problem. There are three places you can fit an extractor fan: in a window, in a wall and in the ceiling, where ducts carry the stale air to the outside. In a kitchen, an extracting cooker hood can serve the same function, provided it is ducted to the outside; a recirculating cooker hood only filters the air.

It is important that an extractor fan is positioned so that the replacement air, which normally will come through and around the door leading to the remainder of the house, is drawn through the room and across the problem area. In a kitchen, the problem areas are the cooker and the sink; in a bathroom, they are the toilet and shower unit.

Window fans

If a simple window ventilator already exists in a fixed window, you may be able to replace it with an extractor fan. If not, you will have to cut a hole in one of the window panes. However, this will not be possible if the glass is toughened or laminated. The same applies to double-glazed units; they must be ordered with the hole pre-cut. The only window you can cut a hole in is one made from normal glass in a single-glazed frame, and even here you may prefer to order a new pane from a glass supplier with the hole already cut. That way, the only work you will have to do is to take out the old pane and fit the new one.

To cut the hole in the glass yourself, you will need a beam circle cutter as well as a normal glass cutter. Use the beam cutter to score two circles: one the correct size for the extractor fan and one slightly smaller inside it. Then use the normal glass cutter to make cross-hatched lines inside the inner circle, and single radial lines between the two circles. Tap out the glass from the inner circle, then use the glass breaker rack on the glass cutter to snap off the remaining margin of glass. Smooth the edge with fine abrasive paper wrapped around a circular tool handle or piece of thick dowelling rod. Once you have a hole of the correct size, fitting a window

Fitting a window fan

ABOVE If no ventilator is fitted, you will need to cut a hole in the glass to fit an extractor fan.

ABOVE If the window already has a simple ventilator, remove this to fit an extractor fan.

fan is simply a matter of following the instructions.

Wall extractor fans

Most designs of extractor fan will require a circular hole to be cut through the house wall. The best tool to use for this is a heavy-duty electric drill fitted with a core drill bit, both of which you can hire. This will cut a hole of exactly the correct size. Make holes in both leaves of a cavity wall and fit the sleeve supplied with the extractor fan. Some fans require a rectangular hole to be cut, which may mean removing a whole brick. Fitting the fan is easy – simply drill holes for wallplugs to take the fan on the inside wall, and fit the outlet on the outer wall.

Ceiling fans

A wall outlet for the ducting from a ceiling fan is fitted in the same way as for a wall extractor fan. It is often the easiest type to fit, as all you need to do is cut a circular hole in the ceiling with a padsaw, taking care to avoid the ceiling joists. From the fan, plastic ducting needs to be taken to an outside wall or to the eaves, where it is connected to an outlet. At the eaves, it is fitted into the soffit in the same way as a soffit ventilator.

Wiring

An extractor fan needs to be wired up via a fused connection unit to the nearest power supply circuit. If you are not sure how to do this, employ a qualified electrician to do the job. In a bathroom, or room containing a toilet, with no opening window, a fan is a compulsory requirement and it must be wired via the light switch so that it comes on with the light and remains on for 15 minutes afterwards.

Fitting a wall extractor fan

1 The first step in fitting a wall fan is to mark the exact position of the wall sleeve.

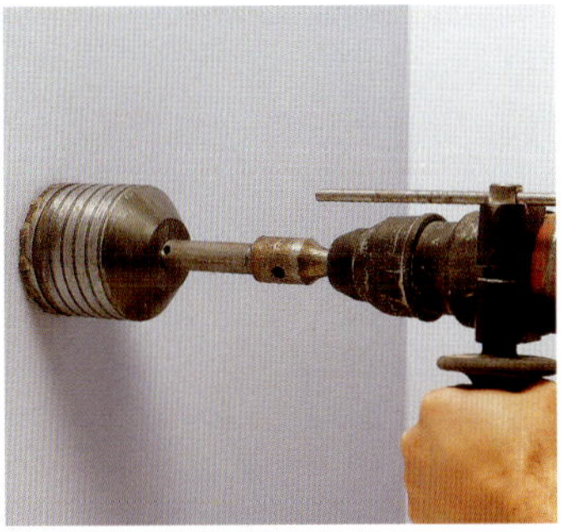

2 Use a core drill bit (with a heavy-duty drill) to cut a hole of the correct size.

3 Fit the sleeving right through the wall, cutting it to the correct length if required.

4 Drill holes for wallplugs so that you can screw the extractor fan to the wall surface.

5 Wiring comes next (get help with this if necessary), after which the cover is put on.

6 Finally fit the outlet on the outside wall (sometimes this just pushes into the sleeve).

Damp and Condensation

This can ruin decorations, destroy floorcoverings, damage walls and plaster, and cause woodwork to rot, so it is important not only to treat the symptoms, but also to track down the causes. These could vary from rain coming in through the roof or walls, condensation, moisture being absorbed through the ground or a mixture of these.

Penetrating damp

This is caused by moisture getting in from the outside, often because of wear and tear to the structure of your home, but it may also affect solid walls that are subjected to strong driving rain. The first sign of penetrating damp appears after a heavy downpour and can occur almost anywhere, although it may be some distance from the actual leak; mould often forms directly behind where the problem lies.

Causes of penetrating damp

- Damp on ceilings upstairs may be caused by broken or loose roof tiles, or damaged copings.
- Damp on a ceiling spreading from a chimney breast (fireplace projection) or rooflight, under the junction of two pitched roofs, or in corners that adjoin a single-storey extension, is usually caused by flashing that has parted company with masonry, or cracked and crumbling mortar fillets.
- When damp patches are high up on an upstairs wall, look for blocked, defective gutters or downpipes and a build-up of leaves.
- With widespread damp on a wall, look for cracked or porous bricks.
- Isolated damp patches on walls are caused by crumbling pointing and cracked or blown patches of render (large damp patches), or mortar-encrusted wall ties (small spots).
- Rotten woodwork and damp patches around door and window frames are caused by gaps between masonry and frames, missing weatherboard or a drip groove encrusted with paint or moss.

ABOVE LEFT A patch of mould on the inner face of an external wall is usually the first sign of penetrating damp.

ABOVE Poor ventilation will make condensation problems worse.

BELOW FAR LEFT Crumbling mortar and defective flashing can cause penetrating damp.

BELOW LEFT Overflowing or broken gutters allow water to seep through masonry.

BELOW A defective roof leaking through cracks and gaps and soaking structural timbers will cause major problems, such as damp, wet rot and dry rot.

Rising damp

This is caused by water soaking up through floors and walls, and is usually confined to a 1m (3ft) band above ground level. It is a constant problem, even during dry spells.

The main areas to check for rising damp are the damp-proof course (DPC) around the foot of walls, and damp-proof membrane (DPM) in the ground floor. Older properties were often built without either, which can lead to widespread damp. If existing materials have broken down or structural movement has caused defects, there may be isolated, but spreading, patches of damp where water is penetrating. A DPC that is less than 150mm (6in) above ground level will allow rain to splash above it and penetrate the wall, which may cause damp patches at skirting (baseboard) level. If a DPC has been bridged, either by exterior render or interior plaster, there will be damp just above skirting level. A cavity filled with rubble, soil or plants growing against the wall may also allow damp to penetrate.

Condensation

When warm, moist air reaches a cold surface, such as a wall exposed to icy winter winds or ceramic tiles, the result is condensation. It is most likely to occur in bathrooms and kitchens where the main activities are bathing, washing and cooking. Controlling condensation requires a fine balance between good ventilation and adequate heating, but while the modern home is warm, it is also well insulated and draughtproofed, so the level of ventilation is often poor. The key to success is to provide sufficient ventilation, without allowing expensive heat to escape.

ABOVE LEFT Gaps between masonry and woodwork around windows will let in rain, causing patches of damp to occur.

ABOVE Injecting an interior wall with silicone – you will need to get professional help to do this.

BELOW LEFT Water vapour from everyday activities can cause condensation.

BELOW Condensation is feature of our modern well-insulated and draughtproofed homes, but keeping it under control is essential to the health of your house and family.

Is it damp or condensation?

If you are not sure if a moisture problem is due to condensation or damp, lay a piece of aluminium foil over the patch, seal the edges with adhesive tape and leave it for 48 hours. Condensation will cause beads of moisture to appear on the surface of the foil; penetrating or rising damp will produce beads of moisture underneath the foil.

ABOVE Test with aluminium foil to determine whether the problem is damp or condensation.

Overcoming Damp and Condensation

Damp and condensation should never be ignored, as these unchecked problems will not go away and may well indicate more serious problems. Often the remedy is quite straightforward and inexpensive, but the after-effects can linger for some time, and then real effort is required when it comes to cleaning up and making good afterwards.

Damp-proof courses

The first line of defence against damp is an effective damp-proof course (DPC) combined with a good damp-proof membrane (DPM), backed up by well maintained rainwater systems and plumbing. Ventilation is the key to preventing condensation problems. An adequate airflow should be maintained through the fabric of the house, using soffit vents and airbricks, while extractor fans will deal effectively with the warm, moist air created by everyday activities such as cooking, laundry and bathing.

Dealing with damp

Once the cause of penetrating damp has been traced and repaired, the problem will be eradicated. The remedy for rising damp caused by a non-existent or defective DPC or DPM is not so easy; the only solution is to install a replacement or make thorough repairs.

ABOVE A damp-proof course should be clear of soil, debris or plants growing up walls.

Waterproofing walls with water seal

1 Brush, clean, and remove any fungal growth from the wall. Fill any surface cracks.

2 Apply the water seal by brush, working from the bottom up, coating the whole wall.

However, dealing with a DPC that has been bridged is quite straightforward. If the ground level is the cause, digging a 150mm (6in) wide trench between a high patio or path and the house wall, then filling it with gravel, will allow rain to drain away more rapidly. When you suspect that debris in the cavity, or a dirty wall tie, is the cause, removing a few bricks will give access to remove the rubble, or chip away encrusted mortar. Apply a coat of liquid water repellent to the area once the bricks have been replaced.

The after-effects

Walls and floors can take up to a month for each 25mm (1in) of thickness to dry out, while old plaster may be heavily contaminated with mineral salts from rising damp, which will continue to absorb moisture from the air. Replastering is recommended in extreme cases as part of the cure, but this should be delayed for as long as possible to allow walls to dry out. Use a mould killer to remove any patches of mould from interior surfaces caused by damp or condensation.

Damp-proof courses

There are many ways of installing a damp-proof course, ranging from physical DPCs that are cut into the brickwork to chemical slurries, which are pumped into a series of drilled holes.

In theory, it is possible to do the job yourself, but dealing with rising damp is rarely simple. It is worth seeking the advice of professionals. If there is a mortgage on your home, the lender may also require a guarantee of workmanship, which rules out tackling the job yourself. The standard of workmanship is as important as the system used, so choosing a reputable company that offers an insurance-backed guarantee is essential and often compulsory.

Installing a damp-proof membrane

This is a job that a competent do-it-yourselfer can tackle. Laying a new damp-proof membrane (DPM) involves digging up and re-laying the old floor slab, which is hard work, but the most effective method of damp-proofing a concrete floor. A floor can also be damp-proofed by applying several coats of moisture-curing urethane, but it is essential that any leaky patches are sealed completely first with a hydraulic cement.

A third option is to apply two coats of rubberized bitumen emulsion to the old surface, then cover this with a cement-sand screed, which will raise the level of the floor by about 50mm (2in).

Whichever method you choose, the DPM material should be taken up the adjoining walls to meet the DPC, if there is one. The problem of damp floors caused by rising ground-water levels, which typically affects basements, is more serious and requires structural waterproofing or "tanking", which is certainly a job for the professionals.

Coping with condensation

Steam from cooking can be removed by a fully vented cooker hood, but where a great deal of steam is produced, when you take a shower for example, the best way to remove it is with an extractor fan.

To be quick and efficient, the fan must be sited properly and it should be the correct size for the room. In a kitchen, a fan must be capable of 10 to 15 air changes per hour, and in bathrooms 6 to 8 air changes per hour, which should be increased to 15 to 20 air changes for a power shower. Simply multiply the volume of the room by the number of air changes required and look for a fan that offers the same cubic metre/foot capacity per hour (m^3/hr or ft^3/hr).

An extractor fan should be installed as high as possible on the wall, and as far as possible from the main source of ventilation, usually diagonally opposite the main door is ideal.

More widespread condensation can be alleviated with an electric dehumidifier, or prevented with a thermostatically controlled whole-house ventilation system.

ABOVE A cooker hood removes steam from cooking at source.

Practical tips

- In bathrooms, keep the door shut when taking a bath and run cold water first to minimize the amount of steam it creates.
- Where condensation occurs in a confined space, such as a built-in wardrobe, causing mould and mildew, use silica gel crystals to absorb excess moisture from the air.
- In kitchens, make sure a tumble drier is properly vented.

Installing a damp-proof course

1 A chemical damp-proof course is injected into a line of drilled holes about 115mm (4½in) apart.

2 Once injected into the drilled holes, the chemicals overlap to form a continuous impermeable barrier.

3 When the fluid is dry, the drilled holes are filled with mortar and then a rendered surface can be painted.

Woodworm, Dry Rot and Wet Rot

Rot and woodworm are the enemies of timber and every homeowner's nightmare, yet by taking a few simple steps both can be prevented. In addition, once discovered, repair can often be a do-it-yourself proposition. At the first sign of infestation, act quickly and try to identify and eradicate the problem before it seriously damages your home.

Woodworm

This mainly affects structural woodwork, such as roof timbers, staircases, floorboards and joists, and unprotected parts of furniture, such as drawer bases and the backs of cabinets. It will also attack plywood and wicker.

The most common menace is the furniture beetle, whose larvae create fine boreholes 1–2mm (1/16in) in diameter. Larger holes are likely to be caused by the house longhorn beetle larvae, which prefers softwood and creates boreholes 3–6mm (⅛–¼in) in diameter, and the deathwatch beetle larvae, which makes substantial boreholes and has an appetite for structural timbers.

It is possible to treat infestation in furniture and localized outbreaks in structural timbers with woodworm fluid, but if the wood is crumbling, the only remedy is to remove and replace the affected areas.

Woodworm fluid will not penetrate a polished surface, so treat boreholes with an aerosol spray or nozzle applicator. Boreholes are connected by a series of tunnels, so you only need to do this every 75mm (3in) or so. Leave the timber to dry for at least 24 hours and then wipe off any excess.

Seek professional help to deal with a large-scale infestation, or if it has compromised the strength of structural timbers.

Preventative action

- Inspect all second-hand furniture before buying, and treat with woodworm fluid before bringing indoors, whether it shows signs of infestation or not.
- Protect unpainted wood, the top and bottom edges of doors for example, with insecticide.

ABOVE Check your furniture, and if necessary, treat it with a proprietary woodworm fluid.

Wet rot

This thrives on wet timber and frequently appears where timber is close to the ground or near leaking plumbing, and in woodwork where the protective paint coating has broken down. Skirting (base) boards may also be affected where a DPC is defective or non-existent.

Wet rot can be due to a number of species of fungus, but the most common consist of brown or black strands that appear on the surface, causing the wood to crack and eventually disintegrate. Affected wood tends to look darker than healthy wood and feels spongy.

Once the cause of the damp conditions that have led to the problem is eliminated, wet rot fungus will die. Treat small areas, such as window frames, with proprietary wood hardener solution and insert preservative tablets into holes drilled into the wood to stop

ABOVE Woodworm can be identified by tiny holes. Check the extent of the infestation by inserting a knife into affected timber.

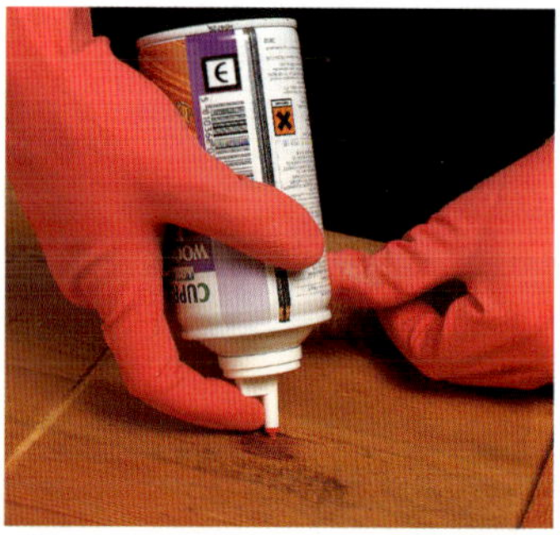

ABOVE Woodworm fluid should be sprayed on to all surfaces of structural timbers. On small areas, apply two coats of woodworm killer.

any recurrence. Where damage is extensive, the affected wood should be cut out and renewed.

Dry rot

The fungus that causes dry rot loves moist, humid conditions and has a taste for resins and silicones in untreated wood. However, the grey strands are fine enough to penetrate masonry, which means that it can spread rapidly from room to room.

Untreated dry rot will destroy floors, doors and skirtings, and infect plaster and ceilings. Initially, it manifests itself as a brownish-red dust, but within days the spores will have developed into a fungus that looks like a mushroom growing upside-down and it also gives off a distinctive musty smell. This is the final stage of germination, by which time the fungus will be producing millions of spores to infect surrounding areas.

Dealing with dry rot is a job that should be entrusted to a specialist, as it may recur if not treated properly. Make sure you choose a reputable company that offers an insurance-backed guarantee.

Practical tips

- Make regular checks of plumbing, especially under baths and shower trays and in the roof.

- Many of the chemicals used to treat woodworm and dry rot are flammable or toxic irritants, which create strong fumes that will linger for about a week. This means taking precautionary measures for at least two days after treatment.

ABOVE An example of severe dry rot on a destroyed wooden floor.

ABOVE A sporophore, or dry rot fungus, on a structural roof timber.

ABOVE Inspect your loft space and check for the first signs of dry rot. Ensure there is good ventilation in the loft and under the floors to help prevent the conditions in which dry rot can flourish.

Preventative action

- Make sure that a damp-proof course (DPC) has not been bridged, by looking for tell-tale signs of damp on walls above skirtings.

- Dry rot will not flourish in well-ventilated areas, so make sure there is good ventilation in roofs and under suspended wooden floors. If necessary, fit air vents or extractor fans in soffits and gable end walls. Make regular checks of the airbricks and clear them if they are blocked.

Replacing rotten wooden sills

1 Remove the rotten wood and cut a new wedge-shaped piece to fit.

2 Fix the new wood in place by countersinking the screws.

Home Security

Most burglars are opportunists, and will take a chance if they spot a property that looks as if it offers quick and easy takings. The golden rule is to leave your home as secure as possible whenever you go out. Protecting your home from unwelcome visitors does not have to be difficult or expensive; often the simplest measures are the most effective.

Locks and bolts

The first line of defence is to make sure that all windows and doors are adequately protected with good-quality locks and bolts. Surface-mounted locks and bolts are easy to install, but fittings that are mortised into the frame are much stronger and more secure. The second line of defence is to make your home less vulnerable and less attractive to opportunist burglars.

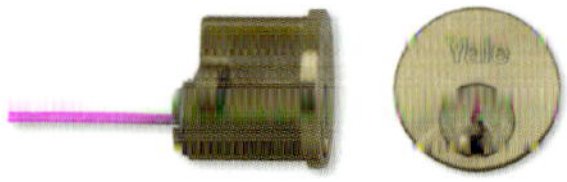

Cylinder rim lock

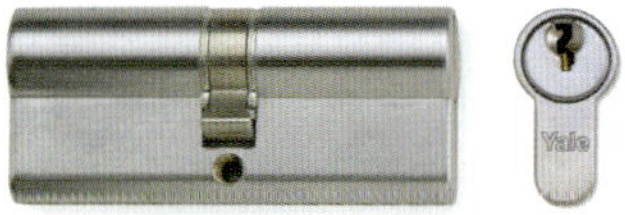

Double-barrel cylinder lock

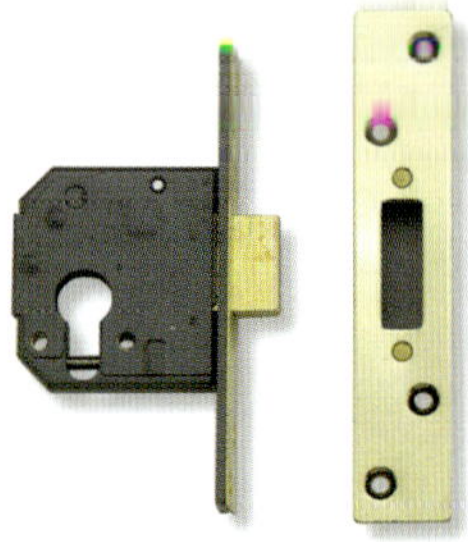

High-security cylinder deadlock

High-security cylinder sash lock

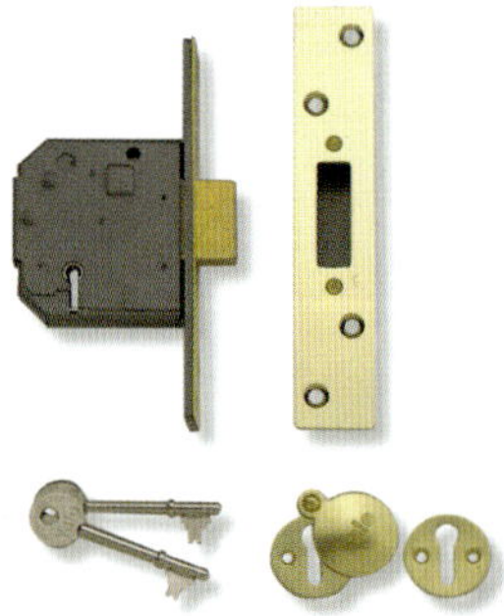

Five-lever mortise deadlock

Secondary security

Doors

- Locks will be ineffective if a door is flimsy or ill-fitting, and a well-fitting, solid wood or blockboard door, at least 44mm (1¾in) thick, offers the best resistance.
- To prevent a door from being lifted off its hinges, fit security hinges, which have lugs that will not come apart if the hinge pin is removed. If the door opens outward, fit hinge bolts.
- For personal safety when you are home, a door viewer will allow you to decide whether or not to open the door to a caller. Choose a viewer with a wide angle of vision, and use it in conjunction with a porch light. You should be able to see someone who is standing to one side of the door, or crouching below the viewer.
- A door chain will give added protection against forced entry. Its effectiveness will depend on how well it is anchored to the door and frame: use the longest and heaviest-gauge screws that you can.

ABOVE Fit hinge bolts to doors that open out.

ABOVE Check out callers with a door viewer.

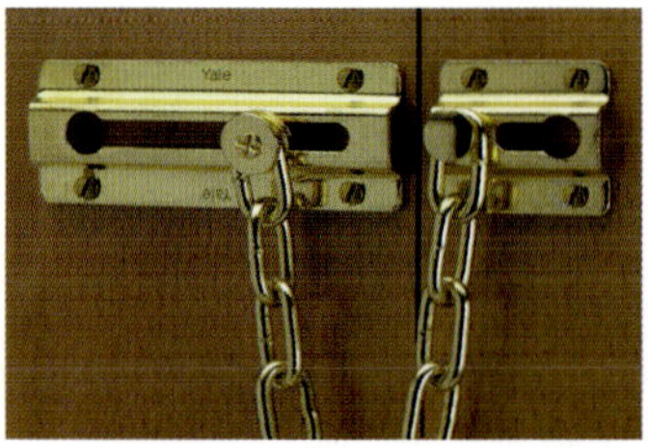

ABOVE Prevent forced entry with a door chain.

Patio doors

- Sliding patio doors are a favourite point of entry, so fit anti-lift devices as well as locks to prevent the doors from being lifted from their tracks.
- A locking bar across the full width of the door will create an immediate, visible deterrent to potential intruders.

Windows

- If casement windows are not fitted with trickle vents or locking handles, replacing the stays with locking stays will provide more security when leaving the windows open for ventilation.

Security systems

A burglar alarm may also deter a thief from choosing your home. Installing a do-it-yourself system is time-consuming rather than difficult, but you should be able to install a wireless alarm in about four hours and a wired system in one or two days. Some wireless systems are not completely wire-free, as the control panel has to be wired to the alarm siren on the outside of the house. However, the latest solar-powered alarm systems have an external siren that has its own integral trickle-charge battery, so that no wiring is required.

Basic alarm kits offer rudimentary protection, so additional components will be needed to provide adequate security. This increases the cost, but do-it-yourself systems nevertheless offer good savings over a professionally installed system. If you cannot afford an alarm system, a dummy alarm box fitted outside may make a burglar think twice.

Protective measures

Glass

- Laminated or toughened glass will make it difficult for a burglar to break in without creating a lot of noise. It may be worth replacing glass panels in vulnerable doors and windows.

Lighting

- Replacing an existing light switch with a photocell switch that will turn lights on at dusk, and off again after a pre-set interval, will keep a potential burglar guessing whether you are in or out. A light that can be programmed to switch on and off at random is convincing.
- Exterior security lights that switch on automatically when movement is detected nearby are also a powerful deterrent in dark areas around your home.

LEFT A security light that will automatically illuminate when someone approaches is an ideal choice for front doors.

BELOW LEFT A passive infra-red detector can be used to monitor a dark passageway or the back yard or garden, turning security lights on automatically when movement is detected.

BELOW A security camera with a built-in passive infra-red detector will detect and record movement, indoors and out.

Practical tips

- Outbuildings and garages should always be locked securely. Not only are they a source of easy takings for a thief, but the ladders and tools inside are perfect implements for breaking into your home.

- Large hedges can screen doors and windows and provide burglars with enough privacy to break in undetected by neighbours, so keep them well trimmed.

- Make vulnerable corners of the garden more secure by planting dense, thorny evergreens. A liberal layer of gravel under windows makes a quiet approach to the house impossible.

Window Hardware and Locks

Over half of all home burglaries occur through a window and even the smallest one is vulnerable, so good locks are very important. The first line of defence is to fit key-operated locks to all ground floor windows, and those first floor windows that are easily accessible. It is also essential to provide secure ventilation around your home.

Basic hardware

The most common items of hardware fitted on hinged windows are a rotating cockspur handle that is used simply to fasten the window, and a casement stay which props it open in one of the several different positions. On sliding sash windows, the basic hardware is a catch that locks the two sashes together when they are closed.

Window locks

A wide range of locking devices for windows is available. Many are surface-mounted using screws and are quick and easy to fit, although for some types a drilled hole for a bolt or recess chiselled for a keeper plate may be required. Mortised locks and dual screws that fit into holes drilled in the window frame take longer to install, but they are very secure.

All window locks are supplied with fixing screws but these should often be discarded in favour of longer, more secure fixings. For extra security, it is also a good idea to fit two locks on casement windows more than 1m (3ft) high and all locking devices for sash windows are best used in pairs.

For ventilation, if the window has a stay pierced with holes, you can replace the plain peg with a casement stay lock. Attach the screw-on lock to the threaded peg with the key supplied. You can now secure the window in position.

Fitting a window handle and stay

1 Choose the position of the cockspur handle on the casement and make pilot holes through it with a bradawl. Then screw the handle to the casement.

2 Fit the striking plate (keeper) to the frame so that it will engage with the cockspur. Drill out the frame to a depth of 20mm (¾in) through the slot in the plate.

3 Fit the casement stay by screwing its base-plate to the bottom rail of the casement about one-third along from the hinged edge.

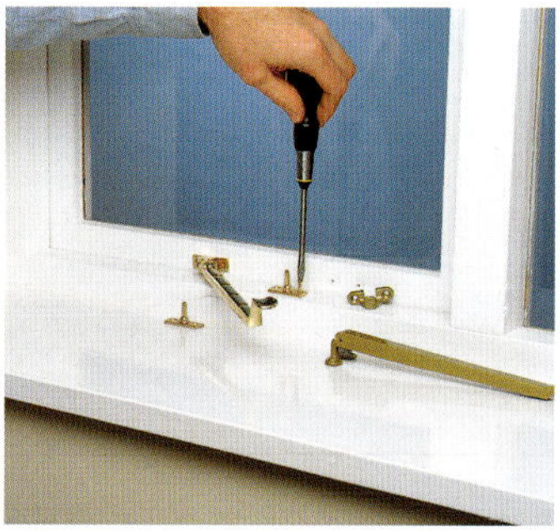

4 Open the window to find the right position for the pins on the frame. Attach the pins, then fit the stay rest on the casement rail.

If fitting lockable window catches and stays, do not leave keys in the locks where they might be seen by an intruder or in case they fall out as the window is opened and closed. Instead, hang them on a hook close to the window.

Practical tip

- Ensure you have the right screws: a lock for wooden frames requires wood screws and metal windows require self-tapping screws.

Casement locks

Locks for wooden casement windows may be surface-mounted or set in the frame. In the former case, the lockplate is attached to the fixed frame and the body of the lock to the opening frame. With the window closed, mark the positions of the lock and plate on both frames, then screw them in place. For those with a locking bolt, you will have to cut a rebate (rabbet) or drill a hole to receive the bolt. Some surface-mounted locks are also suitable for metal casement windows. Check the instructions.

Locks that are set in the frame normally require holes to be drilled in both fixed and opening frames. Also, a hole must be drilled through the face of the frame for the key.

Sash locks

Some types of casement-window lock will also work with sash windows. Another option is key-operated dual screws, which bolt both sashes together. Use a flat bit the width of the lock barrel to drill through the inner meeting rail into the outer rail to the required depth, then tap the barrels into place with a hammer and piece of wood. Fit the longer barrel into the inner rail, the shorter into the outer rail, and screw the bolt into the barrel with the key.

Fire safety

Wherever possible, fit window locks that all use the same standard key so that any key can be used to open a window in the event of an emergency. Keep the key in an accessible position.

Fitting a casement lock

1 With the lock assembled, mark the position on the fixed and opening frames.

2 Separate the two parts of the lock and screw the body to the opening frame.

3 Fit the cover plate and insert the screws. You may want to use longer screws.

4 Some makes come with small covers to hide the screws. Tap these into place.

Fitting a sash window lock

1 Mark the drill bit with tape to the required depth and drill through the inner meeting rail of a sash window and into the outer rail.

2 Separate the two sections of the lock and tap the barrels of the dual screw into place in the meeting rails (mullions).

Door Locks

Doors, especially those at the rear of the house, often provide an easy entrance and exit point for intruders. Good locks properly fitted to a strong door and door frame are the basic requirements for ensuring that house doors are secure, while additional security devices may help you feel safer at home. The doors of garages and outbuildings are also at risk and need to be protected too.

Installing mortise locks

Align the mortise lock with the centre rail of the door and use the lock body as a template for marking the top and bottom of the mortise.

Draw a line down the middle of the door edge and, using a drill bit the width of the lock body, drill a series of overlapping holes along the centre-line to the depth of the lock. Chisel out the mortise so that the lock body fits snugly. Insert the lock, mark the outline of the faceplate with a marking gauge and chisel out a recess so that it fits flush with the door edge.

Mark the positions of the key and spindle holes, then drill them using a twist drill of the same diameter; enlarge the keyhole with a padsaw. Assemble and check the lock works.

With the latch and bolt open, mark their positions on the door frame. Measure from the outside of the door to the centre of the bolt, mark that distance on the jamb and cut mortises in this position. Chisel a recess for the striking plate and check that the door closes properly before screwing it in place.

Practical tip

• "Measure twice and cut once." Accuracy is vital when measuring out for door locks, so take your time with this part of the job and you will have fewer problems later.

Fitting a mortise lock

1 Mark out the dimensions of a mortise lock on the door edge.

2 Draw a vertical line in the exact centre of the door between the marked lines.

3 Drill a line of holes through the centreline to the depth of the lock body.

4 Insert the lock, then mark and chisel out the recess for the faceplate.

5 Using the lock as a guide, mark the position of the spindle and keyhole.

6 Drill, then use a padsaw to form the keyhole, then fit the covers.

7 Cut out mortises for the latch and the deadbolt on the door jamb.

8 Cut out a recess for the striking plate (keeper) so that it fits flush in the door jamb.

Fitting a rim lock to a door

Mark the position of the lock on the door, using any template provided, and bore a hole with a flat bit for the key cylinder. Push the cylinder into the hole, connect the backplate and secure it with screws. The cylinder connecting bar will protrude through the backplate. If necessary, cut it to length using a hacksaw.

Mark and chisel out the lock recess in the door edge, then fit the lock and screw it to the door, making sure that the cylinder connecting bar has engaged in the lock.

With the door closed, mark the position of the striking plate (keeper) on the jamb, then chisel out the recess so that the plate fits flush with the frame. Fix the striking plate with screws and check that the door closes properly.

Fitting rack bolts

Mark the position of the rack bolt in the centre of the door edge and on the inner face of the door, using a try or combination square to ensure that the two marks are level. Drill horizontally into the door edge to the depth of the body of the bolt.

Push the bolt into the hole, mark the outline of the faceplate, then withdraw the bolt and chisel out a recess for the plate. Hold the bolt level with the guideline on the inside of the door, and mark and drill a hole for the key.

Fit the bolt, following the manufacturer's instructions, check that it works properly and screw the keyhole plate to the door.

Close the door and wind out the bolt so that it leaves a mark on the jamb. Drill a hole at this point and fit a recessed cover plate.

Fitting a rim lock

1 Mark the position of the cylinder on the door and drill its hole.

2 Insert the barrel of the cylinder into the drilled hole.

3 Fit the backplate to the door and secure it tightly with screws.

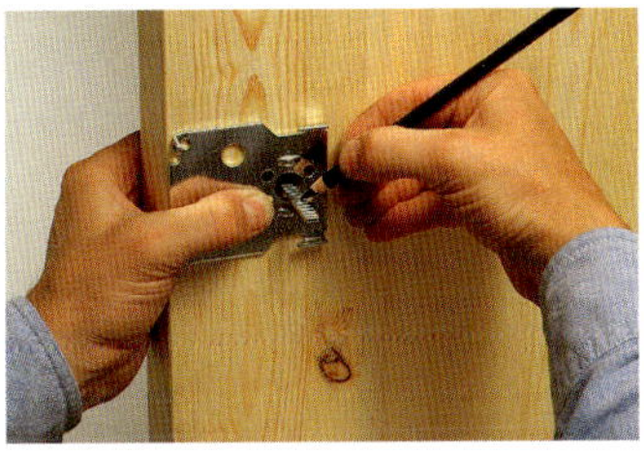

4 Mark the length of the connecting bar to be cut off if necessary.

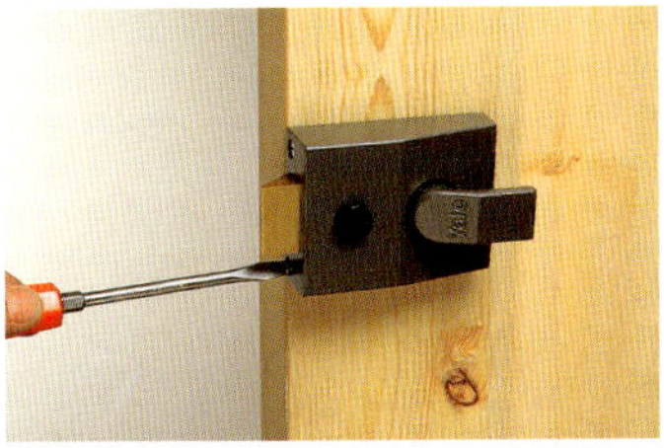

5 Fit the lock case on to the connecting plate and screw up.

6 Mark the position of the striking plate. Chisel out the wood to fix to the frame.

Fitting a rack bolt

1 Use tape to mark out the drilling depth and keep the drill bit horizontal. Push in the bolt.

2 Mark the outline of the faceplate then withdraw the bolt to chisel out the recess.

Carpentry and Practical Projects

Developing your practical skills will allow you to tackle a wide variety of tasks around the home – from putting up the simplest of fixtures, to making all manner of repairs and assembling quite complex structures. Many involve working with wood, which can be a satisfying pastime in its own right. Woodwork is involved in many creative projects, such as repairing all sorts of fittings around the house, easing sticking doors, changing locks, putting up cabinets and shelves and fitting new architrave (trim), picture or chair (dado) rails.

Making Basic Joints

The techniques of joining wood have been developed over centuries, and there is satisfaction to be gained from employing these tried and tested methods. Patience, care and attention to detail provide the key to making accurate joints; an understanding of how they work will allow you to choose the correct type for a given job. The basic joints shown here are suitable for many projects.

Dowel joints

Beech dowels offer a quick and simple means of strengthening corner joints and aligning two components to prevent them from twisting. Three common sizes are available: 6mm (¼in), 8mm (5⁄16in) and 10mm (⅜in). Choose the diameter to suit the material; as a general rule, do not exceed half the thickness of the timber. There are several easy methods of locating them accurately.

Centre-point method

Small brass or steel centre-points that match the dowel diameter come in dowelling kits that are available from hardware stores and also include a drill bit and dowels.

Mitred joints

A frame with mitred corners can be reinforced with biscuits if the parts are thick enough to accommodate them. A versatile jointing machine can save time and improve accuracy in many applications.

Making a dowel joint

1 Use a dowel drill bit, also called a spur-point bit, to centre each hole. A strip of tape wrapped around the bit makes a depth gauge. Hold the drill truly vertical.

2 Insert the centre-points in the holes and push the adjacent component toward them, making sure that it is in its correct position. Use a square to check the edges are flush.

3 Clamp the second piece in a vice and drill to the correct depth for the dowel.

4 Apply glue to the dowels, insert in the holes and tap the joint together.

Making a mitred joint with biscuits

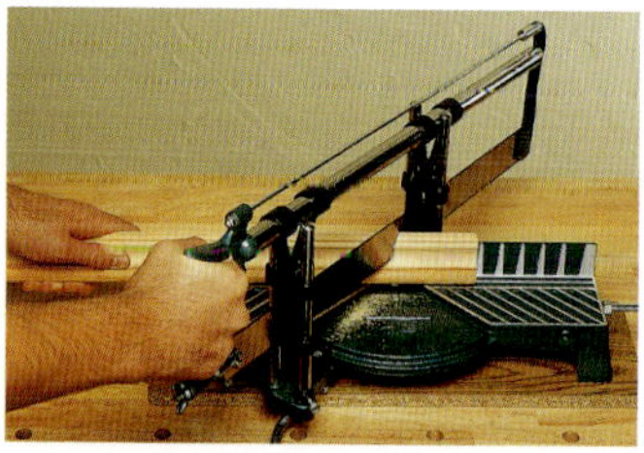

1 A mitre saw will cut through the timber easily and accurately.

2 Use a try or combination square to align the corners accurately when marking.

3 The oval shape of the biscuit automatically centres the mitred joint as it fits together.

Joining boards and knock-down fittings

Manufactured sheet materials are available in large sizes, but occasionally it is necessary to join them together neatly. Because they lend themselves to machine-made joints, there are several options to choose from. Knock-down (K-D) fittings are used extensively in the furniture industry for manufacturing self-assembly units. They are useful for furniture that needs to be reassembled easily.

Lap joint

A lap joint is easily made with a router machine and is useful when matching veneered boards to make decorative panels.

Loose-tongued joint

An even stronger bond can be achieved by using a "loose tongue", which acts as a key for the adhesive. This type of joint takes little time to fabricate.

Scarf joint

Two panels can be joined with a feather-edged scarf joint, which will provide a large surface area for the glue. When made correctly, this type of joint will allow the completed panel to be formed into a curve without the joint separating or kinking.

Practical tip

- Use special construction screws when joining chipboard (particle board) panels. They have a coarse thread designed to grip the fibres in the panels without splitting them.

Making a lap joint

1 Use a router fitted with a fence to form the lap, cutting it to exactly half the thickness of the material.

2 Apply glue and clamp the boards together. When the veneers are well matched, the seam will be almost invisible to the eye.

Making a loose-tongued joint

1 Use 6mm (¼in) plywood for a loose tongue. The cross-ply structure is stronger than a long-grained section of hardwood. Apply glue and insert into a routed groove.

2 Firmly clamp the two panels flat to the bench before applying longitudinal pressure to the joint. This will keep it perfectly flat and produce a strong bond.

Making a scarf joint

1 This straightforward joint can be made easily with hand tools. Make up a simple wooden jig on the workbench to control the angle of the plane.

2 Before clamping the joint together, drive in a few panel pins (brads) to prevent the boards from sliding around. Remove them when the glue has dried.

Fitting Lightweight Fixtures

Installing new fixtures and fittings is a basic do-it-yourself activity that covers a variety of tasks, such as hanging a picture, fitting drawer and door handles, putting up lightweight shelving, and fitting hooks, locks, clasps and catches on all manner of items. Many are very straightforward jobs, which involve simply screwing, pinning or sticking the fixture in place.

Supporting lightweight hooks and shelving

Fixtures of this kind include coat hooks, cup hooks and dozens of other quickly fitted aids and clips of all types. Threaded hooks and eyes need a pilot hole to be made with a bradawl (awl), after which they can be screwed in place with finger and thumb. Small shelves can be supported in a variety of ways, including using screw eyes, dowels and lengths of wood. All these methods are suitable for shelving that will carry little weight.

BELOW A variety of lightweight hooks.

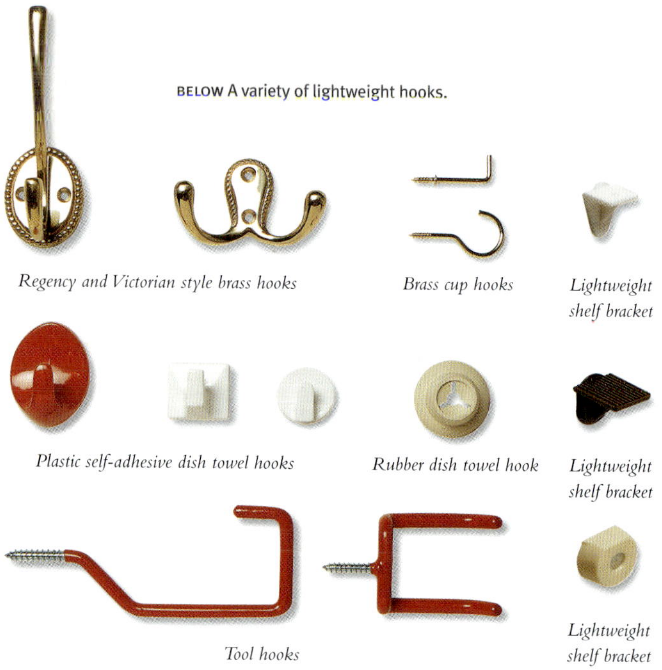

Fixing hanging rails to walls

When attaching a clothes or towel rail to a plaster or plasterboard (gypsum board) wall, it is best to fix a small wooden block to the wall at each end, using a single, central screw, then screw the rail brackets to the blocks.

This avoids the need to drill closely-spaced holes in the wall for the fixing plates, which could cause the surface to crumble, or for the holes to merge into each other.

ABOVE When fixing hanging rails, insert a wooden block between the fitting and the wall.

Hanging a cabinet

A good way to hang a small cabinet is with a wooden batten (furring strip) fixed to the wall with screws and plugs. The tapered top edge of the rail engages with a recess in the back of the cabinet, providing a safe mounting, yet allowing the cabinet to be lifted down when required. It is essential to ensure that the angles of both nails are the same for a good and secure fitting.

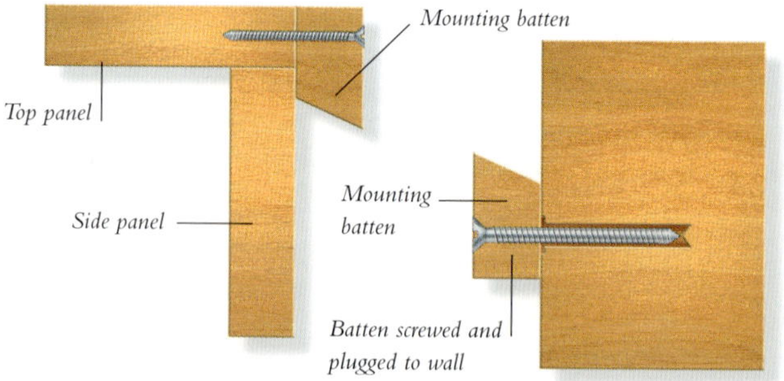

LEFT Hanging cabinets with battens into studwork or brickwork.

Hanging a picture

When hanging any artwork, it is important to consider the weight and size of the frame. Use picture wire or strong cord to hang any weight of frame. Light pictures can be hung with a single picture hook, which incorporates a hardened pin rather like a masonry nail and is driven directly into the wall. Single or double D-rings are strong fixings for light to medium-weight frames, but you should use strap hangers for heavy or large frames. These are screwed on to the back section of the frame and wire or cord can be attached in the same way. However, if the frame is very heavy, it is recommended to hang the picture from the loops of the strap hanger on to screws inserted directly into the wall. Anti-theft devices (ATDs) and mirror plates work in much the same way as strap hangers. The straight section is screwed into the back of the frame, and the curved section is screwed to the wall.

LEFT 1 Picture wire
2 Mirror plates
3 Anti-theft devices
4 Screws
5 Rivets or butterflies
6 Strap hangers
7 Spring clips
8 Picture cord
9 Double D-rings
10 Single D-rings

Setting a striking plate (keeper) for a door catch

Fitting a striking plate incorporates the tasks likely to be encountered in the fixing of many small fittings: accurate positioning and marking, skill in cutting recesses to different depths, and the accurate fitting of countersunk screws. You should offer the striking plate to the timber, making sure that it is in the correct position and square with both the lock and the door frame. Scribe around it, including the hole in the centre. Carefully chisel along the marked outline, starting with the cut across the grain at each end. Then chisel out the waste to the depth of the plate. You will need to cut deeper with the chisel to create the mortise for the catch. Hold the plate in position and use a bradawl (awl) or gimlet to prick the positions of the screw holes. Drive in the screws, making sure that they fit flush into the countersunk holes in the plate.

Surface-mounted catches

The roller catch is often used on small cabinet doors, especially those in a kitchen. Offer up the striking plate first, marking the screw positions, drilling pilot holes and screwing the plate to the frame. Both striking plate and roller have elongated holes to allow for adjustment. The roller is fitted in the same way and adjusted accordingly.

The magnetic catch is also common. This is even simpler to fix, since it can be placed in a variety of positions on the door. Large doors may be fitted with two catches, one top and one bottom. Slotted mounting holes allow adjustment so that the catch works efficiently.

ABOVE A striking plate set in an internal frame.

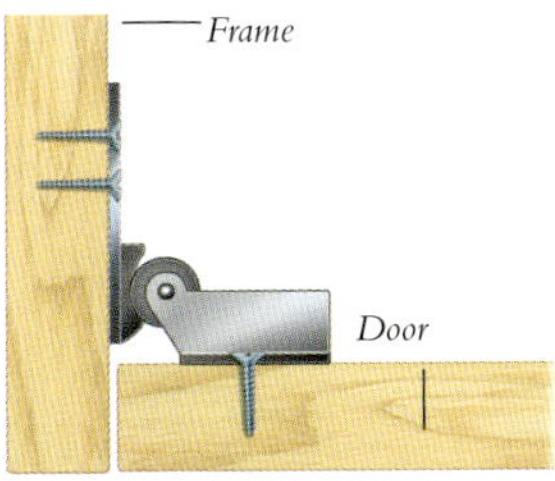

ABOVE Use roller catches on cabinet doors for a smooth opening action.

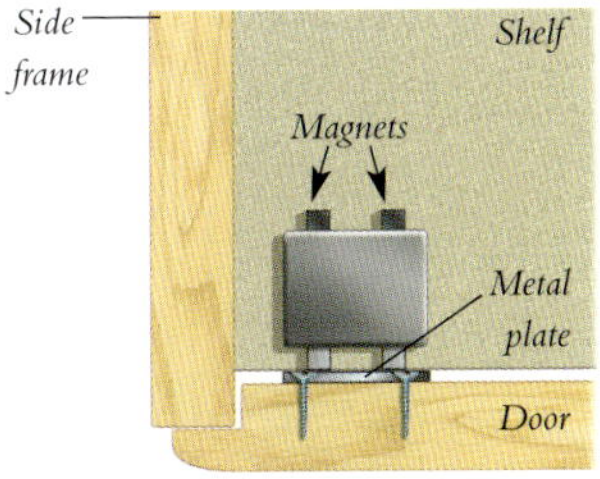

ABOVE A magnetic catch is easy to fit but you may need to use more than one on large doors.

Fitting Heavyweight Fixtures

Heavyweight fixtures around the home tend to be of a permanent nature. Items such as sturdy shelving for books, and cabinets, wall-mounted televisions and cabinet speakers are very heavy, need a lot of support and tend to remain where they are installed originally. For this reason, heavy wall fixings are designed to be permanent.

Obtaining a good fixing

A frequently encountered problem with heavy fixtures is obtaining a good fixing in masonry. A traditional method, which is quite acceptable, is to drill and plug a wall with home-made tapered wooden plugs, driven in hard, and then screw into them.

There are some useful commercial products, too, such as the rawl bolt, which expands inside the hole as it is tightened and will provide a secure fixing for heavy shelving or wall units.

Post anchors are another option, although they are designed mainly for vertical posts outdoors. Some are adjustable to take either 75 or 100mm (3 or 4in) posts and can be used horizontally to fix the frames for stud (dry) walling to concrete or stonework. Hanger screws are an easy method of fixing into woodwork to leave projecting studding, which can be used to secure heavy bookcases and room dividers, yet allow them to be removed simply by undoing the nuts.

Angle brackets

Many sizes of angle and straight steel bracket are available, and they have a variety of uses. Among them are fixing the top and bottom frames for wardrobes. They should be fitted inside the framing so that they cannot be seen. The top brackets should be screwed into the ceiling joists, which you might have to locate by prodding with a sharp tool through the plaster, while the floor brackets should be screwed directly to the floorboards. Much the same applies to fitting the sliding rails for the doors.

BELOW A selection of heavy-duty wall bolts.

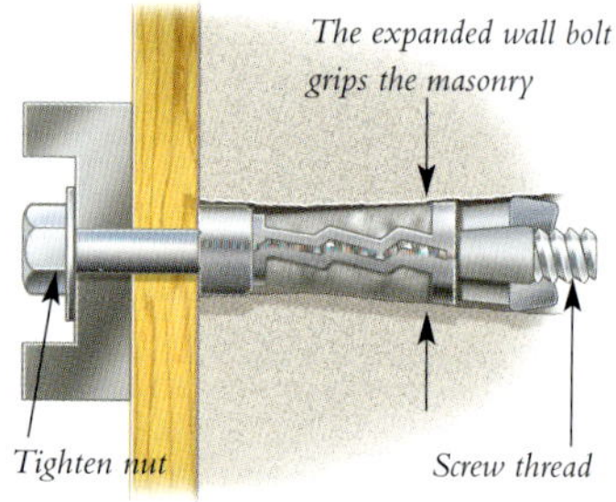

ABOVE How to fix a wall bolt.

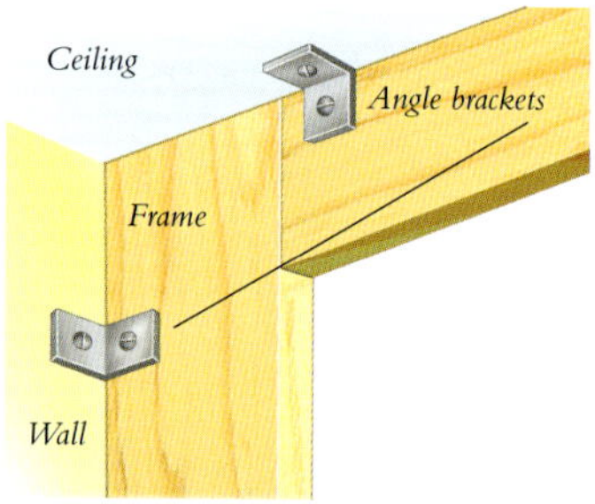

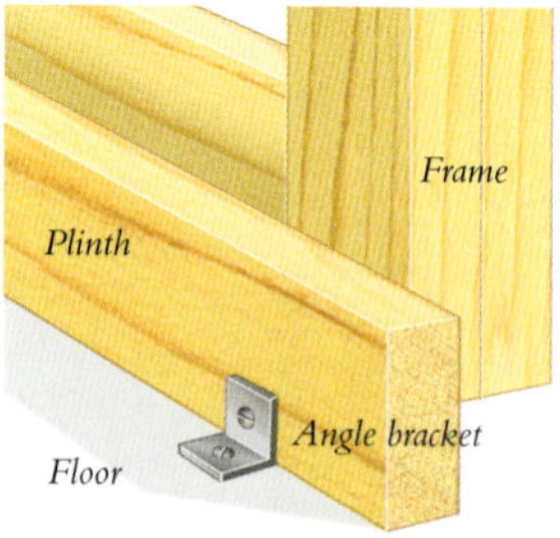

ABOVE Angle brackets positioned as above ensure stability and squareness.

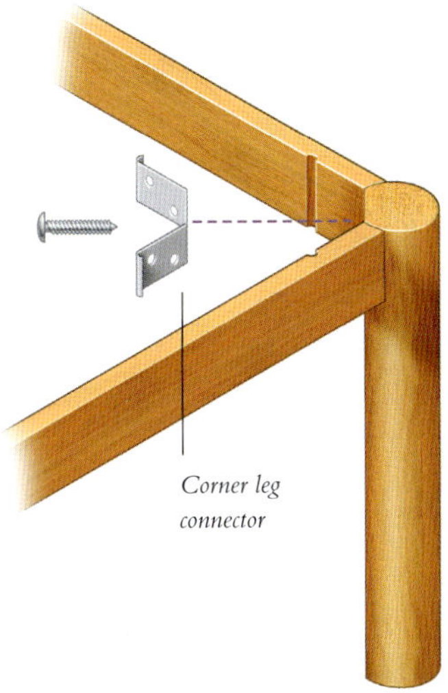

ABOVE Steel angle plates or brackets, or knock-down fittings, can be used to strengthen joints, as well as allowing a piece of furniture to be taken apart if required. These ingenious corner brackets are used to fix the detachable legs and connect the side rails at the same time.

Heavy-duty brackets

There are many heavy-duty brackets to choose from, making all manner of joints possible. One of the most frequently used in the home is the joist hanger. This may be nailed or screwed to an existing timber beam to carry flooring joists, very heavy shelving or similar constructions. Some joist hangers are designed to lip into brickwork. Simple angled plates can be used for bracing the frames of stud walls. They may be nailed or screwed in place. You can also buy heavy-duty fixings for putting up bicycles, racks and ladders in garages. Most are simply bent angle irons with pre-drilled holes.

Fitting a television shelf

In a small room, a television is best mounted in a corner, otherwise it will have to be fixed high on the wall, which will make viewing difficult. When installing a television (or microwave) shelf, always follow the manufacturer's instructions, but generally you should offer the backplate to the wall at the desired height, making sure the television can swing around to the angle required, and mark its position. Drill holes for the bolts, screw them into place and add the movable shelf. Position the television and arrange the wiring so that it will not tangle.

ABOVE A heavy steel bracket can be used for bracing a frame joint.

Steel angle brackets are usually pre-drilled

Heavy brackets (above and below) with multiple fixing options

BELOW A selection of heavy-duty brackets.

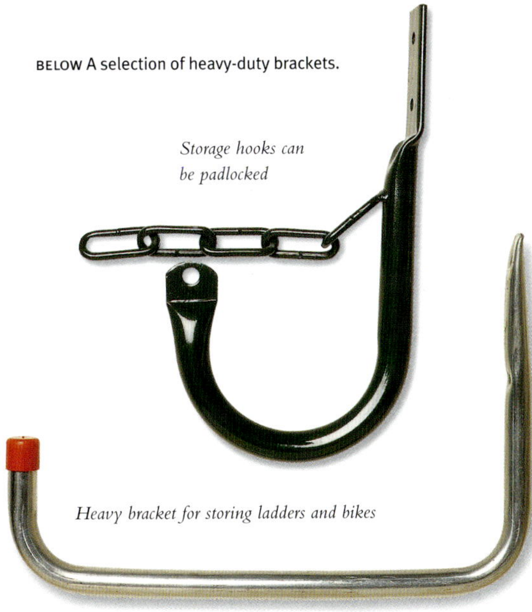

Storage hooks can be padlocked

Heavy bracket for storing ladders and bikes

Fitting Shelves

Putting up shelves is a fundamental do-it-yourself task, and is probably one of the first jobs the newcomer will tackle. With a little thought, shelving can be made to be decorative as well as functional, and a variety of materials, including wood, metal and glass, can be used to good effect. All require firm wall fixings and always use a spirit (carpenter's) level when fitting shelves.

Simple Shelving

Ready-made shelving systems can be employed, both wall-mounted and freestanding. The basic methods of fitting shelving are the same, no matter what material is used. Essential requirements are establishing a truly level surface with a spirit level, obtaining firm fixings in the wall, and being able to fit accurately into an alcove.

Use your spirit level to ascertain the height and horizontal run of the shelf, then mark the positions for the brackets. Mark the positions of the screws through the holes in the brackets, drill with a masonry bit and insert wallplugs. Hold each bracket in place and start all the screws into the wallplugs before tightening them fully. This will ensure that they engage properly.

If fitting more than one shelf on an uninterrupted run of wall, mark them out at the same time, using a try or combination square. Cut them to size, then screw them to the shelf brackets.

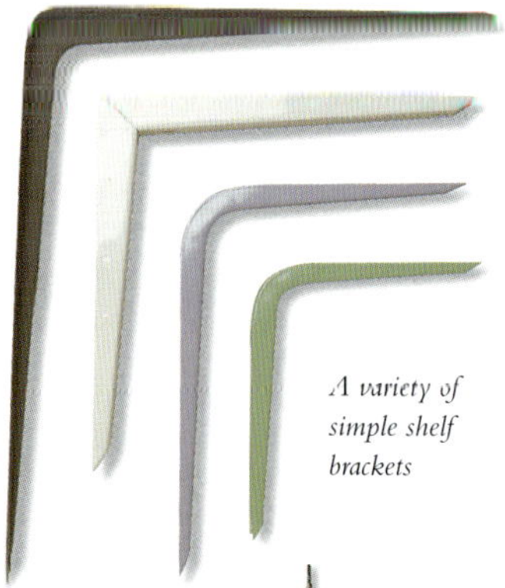

A variety of simple shelf brackets

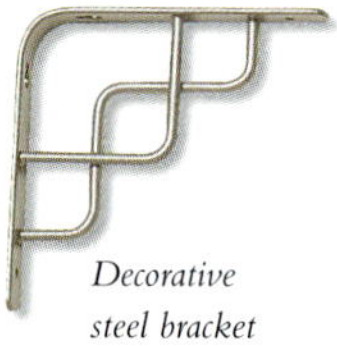

Decorative steel bracket

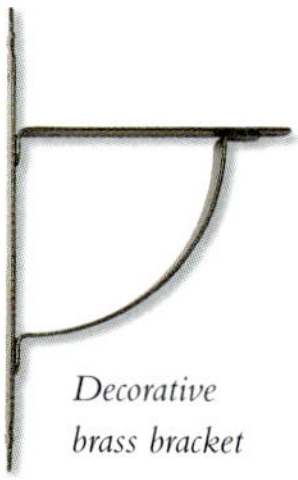

Decorative brass bracket

A variety of very lightweight plastic shelf fittings

Fitting a Simple Shelf

1 Mark the position of the shelf with a level placed on top of a batten (furring strip).

2 Mark the position of the screws through the bracket holes.

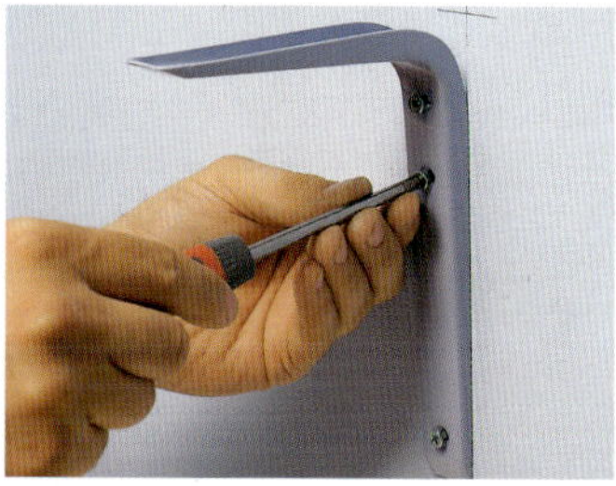

3 Drill and insert your plugs. Start all the screws before tightening up.

4 Screw up the bracket into the shelf to make a secure fixing.

5 You can also attach the shelf to the brackets before mounting the brackets to the wall.

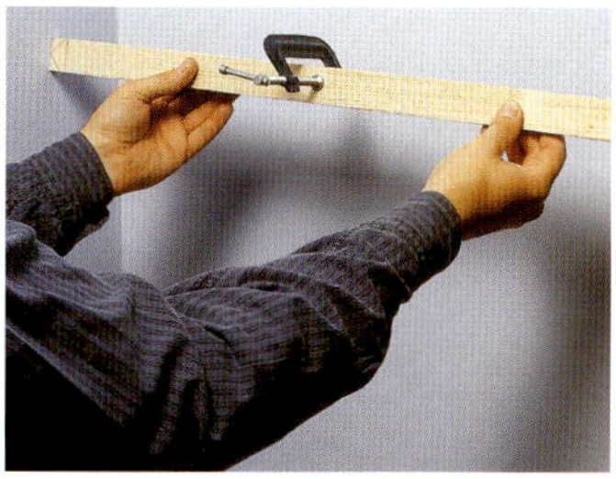

1 Use two battens (furring strips) clamped together to measure in a confined space.

2 Transfer the measurement on to the wood to be used for the shelf and cut to length.

3 Align the position and fit the rear shelf using a spirit level and screw in position.

Alcoves

An easy way to measure the internal width of an alcove is by using two overlapping strips. Allow them to touch each end of the alcove and clamp them together on the overlap. Transfer this measurement to the shelving material and carefully cut it to length.

Establish the position for the back batten with a spirit level. Drill and plug the holes, then screw the batten in place. Using the back batten as a reference point, fit the side battens to the end walls of the alcove.

Drill screw clearance holes in the shelf, place the shelf on the battens and screw it down. When fitting shelves into an alcove, do not cut all the shelves to the same size. If the sides of the alcove are plasterwork, brick or stone, there will almost certainly be some discrepancies in the width from top to bottom, so measure for each shelf individually and cut them separately.

If there is an uneven gap along the back of a shelf, caused by an uneven wall surface, you can hide the gap by pinning quadrant moulding (a base shoe) along the back edge of the shelf.

4 Drill the holes in the side battens and screw into place using the back batten as a guide.

5 Pre-drill the screw holes in the shelf and screw on to the side battens from the top.

Planning shelves

Think of how to make best use of the new storage space. Make a rough sketch of the plans, in order to take into account which items are going to be stored, such as the height and width of books, or the clearance that ornaments and photographs require. Aim to keep everyday items within easy reach, which in practice is between about 750mm (2ft 6in) and 1.5m (5ft) above the floor. Position deep shelves near the bottom so that it is easy to see and reach the back. Allow 25–50mm (1–2in) of clearance on top of the height of the objects to be stored, so that they are easy to take down and put back.

Think about weight too. If the shelves are going to store heavy objects, the shelving material must be chosen with care, since thin shelves will sag if heavily loaded unless they are well supported. With 12mm (½in) chipboard (particle board) and ready-made veneered or melamine-faced shelves, space brackets at 450mm (18in) for heavy loads or 600mm (2ft) for light loads. With 19mm (¾in) chipboard or 12mm (½in) plywood, increase the spacing to 600mm (2ft) and 750mm (2ft 6in) respectively. For 19mm (¾in) plywood, blockboard, MDF (medium-density fiberboard) or natural wood, the bracket spacing can be 750mm (2ft 6in) for heavy loads, 900mm (3ft) for light ones.

Fitting Shelving Systems

Storage can be provided in one of two ways. One is to buy or make pieces of freestanding furniture that match the required storage function. The other is to use raw materials such as wood and manufactured boards plus the appropriate hardware to create built-in storage space, arrays of shelving, closets in alcoves, wardrobes and so on.

Buying shelving systems

Shelving systems abound in do-it-yourself stores for those who prefer simply to fit rather than to make the shelving. There is a range of brackets on the market to cater for every need, and these clip into slotted uprights screwed to the wall. The bracket positions can be adjusted to vary the spacing between the shelves to accommodate your needs.

Shelving systems are a versatile way of dealing with changing requirements, and they have the distinct advantage of being portable when you need to move them. They are capable of holding heavy weights, but remember that ultimately a shelf's capacity depends on the strength of the wall fixing employed.

First measure the distance between the shelving uprights, bearing in mind the thickness and material to be used for the shelf. Books can be very heavy, so do not set the uprights too far apart, otherwise the shelf will sag in the middle. About a quarter of the length of the shelf can overhang each end. If necessary, cut the uprights to length. Drill and plug the wall so that you can attach one upright by its topmost hole. Do not tighten the screw fully at this stage. Simply allow the upright to hang freely.

Hold your spirit level against the side of the upright, and when you are satisfied that it is vertical, mark its position lightly on the wall with a pencil. Mark in the remaining screw positions, then drill and plug the rest of the screw holes.

Fitting a shelving system

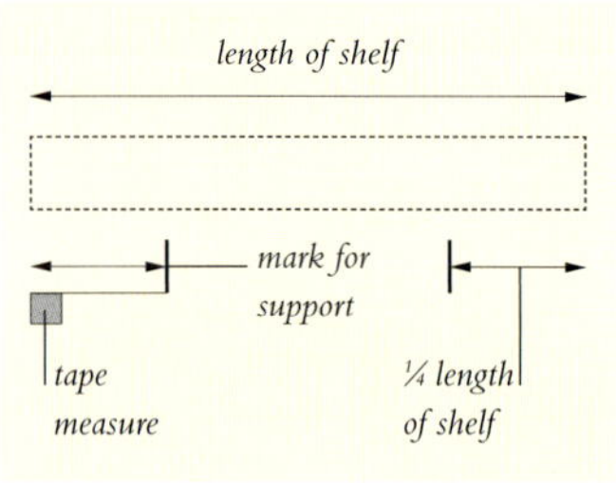

1 Measure the distance between the uprights. Do not set the brackets too far apart.

2 Fix the first screw loosely and let the upright hang.

3 Check the bracket is absolutely vertical with a spirit level.

4 A little packing card may be necessary if the wall is uneven.

5 Mark the position for the second upright using the first as a guide.

6 The shelf brackets can be inserted at different heights and can be easily moved.

You may find that when you tighten the screws, the upright needs a little packing here and there to keep it vertical in the other plane. If these discrepancies are not too large, this adjustment can be done by varying the relative tightness of the screws, which will pull the upright into line. You can mark off the position for the second upright and any others, using a spirit level on top of a shelf with a couple of brackets slipped into position. Fitting the second upright entails the same procedure as before.

ABOVE A well-organized shelving arrangement for a wardrobe system.

Freestanding shelving

These shelving units usually come packed flat for home assembly. They can be very useful and versatile pieces of furniture. They are available in a variety of materials, including pine, manufactured boards and metal. Knock-down joints are often used in their construction.

There is a possibility that boisterous children could pull freestanding shelving over, so it is worth attaching a unit to a wall, if only temporarily until the children are a little older. This can be done with a couple of brackets screwed and plugged to the wall, or with brackets to the floor.

LEFT Knock-down joints are used primarily in symmetrical structures to ensure squareness.

Practical tips

- If there is a gap along the back of a shelf, caused by an uneven wall, you can hide the gap by pinning quadrant moulding (a base shoe) along the back edge of the shelf.
- Select screw sizes according to the load that a shelf will take.

Corner units

A popular form of shelving, corner units represent an efficient way of using what otherwise might be redundant space. They can be made from plywood with some form of lipping applied to the front edge to hide the laminations, or they can be quite ornate and made in an expensive hardwood. Cut the triangular shelves so that the angle at the apex, which fits into the corner, is slightly over 90 degrees. This will ensure that the front edges touch the wall where they will be seen. Mirror plates provide a neat, unobtrusive means of fixing corner units.

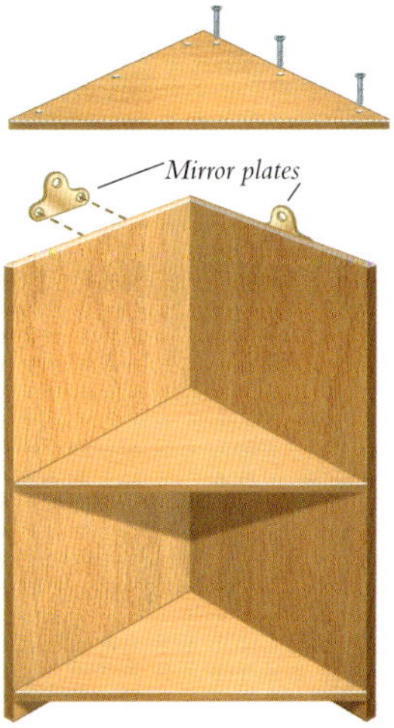

ABOVE Mirror plates hang the cabinet rather than pinning it to the wall.

Hanging Doors

Installing a new door is not a difficult task, but the job does need patience, precision and organization to go smoothly. A methodical step-by-step approach will pay off. The following sequence relates to hanging a new door, and you may only need to trim some of the door. If you are fitting an old door or simply moving one, advice is given in an earlier section of the book.

Types of door

Many modern internal doors are hollow structures with "egg box" centres and solid timber lippings around the edges. They offer little flexibility for trimming to fit frames that are out of square, which often occurs in an old building. For this reason, as well as for aesthetic appeal, use only solid doors in older houses.

Putting in a new door

Measure the frame accurately, top to bottom and side to side, then choose a door that will fit as closely as possible. Even so, it will probably need to be cut to fit.

Joggles, or horns, may project from the ends of the door to protect it in transit. Mark these off level with the top of the door, using a try square. Place the door on a flat surface and carefully cut the joggles flush with the ends of the door, using a hand saw. Offer up the door to the frame, placing wedges underneath (chisels are handy) to raise it off the floor by about 12mm (½in) to allow for a carpet or other floorcovering.

Mark the door in pencil while it is wedged in place to allow for a 3mm

Hanging a door

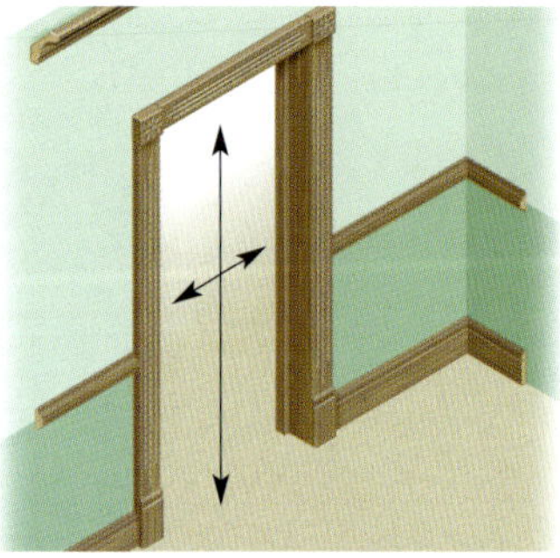

1 Measure the door frame to assess the size of the door you require.

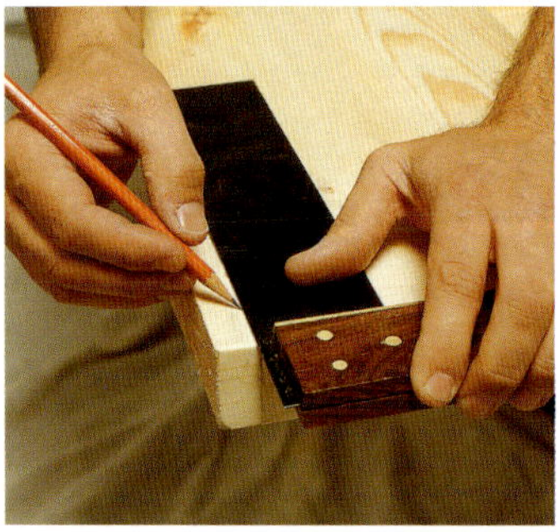

2 If there are joggles, square them off accurately using a try or combination square.

3 Remove the joggles with a hand saw making a clean, square cut.

7 Plane the edges, working in from both sides. Offer the door into the frame to check it fits.

8 Lay the hinge on the door and cut around it with a sharp knife.

9 Alternatively, scribe the outline of the hinge on to the door with a marking gauge.

(⅛in) clearance at the top and sides. Place the door back on the flat surface and saw off the bulk of the waste, leaving the marked lines still visible. Plane down the sides of the door to the marked lines, working with the grain, then plane the top, working in from each side to avoid splintering the wood. Replace the door in the frame, wedging it once more to hold it. If you are satisfied with the fit, you can hang it.

Hold each hinge in position, about 150mm (6in) from the top and 225mm (9in) from the bottom of the door, with the knuckle projecting just beyond the face of the door; mark it with a knife. For a heavy door, a third hinge will be needed, positioned centrally between the other two. Working around the marked outline, cut vertically down into the wood to the depth of the hinge flap with a chisel.

Make a series of cuts across the width of the recess, to the same depth, and remove the waste with a chisel. Place the hinge in the recess, drill small pilot holes for the screws, but fit only one screw at this stage. Repeat with the other hinge.

Open the hinges and offer the hinge side of the door to the frame, placing wedges under it to raise it to the correct height. Press the free flap of each hinge against the frame and mark around it in pencil. Cut the recesses. Drill pilot holes and hang the door, again fitting only one screw in each hinge flap. When you are satisfied with the fit and operation of the door, insert all the screws, making sure that the heads lie flat in the countersinks of the hinges, otherwise the door will not close properly.

Practical tip

- When hanging a door, you'll need someone to help with positioning.

4 Offer the door into the frame. Use a wedge to square up if need be.

5 Mark the clearance on to the frame using a pencil and a 3mm (⅛in) washer as a guide.

6 Saw off the bulk of the waste using your knee as a support on the end of the door.

10 Chop out the waste with a sharp chisel working along the scribed line.

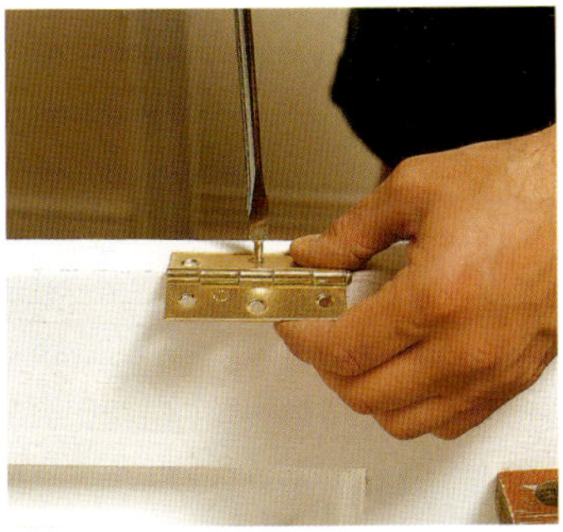

11 Insert the hinge into the recess and screw up tightly.

12 Mark the other part of the hinge on to the door frame with a pencil.

Replacing Cabinet Doors and Drawers

Old and tired-looking cabinets can often be revived by a coat of paint, the addition of stencilled patterns or the application of decorative laminates, however, sometimes the only way to revive them is to renew the doors and drawer fronts themselves. This is neither a complex nor very expensive job and it can be fun to do.

Replacing chipboard doors

This may also be necessary if the hinges have failed in chipboard doors, which can occur with kitchen furniture after a number of years because of its heavy workload. If you replace old chipboard doors with new ones, they must be exactly the same size and be hung in the same way as the originals, since they cannot be trimmed to fit. Doors such as these are readily available, along with the chipboard hinges necessary to fit them. It is important to ensure that the hinge positions are perfectly accurate and that their recesses are of the correct depth, so careful measuring and a reliable drill stand or pillar drill is essential.

Remove the old door from the hinge baseplates by slackening each retaining screw, not the adjuster, and sliding the door off. Then release the two retaining screws and remove each hinge from the door, leaving a circular hole.

Place the new door over the old one so that the top edges are aligned, then measure down to the centre of each hole. Next measure to the centre of each hole from the edge to locate their positions exactly.

ABOVE Revive tired-looking kitchen cabinets with a new coat of paint or new doors.

Use a combination square as a gauge to take the centre position from the old door and transfer it to the new one. Mark the positions of the hinge holes on the new door with a centre punch. Bore the hinge recesses with a pillar drill or a drill mounted in a drill stand for accuracy. Be sure to set the stop to the correct depth.

Insert the hinges, making sure they are square to the edge of the door and screw them in place. Replace the door, using the adjustment screws to obtain a perfect fit with the face of the unit.

Replacing a door

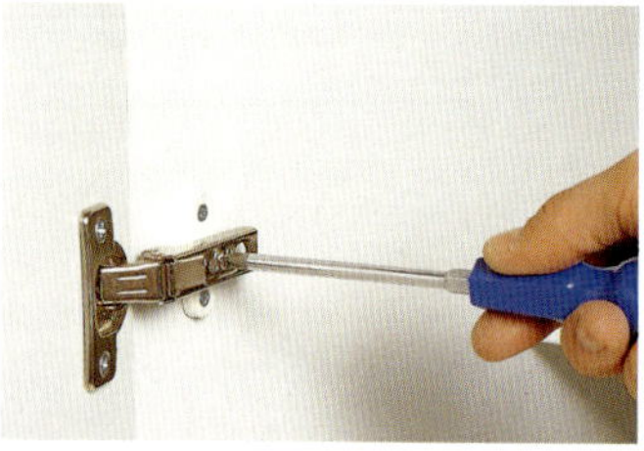

1 Take off the old hinge simply by unscrewing it from the side.

2 Measure accurately from the edge of the old door to the hinge hole.

3 Transfer the mark to the new door to ensure a perfect position for the new hinge.

4 Drill out a new hole, preferably using a static drill stand for accuracy.

5 Attach the new hinge in the same position on the new door as the old.

Replacing a drawer front

1 Remove the old drawer front by unscrewing it from behind.

2 Drill the new front using the existing holes as a guide.

3 Screw the new drawer front into position from behind.

Drawer fronts

The drawers of modern furniture are often made with false fronts that allow a basic carcass to be used in a number of different styles. To replace, open the drawer or, better still, remove it completely. From inside the drawer, slacken the screws holding the false front to the carcass and remove it. Place the old front over the new one, aligning it exactly, drill down through the screw holes and into the new front to make pilot holes for the screws. Take care not to drill right through the new face and spoil the finish. Use a depth stop to prevent this. Finally, screw the new front to the carcass from the inside.

Practical tip

- When fitting screws in hardwood doors, always drill pilot holes for them, otherwise it may be impossible to drive them in completely. Brass or small gauge screws may even snap.

Fitting a louvre door

1 Fit a flush hinge to the door. Surface mounting makes this easy.

2 Screw a magnetic catch beneath the bottom shelf of the cabinet.

3 Screw a magnetic catchplate to the door, both the top and bottom.

4 Change the handle or knob to suit the style of your door.

Fitting solid wood doors

With solid-timber-framed cabinets, an attractive option is to fit louvred doors, which are made of solid timber and are available in a host of standard sizes.

Fitting louvre doors, or other solid wooden doors, to cabinets follows the basic procedures for hanging any door. First fit the hinges to the inside of the door, then open the hinges and fit them to the cabinet stile. Note that fitting a cabinet door with butt hinges is only recommended for solid timber framing.

Cabinet doors can be fitted with a variety of handles and knobs to suit the style of furniture. Often, changing the handles alone can improve the appearance of a cabinet considerably. A small brass handle, for example, makes a nice finish or use stainless steel for a modern look.

Replacing Wall-mounted Boards

Skirting (base) boards receive a lot of wear and tear from scuffing by feet and furniture, which is why they are there in the first place, of course. From time to time, the damage may be so great, such as after replacing flooring, including woodstrip or laminate flooring, that sections of skirting or even complete lengths of it need to be replaced.

Types of boards

Skirting boards may vary from simple rectangular sections of timber to quite ornate moulded profiles. Similarly, picture rails and dado rails, sometimes called chair rails because they protect the walls from damage by chair backs, may need to be renewed or repaired. In many ways these tasks are similar.

Dealing with corners

When fitting a moulded shape with concave curves into a corner, the correct way to achieve the joint is to scribe it. This is done by marking the profile of one board on to the back of the other with the aid of a small offcut of the moulding. Then a coping saw is used to cut along the marked line, allowing the board to fit neatly over its neighbour. This technique avoids the mismatch of ends that can occur when some mouldings are mitred at 45 degrees, using a mitre box or mitre saw. However, to cut an external mitre for a wall return, use a mitre saw or mitre box in the normal way.

Skirting board

In a rectangular room, it is always best to fit the two long sections of skirting board first and then fit the shorter ones to them. It makes handling, lifting and fixing much easier. To fit the boards, first prise the old board partially away from the wall, using a crowbar (wrecking bar), then insert wedges to hold it far enough away to allow you to get at it with a saw. Place a mitre block

> **Practical tip**
>
> • Many skirting boards are fixed with flooring, or cut-nails, which are square-edged and grip extremely well. Almost certainly they will split a small section of replacement skirting, so use masonry nails instead and drill pilot holes in the skirting.

Replacing a section of skirting board

1 Prise away the old skirting board with a crowbar (wrecking bar) and a wedge.

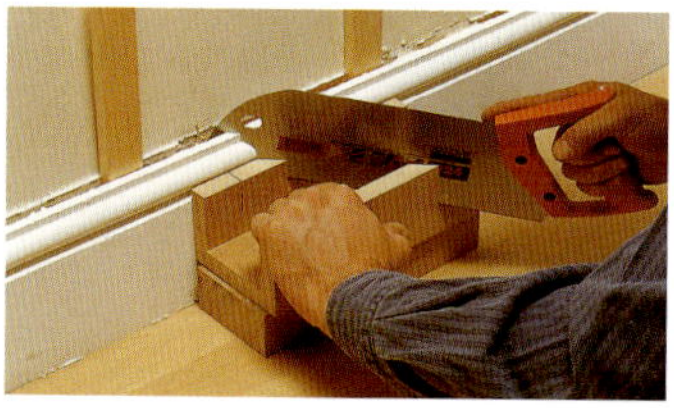

2 Cut away the damaged section with a mitre box and a saw.

3 Mark each end of the new section of board and mitre the ends.

4 Hammer nails into the new section of board while holding a plank against the wood.

ABOVE Internal and external mitres of a skirting board.

1 Prise away the old rail from the wall using a crowbar.

2 Remove any residual nails in the wall or plaster with a pair of pincers.

3 Fill any cracks or holes in the plasterwork with filler.

tight against the board and, with a tenon saw, nibble away at it at 45 degrees until the board is cut in half. Repeat the 45-degree cut at the other end of the section to be replaced and remove the length of old skirting. Then offer up the replacement section, mark each end with a pencil and mitre accordingly.

A good way to hold the new section in position is to lay a plank so that it butts up against the skirting and kneel on it while driving the nails home.

REPLACING A PICTURE OR DADO (CHAIR) RAIL

Use a crowbar to prise the old picture rail away from the wall, inserting a block of wood under its head to protect the plaster and to give extra leverage.

Remove any nails that remain in the wall with a pair of pincers, again using a block of wood to protect the wall. Make good the nail holes with filler, leaving it slightly proud at this stage. When the filler is completely dry, sand it down with abrasive paper wrapped around a cork block or block of wood to give a perfectly flat, smooth surface. Fit the new picture rail, scribing or mitring the ends as necessary.

4 Sand off the dry filler with abrasive paper to get a smooth finish.

5 Fit the new rail to the wall, making sure it is properly level.

FIXING METHODS

Cut-nails, such as those used to fix skirting boards, have long been used to fix picture rails, Delft rails and the like, but you may find that they are not available in your local store. Any ordinary wire lost-head nail is a good alternative when fixing through plasterwork into stud (dry) walling, as long as you know where the studs are.

CUTTING A SCRIBED JOINT

Use a scrap of the board as a guide. Grip a pencil against the scrap of wood and run it down the surface of the back of the board to transfer the outline. Cut it out with a coping saw.

Working with Mouldings

A moulding is the term used to describe any section of wood that has been shaped, either by hand or by machinery, to alter the square profile of the original piece. This may range from rounding over the sharp edges of the finished work to adding more decorative detail. Alternatively, profiled cutters can be fitted in a router to make your own mouldings and create a range of decorative effects.

Cutting angles

In most applications, mouldings are not difficult to fit, but there is a small range of handy aids that make cutting accurate angles a simple process. The most basic of these is the mitre box or block. Essentially, this is a small jig with slots, in most cases cut to 45 and 90 degrees since these are by far the most commonly used angles for saw cuts. The slots hold the saw blade at the correct angle for making the required cut through the moulding. Normally a tenon or backsaw is used. More complex is the hand mitre saw, the blade of which can be set to any required angle, although usually stops are provided for the most commonly used ones: 90, 45 and 22.5 degrees.

This tool can be used for cutting mouldings, lippings, architraves (trims), picture rails and skirting (base) boards. The most sophisticated aid is the powered mitre saw, which will do all that the hand mitre saw can do and cut compound mitres as well. These saws produce perfectly angled cuts and are often used by picture framers.

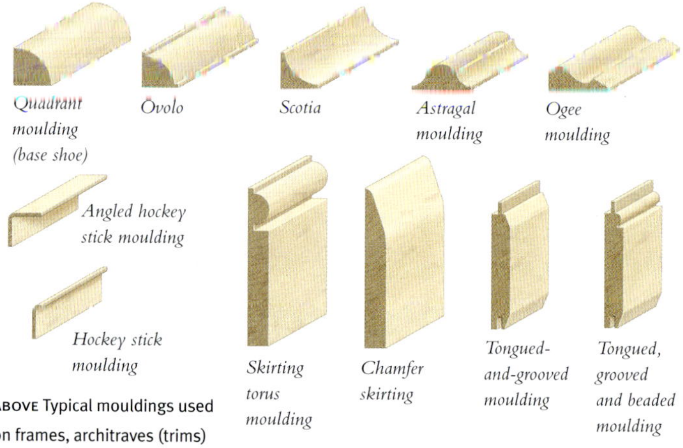

ABOVE Typical mouldings used on frames, architraves (trims) and skirting (base) boards.

Fitting a shelf moulding

1 Using a try or combination square, check that the edge of the board is square.

2 Cut the mouldings at 45 degrees to go around the edges of the board.

3 Glue and fix the mouldings to the board with masking tape. Leave overnight to dry.

4 Clamp the board and carefully clean up any rough edges with a plane.

Fitting a moulding without nails

Small-section mouldings can often be fixed with glue rather than nails. First, establish that the edges of the panel to which the mouldings will be attached are true, using a try square. Cut the mouldings to length, mitring the ends at 45 degrees.

Fitting an architrave (trim) around an internal door

1 Remove the old architrave with a crowbar (wrecking bar).

2 Scrape away any old filler or paint from the face of the frame.

3 Measure the internal door frame width and cut the top of the architrave. Mitre the ends.

4 Pin the new piece of architrave in place about 6mm (¼in) above the bottom of the top member.

5 Measure, cut and fit the side pieces of architrave and pin in position.

6 Any gaps between the mitres can be filled with wood filler and sanded down.

Attach the mouldings to the edges of the panel using wood glue and hold them in place with masking tape. Alternatively, special edging clamps are available that grip the panel and allow pressure to be applied to the moulding.

When the glue has dried, trim the moulding with a plane, or sand it, so that it is flush with the panel.

Fixing mouldings

Generally speaking, it is wise to drill pilot holes in hardwood mouldings before nailing, especially when fixing close to the ends, since small-section hardwoods, especially ramin, which is often used, will split readily.

Softwoods are far more forgiving, and it is unnecessary to drill a softwood architrave (trim) before nailing. Simply drive the nails in, punch the heads below the surface, and fill before finishing. Panel pins (brads) or lost-head oval wire nails are the preferred fixings for architraves: they should be spaced at intervals of 230–300mm (9–12in).

Typical applications

Mouldings are ideal for improving the appearance of a fireplace surround, which is usually the focal point of a room. Metal brackets holding the mantel shelf can be hidden with cornice (cove) moulding, while half-round nosing applied to the front of the shelf will soften the overall effect.

Fitting internal architraves

The range of mouldings includes larger-section profiles such as architrave, which can be ornate. Fitting architrave is fairly straightforward. Measure the internal width of the door frame and mark out the top piece of architrave so that its bottom edge is 12mm (½in) longer. Mitre the ends at 45 degrees, using a mitre box or mitre saw, so that the top edge is longer than the bottom.

Pin the top piece of architrave to the top of the frame so that it projects by an equal amount each side and is 6mm (¼in) up from the bottom edge of the top frame member. All architrave should be set about 6mm (¼in) back from the inside edge of the door frame.

Measure for each side piece separately, as they can vary quite considerably over the width of a door, especially in older houses. Cut each to length and pin in position.

Fixing Cladding

Wooden cladding may be fixed to walls and ceilings for a variety of reasons. These include: cosmetic, to hide the existing finish; acoustic, to deaden sound; and thermal, to insulate against heat loss. Sometimes cladding has a structural quality, for example, when it is part of a stud (dry) wall, in which case all three qualities may be desirable.

Types of cladding

Cladding can take the form of manufactured boards such as chipboard (particle board), plywood and hardboard, often faced with either melamine in coloured patterns or imitation woodgrain, or wood veneers. It can also be solid timber such as shiplap or tongued-and-grooved, V-jointed boards, which come in different profiles, widths and thicknesses.

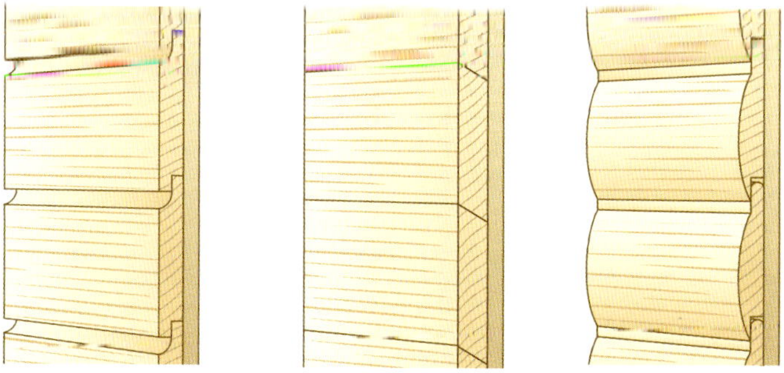

ABOVE Cladding comes in a range of profiles and can be fixed to a framework of battens using nails, screws or adhesive.

Basic requirements

Cladding is only as good as the framework to which it is attached, so it is essential to ensure that any wall is solid and properly prepared with a framework of battens (furring strips), or that a sturdy stud frame is built before proceeding. The positioning of battens and studwork, both vertically and horizontally, is critical when using standard sheets of manufactured board. Each sheet should finish in the middle of a frame member to allow the adjoining sheet to butt against it for nailing. Allowing for likely cable positions, if any, is also advisable.

It is recommended that any wall cladding affixed to the inner surface of an exterior wall should be fitted with a barrier of building paper and insulation material, such as glass fibre, during construction.

Battening a wall

Drill pilot holes in the battens for the masonry nails, as this will prevent the wood from splitting, if it is a thin section. Hammer the masonry nail home at one end. Level the batten with a spirit level and drive home the nail at the other end. Finish by driving in more nails along the length of the batten. If the wall is crumbly, you may prefer to attach the battens with screws and wall plugs. The security of the battening is essential for a good job.

RIGHT Finish the sheet of manufactured board in the centre of the stud.

ABOVE The framework of battens has to be tailored to suit the size and position of obstacles such as doors, windows and electrical fittings. Shown are positions for vertical cladding (left) with a likely cable point and batten positions and for horizontal cladding (right).

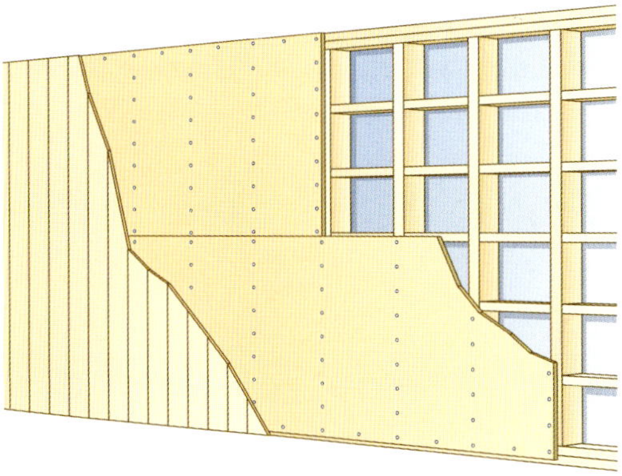

ABOVE Plywood panelling fitted to stud walling with an optional intermediate backing board. Note how the sheets finish in the middle of the studs.

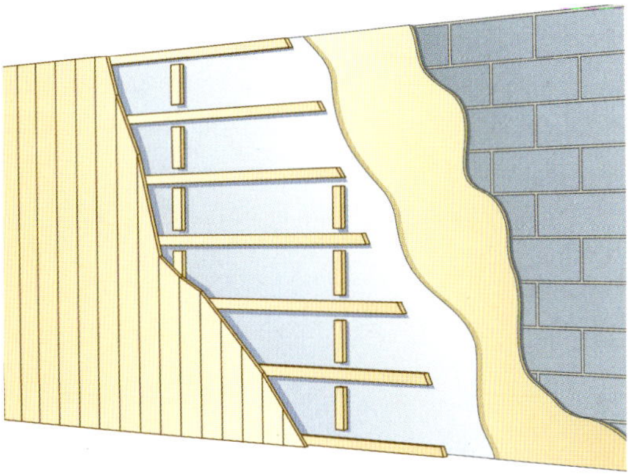

ABOVE A section showing plywood cladding fixed to battens that have been attached to a masonry (plaster and brick) wall.

Fitting sheet panelling

Cladding can be fixed to the framework of battens (furring strips) using either nails or screws. If screws are used, especially brass ones, a feature can be made of them, so they should be equally spaced in a pattern formation.

Alternatively, a panel adhesive can be used for fixing cladding. Apply this to the battens and push the sheet firmly into place. If it fails to adhere immediately, tap nails part way through into the battens. The nails can be removed when the panels are secure.

To cut cladding, use either a hand saw or power saw. If using a hand saw, have the decorative face uppermost and cut on the downstroke to limit the chances of damaging it. With a power saw, turn the decorative face of the wood downward. Ensure that the cladding is resting on a firm, level surface. Before using the saw, score the cutting line carefully using a straightedge as a guide. If you need to leave a perfectly straight edge to a cut sheet, where it is to be butted up against another board, then clamp a straightedge to the board as a guide for the saw.

After cutting, use a fine abrasive paper wrapped around a wood or cork block to smooth down the rough edges.

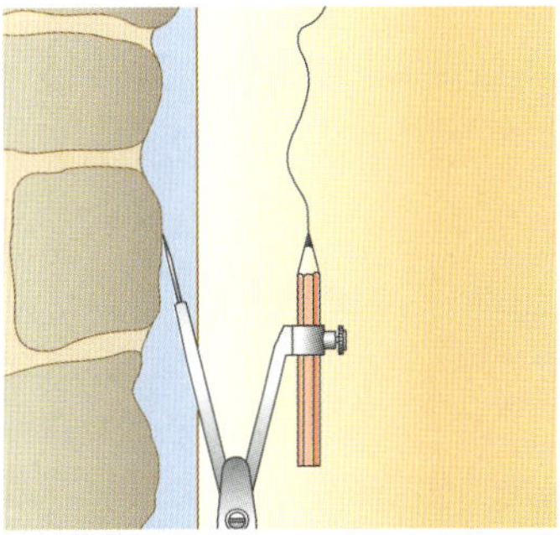

ABOVE A pair of compasses is useful for scribing the edge of a panel where it butts against an uneven surface such as stonework.

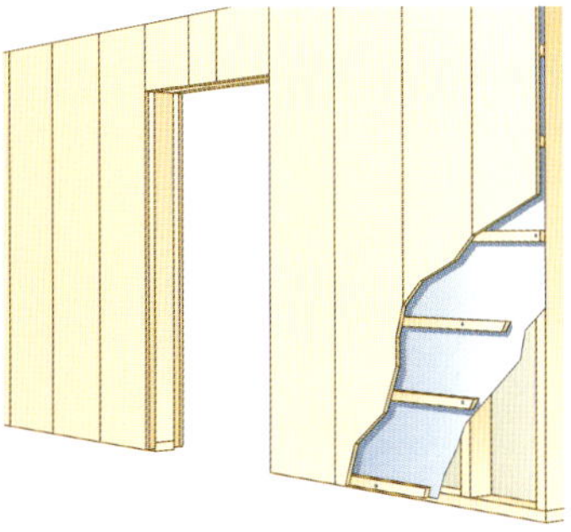

ABOVE Work from each end of the surface to be covered, using cut panels in the middle to retain symmetry.

Foot fulcrum

Using two pieces of wood as a foot fulcrum, pivoting one on top of the other, simplifies holding a panel off the floor for fixing. Wedges can be used, but they are not as versatile.

TONGUED-AND-GROOVED BOARDING

Fitting tongued-and-grooved boarding is more time-consuming than using sheet materials, but the supporting framework can be made simpler because the boards are relatively narrow and rigid. As with all cladding, it is essential to ensure that the battens (furring strips) are laid securely, and are reasonably spaced for adequate support.

TYPES OF BOARDING

For vertical boarding, only horizontal battens (furring strips) are required; for horizontal boarding, vertical battens are needed. The spacing of the battens is not critical unless you intend having staggered joints in alternate rows of boarding, in which case you must make sure that a batten runs beneath each joint position to allow for fixing.

You can also fit boarding in diagonal patterns, which is not too difficult, but it pays to keep things simple by using only 45-degree angles. This can be done in several well-known configurations.

Tongued-and-grooved, V-jointed boards are usually referred to as TGV, and a common size is about 9 x 100mm (⅜ x 4in); allowing for the loss of the tongue in the fitting, each board covers an area about 90mm (3½in) wide. Various decorative profiles are available.

Shiplap is normally heavier. A typical size is 12 x 121mm (½ x 4¾in), the actual coverage being about 110mm (4⅜in). TGV is usually fixed by secret nailing. Panel pins (brads) are driven diagonally through the base of the tongue and into the framework. Decorative surface nailing can also be used.

Mouldings are commonly used to finish around the edges of cladding. For example, quadrant beading (a base shoe) can be pinned in internal corners, while simple square or hockey-stick beading will fit around an outside edge. Both TGV and sheet materials can be used for cladding ceilings. Battens (furring strips) can be fixed directly to the joists above through the ceiling, or a suspended framework installed to support the cladding and lower the ceiling at the same time. This treatment can be attractive, help to conserve heat and add a feeling of cosiness to a room.

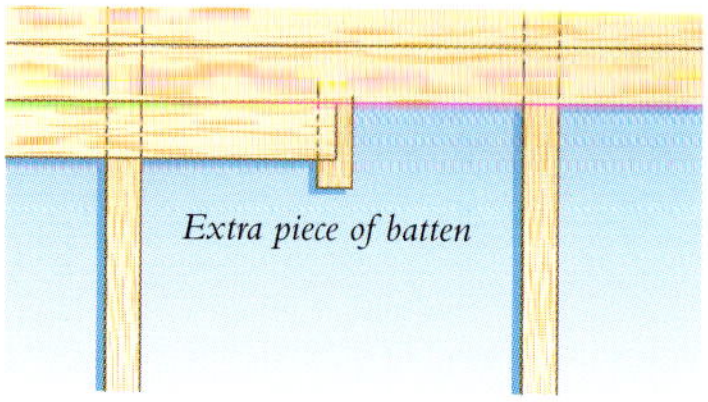

ABOVE Add in an intermediate batten to pick up any short boards.

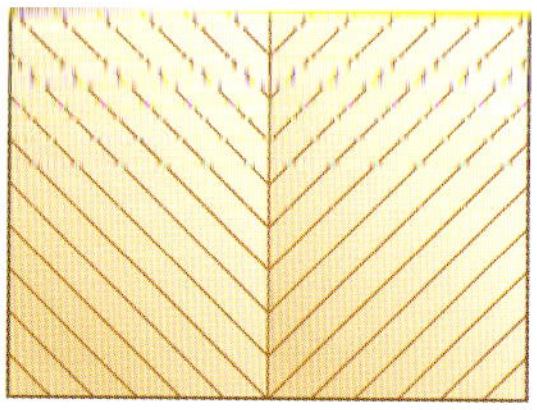

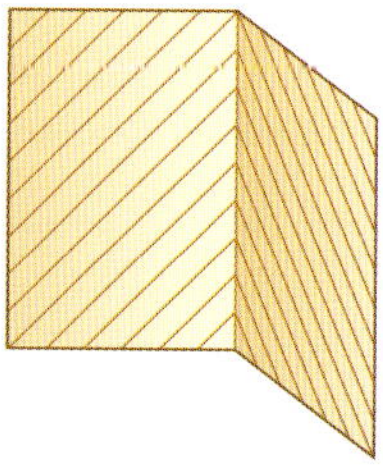

LEFT AND ABOVE Three different options for diagonal cladding.

PRACTICAL TIP

- With a soft or crumbly plaster wall, it is often better to hack off the old plaster and attach battens (furring strips) straight on to the brickwork, rather than try to fix into it. On good flat plaster, battens can be fixed with adhesive.

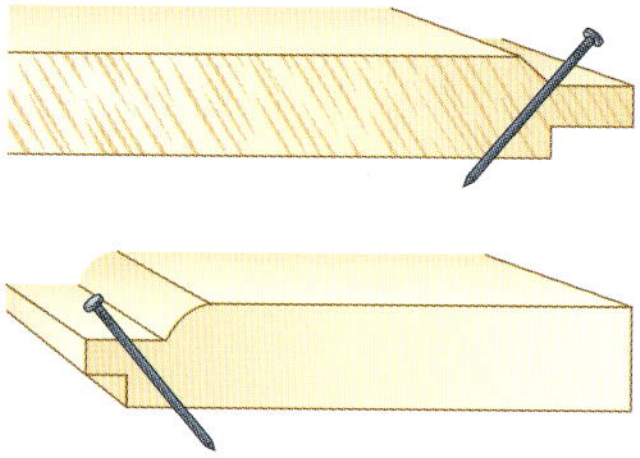

ABOVE Secret nailing through the tongue of the board.

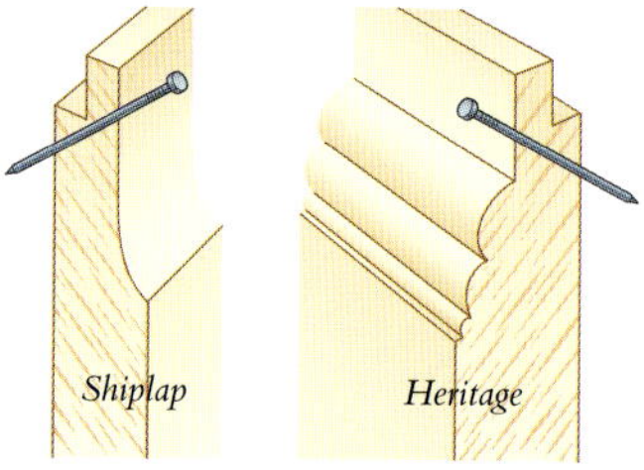

ABOVE Nailing below the tongue can be done when the overlap of the next board is greater.

Fitting the boarding

First, square off the end of the board to ensure that it is at 90 degrees, or 45 degrees if required. Mark off the length of board required with a utility knife or pencil and cut it to size with a tenon saw. Place the board in position on the battens, making sure that the tongue is left exposed for the next board to slot over, and in the case of TGV that the correct face side with the chamfer is showing. Secret nail the board with panel pins. Repeat this procedure with the remaining boards, tapping each firmly home with a mallet and an offcut of the wood to prevent damage to the tongue before nailing. Leave the second to last board slipped over the previous tongue, but before nailing, use an offcut and pencil to scribe the cutting line on the final board if it needs trimming to fit. Cut and plane the board to width. You might need to fit the last two boards by springing them into place, in which case, both will have to be nailed through the face, since the tongues will not be accessible. Punch the nail heads down and fill.

Fitting cladding

1 Tap fixing nails into each support strip at 300mm (12in) intervals. Check that it is level and drive in the nails.

2 If the walls are out of true, insert slim packing pieces between the strips and the wall to keep the faces of the strips level.

3 Scribe the wall outline on to the face of the first board by holding its grooved edge to the wall and running a block and pencil down it.

4 Fix the boards by interlocking their tongued-and-grooved edges and driving nails through the exposed tongue of each board.

5 When fixing subsequent boards, close up the joints by tapping the board edge with a hammer. Protect the board edge.

6 Saw or plane the final board down to the required width and spring the last two boards into place. Secure the last board.

7 Neaten internal corners by pinning or gluing a length of scotia (cove) moulding into the angle. Use this at ceiling level too.

8 Butt-join the two boards that form an external corner, and conceal the joint with a length of birdsmouth (corner bead) moulding.

Boxing-in Pipes

Some people regard visible pipes in the home as an eyesore, but with a little time and minimal woodworking skills they can be hidden successfully from view – and completely concealed if the boxing is decorated to match the room. Be sure to allow for the box work to be easily removed in situations where it may be necessary to gain access, such as around valves.

Accessibility

Bear in mind that stopcocks, drain taps, pumps, hand-operated valves and the like will need to be readily accessible and require some form of removable box system. For this reason, the boxing around them should be assembled with screws rather than nails. If a panel needs to be regularly or quickly removed, turn buttons or magnetic catches are a good idea.

Boxing basics

Steel anchor plates and screws can be used to secure the sides of boxing to walls, and these will be easy to remove when necessary. Battens (furring strips), either 50 x 25mm (2 x 1in) or 25 x 25mm (1 x 1in), can be used to fix boards at skirting (base) board level. Disguise the boxing by decorating it to match the rest of the room. If pipework is running along a panelled or boarded wall, construct the boxing so that it follows the general theme, using similar materials and staining and varnishing the boxes accordingly.

Wall pipes

Measure the distance the pipes project from the wall, taking account of any joints and brackets. Cut the side panels from 25mm (1in) board slightly over this measurement and to their correct length. Fix small

Boxing-in wall pipes

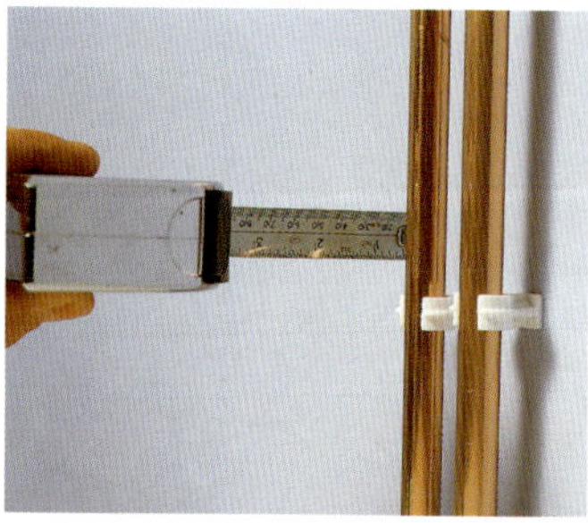

1 Measure how far the pipes protrude from the wall.

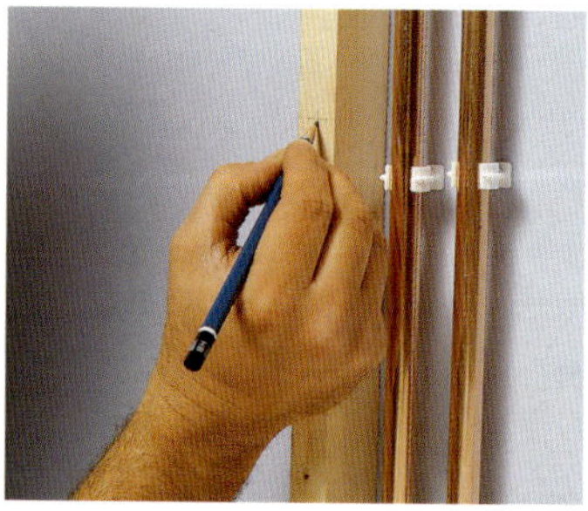

2 With a pencil, mark the positions for the side batten fixings.

3 Attach the side battens, screwing them firmly into position.

4 Cut the front panel of the box to size with a jigsaw. Use 6mm (¼in) MDF.

5 Drill pilot holes and screw the front panel into position, using 19mm (¾in) No. 6 screws.

6 Trim the edges of the front panel with a block plane.

anchor plates flush with the back edge of each panel and spaced at about 600mm (2ft) intervals.

In plywood, you may need to drill pilot holes. Hold the panels against the wall and mark the positions of the screw holes on the wall. Drill the holes and fix the panels to the wall with rawl plugs and screws.

Cut the front panel to size from 6mm (¼in) plywood. Drill evenly spaced screw holes in the front panel and fix it in position with 19mm (¾in) No. 6 screws. Use cup washers under the screw heads to protect the panel if it is likely to be removed often. Trim the edges flush with a block plane.

Floor pipes

Screw battens to the wall above the skirting (base) board and to the floor at the correct distance from the wall to clear the pipes. Screw a 25mm (1in) thick board to the floor batten so that it is level with the top of the wall batten, using 37mm (1½in) No. 8 screws. Fit a 6mm (¼in) plywood top panel to the wall batten and top edge of the front panel with 19mm (¾in) No. 6 screws. Trim the edge flush with a block plane.

When boxing-in pipes at floor level, you may prefer to use a section of skirting board for the front panel. This will help blend the boxing into the overall room scheme.

Waste pipes

Often, where a house has had an extension added, it is possible that the waste-water pipe from a first-floor bathroom will have to be run to the main waste-water drainpipe via a route that will take it across the ceiling line of the ground floor of the extension.

The main problem here is one of noise, as the sound of the waste water flowing away will be clearly audible. In a case like this, the best course of action is to muffle the noise by using 12mm (½in) thick plywood for the boxing, and encasing the pipe by using fibreglass insulation material within the box.

Boxing-in floor pipes

1 Attach wall and floor battens at the correct distance to clear pipes at 60cm (2ft) intervals.

2 Fix the front board to the floor batten, level with the top of the wall batten and screw up.

3 Add the top board and screw into position so that it can be easily removed.

4 You may find it better to use a piece of moulded skirting (trim) to match the room.

Practical tips

- If you intend using solid wood for boxing-in pipes, try to store it in the room in which it will be used, lying flat, for about two weeks before starting work. This will condition it to the room, helping it remain straight and resist further shrinkage when close to hot pipes. Plywood and MDF (medium-density fiberboard) are stable boards.

- Chipboard (particle board) is not a suitable material for boxing-in. Most of the fixings will be close to the edges and its crumbly nature will cause problems; use plywood, MDF, softwood or hardboard for top panels.

- If a panel has to be removable for access, use dome cup covers to conceal the screws.

Wood Finishing

Although there are many techniques for finishing wood, a number of basic steps are common to all of them. Carry out preparation work well away from the finishing area, and be prepared to move the work back and forth several times as you apply and rub down successive coats. Remember that any finish on wood will enhance defects as well as good points, so preparation is important.

Preparation

Not often mentioned is the fact that wood must be dry, regardless of the treatment applied. Another requirement is that when several applications of a finish are called for, they must be rubbed down, or "flatted", between coats.

Many different types of wood will need filling. This can be as simple as rubbing in a grain filler, which will give a more even and less absorbent surface. It may involve using a wood filler, which can be bought to match the colour of the timber being used, to fill cracks, blemishes and knot holes. Soft interior stopping is fine for tiny cracks, and a two-part exterior-grade wood filler for making-good large holes.

The tools required for finishing are simple, and most of the work can be done entirely by hand. A few scrapers, some sandpaper in various grades, wire (steel) wool, soft cloth, a cork sanding block and some filler or stopping are the basic requirements.

LEFT *(Clockwise, from top left)* Wire (steel) wool, filler, spatula, soft cloth, sanding block, a selection of abrasive papers and cabinet scrapers.

Typical finishing processes

Apply any filler that is necessary to knot holes and blemishes in the wood, allow to dry and remove the excess gently with a chisel. With this done, the wood can be rubbed down with sandpaper wrapped around a cork block, working along the grain.

Wipe over the surface with a clean, damp rag to raise the grain very slightly, allow it to dry, then cut it back lightly with 400-grit sandpaper, again working along the grain. If you want to stain your timber, test the stain on a spare piece of the same wood to check the final colour and depth.

Remember that end grain will absorb a lot more of the stain and will be much darker. Stain can be applied with a soft cloth or brush. Keep a wet edge all the time to avoid a patchy finish. Apply the stain in short circular motions.

Filling in wood

1 Apply filler to match the colour of the wood. Cut away any excess with a sharp chisel.

2 Sand down with sandpaper wrapped around a cork block, working along the grain.

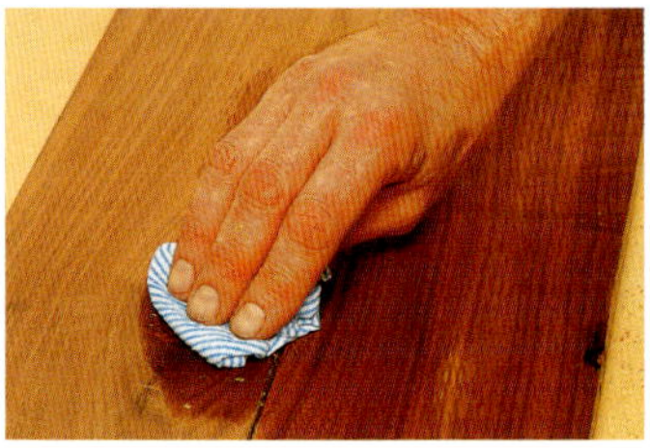

3 To remove dust, wipe down with a soft cloth, using long strokes parallel to the grain.

Applying stains and varnish

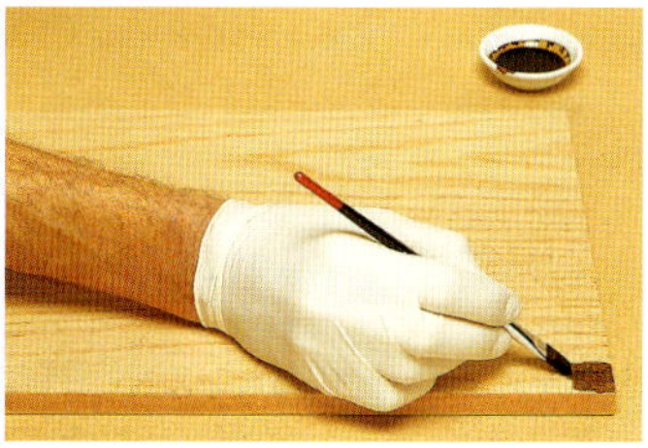

1 Use a small brush to test the colour. Dilute the stain when treating end grain.

2 If satisfied with the colour, apply the stain with a soft cloth in quick, circular motions.

1 For large panels, use a wide brush to apply varnish using long strokes.

2 Rub down the surface using 320-grit silicon-carbide paper, varnish and repeat.

Varnishes, such as polyurethane, or acrylics, which are quick drying, should be applied along the grain with a soft brush. Be sure to get into all corners and recesses but do not leave pools of liquid. Make sure there are no runs, allow to dry and flat down with 400-grit sandpaper or a fine grade of wire wool.

Wax and oil finishes

With the wood sanded down, apply a coat of sanding sealer, lightly rubbing it down when dry. This gives a good base for the oil or wax. Apply the wax or oil with a ball of fine wire (steel) wool, using a circular motion to work it well into the grain. Polish off with a soft cloth.

Types of stain

Take care when you are choosing wood stain to ensure that the type of stain is compatible with the finish. The colour is often labelled according to wood species, such as pine, mahogany or oak. This can be misleading, as the result depends on the base colour of the wood to which it is applied. Test the colour on a small piece of scrap wood.

Practical tip

- Varnish is best applied in a cool environment: otherwise problems with a "ripple" finish can occur.
- To achieve a better finish with wax and oil, build up layers slowly.

Waxing wood

1 Apply a thin coat of clear shellac to provide a stable base for the wax. Leave to dry.

2 Apply the wax with a ball of fine wire (steel) wool in a strong circular motion.

3 Buff the wax vigorously with a polishing pad made from a soft duster. Add more coats.

DECORATING

Starting a new decorating project is always an exciting time. Once all the clutter has been cleared away, you have a blank canvas on which to imprint your unique ideas. You can follow current design trends or let your imagination guide you.

Paint Preparation

Proper groundwork is essential for decorating. Never be tempted to cut corners, as the results will be disappointing. Indeed, preparatory work may sometimes take longer than the time spent on painting, but by paying attention to detail in the early stages the whole decorating process will be made much easier and you will achieve a more professional finish.

ABOVE Keep all your tools and equipment close to your work area.

Preparation

Start by giving yourself room to manoeuvre. Clear the room of as much furniture as possible, pack away ornaments, and remove curtains, shelves, mirrors and pictures. Large items of furniture should be moved to the middle of the room and covered with dust sheets (drop cloths) to protect them from splashes.

Use masking tape to protect light switches and the like from paint droplets, and cover radiators with dust sheets. Old bed sheets are good for protecting the floor; plastic dust sheets should be avoided, as it is easy to slip on them. Keep all your tools and equipment close to hand as a lot of time can be wasted if you need to make excursions to other rooms to find essentials. It will also help to choose a stepladder with an integral tray for holding paint cans and small tools. Alternatively, you can buy a clip-on metal hook to hold a paint can securely.

ABOVE Use masking tape to protect light switches and fittings from paint splashes.

Basic procedures

For the best results, surfaces to be painted must be clean, even and blemish-free. If plasterwork is damaged beyond repair, you may have to consider a professional replastering job. New plasterwork must be allowed to dry for at least four to five weeks, then a plaster primer or PVA adhesive (white glue) thinned with water should be applied before the area can be decorated. If a new-plaster emulsion (latex) paint is used, painting can take place almost immediately.

Plasterboard (gypsum board) surfaces should be primed initially, or painted with a thinned coat of emulsion paint before applying the top coat. Cracks and gaps in plasterwork must be filled with a general-purpose filler. Apply it so that it is slightly proud of the surface, then sand smooth when dry. Tiny cracks and scratches will usually disappear when you apply a standard emulsion. Tackle large holes by applying the filler in a series of layers, allowing each to dry before applying the next one.

Practical tips

- Always wear safety goggles when you are cleaning ceilings to prevent any detergent from splashing into your eyes.
- Old properties may have been decorated with lead paint. Take great care when removing this finish. Never use a heat gun to strip off lead paint. For safety, use wet abrasive paper when sanding down to keep dust levels to a minimum, and wear a face mask.

If you are working on walls that have been painted before, wash them thoroughly with a solution of sugar soap (all-purpose cleaner), then rinse with tepid water and allow to dry. Lightly sand the surface to provide a key before applying the new coat of paint. Clean the ceiling with a long-handled mop and detergent mixed with water. Rinse with clean water.

Scrape off flaking or blistered paint with a wallpaper scraper, then sand lightly and remove all traces of dust before applying a new finish. If there is mould growth on the walls, wash the area with a detergent solution and also treat with a fungicide before painting. If the area remains untreated, stains will soon show through the new paintwork.

Older properties may have been decorated with distemper, which is powdered chalk mixed with water and size. Before over-painting, brush away any dust or debris and seal with a stabilizing primer.

Ideally, all old wallcoverings should be removed before painting. Often, however, sound paper surfaces can be covered successfully. Do not attempt to paint over a vinyl wall-covering: it peels off easily to leave a ready-made lining paper in place. Start at the bottom of each length and loosen the top layer at each corner. Pull the vinyl firmly toward you and work steadily upward, removing as large a section as possible. Remove stubborn fragments of vinyl with a scraper.

Large cracks

Use a paintbrush to remove dust from large cracks prior to filling, then rinse and work the damp bristles into the crack to promote good adhesion.

ABOVE Ensure filler adheres well in deep cracks or holes with careful preparation.

Preparing walls and ceilings

1 Strip wallcoverings with water or steam and scrapers. Peel off the top layer of vinyl types.

2 Remove flaking paint with a narrow or wide-bladed scraper.

3 Fill any cracks and gaps in plasterwork with all-purpose filler.

4 Sand the filled area smooth when dry with a fine abrasive paper.

5 Give the walls a thorough wash with a solution of sugar soap (all-purpose cleaner).

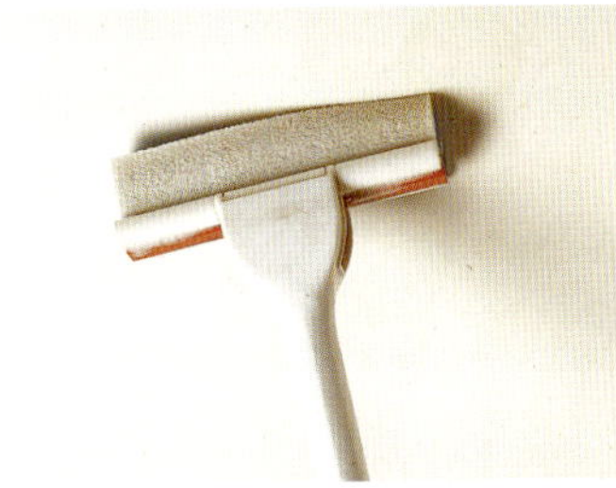

6 Use a squeegee mop to clean ceilings so that you can work at ground level.

Brushes, Rollers and Pads

Paint, whether water-based or oil-based, can be applied with brushes, rollers and paint pads. Each has its advantages and disadvantages, but all have a place in the decorator's tool kit. It is important to use the correct application techniques in order to get the best out of your equipment. Look after your tools, cleaning and drying them as described here, and they will last for a long time.

Brush techniques

Use a thin, straight piece of wood to stir the paint thoroughly, unless it is a non-drip variety. Decant about a third of the can into a paint kettle (pot), which will be lighter and easier to work with than the can itself. Dip the brush into the paint to about a third of the length of the bristles, and remove any excess by dabbing lightly inside the container. Start at the top of your work area and use light, criss-cross strokes for good coverage when using emulsion (latex) paints. Emulsion paints can dry very rapidly, resulting in hard edges. Work quickly and use the "laying off" technique to prevent this. Simply complete each application with feathery, upward strokes. These should blend into the fresh paint when you start again.

Oil-based paints take longer to dry and require a different technique: start by painting a series of vertical lines, then blend them together with an almost dry brush. This should prevent any joins from showing.

Cleaning brushes

First remove excess paint by scraping the brush with a spatula or knife. Cold water is all you need to remove water-based paints: simply hold brushes under a running tap and wipe clean with a cloth.

Oil-based paints are more difficult to remove. Decant some white spirit (paint thinner) or paint cleaner into a jar and leave the brush to soak. Drilling a hole through the handle allows you to suspend the brush in the white spirit so that the bristles are clear of the sediment that collects in the bottom of the jar. Finally, clean it with soapy water, then rinse well and dry with a cloth.

ABOVE Always clean your brushes thoroughly.

Using a roller

For speed of application, a paint roller is the natural choice. However, it cannot deal with corner details and edges; you will need to paint these areas with a small brush before tackling the main job. Fit the roller with a suitable sleeve. Then pour a small amount of paint into the deep section of the roller tray, dip in the roller and run it lightly over the raised section. Do not overload the roller. Apply the paint in a zigzag pattern, keeping the roller in contact with the surface all the time. A common mistake is to let the roller rotate rapidly as you finish a section; this will send out a shower of paint.

Cleaning rollers

First, run the roller over newspaper to remove excess paint. Then use cold running water to remove water-based paints, and white spirit or brush cleaner for solvent-based

Practical tips

- A small roller, typically 100mm (4in) long, is excellent for painting doors and similar areas.
- Aim to complete a whole wall in one session for a seamless, professional look.

Using a paintbrush

1 Dip the first third of the brush in paint, and wipe off the excess.

2 Finish the area of painting with a light, upward stroke.

Using a brush and roller

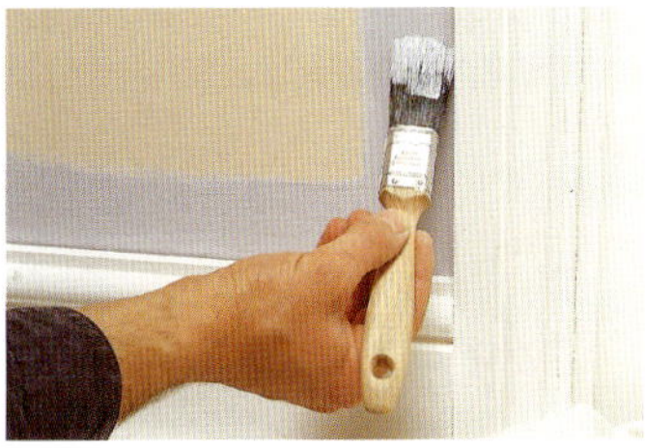

1 Use a brush to cut in around the edges of walls and ceilings, where a roller cannot reach.

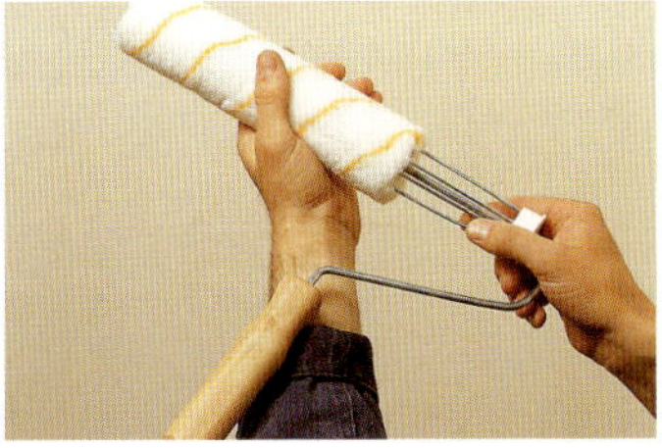

2 Slide your chosen roller sleeve on to the roller cage.

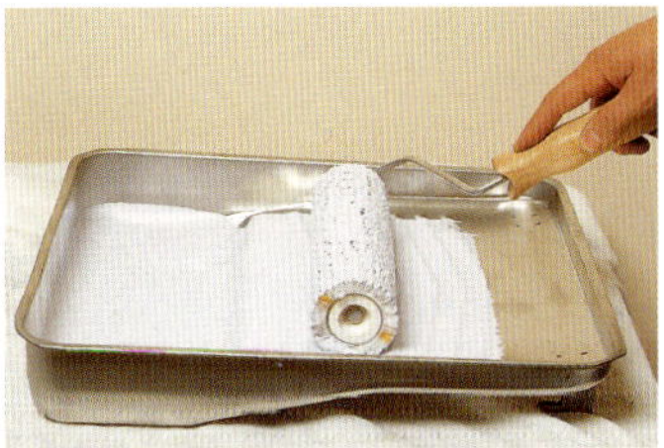

3 Load the roller with paint and then run it over the raised section.

4 Apply the paint in a zigzag formation and do not lift the roller as you work.

Mess-free trays

A easy way of keeping a clean roller tray is to line it with aluminium foil before you use it, then lift it out and discard it when you have finished.

Clean the roller as outlined here and in accordance with the type of paint used and the manufacturer's instructions.

Above Use foil to line the tray and there will be less mess to clear up afterwards.

paints. In the latter case, finish off with soapy water and leave to dry.

Painting with pads

Paint pads tend to apply a thinner coat than rollers and brushes, but they give rapid results and are good for covering large areas. Pads are usually sold with their own tray, but you could pour some paint into a roller tray. If you are using a special pad tray, run the pad over the integral roller. Alternatively, run it over the shallow section of the tray. Wipe off excess paint before you start. Keep the pad in contact with the wall and move it lightly in a criss-cross pattern.

Cleaning pads

A pad can be cleaned in the same manner as a roller, depending on the type of paint being used. Do not leave it to soak in a jar of brush cleaner or water, however, as the fibre pad could separate from its backing. Store the paint pad in an upright position to dry.

Using a paint pad

1 Apply paint to the paint pad and remove the excess on the integral roller.

2 Use a small paint pad to cut in around the edges of the walls and ceiling.

3 Fill in with a larger pad, applying paint in a criss-cross pattern.

Painting Ceilings and Walls

If you are planning to paint a room completely, there is a logical order to follow. The basic technique is to start at the top and work down, with the exception of cornices, which, if they are to be painted a separate colour, need to be completed at a later stage. By breaking a room into workable sections you will do the job more efficiently and create the minimum of mess and disruption.

Ceilings

For obvious reasons, start with the ceiling to avoid rivulets of paint running down freshly painted walls. Then paint the walls and finally the woodwork, such as window frames and doors. Skirting (base) boards and floors are last on the agenda.

The simplest and quickest way to paint a ceiling is with a roller on an extension pole, allowing you to remain at floor level for the majority of the work. First, however, the edges of the ceiling will need to be cut in with a paintbrush, working from a stepladder.

If you prefer to be nearer the ceiling, a work platform is a good idea. For a reasonable outlay, you can hire a platform and support trestles or a mobile workstation with locking castors that can be moved to wherever you need it. Alternatively, place a strong plank between two stepladders.

LEFT It is best to paint ceilings in bands from one wall to another.

If the original paintwork is sound, wash thoroughly and let it dry. Any staining should be treated at this stage with a primer/sealer. First, paint a border around the perimeter of the ceiling with a small brush. To make the most of the available light, start from a corner close to a window area and work inward.

Paint in strips from one wall to another, then back, working quickly so that the edges do not have time to dry. If you prefer a brush to a roller or pad, make sure that it is at least 100mm (4in) wide. Use a small cutting-in (sash) brush around features such as light fittings and ceiling roses. Complete the work in

ABOVE Platforms supported by trestles are a safe way to paint from a height.

LEFT A moveable workstation simplifies the process of painting ceilings and high walls.

ABOVE Use a small cutting-in (sash) brush to paint around light fittings.

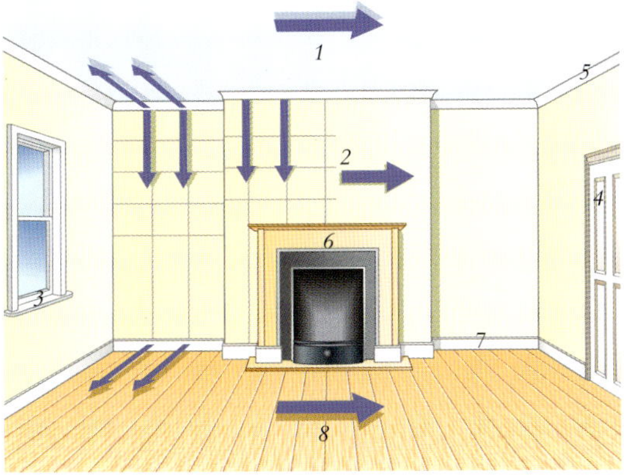

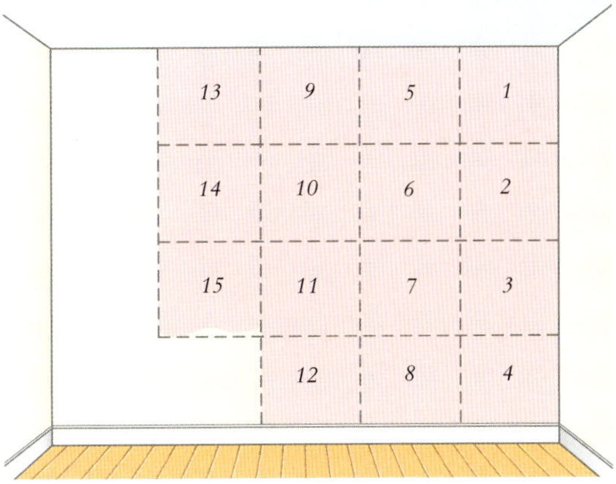

one session to avoid hard paint lines that will show in the finish. Then apply a second coat when the first is dry, unless using a one-coat product.

Walls

As with the ceiling, start in the lightest corner of the room, working from the top of the wall down. If you are right-handed, begin on the right-hand side of the wall, or the left if you are left-handed.

When you are using a roller, paint horizontal strips across the wall, but still using the zigzag technique, take care to blend them carefully to avoid join marks. With a brush, paint in vertical blocks around 600mm (2ft) square, and complete an entire wall before taking a break.

ABOVE Pale colours, such as blue or pale lilac, can make a room look larger.

Textured paints

When walls and ceilings have lumpy or uneven surfaces, consider using a textured paint to hide the irregularities. Essentially thick versions of emulsion (latex) paint, they may tear into delicate foam rollers, so they are best applied with a brush or dense-pile roller. You can buy a range of rollers designed for use with this type of paint to create textured patterns such as diamonds and stripes. On the negative side, textured paint finishes can be difficult to clean and remove.

Practical tips

- Cover your head and wear goggles if you are using a standard emulsion (latex) paint on a ceiling. Alternatively, use a non-drip version to reduce splashes.

- Use colour to create visual illusions in your room. A deep shade on the ceiling will appear to reduce the height, whereas a light shade will have the opposite effect. A dark colour on the walls will make the room seem smaller; a light shade will create the illusion of space.

ABOVE LEFT The correct order to paint a room.

ABOVE Mentally divide each wall into a grid and paint one area at a time as shown.

ABOVE Textured paint finishes can create a variety of effects.

Decorative Paint Effects

Why settle for plain, "flat" paintwork, when you can create an attractive effect with a decorative paint finish? The beauty of paint effects is that they can be used on a variety of surfaces, including walls, ceilings, furniture and floors. Even beginners need not feel apprehensive about tackling the most popular techniques, and there are special paints and tools available to make the job easier.

Sponging

This is a simple technique. It works well with emulsion (latex) paints and oil-based glazes. A natural sponge will give a more subtle effect than a synthetic type.

Begin by applying a base coat with a standard emulsion paint and allow to dry. Soak the sponge in water, then squeeze out as much moisture as possible. Select a second emulsion for the top colour – it is best to choose one that is similar in tone to the base coat. Pour a little of the emulsion into a tray and dip in the sponge. The overall effect should be as subtle as possible, so wipe off any excess paint on the raised area of the tray or a clean sheet of paper.

Start at the top of your work area and begin dabbing paint on to the base colour. Turn the sponge around as you work to vary the effect, aiming for a continuous pattern with no "rivers" of base coat showing through. Once this coat is dry, you can add a second if desired. Up to four additional colours can be added to give depth, but make sure you do not obliterate the base colour.

Colourwashing

This gives a natural, almost transparent, look to walls and is relatively easy to do. You can either buy a ready-made glaze for the top coat or create your own. There is no set rule as to which tools to use – a roller, brush or a cloth can give equally good results. Apply the base coat, using an eggshell finish if you intend adding an oil-based glaze on top. When the undercoat is dry, dip a brush into the topcoat and wipe off the excess with a cloth. Apply the paint in random, sweeping movements over an area of about 1sq m (11sq ft) at a time. The overall effect is meant to be uneven, so do not be too concerned by irregularities. Go over the whole wall with a dry paintbrush to soften the appearance.

Practical tips

- Wash decorating sponges regularly; dried paint is very difficult to remove.
- Stencil cards have a limited life, so make copies of your favourites.
- Try two effects on one wall: for example, sponging below a dado (chair) rail and stencilling above.

Using a natural sponge

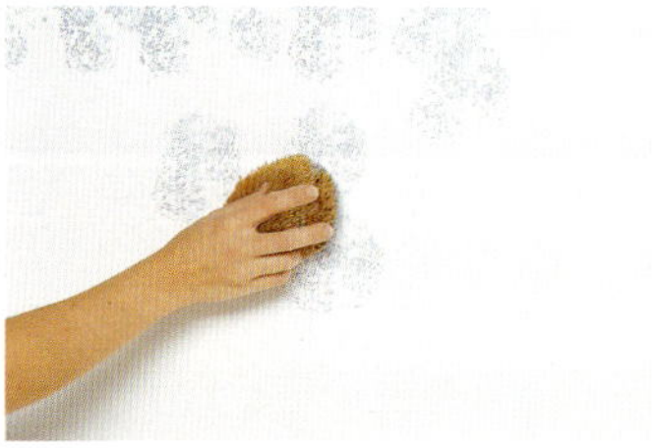

1 Dip the sponge into the paint and scrape off any excess. Lightly dab on the paint.

2 Add more paint, continuing to work over the surface. Fill in any gaps.

Sponging two layers

1 Apply a single layer. When you apply two colours, the second layer softens the effect. Allow the surface to dry completely.

2 Wash the sponge out. Dip it into the second colour paint. Do not over apply it as the first layer must not be totally covered.

Colourwashing two layers

1 Mix the paint using 50 per cent emulsion (latex) paint and 50 per cent wallpaper paste (premixed to a thin solution).

2 Continue painting over the whole surface. When the first layer is completely dry, repeat step 1 using a second colour of paint.

3 Add more paint and soften the joins. The overall colourwash effect will be much softer than when using just one colour.

Stencilling

This does not require a great deal of specialist equipment; many of the items used are commonly found in most households, but it is worth investing in a good stencil brush. The ends of the brush should be flat and the bristles firm.

If you buy ready-made stencils, most of the hard work is done. However, it's fun to make your own stencils, and useful too, should you need to make a copy of a pre-cut one that is wearing out. You can apply the paint with a brush or sponge. Proper stencil brushes have short, stiff bristles and are used with a dabbing action rather than a brushing motion, ensuring that the paint does not creep under the edge of the stencil.

To apply the stencil, draw a pencilled guideline at the midpoint of the wall. Place the stencil on this and secure it with masking tape. Pour a small amount of paint into a saucer or shallow tray. If using a sponge, moisten it with water, then squeeze it almost dry. Lightly coat the sponge with paint, then wipe off the excess.

Start painting at the outside of the image with either the sponge or a stencil brush and work toward the centre, dabbing the paint on with light, even touches. It is better to build up the colour gradually than to use too much paint initially. Gently lift one corner of the stencil to monitor your progress.

When you have completed the pattern, carefully remove the stencil and reposition it to your left or right. Continue in this way until you have completed the stencilled pattern. Wait for the paint to dry before adding subsequent colours.

Transferring a stencil template

1 Place a piece of tracing paper over the design and draw over it with a hard pencil.

2 Turn over the tracing paper, and on the back rub over the lines with a soft pencil.

3 Turn the paper back to the right side. Carefully draw over the original lines using a hard pencil.

4 Place the stencil on to a cutting mat or piece of thick cardboard and tape in place. Use a craft knife or scalpel to cut it out.

Ragging, Dragging and Stamping

Many paint effects require the minimum of tools and special equipment. To try ragging techniques, you simply need a clean rag and a choice of water- or oil-based paints. Beginners should start with ragging on, ragging off and stamping, before progressing to the more challenging techniques of rag rolling and dragging, as confidence grows.

Ragging

There are three different ways of creating an attractive mottled effect with rags: ragging on, ragging off and rag rolling. Each is fairly easy to do, but the last requires steady hands to achieve the best results. A light base colour with a deeper shade of paint on top is a popular choice for these methods. You can use an eggshell base topped by a glaze, or emulsion (latex) paints for both base and top coat.

Using the ragging on technique

1 Pour your choice of paint into a roller tray. Scrunch up a rag, dip it into the paint, wipe off any excess and dab the rag on to the wall.

2 Continue rescrunching the rag and dabbing it on to the wall until the wall has an even cover of paint.

Ragging on

Paint on your chosen base coat and let it dry. Mix 50 per cent emulsion paint with 50 per cent water or wallpaper paste in a paint kettle (pot) or pour a small amount of the top coat into a paint tray. Scrunch up a rag or chamois, dip it into the paint and dab off any excess on the side of the tray, then apply to the wall with a light dabbing motion.

Ragging off

You may need disposable gloves for this method, as it can be messy. Apply a base coat and allow to dry, then paint on the top coat; if using emulsion, thin it with water.

Crumple up a clean rag – cotton works best – and press firmly on to the wet top coat to remove some of the colour and expose traces of the base. Open out the cloth and scrunch it up again to vary the pattern. When the rag becomes saturated with paint, change it for a new one. Paint-soaked rags are highly flammable so allow to dry before discarding them.

Rag rolling

Allow the base coat to dry – an eggshell finish works well. Roll a lint-free cotton rag into a sausage

Using the ragging off technique

1 Mix 50 per cent emulsion (latex) with 50 per cent water or wallpaper paste (premixed to a thin solution) in a paint kettle (pot). Brush the wash on over a large area.

2 Take a rag or chamois, scrunch it up into a ball and dab on to the wall to gently remove small areas of paint. Vary the angles with each dab.

3 Continue working over the surface until the entire effect is even. If you are taking off too much paint, apply more with a brush and then dab the chamois over the surface again.

shape, then dip it into a glaze mixture and squeeze out the excess. Starting at the bottom of the wall, roll the rag upward in a straight line. Reshape the rag if you want to vary the pattern. Dip it into the glaze again, hold the rag so that it overlaps the completed section slightly and repeat the process.

Dragging

This effect works best on very smooth surfaces, as it will highlight every bump. Beginners should practise on a small area first to perfect the technique. An oil-based top coat, such as scumble glaze, will remain workable for longer than emulsion and is the best medium to use if this technique is new to you.

You can buy a ready-made glaze or mix your own. For the latter, simply mix one part glaze with two parts white spirit (paint thinner), adding colour with a little artists' oil paint. It may be difficult to duplicate the exact colour again, so make a generous batch to ensure that you have enough to finish the job.

Paint on an eggshell base coat and leave to dry. Then apply a line of glaze, about 600mm (2ft) wide, along the length of the wall. Begin at the top of the wall and drag a long-bristled brush down through the glaze to create a narrow, striped effect. Wipe the brush clean, then repeat the procedure until you have completed the wall.

Stamping

This technique is quick, easy, fun and an effective way of repeating a design on a wide variety of surfaces, using many different mixtures of paint and inks. There are lots of motifs to choose from, usually mounted on wooden blocks, and the effect has endless design permutations. Stamps are easy to make yourself from foam or sponge. Practise on paper before progressing to more ambitious projects.

You can use a black or coloured paint pad, or decant a little paint into a shallow tray. If using the latter, coat a mini-roller lightly with paint and roll it over your stamp.

Apply the stamp with a firm hand, holding it in place for a few seconds before removing. Repeat the process for every fresh imprint.

Cutting a stamp

1 Draw the design straight on to a low-density sponge using a marker pen.

2 Cut out the shape with sharp scissors and cut away the unwanted background areas.

3 Apply a small amount of paint using a sponge roller until you have an even covering.

Dragging

1 Apply the base coat and leave to dry. Mix emulsion (latex) paint with 50 per cent wallpaper paste or water. Apply the glaze in lengths, working on a small section at a time.

2 Dampen the dragging brush with the glaze before use. Take the brush in one hand and flatten the bristles out with your other hand. Pull the paintbrush down in a straight motion.

Practical tips

- Try the dragging technique on door edges to give a grained effect.
- Keep a rubber stamp clean for sharp images. Wash it in water or solvent depending on the type of paint used.
- When changing your ragging cloth, choose a near identical one to produce a uniform effect.

Preparing Woodwork for Paint

The secret of a good painted or varnished finish on wood is to spend time preparing the surface before you get down to the job itself. Wood must be sound and blemish-free, and any knots, common in softwoods such as pine, will need treating with a knotting solution (shellac) to prevent resin from seeping out and ruining the finish.

Pre-painted wood

If the existing paintwork is sound, there is no need to strip it back to bare wood. Simply wash the area carefully with a sugar soap (all-purpose cleaner) and water solution, lightly sand with abrasive paper, then remove any traces of dust before painting. Where there are patches of bare wood, apply primer, then undercoat as normal. Finally, you should sand lightly before painting on the top coat.

However, if the paint or varnish is chipped or blistered, you will have to remove it. Use a scraper to get rid of loose fragments; a triangular scraper, known as a shavehook, is handy for getting into tight corners and mouldings.

For stripping large areas of wood, the choice is between a chemical stripper and a hot-air gun. If you opt for the former, you will need to neutralize the surface, as recommended by the manufacturer, once the old paint has been removed. A hot-air gun will make light work of removing large areas of paint, but take care around windows, as the heat may damage the glass.

If you plan to paint over a faded woodstain, you will not be able to remove the old finish. In this case, simply sand the area, remove the surface dust, then apply one or two coats of an aluminium-based primer before over-painting.

If knots are showing through the painted woodwork, sand the paint film back to the bare wood and apply a knotting solution (shellac) to the knot, then prime and undercoat to bring the new paint film level with the surrounding paintwork. Sand between coats. Knots in bare wood should always be treated with a knotting solution.

Bare wood

There is a three-step sequence to painting bare wood:

- First, coat with a primer and lightly sand when dry. Wipe the surface with a lint-free cloth and white spirit (paint thinner).

- Apply an undercoat as specified by the manufacturer of the top coat you'll be using, and sand again. Remove any traces of dust with a lint-free cloth moistened with white spirit.

- Paint on the top coat. Normally, this will be a gloss finish, as it is hardwearing and easy to maintain. When varnishing bare wood, sand away any rough edges, wipe off the dust, then apply the finish.

Using liquid stripper

1 Wearing gloves, brush the stripper on to the painted surface. Leave it until the paint starts to bubble, following the instructions.

2 Scrape off the peeling layers of paint with a paint scraper. Use a shavehook for more intricate mouldings.

3 Wash the surface with water, white spirit (paint thinner) or neutralizer, as recommended by the manufacturer.

Using a heat gun

1 Move the heat gun over the surface so that the air stream heats and softens the paint evenly. Scrape off the paint as you work.

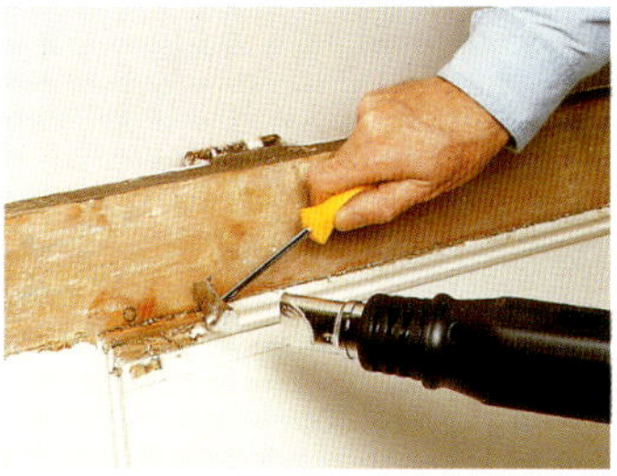

2 Be careful not to scorch the wood. Use a shavehook to scrape out the paint from intricate mouldings.

3 Rub off any remaining traces of paint with wire (steel) wool, soaked in white spirit. Work in the direction of the grain of the wood.

Filling defects in wood

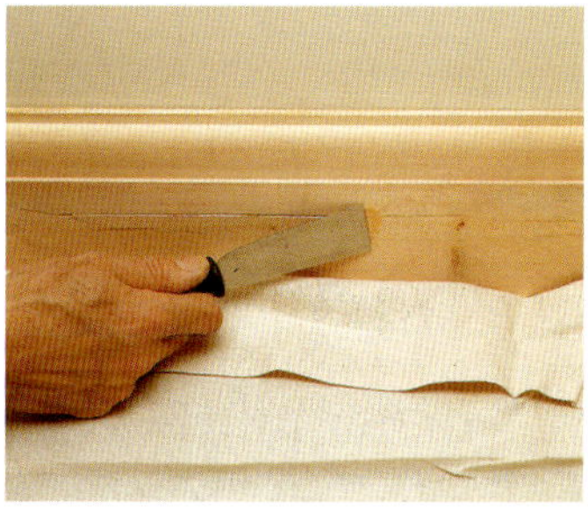

1 Fill splits and dents in wood using all-purpose filler on painted surfaces, and tinted wood filler on new or stripped wood.

2 Use the corner of a filling knife or a finger to work the filler into recesses. Smooth off the excess before it dries.

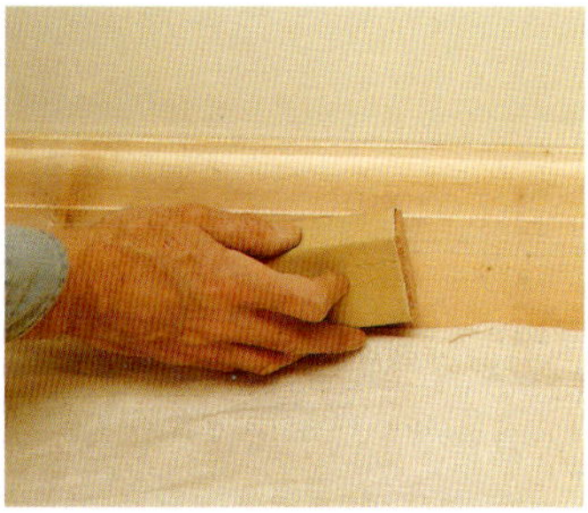

3 When the filler or wood stopper has hardened, use abrasive paper wrapped around a block to sand the repair down flush.

Preparing painted woodwork

1 Use fine-grade abrasive paper to remove "nibs" from the paint surface and to key the paint film ready for repainting.

2 Wash the surface thoroughly with a solution of detergent and rinse with clean water so that no residue is left.

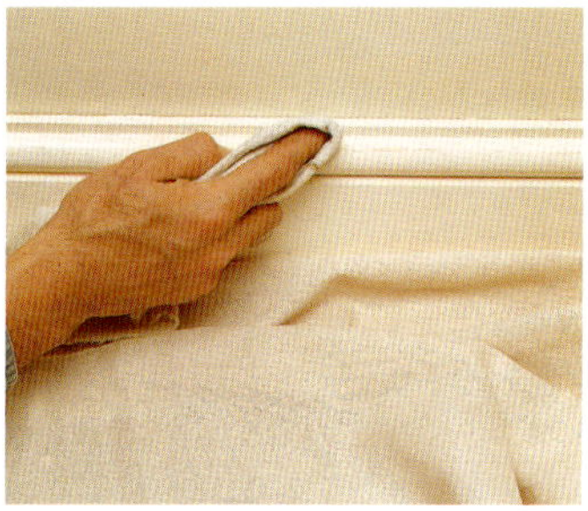

3 Use a clean cloth moistened with white spirit (paint thinner) to remove dust from recessed mouldings and corners.

Painting Windows, Doors and Stairs

Windows and doors are key elements in the appearance of a house exterior. Flaking or badly executed paintwork will deter potential buyers and generally create a poor impression. Planning can be just as important as the mechanics of painting itself; discipline yourself to follow tried and tested painting techniques to ensure your home is presented to its best advantage.

The correct sequence

It is tempting simply to get on with a painting job to complete it quickly. However, there are logical sequences for painting windows and doors, which will streamline the process and give the best results. For instance, by following the illustrated guidelines for painting a panelled door, you will be joining a series of wet edges, allowing the paintwork to be blended completely before it dries. When using gloss paints, work with the grain and, since areas to be covered are typically small, aim to complete the job in one session.

Order of painting windows

When painting a casement window, keep the casements wide open as you work. Start with the glazing bars, followed by open casements, then paint the window frame last.

With sash windows, you will need to move the sections up and down to paint the various components. Paint the base of the top sash first,

LEFT The correct order of painting a casement window. It is best to keep the casements wide open while you work (see below).

Preparing windows for painting

1 Unscrew all old or existing window fittings, prior to painting.

2 Screw a woodscrew into one of the holes to make a temporary handle.

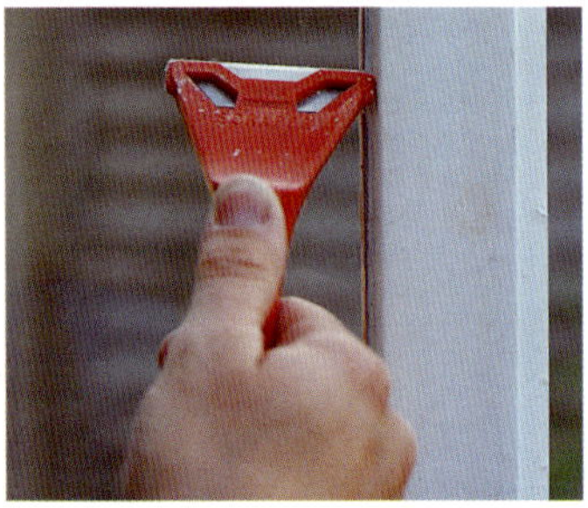

3 Carefully scrape off any traces of old paint.

4 Apply masking tape, leaving a 1.5mm gap.

Practical tips

- Paint windows early in the day, so that they will be dry enough to secure firmly by night-time.
- Try painting the treads and risers of stairs in shades that tone with the general decor, or use a co-ordinating stencilled effect on stair risers and walls.

ABOVE Always remove door furniture.

ABOVE The correct order of painting a sash window.

then finish the rest of this section. Next concentrate on the bottom sash, and finish off with the outer framework – take care not to splash paint on to the sash cords; it will be very difficult to remove.

Order of painting doors

The order for painting a door will depend on its construction. There is one set of rules for flush doors and another for panelled doors – see the numbered illustrations on the right. Complete a flush door in one session, starting at the top left-hand corner and finishing at the bottom right of the door.

ABOVE The order of painting a panel door.

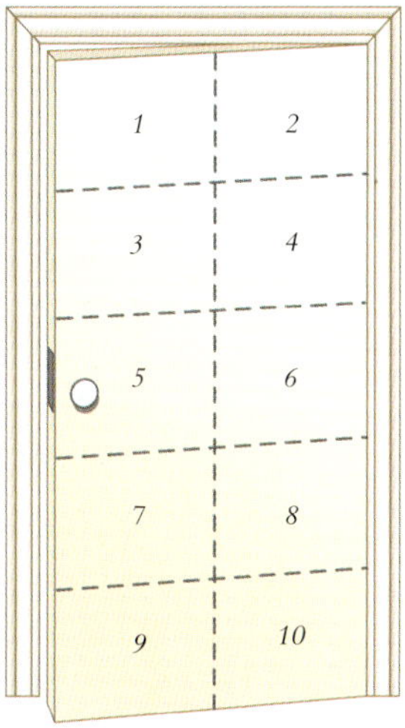

ABOVE The order of painting a flush door.

Order of painting stairs

For each stage, start at the top and work downward. Begin with the banisters and bottom rail, followed by the newel posts, top rail and handrail (if painted). If you are laying a stair runner and want a painted border either side of it, paint the edges of the treads and risers next. Allow the painted areas to run 50mm (2in) underneath each side of where the carpet will lie so no bare areas will be visible. Continue with the skirting (base) board and finally the side of the stairs.

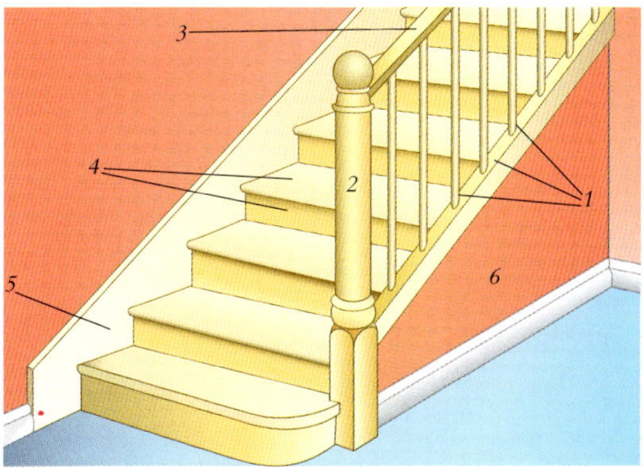

LEFT The correct order of painting a staircase.

Preparing Exterior Surfaces

First impressions are of paramount importance, so the upkeep of the outside of your home should be at the top of your list of do-it-yourself priorities. As with interior decorating, time spent on essential preparation work will ensure the best possible result. It is best to start work at the top of the house and work down to the bottom.

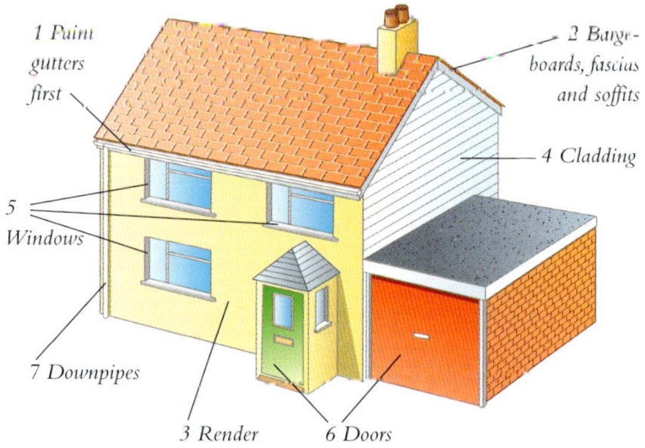

LEFT Preparation and painting order of a house exterior.

Gutters and downpipes

Clear away any rubbish that has built up and pour one or two buckets of water into the gutter to clean the system. Modern plastic gutters should require little additional preparation, but older cast-iron systems are prone to rusting, which can leave ugly deposits on brickwork and render. Remove the rust with a wire brush, before priming and painting. When it comes to repainting the walls, the rust stains should be treated with a metal primer, otherwise they will show through the new finish.

Painted woodwork

Exterior painted woodwork includes features such as fascias, soffits and bargeboards, as well as entire surfaces such as weatherboarding (siding).

New woodwork should be sanded lightly, working with the grain. Remove any dust, then wipe with a cloth moistened with white spirit (paint thinner). Seal any knots with knotting solution (shellac), and fill holes or cracks. Existing paintwork should be washed down with a solution of sugar soap (all-purpose cleaner) and water, sanded and wiped off with a cloth moistened in white spirit. Scrape off flaking paint and any bare areas should be primed and undercoated in the normal way.

For weatherboard surfaces, wash down with a solution of sugar soap, using a hose and car-wash brush attachment to get up high. Leave to dry for a week. Replace any severely damaged sections and fill smaller cracks with a sealant (caulking). Punch in any protruding nails and cover with metal primer. Then prepare as for other woodwork.

Walls

Mould growth is a common problem on walls. Look out for small white, orange, yellow, green or black marks and tackle them immediately.

ABOVE Prime rust stains caused by faulty guttering with a metal primer.

Cleaning brick surfaces

1 Hose masonry down with water or a bleach mixture to get rid of dirt, dust and mould.

2 Apply paint stripper to remove any unsightly paint spillages.

Apply an approved fungicide, or clean with a bleach solution in the ratio of four parts water to one part bleach. Leave the former for 24 hours, then wash off with clean water; bleach should be left for 48 hours before rinsing off.

Mould and fungal deposits are often signs of a more severe problem, usually damp. Check the condition of any damp-proof course, and look for leaky downpipes, defective rendering and problems with brickwork.

Persistent white patches, known as efflorescence, are easy to tackle. They occur on new masonry as it dries out and can be removed with a stiff brush. However, if efflorescence occurs on old masonry, it indicates an underlying damp problem, which must be tackled before any redecoration is attempted.

Masonry surfaces

A sound brick finish can be very attractive, so resist the temptation to obscure it with a coat of paint on a whim. Porous walls will need treating with a clear water repellent to prevent rainwater from seeping into them, but this may be the only treatment necessary.

Rendering

If existing render is in poor condition, cosmetic repairs may be made with an exterior-grade filler, while tiny cracks will normally disappear with the application of masonry paint. Many do-it-yourself

ABOVE A Tyrolean finish rendering can be applied with a hired Tyrolean machine.

enthusiasts will also feel confident about tackling larger areas of damage with a mortar mix. However, rendering a large area or a complete wall will be beyond the ability of most, and professional help should be sought.

The one exception to this rule is the application of a Tyrolean finish, which is produced with a light cement mixture. This is sprayed on with a hand-cranked Tyrolean roughcast applicator, which can be hired. It is possible to control the texture of the finish by varying the distance between the applicator and the wall. Similarly, you can vary the angle of application to create different effects.

Windows and doors

Exterior windows and doors can be treated in much the same manner as other outdoor wood. Start by filling and sanding any cracks or holes in the wood. Bare wood should be primed and undercoated, while old or defective paintwork will need sanding before over-painting. If the existing paintwork is badly cracked or blistered, it should be stripped off completely and a new primer, undercoat and top coat applied.

Preparing windows

1 Remove any old putty from a window frame with a hacking knife.

2 Apply a fresh layer and use a wet finger to smooth it into place.

3 Then smooth the putty with a putty knife, holding it at an angle, and remove the excess.

4 Use a hot air gun to strip off old paintwork. Be careful to avoid heating the glass.

Painting Exterior Walls and Guttering

The best time to tackle exterior decorating is in early summer or autumn, when the weather is fine, but not too hot. Remember that this work will be on a much larger scale than an interior-decorating project, so allow plenty of time to complete it. You may have to spread it over several weekends or take a week or two off work.

Walls

There is a wide range of paints available for painting walls. Choose from cement paints, supplied as a dry powder for mixing with water, rough- and smooth-textured masonry paints, exterior-grade emulsion (latex) paints and exterior-grade oil-based paints for weatherboarding (siding). Masonry paints can typically be used straight from the can, but if you are painting a porous surface with a water-based product it is advisable to dilute the first coat. Use a ratio of four parts paint to one part water.

Exterior paints come in a wide choice of colours, but exercise caution with some of the more flamboyant shades. White, cream, yellow, blue, green, soft pink and terracotta finishes, which blend into the background are generally favoured by house buyers.

ABOVE A typical example of pebbledash rendering. A coat of paint can greatly improve its appearance.

Painting walls

ABOVE Apply smooth masonry paint using a brush with coarse bristles.

ABOVE Apply textured masonry paint in the same way.

ABOVE To protect downpipes from paint splashes tape a newspaper around them.

ABOVE Use a banister brush to paint coarse exterior wall finishes such as pebbledash.

ABOVE Choose a deep-pile roller for coarse surfaces and a medium one for others.

ABOVE For speed, use a spray gun. Mask off surfaces you do not want painting.

Painting doorsteps

Doorstep paint is generally available in shades of red in either matt (flat) or gloss finishes.

When tackling large-scale paint jobs, it helps to break down the job into a series of modules. Aim to complete a sizeable section in one session: for example, an area defined by first-floor windows, stretching from one side of the building to the other. Work downward, using fixtures such as gutters, windows and door frames to dictate where you finish. Hard paint lines will not be noticeable in these areas when you start work again.

Use a banister brush to paint very coarse textures such as pebbledash. Apply the paint using circular strokes and work well into the surface. To ensure good coverage on a medium-textured finish, use a coarse-bristled paintbrush and apply the paint with a firm dabbing motion or use a medium roller. On smoothly rendered surfaces, a large brush or medium roller are ideal. For the best results, apply paint in vertical bands crossed by horizontal strokes.

Using spray guns

This is one of the fastest ways to paint a wall, but it can be very messy. Always mask off areas you do not want painted and do not hold the gun too close to the wall: a gap of 225mm (9in) is generally recommended. Move the gun along the wall in vertical strips, and overlap each one by 100mm (4in) for a seamless finish.

Pipes and gutters

New plastic pipes and gutters do not generally need to be painted. Older systems may be discoloured, in which case a coat of paint will rejuvenate them. Clean the surface with turpentine, then lightly sand and remove dust before applying paint. Metal pipes and gutters should be primed, then an undercoat and top coat applied. Begin at the top of the work area and work downward.

If the pipework and guttering have an existing bituminous paint finish, you will need to apply an aluminium primer before over-painting to prevent the old finish from bleeding through.

Practical tips

- Paint splashes are as problematic outdoors as in. Protect all vulnerable areas with dust sheets (drop cloths).
- Given the large areas to be covered, it makes sense to use a substantial brush, either 100mm (4in) or 150mm (6in), for exterior decorating jobs.
- A long-handled roller will help reduce the amount of time you need to spend up a ladder.

Painting pipes

1 Start painting pipework from the top and work downward.

2 Use card to protect the wall behind when painting downpipes.

ABOVE Avoid painting brickwork, if possible. Simply protect with a clear waterproofer.

Painting Exterior Woodwork

A wealth of products has been developed for painting exterior woodwork. Never try to economize by using interior gloss paints outside, they will not cope with temperature extremes and will soon flake and split. Do not be afraid to experiment with bright colours on woodwork, but choose a finish that complements, rather than contrasts with, other houses in the neighbourhood.

Fascias, Soffits, Bargeboards and Weatherboards

Choose a dry, calm day to paint and avoid working in direct sunlight, as the glare will prevent you from obtaining good, even coverage. Furthermore, if you are using a water-based (latex) paint, it will dry too rapidly, leaving hard edges.

Start by priming any bare areas, then apply an undercoat and finally one or two coats of gloss. With a standard gloss paint, begin by applying the paint vertically, and then use sideways strokes to blend it well. Work in the direction of the grain, blending in the wet edges for a uniform finish. If you are using a one-coat paint, apply the finish quite thickly in close, parallel strips and do not over-brush. For weatherboarding (siding), paint the undersides first, then the faces, working horizontally.

LEFT Paint bargeboards early on in your work schedule. By starting from the top and working down you ensure that any dislodged dirt or paint droplets only fall on unpainted surfaces.

Windows

Bare wood should be primed and undercoated, while old or defective paintwork will need sanding before over-painting. If existing paint is badly cracked or blistered, it should be stripped off completely and a new primer, undercoat and top coat applied. Exterior windows should be painted in sequence, broadly following the pattern for interior casement and sash window frames. However, when painting a sash window, start with the bottom sash, as opposed to the top in indoor work. Mask windows carefully before starting work, or use a paint shield to protect the glass from splashes. Remember to let the paint extend a little way on to the glass to prevent rainwater from seeping into the frame.

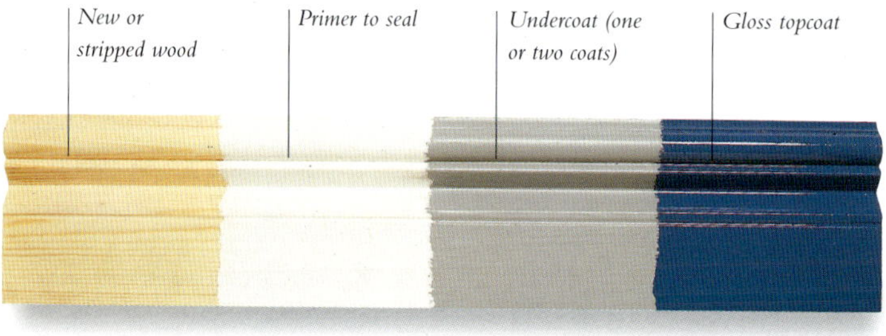

ABOVE The sequence for painting wood.

Doors and Fences

If you have an attractive hardwood door, think twice before covering it with several layers of paint. You may prefer to let the natural beauty of the wood show through by applying a stain or varnish.

Stains may be water-, oil- or spirit-based and are applied directly to the bare wood. Teak and Danish oils are also popular for hardwood doors. They give a waterproof, durable finish and enhance the natural look of the timber. Apply with a clean cloth or brush. The final

Painting a door

1 Remove old paintwork, then smooth the surface with a palm sander.

2 Apply a suitable primer and allow to dry completely before over-painting.

3 Apply one or two undercoats and lightly rub down with abrasive paper between coats.

4 Apply topcoat to mouldings and panelled areas first, then move on to cross rails.

5 Finally, replace the door furniture. The finished door should last for years; simply give the paintwork an occasional wipe-down to keep it in good order.

coat can be applied with a scouring pad or 000-grade wire (steel) wool. If you want a particularly hardwearing paint finish on an exterior door, consider a high-gloss enamel. With this type of product, you will obtain the best results by applying paint sparingly.

For fences and outbuildings, there is a wide selection of exterior wood stains and paints in all shades. Many are water-based and plant-friendly, while being tough enough to withstand the rigours of quite harsh climates. Special paints and stains have also been developed for decking with a greater resistance to scuffing and cracking.

Painting a weatherboard (siding)

1 It is easy to miss sections of exterior weatherboarding, paint the undersides first.

2 Paint the facing boards next, and finish off with the end grains.

ABOVE Fences and gates can be painted in all shades of bright colours.

Wallpaper Preparation

Preparing surfaces for decorating can often take longer than actually papering them, but it is essential. Before you start work, clear the room of all movable items to ensure that you have plenty of workspace and put down protective dust sheets (drop cloths). For reaching ceilings and high walls, make sure that you have the appropriate access equipment.

Removing wallpaper

Ordinary wallpaper is not difficult to remove and requires only wetting and soaking for 10–15 minutes before stripping with a broad-bladed scraper. Adding wallpaper stripper or a few drops of dishwashing detergent to the water will help it to penetrate the paper. Wallpaper that has been over-painted or that has a washable finish needs scoring with the edge of a scraper before soaking, but hiring a steam stripper is the easiest method, and you are less likely to damage the plaster surface.

If walls are faced with plasterboard (gypsum board), take care not to saturate the surface or hold a steam stripper in place for too long. Dry-strippable papers can simply be peeled from the wall, leaving the backing paper in place. If this is still adhering well and remains intact, a new wallcovering can be hung over the top, but if it tears, the backing should also be removed.

Stripping old wallpaper

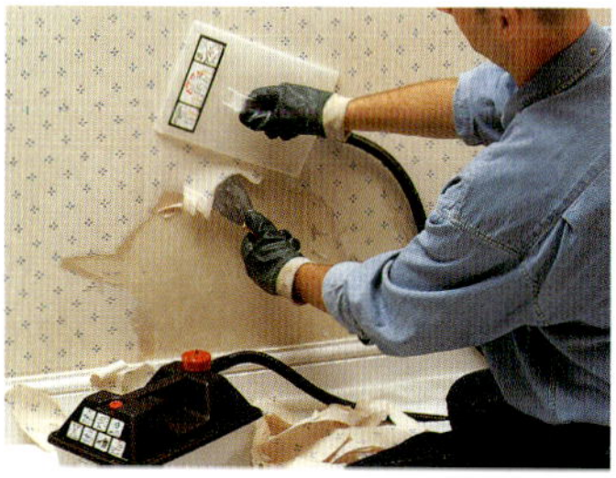

ABOVE Stubborn wallpaper will be easier to remove with a steam stripper.

ABOVE Vinyl wallcoverings can usually be stripped dry and will peel off the wall.

Preparing surfaces

Once all the old paper has been removed, walls should be washed thoroughly with a solution of sugar soap (all-purpose cleaner) to remove dust, grime and traces of old adhesive. Rinse and allow the surface to dry. Cracks and gaps should also be repaired, and any stains that remain after cleaning should be sealed. For settlement cracks between walls and the ceiling or woodwork, use a flexible decorators' filler, and seal stains with an aluminium primer or aerosol stain block.

New porous plaster and old walls that are dusty will require sealing. A PVA adhesive (white glue) solution of 1 part PVA to 5 parts water is ideal for sealing these surfaces and will act as a size before papering. A coat of size ensures good adhesion of the wallcovering and allows paper to be manoeuvred freely on the wall.

Preparing walls

1 Use a sanding block to remove any remaining "nibs" of wallpaper.

2 Repair any cracks and seal persistent stains with a stain block.

3 A coat of size will make the wallpaper easier to hang.

ABOVE The correct sequence of work when hanging lining paper.

WORK PLATFORMS

For comfort, adjust a work platform so that the top of your head is around 300mm (12in) from the ceiling.

ABOVE A work platform can be made from trestles and sturdy planks.

LINING PAPER

This helps to disguise surface blemishes and provides a good surface for decorating. It is usually hung horizontally so that the joints do not coincide with those of the decorative paper, but hanging vertical lengths will be easier in narrow alcoves and where there are wall fixtures such as pipes. On poor walls, two layers of lining paper may be necessary; the first layer is hung vertically, the second horizontally.

The basic paperhanging techniques shown on the following pages can also be used for lining paper, but it should be left to soak for only five minutes to become pliable. Treat each surface separately and trim the paper to fit into internal corners. Do not use a ceiling as a guideline assuming it is level; mark a horizontal guideline for the lower edge of the first length with a spirit level. If you are lining both walls and ceiling, start with the ceiling.

PRACTICAL TIPS

- Allow at least 24 hours for lining paper to dry out completely before hanging the final wallcovering.

- Lining paper may shrink as it dries. Fill small gaps between lengths with fine surface filler and sand smooth. In corners, use a bead of flexible filler and smooth with a wet finger.

HANGING LINING PAPER

1 Normally, lining paper is hung in horizontal lengths across each wall.

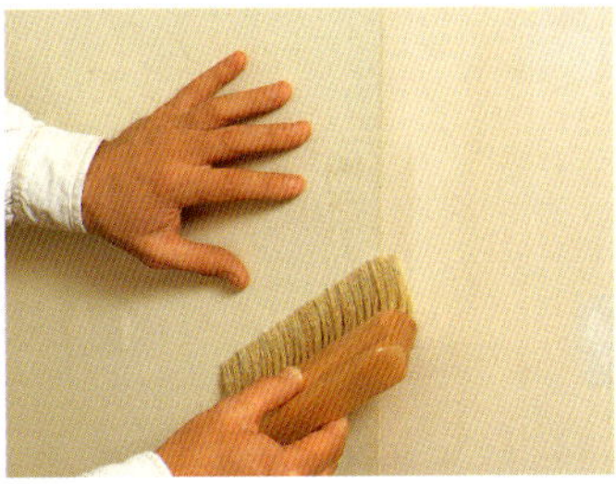

2 Lining paper can be hung vertically in narrow alcoves or behind pipework.

3 To line a ceiling, work across the longest dimension of the room.

Choosing Wallpaper

Although not as popular as it was once, wallpaper still offers a wide range of patterns and colourways, from very traditional to the most modern designs. Choose with care, particularly if you are new to hanging wallpaper, as some will be much easier to hang than others. Check the manufacturer's guidelines before buying to determine the suitability of the paper.

Buying wallpaper

When shopping for wallpaper, ask for a large sample of any design that catches your eye so you can examine it in the room that is to be decorated. Look at the samples in both natural and artificial light, near a window and in a dark corner, as some colours and patterns alter dramatically in different lights.

Test a sample for durability by moistening it under a tap. If it tears easily or the colours run when rubbed lightly, the paper could be difficult to hang and maintain. Avoid thin papers, particularly if you are an inexperienced decorator, as they are likely to tear when pasted and may be difficult to hang.

Never skimp on the number of rolls you buy, and check that the batch number on all rolls is the same, as there may be a slight colour variation between batches that may not be noticeable on the roll, but could become obvious after hanging. However, the batch system is not infallible, so check rolls again for a good colour match before cutting and hanging. It is also worth buying an extra roll. Many retailers offer a sale-or-return service.

Choosing a pattern

Take a critical look at the room you plan to decorate and make a note of any aspects that could make hanging wallpaper difficult. Uneven walls and awkward corners, for example, can make pattern matching particularly problematic, while some types of wallcovering will conceal a poor surface better than others.

Regular patterns, such as vertical stripes, checks and repetitive geometric designs, will emphasize walls that are out of true, whereas random florals and paint-effect papers will not encourage the eye to rest on any one point and, therefore, will help to disguise awkward angles. Trimming can also ruin the appearance of a large pattern, so in a room that has a sloping or uneven

ABOVE Check that the batch number on all rolls is exactly the same.

ceiling, or several windows, cabinets and doors, a design with a small pattern may be a better choice. If a poor surface is the problem, avoid thin or shiny wallpapers, which will highlight every blemish.

If you are not an experienced decorator, avoid complicated patterns, as any mismatching will be obvious; instead consider using one of the many easy-to-hang, freematch designs now available.

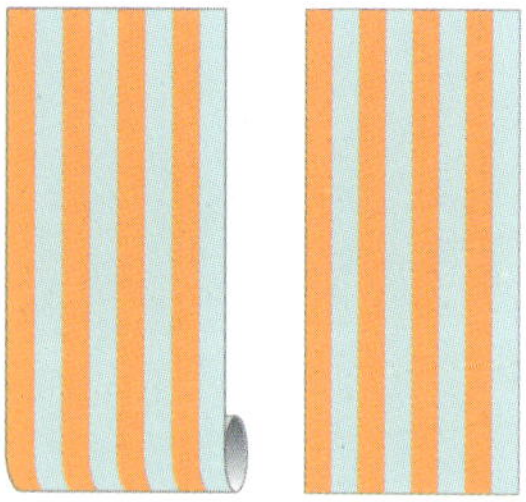

ABOVE A freematch wallpaper or one with a continuous pattern, such as stripes, will not need an allowance for pattern matching.

ABOVE A straight-match pattern has the same part of the pattern running down each side of the paper.

ABOVE An offset pattern has motifs staggered between drops, which must be taken into account when cutting and measuring.

Estimating quantities

Standard wallpapers are sold in rolls that are approximately 10m x 530mm wide (33ft x 21in). Use the tables to calculate the number of rolls required for walls and ceilings, remembering to add ten per cent for waste, especially if the design has a large pattern repeat. Lining paper is usually 560mm (22in) wide and is available in standard 10m (33ft) and larger roll sizes. You can calculate the number of rolls required from the tables, but there is no need to add any extra for a pattern repeat. For walls, measure around the room and include all windows and doors in your calculation except very large picture windows and patio doors. It is easier to measure the perimeter of the floor to calculate the size of a ceiling.

Depending on where they were manufactured, you may find papers in non-standard sizes, so do check. Wallcoverings in the US vary in width and length but are usually available in rolls sized to cover specific areas.

ABOVE Measuring up for wallpaper.

Calculating the number of rolls needed for a ceiling

Measurement around room	Number of rolls
10m (33ft)	2
11m (36ft)	2
12m (39ft)	2
13m (43ft)	3
14m (46ft)	3
15m (49ft)	4
16m (52ft)	4
17m (56ft)	4
18m (59ft)	5
19m (62ft)	5
20m (66ft)	5
21m (69ft)	6
22m (72ft)	7
23m (75ft)	7
24m (79ft)	8
25m (82ft)	8

Calculating the number of rolls needed for walls

	Height of room from skirting (base) board							
	2–2.25m (6ft 7in–7ft 5in)	2.25–2.5m (7ft 5in–8ft 2in)	2.5–2.75m (8ft 2in–9ft)	2.75–3m (9ft–9ft 10in)	3–3.25m (9 ft 10in–10 ft 8 in)	3.25–3.5 m (10ft 8in–11ft 6in)	3.5–3.75m (11ft 6in–12ft 4in)	3.75–4m (12ft 4in–13ft 1in)
Walls	**Number of rolls required**							
10m (33ft)	5	5	6	6	7	7	8	8
11m (36ft)	5	6	7	7	8	8	9	9
12m (39ft)	6	6	7	8	8	9	9	10
13m (43ft)	6	7	8	8	9	10	10	10
14m (46ft)	7	7	8	9	10	10	11	11
15m (49ft)	7	8	9	9	10	11	12	12
16m (52ft)	8	8	9	10	11	11	12	13
17m (56ft)	8	9	10	10	11	12	13	14
18m (59ft)	9	9	10	11	12	13	14	15
19m (62ft)	9	10	11	12	13	14	15	16
20m (66ft)	9	10	11	12	13	14	15	16
21m (69ft)	10	11	12	13	14	15	16	17
22m (72ft)	10	11	13	14	15	16	17	18
23m (75ft)	11	12	13	14	15	17	18	19
24m (79ft)	11	12	14	15	16	17	18	20
25m (82ft)	12	13	14	15	17	18	19	20

Hanging the First Length

Wallpaper can be hung using one of three methods, depending on whether you are using a ready-pasted, paste-the-wall or traditional unpasted paper. However, the most important step with any paperhanging task is to prepare fully before cutting the paper by carefully measuring the lengths and allowing for pattern matching to avoid mistakes.

Preparing unpasted paper

Measure the height of the wall from the ceiling to the top of the skirting (base) board and add 100mm (4in) for trimming the top and bottom. Measure and cut the first drop to length. To ensure a square cut, lay the paper flush with the long edge of the table and use a straightedge to mark the cutting line.

If the ceiling is quite level, you can cut a number of lengths. Match the pattern of each length dry off the roll against the first cut length to avoid problems with pattern matching as the job progresses.

Use the paperhanger's brush to weigh one end down, and line up the edge of the paper with the edge of the pasting table, then apply a thin, even coat of paste brushing outward toward the edges.

Fold the ends of the pasted length in to the centre and leave it to soak, checking the manufacturer's guidelines for the exact length of time. Long lengths of paper should be lightly folded concertina-style.

Ready-pasted paper

To activate ready-pasted papers, fill a trough two-thirds with water and put it at the end of the pasting table. Roll a length of paper with the decorative face inside and immerse for the recommended soaking time. Draw it on to the pasting table patterned side down so that excess water can drain into the trough.

For paste-the-wall papers, apply a coat of paste to an area wider than the paper – it can be hung directly from the roll or using cut lengths.

Cutting, pasting and folding wallpaper

1 Measure carefully, allowing for pattern matching and cut the paper to length.

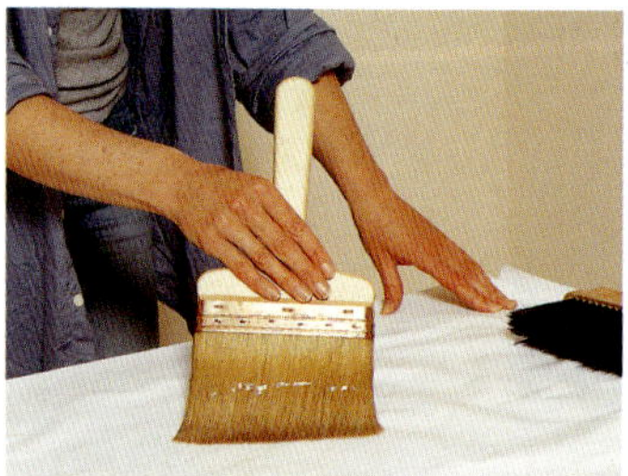

2 Brush an even coat of paste from the centre outwards.

3 Fold short lengths of wallpaper end to end so you can easily carry the paper.

4 Fold longer lengths of wallpaper concertina-style so they are manageable.

Ready-pasted paper

Fill a trough two-thirds full with cold water and put it at one end of the pasting table. Roll the paper with the decorative face inside and immerse for the recommended soaking time.

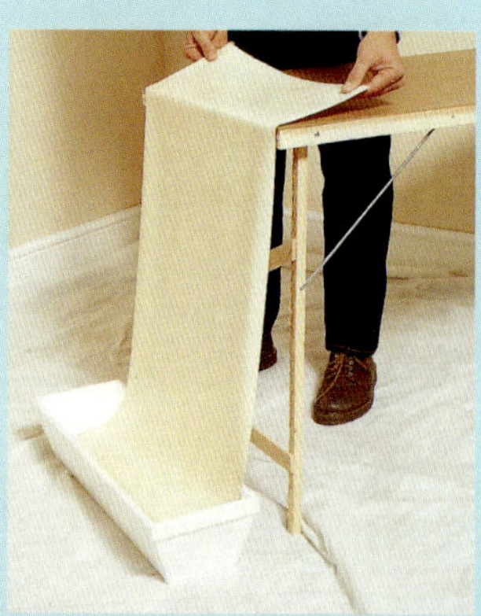

ABOVE Draw the paper over the paste table, pattern side down to drain water.

The first length

Use a plumbline and spirit level to mark a guideline on the wall near a corner. The distance from corner to guideline should be one roll width less 25mm (1in), and the first length should be hung so that you are working away from (and not into) the corner. In rooms with a dominant feature, centre the first length over the focal point and work outward in both directions.

Place the first length next to the guideline, then adjust the top so that there is 50mm (2in) of paper lapping on to the ceiling and slide the vertical edge into its final position.

Lightly brush out the top half of the paper, working downward to expel air bubbles and firmly push the top trimming allowance into the angle with the ceiling. Make sure that the vertical edge is aligned with the guideline then continue to work down the wall, brushing outwards from the centre of the length.

Crease the paper into the junction between wall and ceiling by running the blunt edge of the scissors along the paper, then gently peel back the paper and trim neatly to fit along the creaseline. Brush the trimmed edge firmly back into position.

Ease the bottom half of the paper away from the wall and smooth it into place. Make sure that it is aligned with the guideline, then crease the bottom edge of the paper into the skirting (base) board and trim to fit using scissors.

Hanging the first length

1 Place the length against the vertical guideline and position carefully.

2 Brush out the top half of the paper and push into the angle with the ceiling.

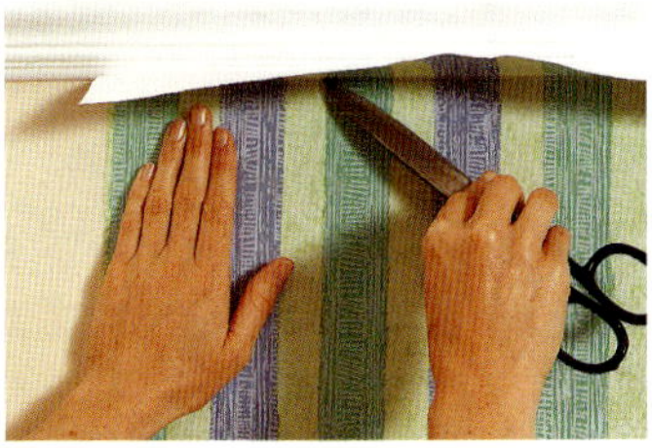

3 Use the blunt edge of the scissors to mark the cutting line.

4 Gently peel back the paper and trim along the crease line.

Where to start

In a room with no focal point, work clockwise around the room. Start and finish near the least obtrusive corner so that any pattern mismatch will not be obvious.

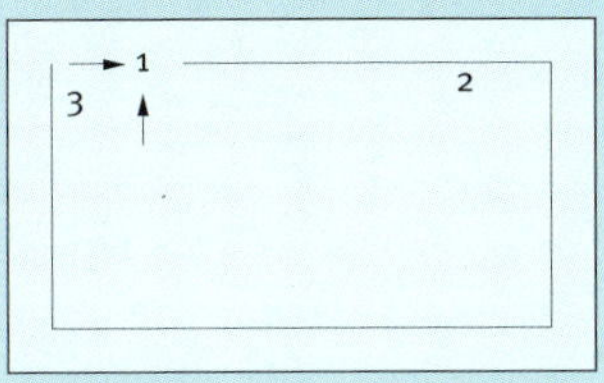

ABOVE Start from a corner of the room and work clockwise around the room.

To ensure the end result is well balanced, centre a pattern over a chimney breast (fireplace projection) or other prominent feature and work outwards in both directions.

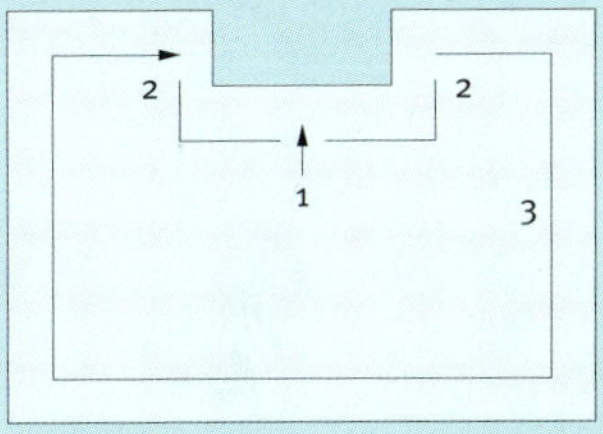

ABOVE Centre a pattern over a prominent feature in the room.

Practical tips

- Hang papers with a large design so that any loss of pattern occurs at floor level not at the ceiling.
- Agitate pre-pasted papers during soaking to expel air bubbles and ensure that all the paper comes into contact with water. Make sure the paper is loosely rolled.

Wallpapering Corners

External and internal corners are unlikely to be completely square, so never try to hang a full width of wallpaper around them as it will not hang straight. Hanging two separate lengths of paper and overlapping them slightly in the corners will produce a far better result, although some small loss of pattern will be inevitable on walls that are not perfectly true.

External corners

Hang the cut length as usual, matching the pattern down the full length, then lightly brush the paper around the corner. Do not apply too much pressure, as the paper could tear but make sure that there are no bubbles and the paper has adhered well along the edge of the corner.

Use scissors to make a release cut top and bottom where the wall meets the skirting (base) board and ceiling. This will allow the paper to be smoothed on to the wall on both sides of the corner and trimmed along skirting and ceiling. Using a craft knife, trim the length vertically to leave an overlap of about 25mm (1in) brushed around the corner. Discard the waste.

Cut another length and hang this to a vertical guideline on the second wall so that it overlaps the strip of paper brushed around the corner, with its edge about 12mm (½in) from the corner and the pattern matching as closely as possible.

To do this, you may need to hang the new length so that it overlaps the previous length substantially. The width of the pattern will determine how much the two lengths may have to be overlapped. Trim through both layers with a craft knife and remove the waste. Brush out, then trim to fit the top and bottom as normal.

Papering an external corner

1 Brush the wallpaper smoothly around the external corner.

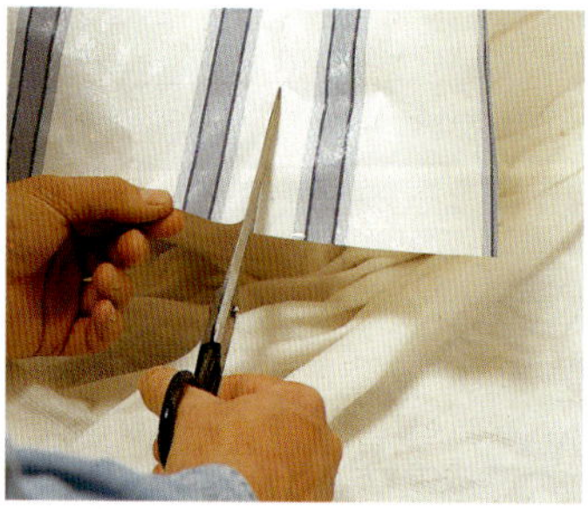

2 Make diagonal release cuts at the top and bottom, into the skirting and ceiling junctions.

3 Trim off the excess paper to leave an overlap of 25mm (1in).

4 Hang a new length so that it overlaps the turned paper and matches the pattern.

5 Trim through both layers of paper using a sharp craft knife.

6 Peel back the edges, remove the waste and brush into place.

1 Measure into the internal corner at the top, middle and bottom.

2 Cut a strip to fit from the next length, but do not discard the offcut.

3 Brush the overlap allowance on to the facing wall.

If the wall is not completely square, the pattern may not match exactly along the full drop where the two lengths cross over. This cannot be avoided and should be taken into account when planning the order of the work. Always aim for the overlap to be where it is least noticeable. On a chimney breast (fireplace projection), for example, the overlaps should be on the side walls, not the face.

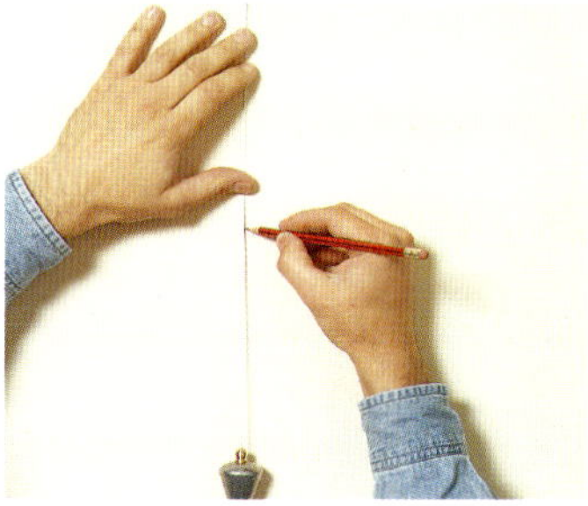

4 Measure the offcut and mark a guideline on the wall with a plumb.

5 Hang the offcut, overlapping the strip turned around the corner.

INTERNAL CORNERS

Hang the last full-width length, then measure the distance from the edge of the paper into the corner, taking measurements from the top, centre and bottom of the wall. Add a 12mm (½in) overlap allowance to the widest measurement and cut a strip of this width from the next full length. Do not discard the offcut (scrap) – put it to one side for use later.

Hang the cut length, brushing the overlap allowance on to the adjacent wall. Make sure the paper is brushed firmly into the corner by dabbing the wallpaper with the tips of the brush bristles.

Measure the width of the offcut and use a plumbline to mark a vertical guideline on the adjacent wall that distance from the corner. If the internal corner is badly out of true, take measurements from the top, centre and bottom of the wall, and adjust the guideline for the offcut so that it will not overlap on to the previous wall.

Hang the offcut against the guideline, overlapping the strip of paper turned on to the wall. Although there will be a slight mismatch of the pattern, it should not be too noticeable. Trim the top and bottom of the length neatly with scissors.

PRACTICAL TIPS

- If an overlap allowance puckers in an internal corner, make small horizontal cuts in the paper so that it lays flat.
- Keep a tube of overlap adhesive handy to ensure that overlapping edges of vinyl wallcoverings adhere properly.
- Paper with a straight-match pattern can be difficult to align in an internal corner. Hold a spirit level horizontally across the corner to check that the design is level.

Papering around Doors and Windows

If you follow the correct sequence for hanging and trimming the lengths of wallpaper, you should be able to paper around doors and windows with little trouble, although small mishaps around windows can often be disguised with window dressings. The techniques described here can be adapted to cope with a variety of situations.

Doors

Mark out the walls in roll widths first so that you know exactly where each length falls. Thin strips beside a door or window will be difficult to hang and are likely to peel, so adjust the starting point if necessary.

Hang a full length so that it overlaps the architrave (trim), matching the pattern to the last length hung. Lightly brush the paper on to the wall where possible, and then use the bristle tips of the brush to press the paper into the top of the architrave.

Locate the external corner of the door frame and make a diagonal release cut into this point with scissors. As you cut toward the corner, press the paper against the wall to prevent it from tearing. Smooth the paper down the wall and brush the vertical overlap of paper into the edge of the architrave.

Make sure the paper does not separate from the previous length as you do this. Crease the paper against the architrave with the back of the scissors, then ease the paper away from the wall and cut along the creases, or trim with a craft knife held at a 45-degree angle to the wall. Trim the top of the door frame first, cutting inward from the outer edge of the architrave. Wipe the paste from woodwork and paper.

Papering around a door

1 Drape the paper over the frame and brush the paper into the top of the architrave (trim).

2 Make a diagonal cut into the external corner of the frame.

3 Brush the paper into the side of the architrave using the tips of the bristles.

4 Trim the paper flush with the architrave using a sharp craft knife.

Practical tips

- Lightly smooth pasted paper on to the wall before trimming so that it does not tear under its own weight when it is damp.
- The junction between wall and door frame is rarely even; trimming the paper so that it overlaps the frame slightly will create a much neater finish.
- If the sides of a reveal are uneven, trim overlapping paper to 50mm (2in) and make horizontal release cuts down the length so that it lies flat, then cut a separate strip to fit.
- Complete all cutting and trimming around doors and windows first, leaving the trimming at the top and bottom of each length to last.

1 Drape the paper over the reveal and cut into the corners of the reveal.

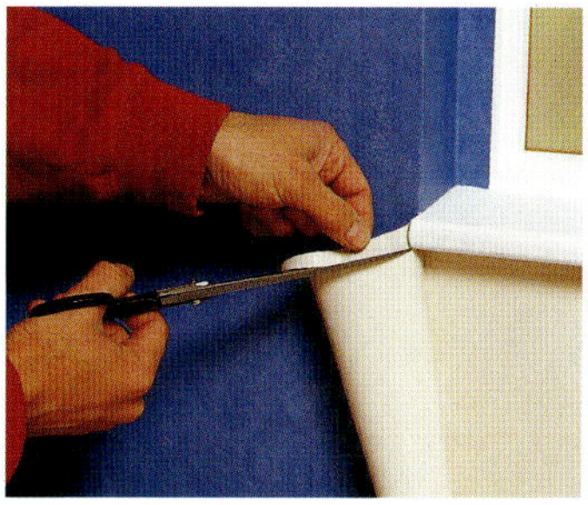

2 Cut along the top of the window sill and make diagonal release cuts around the sill.

3 Brush the remaining flap of wallpaper into the reveal and trim to fit.

4 Ease back the paper, and cut and fit a patch in the corner of the reveal.

5 Cut through both layers and remove the waste to create an unobtrusive butt join.

6 Hang short lengths above and below the window, matching the pattern.

Windows

Hang the first length overlapping the window, matching the pattern to the last length hung. Smooth the paper on to the wall, then make horizontal cuts into the corners of the reveal – the first level with the top of the window sill, and the second level with the top of the reveal.

Locate the corners of the window sill and make diagonal release cuts toward these points so that the paper can be eased around the shape of the sill. Brush the paper below the sill on to the wall, and trim to fit. Brush the remaining flap of paper around the corner into the reveal and trim to fit against the window frame.

Make sure air bubbles are expelled, but do not apply too much pressure. If the overlap is not deep enough for the reveal, hang a narrow strip to fit, matching any pattern.

Cut an oversized patch to fit the head of the reveal, matching the pattern to the paper above the reveal. Make a release cut in the outer corner, then slip the pasted patch into place. Tuck the edges of the patch under the paper above and inside the reveal, and trim through both layers with a wavy stroke. Peel back the paper to remove the waste and brush down firmly – the joint should be almost invisible. Complete the rest of the window in the same way, hanging short lengths above and below the reveal. Lengths above the window can be brushed into the reveal complete provided that it is not deep and the edge is square.

7 Cut lengths large enough to be brushed into the reveal at the top.

Papering Stairwells

When working in stairwells, safety is the main priority. Access equipment suitable for use on stairs may be hired, but you can also construct your own safe work platform. The main problem with papering a stairwell is having to handle the extra-long lengths of wallpaper. Apply paste liberally, so the paper does not dry out while you hang it.

Constructing a work platform

To construct a platform, you will need a sturdy stepladder, a straight ladder and a sturdy scaffold board that is long enough to reach between the two. If you need to bridge a gap of 1.5m (5ft) or more, two scaffold boards placed one on top of the other will be needed, and if the span is greater than 2.4m (8ft), the centre of the boards will require additional support, such as a combination ladder.

The planks should be tied securely to each ladder with stout rope. If the platform has to be erected over balustrading, make sure that the feet of the straight ladder are wedged firmly in place: a strip of wood screwed to one of the stairs is the safest method.

Order of work

Hang the longest length first, and work upward from the foot of the stairs. If you prefer to work from the top of the stairs downward, plan the hanging sequence carefully before you begin. Mark off length widths from the junction of the well wall and head wall, so that the last length will require the minimum of trimming at the head wall.

Hang the top half of each length, but leave the rest of the folded length hanging while you move the work platform out of the way. Then smooth the lower half of each length into place.

When measuring lengths for a well wall, make sure that you allow for the gradient of the stairs – as a rough guide, add the depth of three stair

Practical tips

- Protect the walls from damage by padding the ends of the ladder with soft cloths.
- Where a banister rail is screwed to the wall, try to plan the lengths so that the fixing falls between a butt joint.
- A strip of wood screwed to one of the stairs will ensure that the feet of a ladder do not slip.

BELOW The order of papering for the head wall of a staircase. Note that the ends of the straight ladder have been padded. Adjust the access equipment before brushing the lower half of the wall.

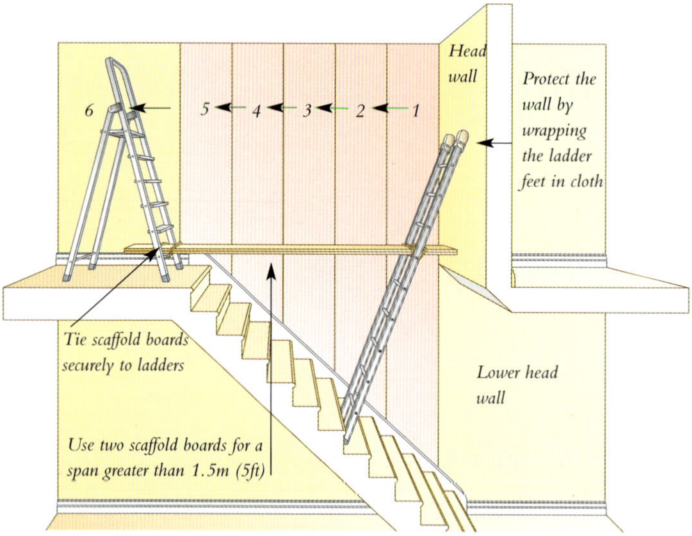

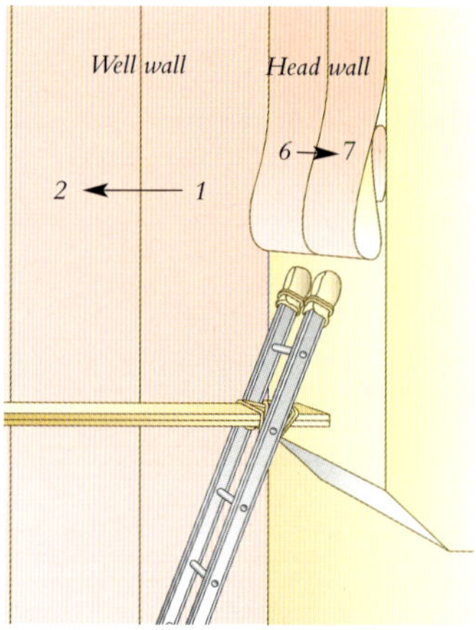

LEFT How to construct a platform for a straight staircase and order of papering for the well wall.

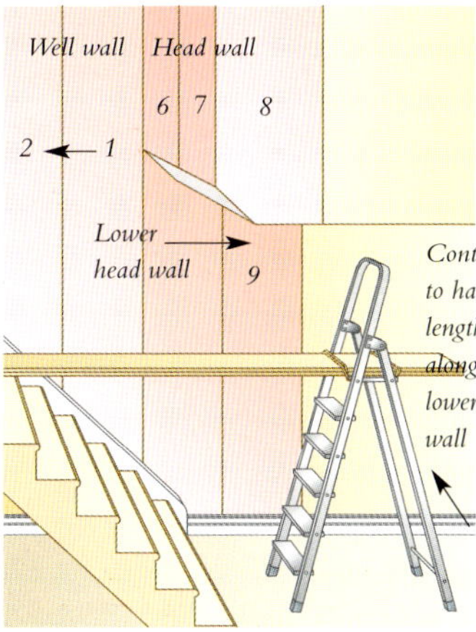

ABOVE The order of papering for the lower head wall of a staircase.

LEFT How to construct a work platform for a staircase with a landing.

risers to your measurement, as well as a trimming allowance.

Tackle the head wall next, hanging the top portions of the two or three drops needed, leaving the remainder of the folded lengths hanging. Adjust the work platform so that the planks rest on one of the stairs and are supported by a stepladder at the bottom of the stairs. Smooth the lower portions of the lengths on to the head wall from this new position, and trim neatly in line with the hallway ceiling. Finally, continue to hang lengths working along the lower head wall from the foot of the stairs.

Handling long lengths

Unless your staircase is divided by a dado or decorative border, the drop from the ceiling to the floor will be considerable in places and the lengths of paper will be difficult to handle alone without tearing.

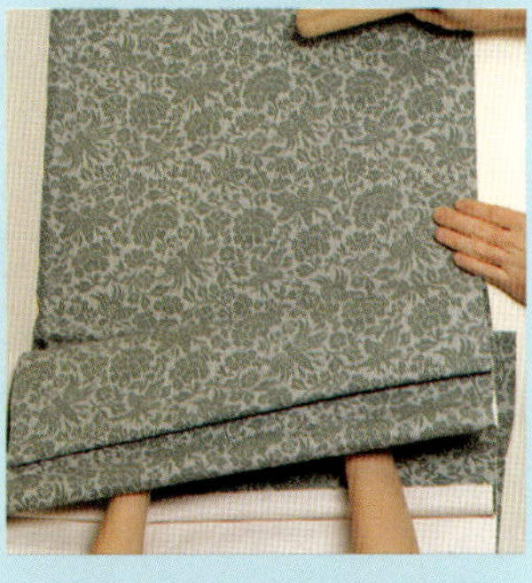

ABOVE When hanging long lengths, ask someone to help support the weight of the lengths of wallcovering while you hang the top portion.

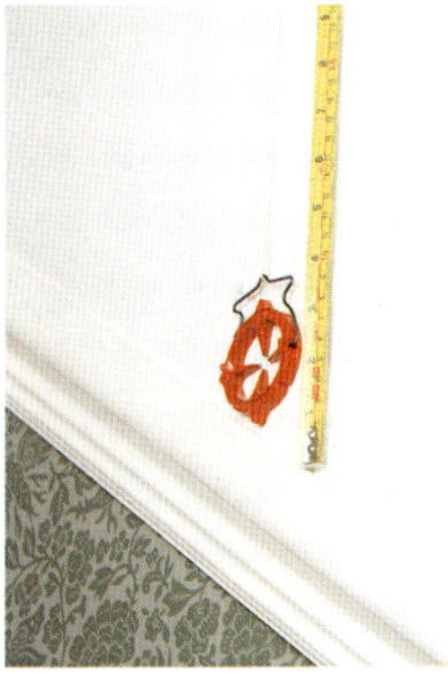

ABOVE Be especially careful to take accurate measurements. Mistakes can be costly when working with very long lengths.

ABOVE Hang the longest length first and work upward from the foot of the stairs. Hang the top half of each length first.

Papering around Obstacles

Hanging wallpaper around any obstacle requires careful trimming to obtain a neat finish, and a sharp utility knife is essential. Make sure that the blade is kept free of paste, and renew it at regular intervals. Wherever possible, remove wall-mounted fittings such as lights, first turning off the electricity supply, as this will make it easier to achieve the professional finish you want.

Fireplaces

Hang a full length so that it drapes over the fireplace and match the pattern above the mantel shelf to the last length hung. Lightly brush the paper into the junction of the wall and shelf and trim. Cut inward from the outer corner of the mantel shelf, and support the rest of the length to prevent it from tearing.

Press the paper against the wall at the point where the corner of the shelf meets the wall, gently easing the paper around the contours with your fingers. Make a series of small cuts to allow the paper to lie flat, then use the tips of a paperhanger's brush to mould the paper into the precise shape. Trim each small flap of paper, then crease and trim the paper down the side of the fireplace and wipe any adhesive from the surface.

Papering around a fireplace

1 Drape the paper over the mantel shelf and trim along the back edge.

2 Ease the paper around the contours of the mantel shelf by making small release cuts.

Radiators

If a radiator is too heavy to remove, turn it off and allow it to cool. Measure and make a note of the position of each wall bracket from the outer edges and top of the radiator, then hang the paper so that it drapes over the radiator. Match the pattern with the last length hung above it. Measure out the position of the wall bracket and make a pencil mark on the wallpaper at this point. Make a vertical slit with scissors from the bottom edge of the paper up to the mark, and use a radiator roller to feed and smooth the paper down on either side of the bracket.

Trim the paper neatly along the skirting (base) board and wipe off any adhesive left on the face of the wallpaper, skirting and radiator. Repeat for the other bracket.

Papering behind a radiator

1 Make a vertical cut from the bottom of the paper in line with the bracket.

2 Use a radiator roller to smooth paper down behind a radiator.

Wall fixings

When removing wall fittings, mark the position of each screw hole with a matchstick (wooden match) and carefully press the tip through the pasted paper before it is smoothed into place.

Papering an arch

1 Trim away excess paper from the arch to leave a trimming allowance of 25mm (1in).

2 Make right-angled cuts to ease the paper around the curve of the arch.

3 Paper the inner face of the arch last, joining strips at the highest point.

Arches

Hang the paper so that it overlaps the arch, matching the pattern to the last length hung, then trim off the waste to within 25mm (1in) from the edge of the arch. Brush the trimming allowance on to the inner face of the arch, making right-angled cuts into the paper every 12mm (½in) around the curve of the arch so that it lays flat. Paper across the rest of the arch, length by length, using the same method of cutting to cope with the curved edge.

For the inner face, cut a strip of paper 35mm (1¼in) wider than the arch. If the paper has a definite pattern, use two strips with a butt joint at the highest point. Align the manufactured edge of the cut strip with one edge of the arch and trim the other edge with a knife once the paper is smoothed into place.

Sockets and switches

Turn off the electricity supply and hang the paper over the fitting. Press it firmly against the faceplate, so that you can see a clear impression and make a pencil mark 6mm (¼in) in from each corner. Make diagonal cuts to each pencil mark with scissors, trimming off the flaps of paper 6mm (¼in) in from the outer edge of the faceplate.

Loosen the screws of the faceplate and ease it from the wall, then use a paperhanger's brush to gently push the paper behind the faceplate and wipe off any adhesive.

Light fittings

Turn off the electricity supply and remove the fitting. Bind the wires with electrical insulating tape. Hang the paper to the cable, mark its position on the paper and make a small incision. Feed the cable through the hole. Allow the paste to dry before replacing the fitting.

Papering around a switchplate

1 Turn off the electricity supply. Mark the corners on the paper overhanging the fitting.

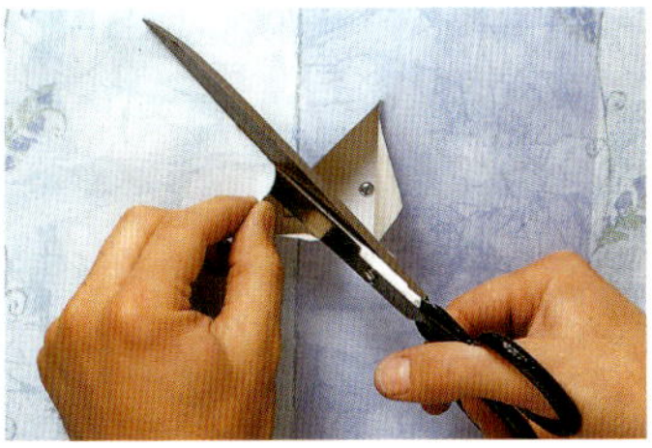

2 Make four diagonal cuts from corner to corner of the faceplate. Loosen the screws.

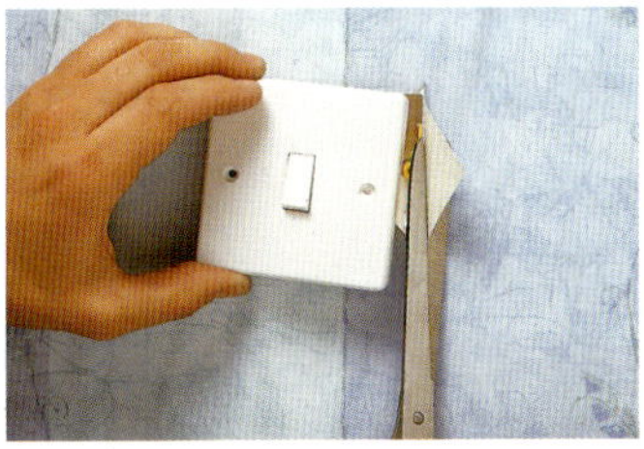

3 Trim off the flaps of paper and push them under the edges of the loosened faceplate.

HANGING BORDERS

A decorative border can add the finishing touch to a wallpaper or paint scheme. You can choose from a wide variety of patterns, colourways and sizes, all of which are quick and easy to hang. The key to a professional-looking result is to make sure that the border is absolutely straight and hung against accurate guidelines, and that all the joins are neat.

BASIC TECHNIQUES

Use a spirit level to mark the position of the border on the walls at 300mm (12in) intervals, joining the pencil marks with a long straightedge. Measure from one corner of the wall to the other and add 50mm (2in) for trimming. Paste by brushing out from the centre, and fold concertina-style, leaving the paper to soak for ten minutes. Brush the back of a ready-pasted border with tepid water, rather than immersing it in a trough. A self-adhesive border needs to be re-rolled so that the decorative face is outwards.

To hang, place 300mm (12in) of the border against the guideline at a time, allowing the folds to drop out as you work. If using a self-adhesive border, peel away the backing paper and smooth it into place. Before cutting and hanging the next length, match the pattern on the roll. Do not attempt to hang a continuous length of border around an external or internal corner, instead use the same technique as for hanging conventional paper.

If you have to use more than one length on a wall, a butt join can be used for borders with a simple repeat pattern. For more complex designs, overlap the two lengths so that the pattern matches exactly and carefully cut around a motif through both layers. When the waste paper has been removed and the cut edges smoothed into place, the join should be almost invisible. Use a seam roller to press down the edges.

CREATING A BUTT JOIN

1 Form a butt join between two lengths of a border that has a simple pattern.

2 Use a seam roller to press edges and joins down firmly.

PRACTICAL TIPS

- Hang a border by working from right to left if you are right-handed, and left to right if left-handed.
- Positioning a border is easier if the guideline is above a horizontal border, and on the inner edge around windows and doors.
- Fix a border below an uneven ceiling and paint the gap to match.

HANGING A CORNER BORDER

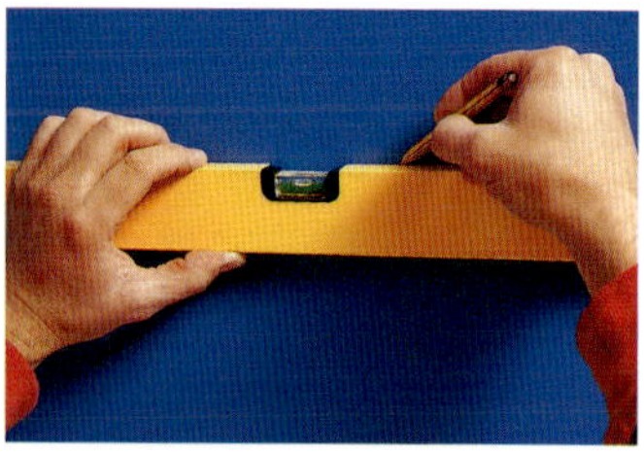

1 Draw a guideline for the border on the wall using a spirit level.

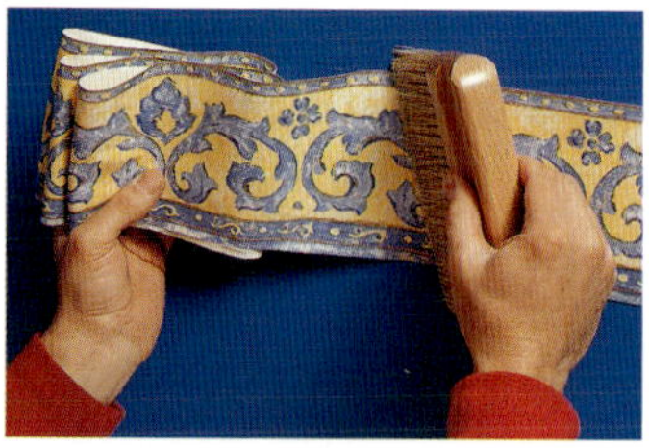

2 Fold a pasted border concertina-style so that it is ready to hang and easy to handle.

3 Match the pattern in a corner using a dry length, before cutting and pasting.

Dividing a wall

1 Hang the two papers so that they overlap the pencil guideline.

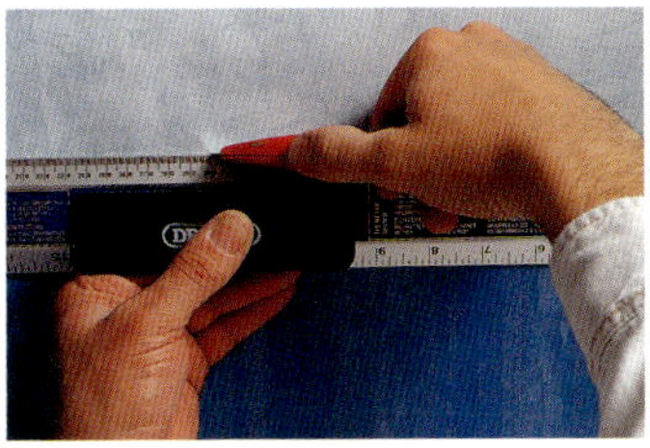

2 Trim through both papers along the guideline and remove the waste.

3 Centre the border over the butt join and wipe away any traces of adhesive.

Dividing a wall with a border

A border will allow two different wallpaper patterns to be applied to a wall, one above and one below, by concealing the joint between them. Mark a guideline on the wall, approximately 900mm (3ft) from the floor, and hang a length of each design at the same time so that it overlaps the pencil line by 50mm (2in). Before hanging the next lengths, hold a long straightedge on the guideline and cut through both layers of paper with a knife. Remove the waste and smooth down the cut edges to form a neat butt joint.

When the room has been papered, the border can be hung. Centre it over the butt join using an overlap adhesive for vinyl wallcoverings.

Around a window or door

Draw a horizontal guideline to the full width of the border above the frame, and then mark a vertical guideline down each side. Cut the horizontal length 50mm (2in) longer than required and hang it, making sure that it overlaps the side guidelines evenly.

Add the vertical lengths, overlapping the horizontal strip squarely at the corners. Use the trimming allowance on the vertical lengths to adjust the border so that you will be cutting through the busiest part of the design. Holding a steel rule at a 45-degree angle, cut through both layers of paper from the external to internal corner of the border, using a craft knife. Peel back the cut edges and remove the waste paper from the wall. Brush the border back into place to create a neat mitred join at each corner.

Creating an invisible join

Disguise a join in an ornate border by cutting around an intricate shape with a sharp knife.

Mitring a corner border

1 Mark out horizontal and vertical guidelines using a spirit level.

2 Overlap strips and cut through both layers from corner to corner.

3 Remove the waste and smooth down cut edges to form a neat mitred join.

Papering Ceilings

Wallpapering a ceiling is not as difficult as it may appear. The techniques used are the same as for walls and there are few obstacles or awkward angles to deal with. Although the job will be easier with two people, it is possible to achieve good results on your own. Adequate access equipment, however, is essential and will make the job very much easier.

Hanging the first length

Assemble your work platform across the main window of the room. Ceilings should be papered by hanging lengths across the room parallel to the window, working away from the light so that you are not in your own shadow and daylight will not emphasize the joins between lengths.

To mark a guideline for the first length, measure one roll width less 25mm (1in) out from each corner and drive in a nail at each point. Tie a taut, chalked line of string between the nails, then snap the string against the ceiling to create a guide for the first length. If hanging paper on a white ceiling, make sure you use coloured chalk to coat the string.

Cut the first strip of paper to length, allowing an extra 100mm (4in) for trimming, then paste and fold it accordion-style. Place one end so that about half of the trimming allowance laps on to the wall and the edge of the paper is aligned with the chalk line, then brush it firmly into place.

If you are papering around a bay window or alcove, make diagonal release cuts at the external corners to allow the paper to lay flat. Brush the paper into the side wall of the recess and trim to fit along the edge of the ceiling.

Once the first length of wallpaper is in position, crease and trim the long edge into the angle between the wall and ceiling first, followed by each end, using normal wallpapering techniques.

Completing the job

Hang subsequent lengths in the same manner, butt joining the long

Papering a ceiling

1 Measure out from each corner and mark the positions with nails.

2 Tie a chalked line of string between the nails and snap it against the ceiling.

3 Hang the first length against the chalk line, brushing it into place as you go.

4 Use the bristle tips to ease the paper into the angle between the wall and ceiling.

5 Crease and trim the long edge, then each end of the length.

edges. If there is a ceiling rose, turn off the electricity supply before brushing the paper over the casing and then locate its exact centre with your finger. Make a small cut in the paper at this point and gently pull the pendant through the cut, taking care not to tear the paper.

Ease the paper around the shape of the rose by making a series of small radial cuts from the centre of the rose to the edge of the casing. Smooth the paper into place on the ceiling around the rose and finish hanging the remaining paper. Crease the paper into the edge of the rose before restoring the electricity supply. The paper can be trimmed neatly with a knife once the paste has dried but turn the electricity supply off again before doing this. Where there is a large ceiling centrepiece, it is easier to hang and trim paper if a join runs through the middle of the rose.

Cut the last length roughly to the width required plus 25mm (1in) for trimming along the edge of the paper. Hang and trim it in the same manner as the first length.

ABOVE Paper into a bay window or an external corner by making a diagonal cut to ease the paper around the external angle.

Access equipment

Before tackling this job, it is important to consider how you plan to reach the ceiling safely. Access equipment will be needed that allows you to hang a full length across the room. Scaffold boards supported at either end by sturdy stepladders or trestles will create a flat, level walkway spanning the full width of the room, and can be adjusted to a working height to suit you. Use two boards tied together for a distance over 1.5m (5ft) and provide support in the centre.

Papering around a light fitting

1 Turn off the electricity supply. Make a series of cuts into the edge of the ceiling rose.

2 Crease the paper around the edge of the rose, then trim neatly with a knife.

Papering sloping ceilings

Plan the papering sequence so that a paper that has a definite pattern is centralized across the room. A sloping ceiling can be papered either to match the ceiling or the walls, but do not attempt to hang a single length down the sloping surface on to the wall below. Treat the wide angle between the two surfaces as an internal corner.

Handling paper

Long lengths of paper for a ceiling are easier to handle if they are supported with a spare roll of wallpaper or a cardboard tube.

ABOVE A spare roll of wallpaper can be used to support each length.

Solving Papering Problems

Inadequate preparation and poor papering techniques, rather than faults with the paper itself, are the cause of most wallpapering problems. Some minor mistakes are quite easy to remedy, as shown here, but if the problem is extensive, it is better to strip off the affected area and start again. Some situations can be difficult, and here are some tips to make it easier to handle the wallpaper.

Air bubbles

Bubbles that remain after the paste has dried are caused by not allowing the paper to soak for long enough, not having brushed out the paper properly, or by poor preparation, which prevents the paper from sticking to the wall. Cut a cross in the bubble with a knife, apply paste to the underside of the paper and smooth on to the wall.

Tears

Often, tears are not as bad as they look. If the tear is small, carefully apply some overlap adhesive to the torn piece and ease it back into place with the tips of a brush.

When faced with a large tear in wallpaper, remove loose and damaged paper by tearing it gently from the wall. Tear, rather than cut, a patch from a new piece of paper so that the pattern matches the surrounding area, then feather the edge by tearing away a 6mm (¼in) strip from the back. Paste the patch and lightly brush it into place.

With a vinyl wallcovering, cut a patch so that the pattern matches the surrounding area and tape it to the wall over the damage. Cut through both layers to form a square, remove the damaged vinyl from the wall, then paste and fit the patch.

Ceiling rose

Work out the position of ceiling strips so that a joint passes through the middle of a large centrepiece.

Expelling air bubbles

1 Make diagonal cuts in an air bubble with a sharp knife.

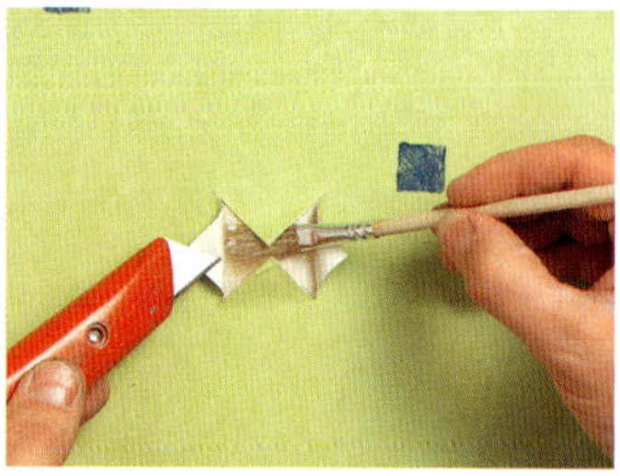

2 Brush adhesive under the cut flaps of paper and press down.

Repairing damaged wallcoverings

1 Carefully tear away any loose or damaged wallpaper, feathering the edges.

2 Make a matching patch by carefully tearing the paper. Feather the edges.

Repairing vinyl

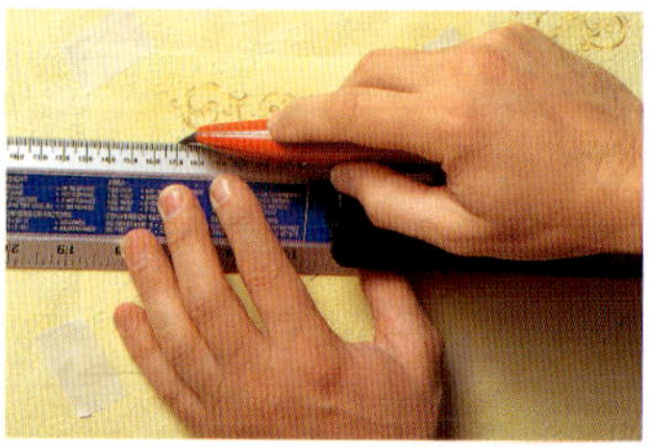

1 Cut out damaged vinyl and a new patch taped on to the wall to match in one go.

2 Remove the old vinyl from within the cut square and apply the patch.

Bulky overlaps

Overlapped edges can create bulky seams in relief and embossed wallpapers. Feather the trimming allowance by carefully tearing down the edge, then flatten the torn paper with a seam roller before hanging the overlapping length.

Gaps in seams

Paper shrinking as it dries, due to poor pasting technique or poor butt joins can cause gaps at the seams. To avoid this, disguise the gaps with a fine felt-tipped pen or crayon in a similar shade to the base colour.

Curling edges

These are caused by inadequate pasting, paste drying out during hanging or, on overlapped vinyl, the wrong paste having been used. Lift the edge of the paper with the back of a knife blade and apply a small amount of paste with a fine brush. Smooth the paper firmly into place with a damp sponge. For overlapping edges on vinyl wallpaper, use vinyl overlap adhesive.

Poor pattern match

Usually the result of inaccurate cutting and hanging, patterns not matching may be caused by variations in the paper along the seams. Check the whole batch and return faulty rolls to the retailer. Straight-match patterns can be difficult to match, especially in internal corners where the edge has been trimmed. Use a level to check that prominent motifs are level across the corner.

Shiny patches

Brushing matt finish wallpapers too vigorously can cause shiny patches. Normally, they cannot be removed, but rubbing gently with a piece of fresh white bread may disguise them. Bread is also useful for removing greasy fingermarks from non-washable papers.

Stains along seams

Paste that has been allowed to dry on the face of the paper can result in stains. These are difficult to remove, but if the paper is washable, try wiping with a sponge and a solution of mild detergent.

Practical tip

- Decorating equipment that has not been well cared for may spoil new wallpaper the next time it is used. Old dry paste will blunt the cutting edges of knives and scissors and make the bristles of a paperhanger's brush stiff to use. Wash all equipment and dry well.

ABOVE Centre a joint over a decorative rose and make radial cuts into the edge to trim.

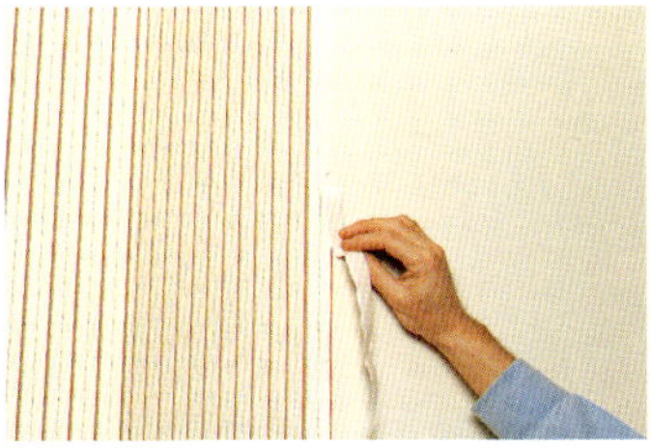

ABOVE Feather the edge of relief wallpaper at external and internal corners.

ABOVE Disguise gaps with a felt-tipped pen, a crayon or watercolour paint.

ABOVE Apply wallpaper adhesive to curling edges with a fine brush.

ABOVE Use a spirit level to check that motifs are level across a corner.

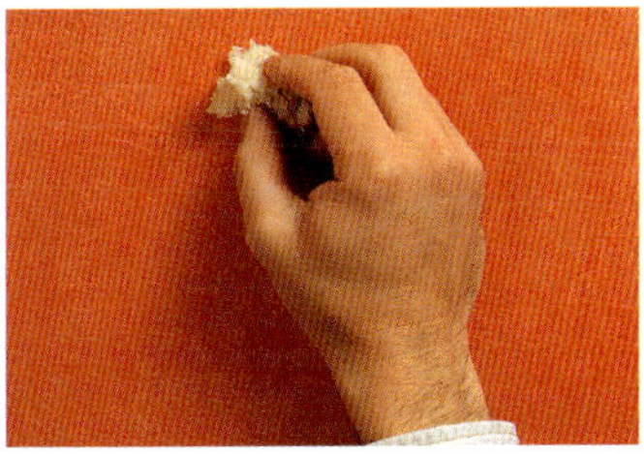

ABOVE Rubbing with a ball of white bread may make shiny patches less obvious.

PREPARING FLOORS

Do not ignore the decorative potential of the floors in your home. There is a wide range of attractive materials from vinyl and cork to ceramic and parquet tiles, but all need laying on a sound, stable surface. Cheapest of all are the floorboards beneath your feet, which, sanded and sealed, can be decorated to suit your colour scheme.

BASIC REQUIREMENTS

The flooring is often the most expensive item in a room, so it must be laid and fitted correctly. All flooring requires a smooth, dry and level base, and a sub-floor will be needed over floorboards if sheet vinyl, parquet, or vinyl, cork, woodstrip, laminated or ceramic tiles are chosen.

Sheets of 3mm (⅛in) thick hardboard will be adequate for lightweight flooring such as cork and vinyl, but ceramic tiles will require a stronger base of plywood 6–12mm (¼–½in) thick. In bathrooms, it is worth paying the extra for marine ply, which offers greater resistance to damp.

Where flooring is to be laid directly on to floorboards, make sure that the surface is in good condition. Any protruding nails should be hammered in and loose floorboards secured with screws. A solid floor that is uneven or damaged should be repaired with a proprietary self-levelling compound.

ABOVE Punch any protruding floorboard nails below the surface of the wood to prevent them from damaging the new floorcovering.

LAYING A HARDBOARD SUB-FLOOR

1 To ensure a secure fixing for hardboard or plywood, use annular (spiral flooring) nails.

2 Condition the hardboard sheets by brushing or spraying with water before laying.

3 A piece of wood cut to size will allow you to space nails correctly and rapidly.

4 Use the offcut (scrap) from each row to start the next so that joins are staggered.

LAYING A SUB-FLOOR

Before laying, condition the boards by spraying the textured side of each sheet with 450ml (¾pint) of water. Stack the sheets back-to-back flat, separated by strips of wood, on the floor of the room in which they are to be laid. Leave them for 48 hours.

Begin laying boards in the corner farthest from the door, fixing each sheet in place with 19mm (¾in) annular (spiral flooring) nails. Start to nail 12mm (½in) in from the skirting (base) board edge. To ensure the boards lay flat, work across the surface in a pyramid sequence, spacing the nails 150mm (6in) apart along the edges and 230mm (9in) apart in the middle.

Butt boards edge to edge to complete the first row, nailing the meeting edges first. Use the offcut from the first row to start the next row, and continue in this way, staggering the joins in each row.

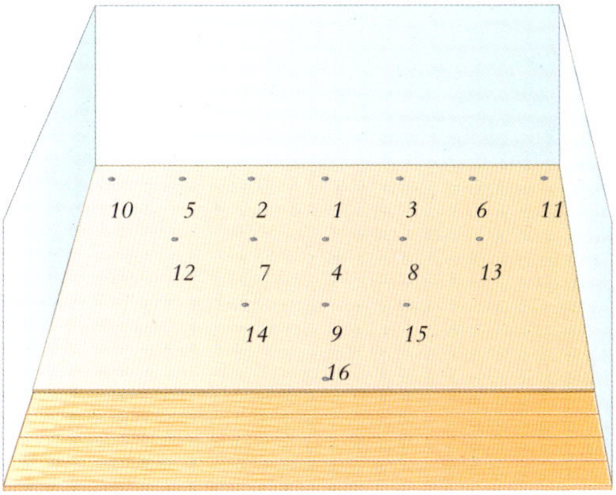

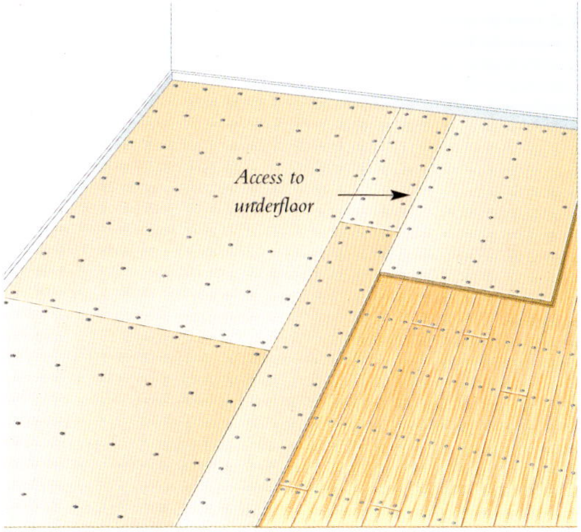

ABOVE Nail across a hardboard sheet in a pyramid sequence to avoid creating bulges. Nails should be 150mm (6in) apart along the edges and 230mm (9in) apart in the middle.

ABOVE If there are plumbing pipes or electric cables under the floor, lay narrow strips of board over pipe runs to ensure easy access for future maintenance.

Calculating quantities

Before buying new floorcovering, take note of any aspects that could make laying difficult.

Sheet materials (carpet and vinyl) Measure the length and width of the room at its widest points, taking the tape right into alcoves and to the halfway point under doors.

Multiply these two figures together to obtain the floor area, which will give you an idea of the amount of flooring needed. Draw up a rough sketch of the room showing all the dimensions and take it to your flooring retailer, who will calculate the quantity required and advise on how to minimize wastage and plan any necessary seams.

Small-unit flooring (tiles, slabs and panels) Measure the room and multiply the width by the length to obtain the floor area. If the room has a bay or recesses either side of a chimney breast (fireplace projection), measure and calculate these areas separately and add to the total.

Hard floor tiles and slabs may be sold by the square metre or square yard. Purchase the quantity required plus a ten per cent allowance for wastage and breakages when cutting. Soft floor tiles and parquet panels are sold in packs. To work out the number of packs required, divide the floor area by the area that one pack will cover, rounding up to the next whole pack.

Strip flooring (woodstrip and laminated boarding) Measure the room and obtain the floor area as discussed above.

Strip flooring is sold in packs to cover a given area. To calculate the quantity of packs required, multiply the length of the room by the width to give the area of the room and divide by the area that is covered by one pack, rounding up to the next complete pack if necessary. Different makes of woodstrip vary slightly, so follow the manufacturer's guidelines when laying the floor.

Practical tips

- Boards can be nailed in place quickly if you cut a length of wood to the correct length as a guide for spacing the nails.
- Lay hardboard with the textured side up. This provides a good key for adhesive, while nail heads will be concealed.
- In an irregularly shaped room, set out the stringlines and adjust the starting point so that any obvious pattern is centred in the main part of the room.

Sanding and Finishing Floorboards

A natural wooden floor will allow you to appreciate the true beauty of the wood grain and can transform a room. A few simple checks will soon tell you if the floorboards beneath your feet are worth renovating. While the work itself is quite straightforward, do not underestimate the amount of time that may be needed to complete the job.

Assessing the Floor

A mechanical sander will not only get rid of ingrained dirt, polish and stains, but also remove deep blemishes and ridges between boards. However, the result will only be as good as the base material. Thin and splintering floorboards are not worth the effort of renovating, while a floor that consists of many sizes and types of board will not look attractive unless painted or disguised with dark stain.

Gaps, however, are quite easy to remedy: small gaps can be filled with a neutral-coloured wood filler, while large gaps should be plugged with fillets of wood planed level with the surface. If the problem is extensive, it will be easier simply to lift and re-lay the whole floor. Protruding nail heads and heavy deposits of old polish will tear and clog abrasive paper, and must be dealt with first.

Tools and Equipment

Stripping a wooden floor can be hard work, so make sure that you have the right tools – hire those tools you do not own. You will need a drum sander for stripping the main part of the floor, an edge sander to reach right up to the skirting (base) boards as well as different grades of abrasive paper, a shave hook (triangular scraper) and a hand sanding block for getting right into tight corners.

A nail punch, hammer and screwdriver will be needed to knock in protruding nail heads and screw down loose boards.

ABOVE Sanding floors is a noisy, messy job. Protect your clothes and yourself with the right equipment.

Practical Tips

- Using a sander creates dust, so wear a facemask and goggles.
- For safety, drape the electrical cable of a mechanical sander over your shoulder, and keep it behind you at all times. Use all power tools with a Residual Current Device.

Preparing the Floor

1 Seal doors with masking tape to prevent dust from seeping into the rest of the house.

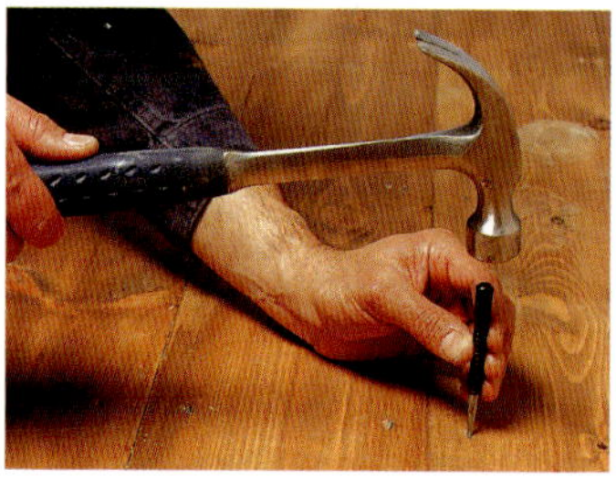

2 Screw down loose boards and punch down protruding nails.

3 Fill gaps between boards with a matching offcut (scrap) of wood or wood filler.

4 Remove traces of old polish with wire (steel) wool and white spirit (paint thinner).

Sanding

To remove the worst of the dirt, fit coarse sandpaper to the drum sander and work diagonally across the boards, overlapping each sanded strip by about 75mm (3in). If the boards are badly blemished or warped, vacuum to remove dust, then repeat this step, working diagonally in the opposite direction. Vacuum again, then fit medium-grade sandpaper to the machine and work up and down the boards along the grain, overlapping each strip as before.

Finally, repeat this step, after vacuuming, using fine sandpaper. Around the edges, use an edge sander along the grain, and finish corners with a shave hook and sanding block, or a disc sander.

If you are not careful, a floor sander can run away from you, and if used incorrectly it can spoil a floor. Therefore, it is important to know how to use it properly.

With a drum sander, tilt it back on its wheels, switch on and gently lower the belt on to the floor. Allow the machine to move forward slowly and do not try to hold it back or in one spot, or it will create grooves in the floor. Raise the machine back on to its wheels at the end of each pass, and do not be tempted to "spot sand" stubborn marks as you may end up with a deep groove.

Lay an edge sander on its side, switch on, lift it and lower it on to the floor. Keep the machine moving, otherwise it will create swirl marks.

Finishing and sealing

Once stripped and sanded, floorboards must be sealed with a flooring grade wax, oil, and polyurethane varnish or paint.

Wax is the most traditional treatment, although it attracts dust and is not particularly durable, so it is best used in low-wear areas. Brush-on liquid floor wax is the easiest to use, but must be applied in several thin coats, otherwise it will stay soft and look dull.

Floor oils are very easy to apply and form a hardwearing, water-resistant finish, but will darken the surface colour of the wood slightly. Rub with wire wool before the final coat. Follow the manufacturer's instructions for the best finish.

Sanding a wooden floor

1 Sand diagonally across the boards, using coarse sandpaper.

2 Use a medium-grade sandpaper, working along the grain. Finish with fine-grade paper.

3 Use a belt sander to tackle edges. Use a disc sander or sanding block for the corners.

4 Remove all traces of dust with a brush and then a damp sponge or cloth.

5 Sand down any remaining rough spots by hand with a sanding block.

6 Build a new protective finish with several thin coats of varnish, applied along the grain.

Painting and Varnishing Wooden Floors

A wooden floor makes an attractive feature in itself, but it can take on a whole new dimension when you experiment with colourful paints, stains, waxes and varnishes. Bare floorboards in pristine condition cry out for innovative treatment. If you prefer traditional treatments, look at oak, mahogany, or beech stains coupled with varnish or a clear wax finish.

Essential preparation

Prepare the surface by vacuuming up all traces of dust, then clean the boards with a lint free cloth moistened with white spirit (paint thinner). If the boards are already painted or varnished, the floor will need sanding. A hardboard floor will look more attractive with a painted finish. Use a primer first, then apply two coats of paint. Allow each to dry thoroughly, sand lightly and finish off with two coats of varnish.

The most important rule when treating a floor is not to paint yourself into a corner. Start at the corner farthest from the door, then work back toward the doorway so that you can make a safe exit while the floor dries.

Limed boards

Liming is an easy technique and a good one for beginners to try. It can be used in conjunction with colour-washing – the colourwash goes on first, then the liming paste – to produce an effect known as pickling.

Strip back any worn or grimy floorboards and apply a coat of shellac to seal the wood. Allow the shellac to dry, then use a wire brush to expose the grains and provide a good surface for the liming paste.

For a very attractive finish, try using pastel shades such as pale green or blue for the background colour.

Practical tip

- Use lacquer on your floor for a bright, durable finish. Keep it scrupulously clean, as every speck of dust will show up on the glossy wooden surface.

Liming a wooden floor

1 Stroke the floorboards with a wire brush, working gently in the direction of the grain.

2 Apply the liming paste with fine wire (steel) wool. Fill up the grain as you work.

3 Working on a small area at a time, rub the liming paste into the boards in a circular motion. Leave to dry thoroughly.

4 Remove the excess by rubbing in some clear paste wax with a soft cloth. Buff the surface with a soft cloth to give a dull sheen.

Wood dyes

For modern schemes, consider colourful wood dyes. These must be applied to a clean, sound, grease-free surface. If the preparation is not thorough, the result will be patchy and unattractive. Wood dyes penetrate deep into timber, but they do not provide a protective surface and must be sealed after application.

It is advisable to test the dye on a similar piece of wood before you start work on the floor as the dye will give varying results on different woods and can change significantly as fresh coats are applied. Finish the test with a coat of varnish.

If you are happy with the finish, apply the dye with a 100mm (4in) brush in the direction of the grain, working rapidly so that hard edges do not spoil the effect. Alternatively, you could use a soft cloth.

Wood stains

These do have a protective function and come in a wide choice of colours, in water- and solvent-based versions. The former dry more quickly, but this may not be an advantage when covering large areas, as patchy sections could develop. When staining a newly stripped floor, seal the surface with a thinned polyurethane varnish first.

Use a brush to apply up to three coats of stain, using the product sparingly and working with the grain. If, at some point in the future, you wish to over-paint a stained floor, you will need to strip the surface back to bare wood, then apply a primer and undercoat.

Floor paints

Specially formulated floor paints give a particularly durable finish, but in practice, many ordinary paints will suffice. The latter will need one or two coats of varnish to protect the surface.

Although paint will conceal the natural grain of the wood, it can produce an attractive, hardwearing finish, which requires less preparation time as floors do not need to be stripped back to bare wood, although they must be clean and grease-free.

Varnishes

These are available in oil- and water-based versions, and in satin, gloss and matt (flat) finishes. Coloured varieties, a mixture of stain and varnish, give you the option of transforming pale floorboards into a rich spectrum of colours, ranging from light honey pine to deep mahogany.

If you are applying a solvent-based product, ensure that the room is well ventilated. Stir the varnish well and use a wide brush to apply it. Apply a minimum of three coats. Rub the floor down with a fine abrasive paper before applying the final coat of varnish. On the minus side, varnish will crack with time. Every two or three years, you will need to sand the floor back to bare wood and treat the boards again.

Applying a wood wash or stain

1 Pour the pre-mixed wash or stain into a paint kettle. Brush the wash or stain evenly on the wood in the direction of the grain.

2 While wet, wipe off any excess. This will even the effect and expose more of the grain. Leave to dry before varnishing, if required.

Applying satinwood paint

1 Dilute satinwood paint with 50 per cent white spirit (paint thinner). Brush on the mixture in the direction of the grain.

2 While wet, wipe down with a cloth to remove the excess and even the effect. Leave the surface to dry before varnishing.

Practical tips

- Colours that work well in wood washes and stains include yellow ochre, blue, Indian red, violet cream and pale green.

- If you use a solution of artist's oil paint and white spirit (paint thinner) to make up a thin wash, make sure you only use a small amount of oil paint, as the pigment produces intensely strong colours.

Laying Soft Floor Tiles

Soft floor tiles, such as vinyl, cork and carpet, are a practical and hardwearing choice for floors, especially for rooms such as the kitchen or bathroom. Not only are they quick and easy to lay, but they are also economical to use in irregularly shaped rooms. The look of the floor can also be varied according to the pattern in which the tiles are laid.

Vinyl and cork tiles

It is vital to achieve a symmetrical layout so that any pattern is centred in the room, and there is an even border of tiles around the edges. The first step is to find the centre of the room by joining the mid-points of opposite walls with lines of string pinned to the floor.

Working from the centre, lay a row of dry tiles along both lines of string until no more whole tiles can be laid. If the border tiles are less than a quarter of the width of a tile, adjust the stringline parallel to that edge of the wall by moving it over half a tile width. Make sure that the lines of string cross at right-angles, then rub chalk on the strings and snap them firmly on the floor to leave a guideline in each direction. Use a notched spreader to apply adhesive to the floor, and place the first tile accurately against the stringlines. To lay self-adhesive vinyl tiles, simply peel off the protective backing paper before placing in position. Work outward in both directions, laying

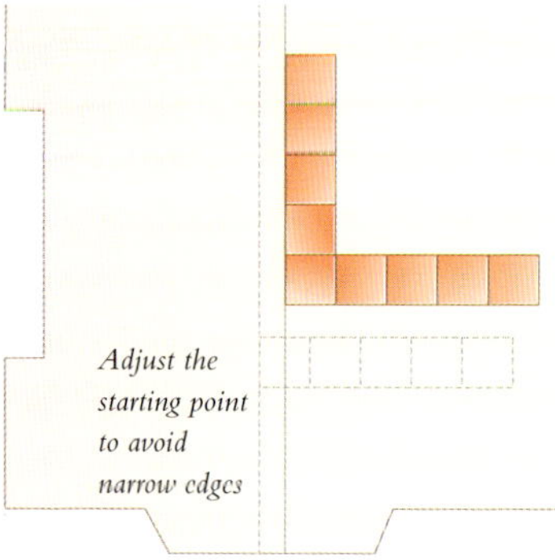

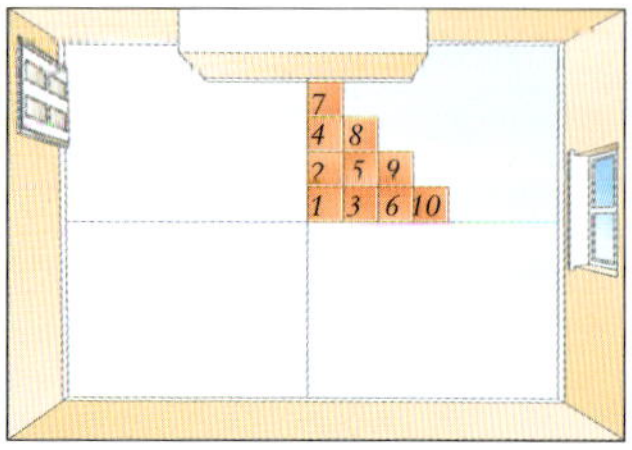

LEFT Lay two rows of dry tiles from the centre of the room and adjust the starting point.

ABOVE Complete a quarter of the floor at a time, laying tiles in the sequence shown.

Laying cork tiles

1 Apply adhesive with a notched spreader to a small area at a time.

2 Lay the first tile accurately against the chalk lines at the centre-point.

3 Mark a border tile for cutting by using the edge of a spare tile as a guide.

4 For a corner tile, first mark one cutting line using the same method as for border tiles.

5 Swivel the tile around the corner and mark the second cutting line.

6 The L-shaped tile should fit neatly around the external corner.

tiles in the sequence shown. Butt cork tiles tightly together to prevent water from seeping between the joins, and wipe off any adhesive that oozes on to the face of the tile.

Complete a quarter of the floor at a time, starting in the section farthest from the door. Once all the whole tiles have been laid, leave the glue to set before laying the edge tiles.

To cut a border tile to size, start by placing the tile exactly on top of the last whole tile laid, then put another whole tile on top of this so that its edge butts against the skirting (base) board. Use the edge of the top tile as a guide for marking the cutting line on the tile below. The same method can be used to cut tiles to fit internal and external corners. Cut self-adhesive tiles to size before removing the backing paper.

At doorways, protect and neaten edges by fixing a binder bar across the centre of the threshold.

If cork does not have a factory finish, it will require sealing with flooring wax or at least three coats of polyurethane varnish.

Carpet tiles

These can be laid loose, but in busy areas, such as a child's room, secure the edges around doors and on every third row with double-sided flooring tape. Carpet tiles are usually laid in a traditional chequerboard pattern by alternating the pile direction; an arrow on the back of the tile shows the direction of the pile.

Cutting techniques

Cut vinyl tiles on scrap board, pressing the knife firmly through the decorative face. Cork should be scored through the face, then snapped along this line. Cut carpet tiles through the backing material, holding the knife at a slight angle away from the pile to create a neat edge.

To cut tiles to fit around obstacles, first make a template. For pipes, slit the tile from the back edge to the position of the pipe, then cut out a circle for it. A piece of pipe with sharpened edges is useful for cutting neat holes in soft floor tiles.

Sub-bases

Carpet tiles can be laid directly over floorboards, but vinyl and cork tiles will require a hardboard sub-floor. Soft floor tiles can also be laid directly on to a level, clean and dust-free solid floor, provided there is a damp-proof course.

Practical tips

- Shuffle packs of cork tiles so that any slight difference in colour is less noticeable.
- Check which way to lay pre-sanded tiles. The underside is rougher to provide a key for adhesive.
- Narrow strips of carpet tile will curl rather than lay flat, so adjust the layout to avoid cutting tiles less than 100mm (4in) wide.
- To remove air bubbles, rub vinyl tiles in a circular movement with your fist, working from the centre of the tile outward.

Cutting soft tiles

ABOVE Cut through the backing of carpet tiles with a sharp knife.

ABOVE Make a template for curved cuts and awkward shapes.

ABOVE Score cork tiles through the decorative face and snap cleanly.

ABOVE Cut a slit from the back edge of the tile to the position of a pipe.

Laying Hard Floor Tiles

Hard flooring, including ceramic and quarry tiles, stone and slate, creates a hardwearing, waterproof finish that is perfect for busy areas of the home. Laid correctly, it will give years of service. This flooring is not as easy to lay as soft floor tiles, so it is worth planning the layout first on graph paper and investing in the correct cutting tools.

Ceramic tiles

Plan the layout of ceramic tiles as for soft floor tiles, then fix two marker battens (furring strips) against the edges of the last whole tiles laid. Use a try or combination square to ensure the battens form a perfect right angle, and on a solid floor secure them with masonry nails.

Apply adhesive with a notched spreader to an area of about 1sq m (11sq ft), and lay the tiles according to the dry run. Use pieces of thick card or floor tile spacers to maintain even gaps for grouting. Lay up to a dozen tiles at a time, using a long straightedge and spirit level to check that the tiles are straight and the surface horizontal. Work across the room in this fashion, then leave the tiles for 24 hours to set before tackling edge tiles.

To mark an edge tile for cutting, follow the technique described for soft floor tiles. A proper floor tile jig will make cutting easier. Apply tile adhesive to the back of cut tiles, not the floor. Leave the floor for 24 hours, then grout it. Apply grout with a dry sponge to 1sq m (11sq ft) at a time, neatening joints with a grouting tool or piece of dowel. Wipe off excess grout with a damp sponge and, when it has set, buff the surface with a clean dry cloth.

Quarry tiles, stone and slate

Plan the layout and set out two guide battens in the same manner as described for ceramic floor tiles. The battens used should be twice the thickness of the flooring.

Dry-lay a batch of tiles and nail a third batten to the floor so that it butts against them and is parallel to one of the other battens. Check that the battens are level, adding packing pieces to adjust them if necessary.

Laying ceramic tiles

1 Mark the outer edges of the last whole tiles with two battens (furring strips).

2 Maintain even gaps between tiles with thick card or floor tile spacers.

3 Lay a batch of tiles at a time, then check that they are straight and level.

4 A proper floor tile jig is needed for making straight cuts in thick tiles.

5 Nibble away awkward cuts with tile nippers, piece by piece.

6 Apply adhesive to the backs of cut ceramic tiles, not the floor.

Mix mortar from one part cement and three parts builders' sand. Lay a 12mm (½in) thick bed for quarry tiles and 18mm (¾in) for stone and slate, levelling it by dragging a notched board across the bay. The cut notches at each end of the board should be the thickness of a tile less 3mm (⅛in).

Sprinkle dry cement over the mortar, then lay all the tiles to complete the bay. Insert floor tile spacers or pieces of dowel to maintain even gaps between machine-made quarry tiles. Use the point of a trowel to form 10mm (⅜in) gaps between hand-made tiles and slabs.

Tamp down the tiles with the unnotched side of the board until they are level with the battens, and wipe any mortar from the face of the tiles before it hardens.

Move the outer batten to form another bay of the same size and work section by section across the room until the main area of the floor is complete. Leave to set for one or two days. When the tiles can be walked on, remove the battens and fit the edge tiles. Apply mortar to the floor and level it first with a small notched piece of board.

Seal joints with a waterproof grout or point with a dry 1:3 mortar mix.

Cutting techniques

To cut ceramic and quarry tiles to fit around obstacles such as pipes and external corners, mark the cutting line on the tile and nibble away the waste with pincers. When most of the waste has been removed, smooth the rough edge with a tile file. Stone and slate must be chipped away with a bolster chisel and hammer. For cutting ceramic floor tiles, hire or buy a floor tile jig capable of cutting thicknesses up to 18mm (¾in).

Sub-bases

Ceramic tiles can be laid on a plywood sub-floor over floorboards, but a suspended timber floor may not be strong enough for other types of hard flooring. Solid floors provide an ideal base, and hard flooring can be laid where there is underfloor heating or no damp-proof course.

Practical tip

- **Tiles with a smooth back can be laid on a thin 3mm (⅛in) bed of adhesive, but tiles with studs will need a 6–12mm (¼–½in) bed.**

Laying quarry tiles

1 Fix and level a third batten (furring strip) to construct a bay for the mortar.

2 Dry-lay tiles along the guide battens in both directions to check for fit.

3 Lay mortar between the battens and level with a notched board.

4 Use spacers or pieces of dowel to maintain even gaps between machine-made tiles.

5 Tamp down the surface with a length of wood to level the tiles.

6 Use a notched piece of board to level mortar for edge tiles.

Laying Sheet Flooring

A roll of sheet vinyl can be heavy and awkward to manoeuvre, but it is not too difficult to lay. The same method can also be used for laying carpet with a synthetic backing. Fitting fibre-backed carpet that needs underlay, however, requires a different technique and is a job best left to the professionals if you want to get the best results.

Planning

Sheet flooring allows a large area to be covered quickly and with the minimum of seams, but in an awkwardly shaped room can result in wastage. Plan the layout so that any joins do not run across or into a doorway. Seams laid at right angles to a window will be less noticeable.

Fitting

Unroll the flooring in the correct position, allowing the waste to lap up the skirting (base) boards. So that it will lay flat, cut away a triangle of material at each internal corner and make a release cut at each external corner. You will also need to make a series of small release cuts to allow the flooring to lay flat around awkward shapes such as door frames. Work around the room and trim away the surplus with a sharp craft knife, leaving 50–75mm (2–3in) lapping up the skirtings.

Start to fit the flooring along two straight adjacent walls, working out from this corner around the room. Use a bolster (stonecutter's) chisel to crease the flooring into the junction between skirting and floor. Then, holding it firm with a long metal straightedge, use a sharp craft knife to trim the flooring to fit neatly against the skirting.

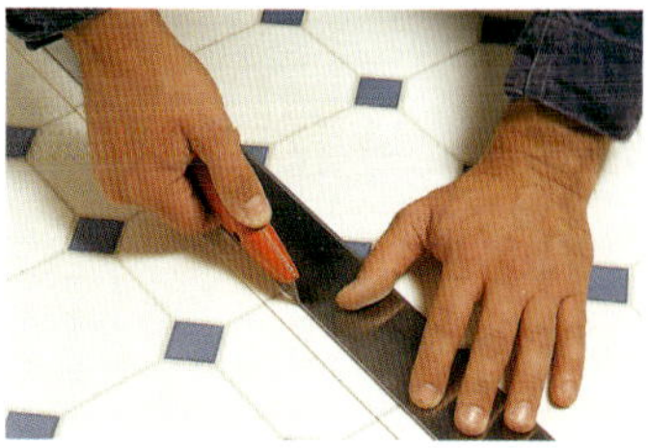

ABOVE To join vinyl, overlap the edges, align the pattern and cut through both layers.

If a join is necessary, carpet edges can be butted together – the pile will disguise minor irregularities. For vinyl, overlap the edges so that the pattern matches and cut through both layers with a sharp knife along a metal straightedge. Secure with double-sided flooring tape fixed to the floor directly beneath the join.

Once the flooring has been trimmed to fit, pull back the edges and fix double-sided tape to the floor all around the room. Remove the protective paper from the tape and press the cut edges of the flooring

Laying the vinyl

1 At internal corners, cut out triangles of flooring so that it will lay flat.

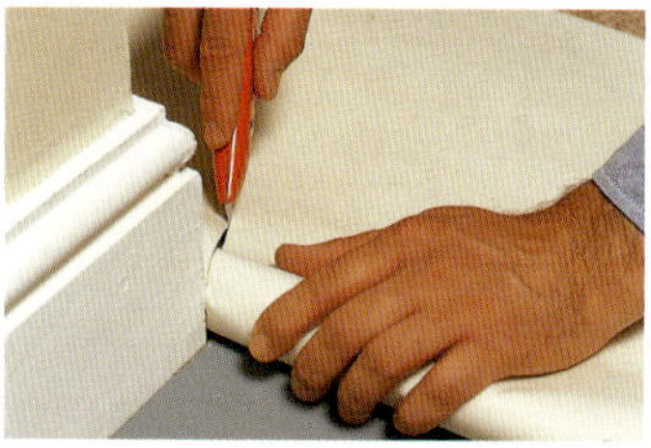

2 To ease flooring around an external corner, make diagonal release cuts.

3 Ease the flooring around door frames by making a series of small release cuts.

4 Trim away excess material, leaving an overlap of 50–75mm (2–3in).

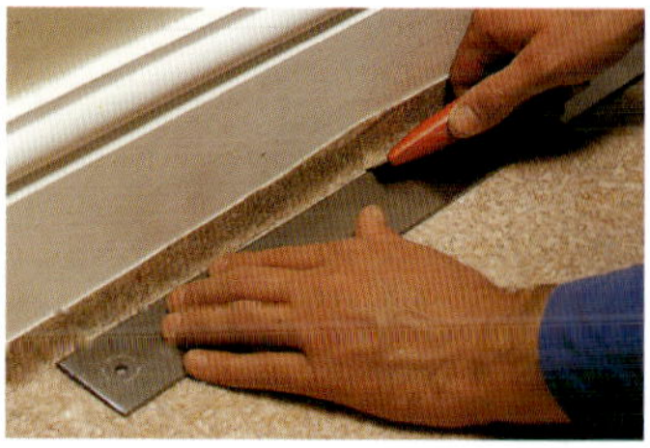

5 Crease the flooring into the skirting, then trim using a metal straightedge as a guide.

firmly into place. Carpet laid over floorboards can be fixed with heavy-duty staples 18mm (¾in) in from the edge at 100mm (4in) intervals, or with 37mm (1½in) carpet tacks every 200mm (8in). When using tacks, cut the carpet slightly oversize, turn the edges under, and drive the tacks through the double thickness. Secure flooring in a doorway with a threshold strip fixed over the centre.

Fitting around awkward shapes

A profile gauge will be useful for marking out small shapes prior to cutting, but for a larger obstacle you will need to make a template. Tape sheets of thick paper or card to the floor, and use a small block of wood and a pencil to scribe the shape on to the template – this will be slightly larger than the size required. Lay the template on the flooring and use the wood block once more as a guide to transfer the cutting line on the flooring. Trim using a sharp knife and make a straight cut in from the back edge of the flooring to fit.

Sub-bases

Carpet can be laid over floorboards, but sheet vinyl will require a hardboard sub-floor. Both materials

ABOVE Secure edges of vinyl flooring around the room with double-sided flooring tape.

can be laid on a level concrete floor that has a damp-proof membrane. Lining paper should be laid under synthetic-backed carpet to prevent dust from rising through floorboards and the carpet from sticking to solid floors.

Laying paper underlay

Roll up the carpet half-way across the room and start to lay the paper underlay 50mm (2in) from the skirting. Work toward the centre of the room, overlapping each strip by 25mm (1in), and staple the paper to the floorboards along the seams and around the edges – use flooring tape on a solid floor. When one half of the room is complete, roll the carpet back into place, then roll up the rest of the carpet to complete the other side of the room.

Using a template

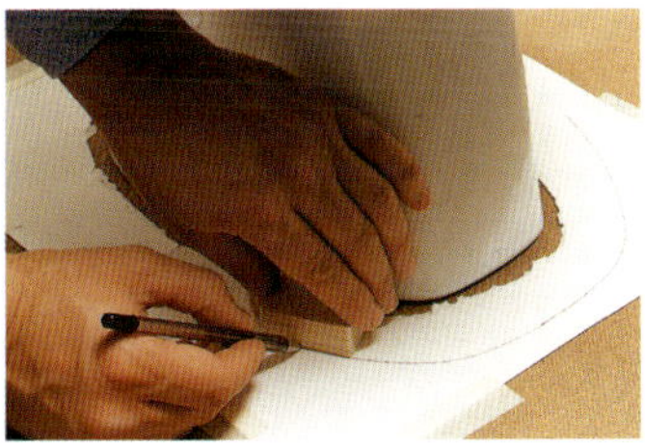

1 Use a block of wood and a pencil to scribe the shape on to a paper template.

2 Transfer the shape on to the flooring using the block of wood as a guide.

Practical tips

- Re-roll sheet vinyl so that the pattern is outermost, then lay it flat for 48 hours in the room in which it is to be laid. This will make it more pliable and easier to lay.
- In a bathroom, it will be easier to start along the wall where the handbasin or WC is installed.
- Dust and fluff impair the adhesion of double-sided tape, so do not remove its protective paper until all of the flooring has been trimmed to fit.
- A carpet should be laid with the pile running away from the main window to prevent uneven shading in daylight.

Threshold strips

Make sure that you buy the correct type of threshold strip. There are various types suitable for joining carpet to carpet, vinyl, cork, wood flooring and ceramics. Remove inward opening doors to make laying floor covering easier.

ABOVE In a doorway, use a threshold strip to secure and protect the cut edge.

Laying Woodstrip Flooring

Woodstrip flooring is suitable for use in most rooms of your home and requires only basic carpentry skills to lay. The method used will vary according to the system you buy. Some strips need to be secret nailed to the floorboards, while others are designed to be a floating floor and may be glued, clipped or simply slotted together.

Expansion gaps

All woodstrip flooring requires an expansion gap around the edges of the room to allow the floor to expand and contract naturally. This can be achieved by removing and refitting the skirting (base) boards so that they cover the edge strips, or by filling the gap with cork strip or covering it with quadrant (base shoe) moulding, which are quicker and easier options. Floor laying kits that contain expansion-gap spacers are available. Laminated strip flooring can be laid in exactly the same manner as woodstrip flooring.

Fitting

Mark a guideline for the first run by snapping a chalked stringline 12mm (½in) away from, and parallel to, the longest or most convenient wall. Normally, woodstrip is laid lengthways in a room, or at right-angles to the floorboards.

Use a strip of wood or spacers to maintain the expansion gap and butt the grooved edge of the first strip

Pull bar from laminated flooring kit

Glue scraper

Tapping block

Spacers

Professional tapping bar

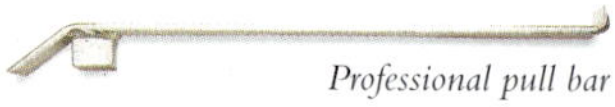

Professional pull bar

Laying a woodstrip floor

1 To allow for an expansion gap, butt the first length against 12mm (½in) spacers.

2 Drive pins at a 45-degree angle through the tongue into the floor.

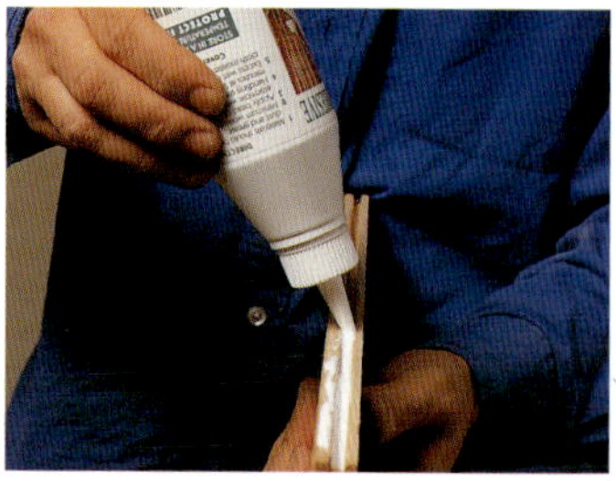

3 If adhesive is recommended, apply glue to both the tongue and groove.

6 To ensure that the floor is strong and stable, stagger the joints.

7 Use an offcut to mark the architrave (trim) for cutting to the correct size.

8 Cut strips to size with a tenon saw and discard the tongue portions.

tightly against it. Lay strips dry to complete the first run and, if necessary, cut a length to fit, marking it with the aid of a try square.

Once the first row has been aligned and is square with the wall, ease the boards apart and fix them in place according to the recommended method. For a glued floor, apply adhesive to both the tongue and groove of adjoining boards, wiping off any that oozes between the boards immediately. Boards held by clips should have them driven into adjacent lengths at 760mm (30in) intervals. If secret nailing is required, drive pins into the floor through the board tongues at a 45-degree angle, spacing them 200–250mm (8–10in) apart, up to 40mm (1½in) from each end.

To lay subsequent lengths, push the grooved edge of one strip on to the tongue of the strip laid previously, tapping it firmly with a hammer and protecting the edge from damage with an offcut (scrap). Lay the second and subsequent rows in this way, staggering the joints. An offcut longer than 300mm (12in) can be used to start the next row.

If a strip needs to be trimmed along its length to fit in the skirting, place it exactly over the last strip laid and put a spare board on top so that its tongue butts up to spacers against the skirting. Use the edge of the top board as a guide for marking the cutting line on the board below, and trim to size with a tenon saw. To ease the last strips into place, use a lever, or fitting tool if supplied, and pull them tightly against the previous row. If the flooring has been fixed by secret nailing, secure the last pieces by nailing through the face of the wood, punching the nails below the surface and disguising them with wood filler. Leave the floor to settle for 24 hours, after which the spacers can be removed and the expansion gap filled with cork strip or covered with quadrant moulding pinned to the skirting. If the flooring does not have a factory finish, it should be sealed as soon as possible with flooring grade wax, finishing oil or polyurethane varnish.

4 Tap each strip into place, using an offcut (scrap) to protect the edge from damage.

5 To mark a cutting line, align strips carefully and use a straightedge as a guide.

9 The last strip will need to be levered into place to create a tight fit.

10 Remove the spacers and fit cork strip into the expansion gap.

Cutting techniques

Cutting wooden flooring to fit neatly around a door frame can be difficult. Instead, use an offcut as a guide to mark a horizontal cutting line around the bottom of the architrave (trim) and frame. Saw through the architrave along the line and remove the narrow portion of wood. The wood strip should slip neatly underneath.

Sub-bases

Woodstrip flooring does not need a hardboard sub-floor, but it may require a paper underlay or polyethylene vapour barrier, so check the manufacturer's installation instructions. Floating floors and direct-fix systems can be installed over floorboards. A floating floor is the best option for a solid floor.

Practical tip

- Doors may need trimming to fit over the new floor, so remove them before you start.

Laying Wood Mosaic Flooring

Wood mosaic or finger parquet flooring is the least expensive type of decorative wooden flooring, and may be veneered or hardwearing solid wood. It is also easy to lay and economical to use, particularly in awkwardly shaped rooms. Some finger parquet is supplied pre-finished, while other types may require sanding as well as sealing after being laid.

Fitting

To mark a guideline for the first row, add 12mm (½in) to the width of one panel and snap a chalked line of string on the floor that distance from the wall farthest from the door. Butt a 12mm (½in) strip of wood or spacers against the skirting (base) board to maintain the expansion gap. Apply adhesive to the floor with a notched spreader, covering an area equal to two or three panels.

Lay the panels one row at a time, against each other. Do not push panels together, as this will force adhesive on to the surface of the wood. Wipe away excess adhesive immediately. Use a straightedge and spirit level to check that each row is straight and horizontal before going on to the next. Level uneven panels by tapping them down with a softwood block and hammer.

Once all whole panels have been laid, cut others to fit around the edges of the room by using a spare panel to mark the cutting line. Butt the top panel up to the spacers against the skirting to allow for the expansion gap. When trimming panels to size, cut down through the decorative face with a tenon saw; apply adhesive to the back before fitting into place.

Attach quadrant (base shoe) moulding to the skirting with panel pins (brads) every 600mm (24in), or fill the expansion gap with cork strip. Punch pin heads below the surface and disguise with wood filler.

Once the adhesive has set, the surface can be sanded if necessary. Use an electric orbital sander, paying particular attention to any uneven joints. Vacuum thoroughly and wipe with white spirit (paint thinner) to remove all dust. Then seal according to the manufacturer's instructions.

Practical Tips

- To reduce the risk of warping, remove the wrapping and leave the panels in the room in which they are to be used for seven days prior to laying so that they will acclimatize to humidity levels.
- Set out panels dry first, adjusting the starting point if you will be left with awkward gaps to fill.
- The grain on parquet runs in different directions, making sanding difficult. To minimize scratching, lightly sand at a 45-degree angle to the grain.

Laying wood mosaic flooring

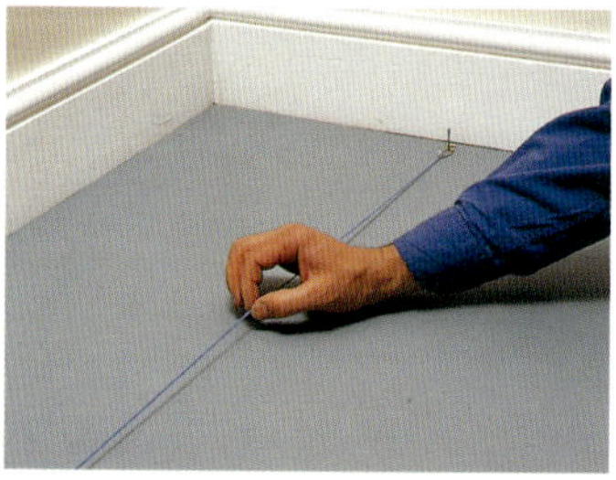

1 Snap a chalked line on to the floor as a guideline for the first row of panels.

2 Mark the expansion gap, and apply glue to the floor with a notched spreader.

6 Cut the wood mosaic panels face upward, using a tenon saw.

7 Wood mosaic can be cut to fit or slotted underneath a door frame.

Cutting techniques

To cut parquet or wood mosaic flooring to fit around a door frame, you can remove part of the architrave (trim) by using an offcut as a guide to saw horizontally through the frame as for woodstrip flooring and slip it underneath, or use a profile gauge to transfer the exact shape on to the panel and cut it out with a fine hacksaw.

To accommodate a pipe, measure and mark the position of the pipe on the panel, then drill a hole slightly larger in diameter than the pipe at that position. Remove a strip of wood between the drilled hole and the edge of the panel so that it can be glued in place, then fit the strip into the gap behind the pipe.

Sub-bases

Wood mosaic flooring must be laid on a clean, dry and level sub-floor. A self-levelling screed should be applied to uneven solid floors, while a hardboard sub-floor will be required over floorboards.

ABOVE Use a profile gauge to transfer the shape of small obstacles to panels.

Cutting curves

Mark out a template on a piece of cardboard and transfer the shape to the wooden panel. Use a coping saw to cut along the guideline.

ABOVE Drill a hole and cut out a strip to fit a panel around a pipe.

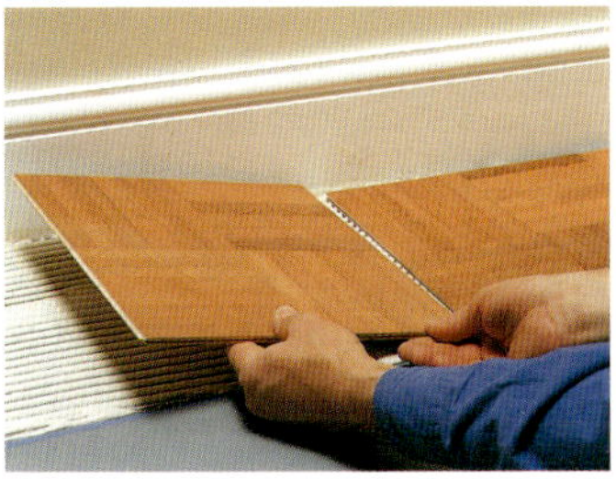

3 Butt panels against each other by aligning the meeting edges first.

4 Work in rows across the room, laying whole panels first.

5 Make sure that you allow for the expansion gap when cutting panels for edges.

8 Fix moulding to the skirting (base) board, not the floor. Punch the pins below the surface.

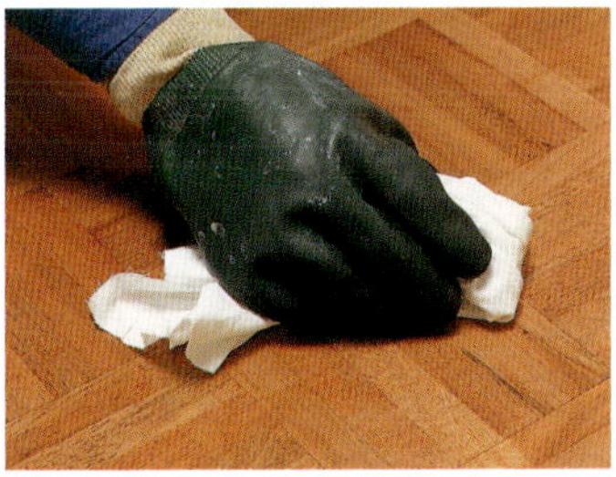

9 Remove all dust by wiping the floor with a cloth moistened with white spirit (paint thinner).

10 For unsealed floors, apply two or three coats of varnish or floor sealer.

Preparing Walls for Tiles

A clean, level surface is essential for all decorating jobs, but especially when tiling. If there is the smallest trace of old adhesive, grease or dust on the surface of the wall, tiles will not adhere properly. Similarly, any unevenness will ruin the alignment of the tiles, and mirror tiles fixed to an uneven surface will produce a distorted image.

Level of difficulty

Beginners may feel confident about painting and wallpapering, but fear that tiling is beyond their level of expertise. However, provided the groundwork is carried out thoroughly, the task is relatively straightforward. If you are completely new to tiling, do not be too ambitious. Do not order top-of-the-range ceramic tiles until you have mastered the basic skills.

Start with a small, manageable area such as a splashback. Set out the tiles so that they are centred on the section you will be working on, and where there will be little tile cutting to do compared with a substantial portion of a wall or an area around a window. Adjust the boundaries of your work if necessary, so that you will only need whole tiles to finish off the job and do not have to cut border tiles.

Once you have succeeded with a simple project, progress to cutting tiles and fitting them around awkward angles. Do not attempt to tile on top of hardboard or chipboard as they do not provide a stable enough background.

Planning

The most important thing to do is to plan precisely where whole tiles will fall. On a flat, uninterrupted wall this is quite easy; simply find the centreline of the wall and plan the tiling to start from there. However, there will probably be obstacles such as window reveals, door openings and built-in furniture in the room, all competing to be the centre of attention. It is necessary to work out the best centre-point to begin work from and care must be taken to avoid having very thin cut tile borders and edges.

Careful setting out is essential to the success of any tiling job. The object is to obtain a balanced look

Preparation

ABOVE Use a scraper to get rid of blistered paint. Fill in any dents or cracks.

ABOVE Absorbent surfaces should be primed with a PVA adhesive prior to tiling.

ABOVE Wash any paintwork with a solution of water and sugar soap (all-purpose cleaner).

ABOVE Use a coat of skimming plaster to smooth out blemishes before you begin.

ABOVE Score the surface of old tiles with a tile cutter to provide a key for the new ones.

1 Tap the broken tile with a hammer protected by a cloth.

2 Carefully chip out the broken tile using a cold chisel.

3 Remove old adhesive. Butter the back of the new tile and slot into place.

on each tiled surface, with the rows of tiles centred on the wall itself or on some prominent feature, much as you would centre a wallpaper pattern. This will ensure that any cut tiles at the margins or around a feature are of equal size. Doors and window openings particularly can cause problems and often require quite a bit of thought.

You will need to work quite quickly, as the adhesive and grout will begin to dry out rapidly. Tackle small sections at a time, cleaning off any excess as you go before it has a chance to harden. This is particularly important with combined adhesives and grouts.

PRACTICAL TIPS

- Never mix floor and wall tiles. The former will be too heavy to adhere to walls. Similarly, wall tiles are far too fragile to use on floors.

- Look for authentic, relief-pattern Victorian tiles to add a little luxury to your decor. Salvage yards and antique shops are a good source.

SURFACES

It is vital to prepare the surface to be tiled properly, so that the tiles will adhere well. The surface for tiling should be clean and dry. It is possible to tile over painted plaster or plasterboard (gypsum board), but old wall coverings should be removed and brick walls must be rendered.

Printed wallpaper can easily be removed because it will absorb water splashed on it immediately; other types will not. With paper-backed fabric wall coverings, it is often possible to peel the fabric away from its paper backing; try it before turning to other methods.

Modern tile adhesives allow tiling over existing tiles, so there is no need to remove these if they are even and securely bonded to the wall surface. Removing tiles might leave you with a time-consuming plastering job before you start. Score the surface of the tiles to provide a key for the adhesive.

Wash wall surfaces down with sugar soap (all-purpose cleaner) or detergent, working from the bottom up, then rinse them with clean water, working from the top down.

TILING CHECKLIST

- Never attempt to tile over old wallcoverings. Remove every scrap of paper and make sure that the wall behind is solid and stable. Remove any flaking plasterwork and repair any cracks.

- Allow new plaster to dry out completely before tiling, then apply a primer sealer to prevent the tile adhesive from soaking into the surface.

- It is possible to tile over existing tiles if they are fixed firmly, although generally it is preferable to remove them. Key the surface of the old tiles by rubbing them down with silicon-carbide paper, score and then wipe clean. Do not line up the old and new tiles. Aim to vary the pattern so that new grout lines are created.

- Painted walls should be washed down, lightly keyed with sandpaper, then all dust removed with a damp cloth.

Planning and Estimating

Successful tiling relies on good planning. Ceramic tiles, the most popular choice for tiling, can be very expensive, especially if you opt for ornate designs or hand-decorated types, and mistakes could prove very costly. Most tiles are produced in standard sizes, so it is a simple matter to work out exactly how many you need to complete a job.

How many tiles?

Our table lists one of the commonest tile sizes, 150 x 150mm (6 x 6in), but tiles come in a wide variety of shapes and sizes, ranging from tiny mosaics to large tiles measuring 400 x 300mm (15¾ x 11¾in) and over.

Begin by measuring the height and width of the space you want to tile, then multiply these figures to give you the overall area in square metres (or square yards). Then you need to establish how many of your chosen tiles will be needed to fill this space. Many manufacturers will specify the number of tiles required to cover a given area. This is invaluable if the tiles have a non-standard shape. Then it is a simple matter to work out the required number for the whole area. For example, if you need to cover a space of 10sq m (10sq yd) and there are 16 tiles to the square metre (square yard), you will need 160 tiles to complete the job. However, you should also allow an extra ten per cent for breakages, which would bring the total to 176.

ABOVE If your tile design is complex, for example, with motif tiles used sparingly in a run of expensive tiles, use graph paper to plan the final layout. Use a large square to represent each tile.

Ceramic coving tiles

These small ceramic tiles offer a neat alternative to plastic strip or waterproof sealants around areas such as shower trays and baths.

Bullnose tile

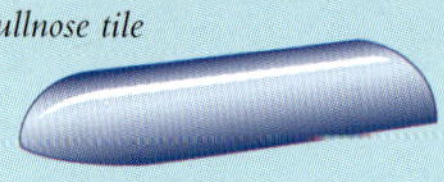

Use this to round off a run of coving tiles.

Quadrant

Neatly fills gaps around the bath.

Mitred tile

Mitred tiles give a neat finish to corners.

Calculating the number of tiles required

Measure the height and width of the area to be tiled and use the chart to calculate how many tiles you will need.

	Approximate number of 15 x 15cm (6 x 6in) tiles required											
2.74m/9ft	36	72	108	144	180	216	252	288	324	360	396	432
2.43m/8ft	32	64	96	128	160	192	224	256	288	320	352	384
2.13m/7ft	28	56	84	112	140	168	196	224	252	280	308	336
1.82m/6ft	24	48	72	96	120	144	168	192	216	240	264	288
1.52m/5ft	20	40	60	80	100	120	140	160	180	200	220	240
1.21m/4ft	16	32	48	64	80	96	112	128	144	160	176	192
0.91m/3ft	12	24	36	48	60	72	84	96	108	120	132	144
0.61m/2ft	8	16	24	32	40	48	56	64	72	80	88	96
0.3m/1ft	4	8	12	16	20	24	28	32	36	40	44	48
	0.3m/ 1ft	0.61m/ 2ft	0.91m/ 3ft	1.21m/ 4ft	1.52m/ 5ft	1.82m/ 6ft	2.13m/ 7ft	2.43m/ 8ft	2.74m/ 9ft	3.05m/ 10ft	3.35m/ 11ft	3.65m/ 12ft

Which tiles?

In general, the cheapest tiles are those with no pattern. However, a large area of a plain colour may look better if enlivened with patterned border tiles or a plaque, comprising a number of tiles that fit together to make a larger picture. Or, pretty motif tiles can be used sparingly on a predominantly plain wall to add colour and interest. Although ceramic tiles are the most popular choice, you could also use vitreous glass, mirror, metallic, mosaic, cork or terracotta tiles for your walls. Buy your tiles in bulk, making sure that any batch number is the same on each box as there can be significant differences in shading between batches. You can also disguise the differences in colour by mixing up all the tiles before you begin.

Tiling gauge

Make a tile gauge from a 50 x 25mm (2 x 1in) strip of wood, cut to about 2m (6ft 7in) long. Place it on the floor and lay your tiles along it. If you are using standard field tiles, allow room for the spacers, then mark the position of each tile on the gauge. Draw a line at the top of the horizontal tiling area and use a spirit level to ensure it is level.

Use your gauging rod vertically to mark off the tiles down the length of the wall. If you need to cut the tiles to fit, they will be much less noticeable at the bottom. Use masonry nails to secure a batten (furring strip) where the last full tiles will be positioned at the base of your work area. The batten acts as a guideline for your gauge and will also support your tiles.

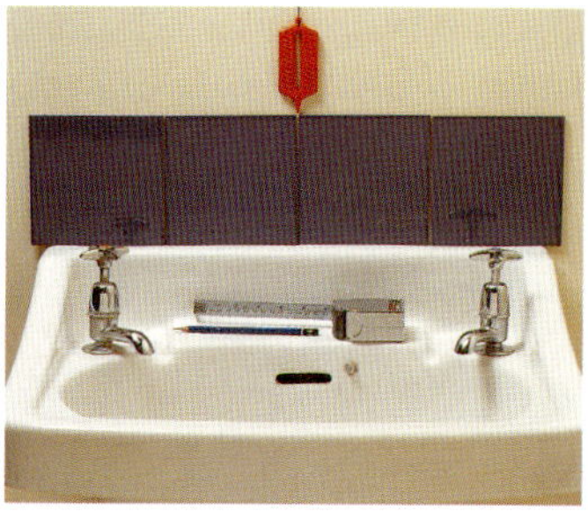

ABOVE If you are tiling a small area, such as a splashback, plan the job so you can position a tile either side of the centre point.

Use a plumbline and mark a vertical line down the centre of your tiling area. Position your gauge rod to work out where the whole tiles will fall on each side of the line. Nail in a vertical batten to indicate where the final vertical row will fall. These two battens form the perimeter of your work.

Fitting support battens

1 Place the tile gauge on the floor. Mark the position of the tiles and spacers on the gauge.

2 Draw a line at the top of the tiling area and use the spirit level to check it is accurate.

3 Using your gauge, mark off the tiles down the length of the wall.

4 Secure the batten (furring strip) to the wall to act as a guide for your bottom row of tiles.

5 Use a plumbline to get a vertical line and mark with a pencil.

6 Nail in a vertical batten with masonry nails to show where the final row of tiles will fall.

Cutting Tiles

Although there are several very good devices to help you cut tiles successfully, you will achieve much better results if you carry out a few practice runs first. Experiment on old tiles or sacrifice a few plain tiles to perfect the technique. It may be worth investing in a tile jig to help you achieve professional results when cutting large quantities of tiles.

Professional results

Badly cut tiles with jagged edges will be an eyesore wherever they are placed. If you find it impossible to obtain consistently good results, approach your tile supplier, as many will be prepared to cut them for you, but make sure you mark them clearly and accurately. When fixing small pieces of tile, use a notched spreader to apply adhesive to the tile itself, rather than the wall. This should keep excess adhesive off adjoining tiles.

Scoring/cutting devices

Straight cuts are the simplest to make. For example, cutting a tile to fit into a corner or to fill the gap at the bottom of a run of whole tiles.

A tile-cutting jig or hand-held cutter will make light work of this, but the former may not be able to cope with diagonal cuts. In which case, a hand-held tool should be used, scoring along the cutting line and snapping the tile in two in the jaws of the tool or over two matches or a pencil.

For irregular and awkward shapes, around basins and pipes for example, you will need to make a template to

Cutting techniques

1 To cut with a hand tool, mark the cutting line, then score along it.

2 Place the tile, face up, over a pencil. Gently press, as shown, to snap the tile in two.

3 Score and cut devices hold the tile in the jaws of the tool. First score along the line.

4 Apply pressure to lock the jaws of the tool on the tile and snap.

Cutting awkward shapes

1 When cutting narrow awkward shapes, use tile nippers to nibble away small amounts.

2 Smooth down any rough edges on cut tiles with a tile file.

Using a tile jig

With a guillotine jig-type tile cutter, draw the cutter across the tile to score it, then firmly press down the handle to cleanly cut through the tile.

ABOVE Although more costly, tile jigs give excellent results with practice.

transfer the shape to the tile. Alternatively, a profile gauge can be used to copy the shape. This incorporates a series of plastic fingers that reproduce the outline of the object you want to copy when you press them against it. Narrow sections of tile can be cut away piece by piece with tile nippers.

Mirror tiles

To cut a mirror tile, place it, face-up, on a flat surface protected by a cloth or newspaper. Mark the cutting line with a straightedge, then run a glasscutter along the line in one smooth stroke.

Place the straightedge under the tile and use the handle of the glasscutter to tap the surface of the tile lightly along the line of the cut. This will ensure a clean break.

Finally, position the tile so that the scored line is aligned exactly with the straightedge. Protect the surface of the tile with newspaper, then place a hand on each side of the straightedge, pressing down firmly to snap it in two. Wear safety goggles when doing this. Alternatively, a local glass supplier will cut the tiles for you, and smooth down any rough edges, for a small outlay.

Cutting a curved shape

1 Trace the shape of the tile on to paper or card. Use it to make a template of the obstacle.

2 Copy the outline of the obstacle on the tile with a chinagraph (wax) pencil.

3 Hold the tile firmly in a vice, then use a tile saw to cut out the circular shape.

4 Remove from the vice and smooth down any rough edges with a flexible tile file.

Mosaic tiles

These are fixed to a mesh backing and are trimmed by cutting through the backing with scissors. Some may have a paper facing, which is also easily cut. Individual tiles can be cut with tile nippers.

Cutting border tiles

Each border tile should be marked and cut individually as walls can often be uneven and the dimensions may vary on a run of tiles. Once the tile is cut to size, file smooth any sharp edges.

Taking measurements

1 Measure the space between the last full tile and the wall or floor.

2 Transfer this measurement to the tile, score and snap to size.

Practical tips

- Wear safety goggles and protective gloves when cutting tiles to avoid fragments that are very sharp and can cause injuries.
- Use adhesive tape to pick up tiny fragments of mirror. Narrow slivers of tile are unsightly and virtually impossible to cut, so avoid them.

Fitting Field Tiles

All tiling jobs begin by filling in the central area to be tiled with whole tiles, known as field tiles. These need positioning accurately and supporting on the wall while the adhesive dries, otherwise they will slip under their own weight. Nailing vertical and horizontal wooden battens (furring strips) temporarily to the wall will provide this support.

Adhesive

Choose the adhesive carefully, making sure you buy a waterproof version for wet areas, such as for shower cubicles and baths. If you opt for a combined adhesive and grout, wipe any excess from the face of the tiles immediately; once dry, it will be very difficult to remove.

Beginning to Tile

Spread on tile adhesive with a spreader or pointing trowel, to a depth of about 3mm (⅛in), covering an area of approximately 1sq m (11sq ft). Then, holding a notched or serrated spreader at an angle of about 45 degrees, pull it across the wall to form even ridges of adhesive. This will provide the best adhesion. Start at the bottom of the work area, in the angle created by the two guide battens (furring strips), and press the first tile firmly in place.

Position the second tile, using tile spacers to ensure a consistent gap if you are using standard field tiles. Simply butt universal tiles together. Carry on until you complete the first row, then start on the next row, working from the edge batten as before. As you work, adjust the tiles to ensure that they are all bedded to the same depth. If any are proud of the surface, apply extra pressure to ease them into place.

Any tile that is slightly out of line should be removed immediately and repositioned; a misplaced tile can ruin the appearance of the entire job. If you have put too much adhesive on the wall, remove it

Fitting the Tiles

1 Spread a layer of tile adhesive with a spreader over an area of 1sq m (11sq ft).

2 Start at the bottom of the work area, in the corner where the two guide battens meet.

3 Position the second tile, using tile spacers to create an even gap with standard field tiles.

4 Complete the first row, then position the next row in line with the batten as before.

5 If you get too much adhesive on the wall at the top of the tiling, remove it with a knife.

6 Continue until the wall is complete. Allow the adhesive to dry and remove the battens.

carefully with a stripping knife. Wipe any adhesive from the face of the tiles with a damp sponge. Continue in this way until all the whole tiles have been applied. Allow at least a day for the adhesive to dry, then remove the support battens, taking care not to damage the tiles. Finally, cut tiles to fit around the edges.

Cut tiles

These often leave a slightly jagged edge which can be smoothed off with a tile file. You can fix the tile in the jaws of a vice or hold it in your hand. If using a vice, use a cloth to protect the decorative face from being scratched by the jaws of the vice. Hold the tile at an angle of about 45 degrees. File only in one direction with the glazed, decorative surface uppermost. Pull the file downwards without great pressure; repeat until the edge is smooth. If needed, you can finish off with abrasive paper wrapped around a wood or cork block.

Tiling around pipework

Inevitably, you will encounter a pipe projecting from a wall. This cannot be avoided. Assuming that the pipe will pass approximately through the centre of the tile, make a cardboard template, in two halves, and when the fit is perfect, transfer the position of the pipe to the tile using a chinagraph (wax) pencil.

Next, draw a cutting line to pass directly through the outline of the hole. Using whatever cutting method you prefer, cut the tile. Clamp each half of the tile in a vice and saw out the semi-circle in each tile. Use a tile file to smooth the edges then fit the two halves on the wall. If the work is done carefully, the joint line will barely be visible.

Mosaic tiles

You can use sheets of mosaic tiles to make a feature among full-sized tiles, as a splashback or to cover an entire wall. Alternatively, you can create an attractive border or dado (chair) rail effect. Individual tiles can be used to create unique patterns on a wide range of surfaces.

If the sheet of mosaic has a net, mesh or nylon backing, apply adhesive directly to the wall in the normal way, then press the sheet carefully into place. Bed the sheets in place by using a mallet to tap lightly against a rectangle of wood covered with carpet. This will soften the impact of the blow and protect the tiles from damage. The space between the tiles is determined by the backing.

Some mosaic tiles are held together by a paper facing. The tiles are fixed in the usual way, then the facing paper is peeled off once the adhesive has set. Soak a sponge with warm water and wet the tiles. Ease off the paper, starting from a corner. Finally, grout the tiles.

Practical tips

- Allow adhesive to dry for at least 24 hours before applying grout. When tiling over existing tiles or a painted surface, allow longer, ideally about three days.
- Leave newly tiled shower areas for at least two weeks before using to allow the adhesive and grout to dry thoroughly.
- To save money, make your own tile spacers using matches or strips of cardboard.

Fitting mosaic tiles

1 If the sheet of mosaic tiles has a net backing, apply adhesive directly to the wall.

2 Bed the sheets in by tapping with a mallet on a piece of wood covered with carpet.

3 Finally, grout the tiles. Wipe off the excess and leave to dry completely.

Tiling Corners and Recesses

Although some tiling jobs are relatively simple, if using only whole tiles to create a splashback, for example, many are more challenging. If tiling more than one wall or a wall with a door or window, you need to know how to fit tiles around corners and awkward angles. Dealing with these situations requires more thought and planning to ensure a professional result.

Internal corners

At internal corners, the edges of the tiles of one wall should be allowed to overlap those of the other wall, producing a neat grouted joint. Normally, the tiles will be arranged symmetrically on each wall, almost certainly leading to cut tiles at the corner. If, however, complete tiles fit into the corner on one wall, make these overlap the cut tiles on the other wall, as this will produce a neater join. On a narrow return wall in an alcove or recess, it may be better to use whole tiles along the external corner and place narrow cut tiles at the internal corner, where they will be less noticeable.

External corners

Special care should be taken when tiling around external corners, as any mistakes will be immediately apparent. A neat solution is to insert a strip of edge trim down the corner. Fix the trim with adhesive first, then tile up to it on both walls. Take care when setting out the battens (furring strips) on each wall that they are aligned perfectly so that the rows of tiles will be even. You could also finish off an external corner with purpose-made border tiles or a wooden moulding with a painted finish.

Finishing an internal corner

1 On internal corners, place the smallest cut tiles in position first, furthest back as shown. Butter the back of the slightly larger tile.

2 Place the tile into position. Apply pressure and remove excess adhesive with a damp cloth or sponge.

Finishing corners

- To create a neat edge finish, let the tiles on the most prominent wall overlap those of the other wall. You must choose tiles with rounded, glazed edges to give a neat profile. In window reveals, the narrow cut tile should be positioned with the cut edges against the frame where they will not be noticed.

Above To finish external corners neatly, use tiles with rounded glazed edges.

Fitting an external corner

1 Fix the single-edge (or double-edge) corner trim in place first.

2 Choose a colour to match your tiles, then line up the two lines of tiles.

Window areas

There are likely to be lots of awkward gaps to fill around a window, especially one set in a reveal. The secret of success is to follow a logical order of work and break the job down into manageable sections. Carry out a dry run to ensure that the arrangement of the tiles will be aesthetically pleasing.

Tile up to the window reveal first, taking care when you are cutting tiles so that they fit neatly. For L-shaped formations, mark in the outline with a chinagraph (wax) pencil and cut out the waste with a tile saw from the outside edge working to the centre.

Score the upright section and discard the waste. Work on the sill portion of the reveal next, leaving the sides and top until last.

For the neatest finish, position tiles with rounded or glazed edges to the front, or fit edge trim around the reveal, and fit cut tiles against the window frame. Take particular care to align tiles within the reveal with those on the main wall.

Tile the sides of the window reveal next, followed by the top section. To tile the top of the reveal, you will first need to construct a temporary wooden support to hold the tiles in place while the adhesive dries.

To make a feature of the window area you could create a frame-effect with attractive border tiles. This effect can be extended around the room at sill level to form a striking dado (chair) rail. Embossed tiles can look particularly effective when used in this way.

As ceramic border tiles can be quite expensive, aim to choose a design that will stand the test of time. Alternatively, experiment with mosaic tiles to create faux dado and picture rails for a smaller outlay.

Practical tips

- Choose edge trim to match your decor. It comes in a range of attractive colours.
- Avoid using a felt-tipped pen to mark cutting lines on tiles. The ink can run into grout lines and is practically impossible to remove.
- Border tiles may save you the chore of cutting lots of plain tiles to fit. You can choose fun designs, such as aquatic themes in bathrooms, to liven up plain runs of tiles.

Tiling around a window

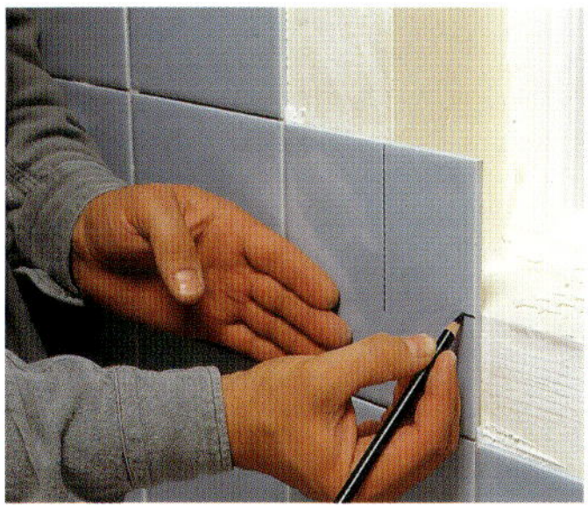

1 Mark the outline and cut from the outside edge to the centre.

2 Tile the window sill portion next. Position the cut portions of half tiles nearest the wall.

3 Ensure all tiles align within the recess with those on the main expanse of the wall.

4 All the grout lines should match up exactly on a finished window recess.

ABOVE Find the mid-point between two windows and let your first tile line up with this.

Fixing Accessories and Grouting

The luxury of having a soap dish or toothbrush holder just where you want it can far outweigh the inconvenience of having to drill holes in a ceramic tile to install it. However, special tiles with pre-fixed accessories are a boon for beginners. Grouting is less daunting for the novice tiler, but it should be approached with the same thoroughness as all the preceding stages

Drilling holes

Drilling into tiles can be daunting for beginners, and while it is not particularly difficult, it is best avoided if there is an alternative. If a lot of time and effort has been spent creating a flawless tiled surface, it can be demoralizing to deal with a cracked tile or a hole that is too large as a result of a drifting drill bit. However, if there is no other option, following the technique described here will make the process a lot less painful.

It is also possible to buy accessory tiles that match the colour and dimensions of some ranges of tiles. These have bathroom fittings already in place, such as tooth mug brackets, toothbrush holders, soap dishes and toilet-roll holders.

Fixing an accessory tile

Leave a tile out of the appropriate row and clean any traces of adhesive. After 24 hours, apply fresh adhesive to the back of the accessory tile and place it in the gap. Use masking tape to hold the tile in place until the adhesive is dry.

Drilling into tiles

If you have to drill your own fixing holes, you can buy a special tile bit that will cut through the glaze with ease. Alternatively, a masonry bit can be used, although it is wise to break through the glaze first by tapping lightly with the point of a masonry nail. A little planning will also make the job go smoothly.

Drilling will create a lot of dust, which can discolour adjacent grout. To minimize the problem, have a helper hold the nozzle of a vacuum cleaner near the hole as you drill.

Decide exactly where you want your accessory to be and mark the spot clearly with a chinagraph pencil. Place a piece of masking tape

Accessory tiles

Some tiles can be purchased with bathroom fittings such as soap dishes, or toothbrush holders in place. To fix one of the above, leave a gap in your tiling and clean away any traces of adhesive. Leave for 24 hours, then apply adhesive to the back of the tile and place it in the gap. Use masking tape to hold it in place until the adhesive is dry.

ABOVE Accessory tiles are heavier but do not require a special adhesive.

Making holes

1 Masking tape will stop the drill bit from slipping on the surface of the tile.

2 There are proprietary fittings that prevent drill slippage and keep the hole square.

3 Push a rawl plug into the wall beyond the back of the tile to prevent any splitting.

over the area to be drilled to stop the drill bit from slipping on the shiny surface. Mark the position of the hole clearly on the tape. Line up the bit carefully and drill through the tile and into the wall. You can now buy a fitting which will help you to drill accurately. To use it, take the sticky-back plastic off the fitting, position it where you want to drill, and use it as your guide.

Take care not to overtighten the screws when fixing the accessory, as you may split the tile.

Grouting

The final task is to fill the gaps between the tiles with grout. Leave a suitable interval for the tile adhesive to dry, typically 24 hours, before applying the grout. It can be purchased in powder form for mixing with water, or ready-mixed. Remember to use a waterproof grout in a kitchen and bathroom.

Apply the grout with a squeegee or damp sponge, working it well into the tile joints. Cover an area of about 1sq m (11sq ft) with each application of grout.

Do not allow the grout to dry on the surface of the tiles, as it will be difficult to remove. Wipe off excess as you work with a damp cloth. If you prefer a concave finish to the grout, run a piece of dowel or a proprietary grout shaper gently along each joint. Allow the grout to dry, then wipe over the tiles with a damp sponge. Finally, polish with a cloth for a gleaming finish.

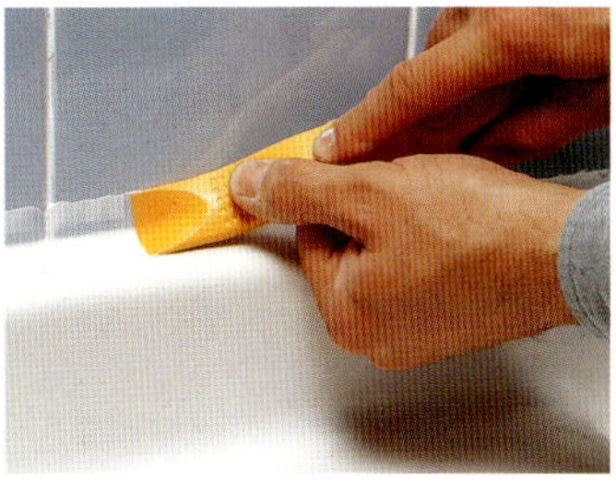

ABOVE You can now buy specially made tools for tidying sealant. Use a sealant specially formulated for the job.

Grouting and sealing

1 Use a squeegee or sponge to work the grout well into the tile joints.

2 While the grout is moist, wipe excess off the face of the tiles with a damp sponge or cloth.

3 Press a piece of dowelling gently into each grout line to give a neat finish.

4 Finish the job by applying sealant to the gap between the tiles and basin or bath.

Grout whiteners

If grouting becomes discoloured, whitening products are available that are simply painted on to create sparkling new grout lines. Clean the area well and allow to dry before applying the new finish. Coloured grout can look very dramatic, especially between white tiles. However, some types are not suitable for use over waterproof grout. Always check the manufacturer's instructions.

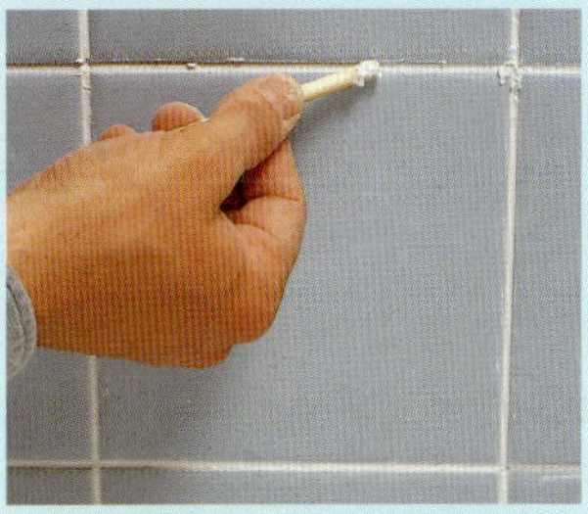

ABOVE For a good finish, use a special grout shaper to joint the tiles.

GLOSSARY

Architrave (trim) A type of timber moulding, used mainly around openings in walls for doors.

Batten (furring strip) A name given to a straight length of timber, used for temporary or permanent support e.g. of roof tiles, wall tiles or for setting concrete.

Bevel An angled edge on, for example, a piece of wood. Also see *chamfer*. Also a carpenter's tool for setting an angle.

Bolster (stonecutter's) chisel A flat-bladed chisel used for cutting masonry. Used widely by electricians, plumbers and paving contractors; can also be used for levering up floorboards.

Building regulations Legal requirements in the UK and other countries for the ways that houses are constructed (and modified).

Butt joint A joint between two pieces of timber when one piece simply meets the other, such as in an L-shape or a T-shape or end-to-end.

Casement window A window (or *light*), which is hinged at one side or at the top.

Caulking gun A device for squeezing sealant or adhesive out of a cartridge.

Cavity wall A method of house construction, where the outer walls of the house consist of two "leaves" (typically one of brick and one of lightweight block) with a gap (cavity) between them.

Centre point The sharp point of a *twist drill bit* or a metal plug put into a *dowel* hole to transfer its position to a second piece of wood.

Chamfer An angled edge to timber, usually smaller than a *bevel*.

Chipboard (particle board) An inexpensive manufactured board consisting of timber scraps and glue.

Clearance hole A hole drilled to take the full size of a screw.

Consumer unit The modern term for an electrical fuse-box. It may contain miniature circuit breakers rather than fuses depending on its age.

Combination ladder A ladder that can be used in two or more ways. Uses include: step-ladder, straight ladder, stair ladder and extending ladder.

Cornice, Cove (crown molding) A decorative timber, plaster or polystyrene (styrofoam) moulding to cover up the join between wall and ceiling.

Counterbore To enlarge a hole, e.g. to take a bolt or screw head.

Countersink An angled recess to take the head of a countersunk screw. Also tool for making the same.

Damp-proof course An impermeable layer put in exterior walls to prevent damp rising up the wall.

Damp-proof membrane An impermeable layer put in floors to prevent damp rising.

Depth stop A device attached to an electric drill to limit the depth of a hole being drilled.

Door furniture A general term for the bits screwed on to doors, such as handles, knockers and knobs.

Dovetail A woodworking joint, where angled pins in one piece of wood fit into identical angled recesses in the other. Also describes fine-toothed backsaw used for making same.

Dowel A circular timber peg used for reinforcing woodworking joints.

Duckboard A low slatted timber platform for standing on.

Eaves A general term for the wood pieces where the roof meets the house walls. Consists of *soffit* and *fascia board*.

Emulsion (latex) paint Water-based paint for covering walls.

End grain The fibres at the end of a piece of wood that are highly absorbent.

Fascia (board) The vertical timber boards at the eaves. Gutters are usually fixed to these.

Fillet A thin narrow strip. Usually applied to strips of mortar used in paving.

Flashing Strips cut from lead or zinc sheet used to seal roofing junctions.

Float glass The modern replacement for sheet glass and plate glass (so called because in manufacture it is floated out of the furnace on molten tin).

Flush panelling Covering moulded doors with hardboard to make them flat.

Former A word for a mould around which something else shapes itself.

Fungicide A chemical treatment for removing mould and algal growth.

Fused connection unit An electrical fitting allowing electric equipment to be permanently wired in.

Gable The pointed walls, sometimes found at the ends of a pitched roof.

Galvanized Coated with zinc to prevent steel from rusting.

Gloss paint An oil-based paint with a shiny finish used on wood and metal.

Grain The texture of timber created by the annual growth of a tree.

Grout A filling to go into the gaps between tiles.

Handed Refers to hinges (e.g. rising butt hinges) attached to either the right or the left of the door.

Hardcore A mixture of stones and rubble used to provide a base for paving and concrete.

Housing (also housing joint) A wood-working joint where one piece of wood fits into a slot (housing) in another piece.

Jamb Vertical timbers that form the sides of window and door frames.

Joists Large pieces of timber used in house construction to support floors, ceilings and flat roofs.

Knot A dark coloured circle in wood where a branch grew out of the tree. It can exude resin or can fall out.

Laminate Wooden flooring made in layers; the thin sheeting applied to the tops of worktops; and glass made with a plastic interlayer.

Lath-and-plaster An old-fashioned way of constructing ceilings and partition walls. The plaster is applied to thin timber strips (laths), which are secured to vertical studs (walls) or horizontal joists (ceilings).

Leaded light A window where small panes of glass are held between lead strips.

Light Another name for a window.

Lipping A thin strip (often of hardwood) applied to the edges of a timber board (e.g. a shelf or a countertop).

Mastic (caulking) A non-setting and flexible waterproof sealant.

MDF Medium-density fibreboard. A manufactured board consisting of timber fibres and resin. Has smooth surface and will take screws and nails, but needs handling with care.

Melamine An easy-to-clean plastic often used for covering *chipboard* (particle board) to make shelving boards.

Mitre A joint made by cutting two pieces of wood at 45 degrees, such as for making picture frames.

Mitre fence A platform on a fixed sander to support mouldings while the mitred end is sanded.

Mortise A deep slot cut in timber, for example, for a mortise lock. A mortise chisel is a strong type for levering out the wood. See also *tenon*.

Ogee A particular shape of ornate moulding or gutter profile.

Oilstone A flat abrasive stone used with oil for sharpening chisels and knives.

Overflow An essential part of a sink, basin or bath or a pipe attached to a water tank.

Party wall The wall between two semi-detached houses or two terraced houses.

Pilot hole A small hole drilled to guide a larger drill or to take the point of a screw that then cuts its own thread.

Pitch The slope of a roof or a staircase.

Planning permission Local authority consent needed in the UK and other countries to build a house or for certain extensions and alterations.

Plasterboard (gypsum board) Sheets consisting of solid plaster contained by heavy paper sheets, used for constructing partition walls and ceilings.

Plywood A man-made board consisting of thin sheets glued together. Alternate sheets have the grain running at right angles giving it exceptional strength.

Pointing Using extra mortar to finish the joints between bricks in a wall.

Polyurethane varnish A very tough varnish (paint without colouring), which will withstand heat and resist stains.

Prime/primer The first coat of paint applied to bare wood or metal.

Punched Applied to nail heads to mean that they are pushed below the surface of timber with a nail punch.

PVA (white) glue Strictly polyvinyl acetate: a type of adhesive used for woodworking, also used in concreting work to reduce the absorbency of surfaces.

Rafters Sloping timber members of a roof.

Rebate (rabbet) A slot cut out of the corner of timber to hold something.

Render A mixture of sand and cement used to coat external walls.

Residual current device An electrical safety device that prevents electric shock.

Reveal The rectangular hole in a wall in which a window or door is fitted.

Rim lock (rim latch) A lock (or latch) that is attached to the surface of a door unlike a *mortise* lock, which fits into a slot cut out of the door.

Rising butts Hinges that lift a door as it is opened.

Router An electrical woodworking tool that cuts a slot or a recess.

Sash A name for a window, usually applied to sash windows where each window slides vertically.

Screed A thin layer of sand and cement applied to concrete floors.

Set The way in which alternate teeth on a hand saw are bent away from the blade to make the cut wider than the saw blade and so prevent the saw from sticking.

Shuttering A framework of timber boards used to hold concrete while it sets.

Silicone A flexible non-setting plastic used in sealants.

Skew (toe) nailing Driving nails in at an angle to provide a stronger bond.

Soffit The horizontal timber boards used at the eaves.

Soil pipe The large vertical drainage pipe in houses taking the toilet waste.

Spigot A projection designed to fit into a recess.

Stile The vertical timber pieces of a door or window.

Stopcocks Valves fitted to water pipes to stop the flow of water through them.

Stopping A filler for use with wood.

Stud A vertical timber strut used for internal partition walls.

Tamping Using something heavy to compact materials.

Template A guide for drilling or cutting.

Tenon A reduced section on one piece of wood designed to fit into a slot (*mortise*) in another.

Tongued-and-grooved A method of joining planks (such as floorboards or cladding) edge to edge – a tongue on one piece fits into a groove in its neighbour.

Trap A device fitted in the waste pipe under a bath, basin or sink to prevent foul air and small animals getting in.

Twist drill bits Drills for making holes in wood and metal.

Veneer A very thin layer of expensive timber attached to a cheaper base.

Waste Any piece of material that is cut off and not used.

Waste pipe The pipe taking dirty water from bath, basins, sinks and showers.

Suppliers and Useful Addresses

United Kingdom

Axminster Power Tool Centre
Chard Street
Axminster
Devon EX13 5HU
Tel: 01297 33656
Power tools supplier

Black and Decker and Dewalt
210 Bath Road
Slough
Berkshire SL1 3YD
Tel: 01753 567055
Power tools supplier

Colour Centre
Offord Road
London N1
Tel: 020 7609 116
Paints and DIY equipment supplier

Foxell and James
Farringdon Road
London EC1M 3JB
Tel: 020 7405 0152
Wax, oil, varnish, and finishing products.

Heward and Dean
Grove Park Road
London N15 4SP
Tel: 020 8800 3447
Tool supplier

HSS Power Tools
25 Willow Lane
Mitcham
Surrey CR4 4TS
Tel: 020 8260 3100

James Latham
Leeside Wharf
Mount Pleasant Hill
Clapton E5
Tel: 020 8806 3333
Timber suppliers

Plasplugs Ltd.
Wetmore Road
Burton-on-Trent
Staffordshire DE14 1SD
Tel: 01283 530303
www.plasplugs.com
Tiling tools, fixings and fasteners

Record Tools Ltd.
Parkway Works
Kettlebridge Road
Sheffield S9 3BL
Tel: 0114 244 9066
Hand tools supplier

Ronseal Limited
Thorncliffe Park
Chapeltown
Sheffield S35 2YP
Tel: 0114 246 7171
www.ronseal.co.uk
Ronseal, Colron, Thompson's products

Spear & Jackson
Neill Tools Ltd.
Atlas Way
Atlas North
Sheffield S4 7QQ
Tel: 0114 261 4242
Tools supplier

Stanley Tools UK Ltd.
Beighton Road East
Drakehouse
Sheffield S20 7JZ
Tel: 0114 276 8888
Tools supplier

Vitrex Ltd.
Everest Road
Lytham St. Annes
Lancashire
FY8 3AZ
Tel: 01253 789180
Tools and clothing

Woodfit Ltd.
Kem Mill
Whittle-le-Woods
Chorley
Lancashire PR6 7EA
Tel: 01257 266421
Furniture fittings supplier

United States

Compton Lumber & Hardware Inc.
P.O. Box 84972
Seattle, WA 98124-6272
Tel: (206) 623-5010
www.comptonlbr.com

Constantine's
2050 Eastchester Road
Bronx, New York NY 10461
Tel: (718) 792-1600
www.constantines.com

The Cutting Edge, Inc.
7123 Southwest Freeway
Houston, TX 77074
Tel: (981) 9228
www.cuttingedgetools.com

Northern Tool and Equipment
Corporate Headquarters
2800 Southcross Drive West
Burnsville, MN 55306
Tel: (800) 533-5545
www.northerntool.com

Australia

BBC Hardware Stores
Hardware House
For details of your nearest store in either of the above two chains, contact (02) 9876 0888.

Mitre 10
For details of your nearest store contact (03) 9703 4200.

Bunnings Warehouse
For details of your nearest store contact (03) 9607 0777.

Thrifty-Link Hardware
See you local state directory for your nearest store.

Useful addresses

British Cement Association
Century House
Telford Avenue
Berkshire RG45 6YS
Tel: 01344 762676
www.bca.org.uk

British Wood Preserving and Damp-proofing Association
1 Gleneagles House
Vernon Gate, South Street
Derby DE1 1UP
Tel: 01332 225100
www.bwpda.co.uk

Conservatory Association/Glass and Glazing Federation
44–48 Borough High Street
London SE1 1XB
Tel: 01480 458278
www.ggf.org.uk

Energy Saving Trust
21 Dartmouth Street
London SW1H 9BT
Tel: 08457 277200
www.est.org.uk

Home Energy Efficiency Scheme
Eaga Partnership
2nd Floor, Eldon Court
Eldon Square
Newcastle-upon-Tyne NE1 7HA
Tel: 0800 316 6011

Kitchen Specialists Association
12 Top Barn Business Centre
Holt Heath
Worcester WR6 6NH
Tel: 01905 726066
www.ksa.co.uk

Laminated Glass Information Centre
299 Oxford Street
London W1R 1LA
020 7499 1720
www.martex.co.uk/prca/condor

National Association of Loft Insulation Contractors
and
National Cavity Insulation Association
PO Box 12
Hazlemere
Surrey GU27 3AH
Tel: 01428 654011
theceed@computer.com

National Fireplace Association
6th Floor
The McLaren Building
35 Dale End
Birmingham B4 7LN
Tel: 0121 200 1310

RIBA (Royal Institute of Chartered Architects)
66 Portland Place
London W1B 1AD
Tel: 020 7580 5533
www.architecture.com

SALVO
(Directory of Salvage Yards)
PO Box 333
Cornhill on Tweed
Northumberland TD12 4YJ
Tel: 01890 820333
www.salvo.co.uk

The Association of Noise Consultants
6 Trap Road
Guilden Morden
Hertfordshire SG8 0JE
Tel: 01763 852958
www.association-of-noise-consultants.co.uk

The Institute of Electrical Engineers
2 Savoy Place
London WC2R 0BL
Tel: 020 7240 1871
www.iee.org.uk

The Institute of Plumbing
64 Station Lane
Hornchurch
Essex RM12 6NB
Tel: 01708 472791
www.plumbers.org.uk

INDEX

ACKNOWLEDGEMENTS

PICTURE CREDITS

The publisher would like to thank the following agencies, individuals and companies for the permission to reproduce the following images.

Axminster Power Tool Centre: 15bc; 16tc; 22r; 34br; 39tc; 40c; 43br; 49c; 112tr. Junckers 8c; Fired Earth 9br; DIY Photo Library: 12bl, br; 13bl, c, br; 51 steps 1–5; 62tr; 104–5 all; 106–7 all; 125cl; 132br; 141bc; 143bl; 143br; 199bl. John Freeman: 144bl; 154–5, 178–9. Simon Gilham: 56bc; 123bl; 136bc, br; 140bl, c, br; 142bc; 143tr; 145bc, br; 147; 196bl. HSS Tool Hire: 16c; 17t, c, r; 55br; 143bc; 197br. Hunter Plastics 58–9. Rentokil: 141tr; 145tc, c, tr. Thompson's (Ronseal): 142tc, tl; 199br. Yale Security Products: 146. Mr. Mark Blewitt: 56tr.

The publisher would like to thank the following individuals and companies for their help with photography and images:

Axminster Power Tool Centre

Burlington Slate Limited
Cavendish House
Kirkby-in-Furness
Cumbria LA17 7UN
Tel: 01229 889661

Canonbury Art Shop
266 Upper Street
London N1
Tel: 020 7226 4652

Colour Centre
(see Suppliers)

David Cropp
Rentokil Initial plc
East Grinstead
West Sussex RH19 2JY
Tel: 01342 830220
http://www.rentokil-initial.com/photos

Dewalt Power Tools

Eternit Building Materials

Heward and Dean (BD) Ltd
(see Suppliers)

Hunter Plastics Limited
Nathan Way
London SE28 0AE
Tel: 020 8855 9851

Marley Roofing Products

Mr. Mark Blewitt
c/o The National Federation of Roofing Contractors

Plasplugs Ltd.

Sandtex
Julie Coleman
ICAS Public Relations
19 Garrick Street
London WC2E 9BB
Tel: 020 7632 2424

Thompson's
Pure PR
PO Box 1430
Sheffield S11 7XH
Tel: 0114 230 9112

Vallance Adhesive and Sealant Range
Stransky Thompson PR
Denton House
40–44 Wicklow Street
London WC1X 9HL

Vitrex Limited

Yale Security Products
UK Limited
Wood Street
Willenhall
West Midlands
WV13 1LA
Tel: 01902 366911

NOTES

Notes

Notes

Notes

Notes

NOTES

Notes

Notes